Globalization and History

Globalization and History

The Evolution of a
Nineteenth-Century
Atlantic Economy

Kevin H. O'Rourke and
Jeffrey G. Williamson

The MIT Press
Cambridge, Massachusetts
London, England

Third printing, 2000

This book was set in Palatino by Achorn Graphic Services, Inc.

Printed and bound in the United States of America.

Library of Congress Cataloging-in-Publication Data

O'Rourke, Kevin H.
    Globalization and history : the evolution of a nineteenth-century Atlantic economy / Kevin H. O'Rourke, Jeffrey G. Williamson.
        p.   cm.
    Includes bibliographical references and index.
    ISBN 0-262-15049-2 (alk. paper)
    1. Free trade—North Atlantic Region—History. 2. North Atlantic Region—Economic integration—History. 3. North Atlantic Region—Emigration and immigration—History. 4. Capital movements—North Atlantic Region—History. I. Williamson, Jeffrey G., 1935–   . II. Title.
    HF1711.O76   1999
    337.1'1821—dc21   99-17963
                                                                          CIP

For
Andrew O'Rourke and Hanne Hjortshøj O'Rourke
Kossuth Mayer Williamson and Martha Hale Williamson

Contents

Figures

Acknowledgments

This book has been stewing ever since 1991 when one of us submitted a proposal on globalization and history to the National Science Foundation. The fruits of that award began to emerge when the two of us presented papers the following year to the Cliometrics Conference (Miami, Ohio) and the National Bureau of Economic Research DAE Conference (Cambridge, Massachusetts). Many technical papers, journal articles, and conferences later, we are ready to summarize what we know for the economist and historian who also finds globalization fascinating but who has not invested quite as much time as we have in learning about it.

A project stretching over eight years tends to accumulate a lot of debts. We start by expressing our gratitude to the National Science Foundation, which supported this project from the start with SES-90-21951, SBR-92-23002, and SBR-95-05656. Next, we are delighted to recognize the role that our collaborators on related projects have played in influencing this book: George Boyer, Bill Collins, Tim Hatton, Cormac Ó Gráda, Alan Taylor, and Ashley Timmer. Their mark is especially deep at the many points in the book where we cite in more detail the collaborations that mattered most. They have been stimulating intellectual partners and fun to work with. In addition, we have received copious comments from six scholars whom the MIT Press asked to referee a previous draft of the book. We are grateful to these six since they spotted errors, guided us away from irrelevancies, and caused us to sharpen the arguments. The six are: Brad DeLong, Giovanni Federico, Tim Hatton, Doug Irwin, Ed Leamer, and Alan Taylor. Alan Taylor's patience and help was especially invaluable in drafting chapters 11 and 12. In addition, the manuscript received detailed critical reviews from Barry Eichengreen, Elhanan Helpman, Charlie Kindleberger, and

Cormac Ó Gráda, and Maurice Obstfeld read the chapters on international capital mobility. The quality of this book has certainly been raised by the attention that these scholars, and our students, have given it. We hope they are not too annoyed if we have sometimes failed to make the changes they suggested or simply misunderstood their points. Patrick Lane also made several helpful comments on the original manuscript, for which we are grateful.

Others who have never read this book made a significant impact on it when the component parts were in the making: Moe Abramovitz, Bob Allen, Jeremy Atack, Dudley Baines, Andy Bielenberg, Michael Burda, Juan Carmona, Roberto Cortés Conde, Kimiko Cautero, Jean-Michel Chevet, Louis Cullen, Don Davis, Lance Davis, Gerardo della Paolera, Kevin Denny, Don Devortez, Steve Dowrick, Mike Edelstein, Toni Estevadeordal, Riccardo Faini, Ron Findlay, Robert Fogel, James Foreman-Peck, Bob Gallman, Hank Gemery, Claudia Goldin, Aurora Gomez, George Grantham, Alan Green, Tom Grennes, Morgan Kelly, Chris Hanes, Knick Harley, Colm Harmon, Ingrid Henriksen, Matt Higgins, Barry Howarth, Ken Kang, Liam Kennedy, Lynne Kiesling, Jan Tore Klovland, Anne Krueger, Paul Krugman, Pedro Lains, Philip Lane, Peter Lindert, Jonas Ljungberg, Deirdre McCloskey, Ian McLean, Marv McInnis, Anthony Murphy, Paul O'Connell, Gunnar Persson, David Pope, Leandro Prados, Jaime Reis, Christian Riis, Sherman Robinson, Dani Rodrik, Tom Rutherford, Jeff Sachs, Steve Saeger, Lennart Schön, Pierre Sicsic, Boris Simkovich, Graeme Snooks, Ken Snowden, Peter Timmer, Gianni Toniolo, Gabriel Tortella, Tony Venables, Max Urquhart, Alessandra Venturini, Brendan Walsh, Andy Warner, David Weinstein, Adrian Wood, Gavin Wright, Tarik Yousef, and Vera Zamagni.

We are especially grateful to our wives, Nancy Williamson and Roseann Byrne, for their tolerance and good humor throughout this project. Nancy provided expert help on computers, without which our transatlantic collaboration would have been in severe trouble, while Roseann was left far too often to cope alone with the pleasant burdens of parenthood. We could not have done this, or much else, without them.

Our first and most important teachers were our parents. This book is dedicated to them.

1   Globalization and History

At the start of the nineteenth century, economic globalization was distant from the minds of politicians, businessmen, and voters in the Atlantic economy. And it was even more distant from the minds of those in Latin America, Africa, Asia, and even most of the Mediterranean basin. A long and expensive war between Britain and France had engaged almost all Europeans for at least thirty-six of the sixty years between 1760 and 1820. Like most other international conflicts, it had made a shambles of normal channels of trade, technological transfer, labor migration, and financial capital movements. Even without the French Wars (as the British called them), the transport costs associated with staple foods and industrial intermediates were enormous, thus choking off trade; in addition, mercantilism and protection were the preferred policies of the day, suppressing trade still further; long-distance migration was even more expensive in terms of both time and money—so much so that it did not influence local labor markets much; and financial markets had led segmented wartime lives for some time. When it was clear that a durable peace had finally arrived in the early 1820s, the world was hostile to globalization forces and globalization policies.

It took a while for members of the Atlantic economy to start moving away from their insular commodity and factor markets, and toward more integrated world markets. We are sometimes presented with the image of a heroic era of regime switch in the late 1840s and early 1850s, at roughly midcentury. Those years included Britain's move toward free trade with the repeal of the Corn Laws in 1846, the first voluntary mass migration triggered by the Irish famine, which started in 1845, and the laying of the first successful submarine telegraph cable under the English Channel in 1851, linking financial markets in London, Paris, and other European capitals. Those dates are convenient and their stories are colorful, but the history is incomplete and misleading. The first half of the century had undergone a spectacular decline in transport costs on sea-lanes and on routes to the interior, British tariffs had drifted down from almost embargo heights, migrations across the Irish Sea and on the Continent had quickened, and European capital, freed from wartime finance, was starting to look for promising returns in distant New Orleans, Chicago, Sydney, and Bombay.

Yet the really big leap to more globally integrated commodity and factor markets took place in the second half of the century. By 1914, there was hardly a village or town anywhere on the globe whose prices were not influenced by distant foreign markets, whose infrastructure was not financed by foreign capital, whose engineering, manufacturing, and even business skills were not imported from abroad, or whose labor markets were not influenced by the absence of those who had emigrated or by the presence of strangers who had immigrated. The economic connections were intimate, poor regions had enjoyed significant convergence gains by erasing part of the gap between themselves and rich regions, and flourishing export sectors enjoyed the benefits associated with the global trade boom. Not everyone was happy with the new global economy. Farmers voiced populist complaints about railroads and bankers. Rich landowners demanded protection from cheap farm products. Workers pointed to unfair competition from imports made with cheap foreign labor and claimed that their jobs were being robbed by immigrants. Capitalists in declining import-competing industries argued that it was only fair that they get compensation for the losses they suffered on sunk investments. And domestic policymakers began to feel that they were losing their ability to manage prices, interest rates, and markets; they felt increasingly vulnerable to financial panic, industrial crisis, and unfavorable price shocks generated in distant corners of the globe.

This characterization should sound familiar since the same language has been used often enough to describe the evolution of the world economy over the past half-century. Globalization seemed remote in 1945 too, although it was all policy alone, rather than the combination of policy and transport costs, that accounted for the segmentation of world commodity and factor markets at the end of World War II. The world economy had lost all of its globalization achievements in three decades, between 1914 and 1945. In the half-century since then, it has won them all back in every market but one; world migration is no longer "mass."

What form did the globalization boom take from the mid-nineteenth century to the Great War? Did poor countries start to catch up on rich countries, and did globalization help contribute to the convergence? Which part of the globalization process had the biggest impact on factor markets and gross domestic product (GDP) convergence? Capital flows? Labor migration? Trade? Technology transfer? Did all the Atlantic economies participate equally? Who gained? Who lost? Did the losers complain loud enough to generate a political reaction?

These are the questions for which this book offers answers. It also serves up the answers while looking explicitly and constantly at modern experience and modern debate. We want this book to speak to today's debates about the growth of trade, the impact of immigration on local labor markets, the sources of inequality, why more capital does not flow to poor countries, whether trade liberalization can lessen immigration pressures in rich countries, why globalization backlash arose in the past, and whether we can expect it again as we enter the next century.

The book begins with Atlantic economy convergence experience over the century or so from 1830 to 1940. Like all other economists worried about convergence, we pay attention to GDP per capita and GDP per worker-hour, but we pay far more attention to real wages. This focus on real wages and other factor prices pervades the whole book since we feel that economists cannot possibly answer the questions raised in the previous paragraph by dealing solely with macroeconomic aggregates. Chapter 3 identifies and measures the spectacular transport revolution that took place across the nineteenth century and generated an equally spectacular convergence in commodity prices. Most of the huge gap in commodity prices quoted between distant markets in 1820 had been erased by 1914, even though rising protection tried hard to mute these globalization forces. Chapter 4 then asks whether Eli Heckscher and Bertil Ohlin were right in predicting that the convergence in world commodity prices would induce a convergence in world factor prices. The next two chapters explore the political economy of tariffs in accounting for the move to "openness" in the middle of the century and then for the subsequent retreat from that short brush with liberalism. Chapter 7 asks why the migrants moved. To be more precise, Was there self-selection? Why were those who had the most to gain so often the last to leave? Would the mass migrations have subsided in the 1920s and 1930s in the absence of the quotas and a great depression? The next chapter assesses the impact of the mass migrations on countries sending the emigrants and those receiving them. The impact was very big: most of the Atlantic economy convergence observed can be attributed to the mass migrations. Chapters 9 and 10 deal with the political economy of globalization. First we establish who lost from these globalization forces by documenting movements in relative factor prices and inequality everywhere around the Atlantic economy. Globalization predictions are confirmed: inequality was on the rise in labor-scarce New World economies, inequality was on the decline in European agrarian economies, and inequality was relatively stable in the European industrial economies. Chapter 6 deals with tariff responses to these distributional events, and chapter 10 completes the globalization backlash story by exploring the fall in immigrant subsidies and the rise in immigrant restrictions in the New World, which occurred long before the quotas of the interwar period. Chapters 11 and 12 turn to financial capital markets. The first establishes that world capital markets were almost certainly as well integrated in the 1890s as they are in the 1990s. The second explores the impact of the capital flows and dwells on two questions: Why didn't more capital flow to poor, labor-abundant countries? When it did flow to the periphery, what was its contribution there? Chapter 13 explores a question that is central to debates about policy: Were trade and factor flows substitutes or complements? The book concludes with a summary of the lessons from history.

This, then, is the agenda. As economists today debate globalization issues, they treat the phenomenon as if it is unique to our time, seemingly unaware of how directly the first great globalization boom speaks to the second. A conversation between the two is long overdue. What follows is a start.

2   Convergence in History

Two important features of the late twentieth-century international economy characterized the late nineteenth century as well. First, the earlier period was one of rapid globalization: capital and labor flowed across national frontiers in unprecedented quantities, and commodity trade boomed in response to sharply declining transport costs. Second, the late nineteenth century saw an impressive convergence in living standards, at least within most of what we would now call the Organization for Economic Cooperation and Development (OECD) but what this book calls the Atlantic economy. Poor countries around the European periphery tended to grow faster than the rich industrial leaders at the European center, and often even faster than the labor-scarce countries in the New World. The poor countries on the periphery of the Atlantic economy that were catching up to the leaders excluded Asia, Africa, the Middle East, and most of eastern Europe, and even around the fast-growing periphery there were some that failed to catch up. While Spain and Portugal lagged behind the leaders, others, like Ireland and the Scandinavian countries, underwent a spectacular catch-up from the Great Famine to the Great War.

Were globalization and convergence connected? This book argues that most of the convergence between 1850 and 1914 was due to the open economy forces of trade and mass migration. By inference it also suggests that convergence stopped between 1914 and 1950 because of deglobalization and the retreat to autarky. These facts are directly relevant to debates over globalization today.

We start with the convergence evidence. The rest of the book offers the open economy explanations for it.

Convergence in the Present

Since the academic literature on the topic has become so plentiful and the issue even gets abundant media exposure, it is hard to imagine any economist who is unaware of the dramatic (unconditional) convergence that the Atlantic economy has experienced since 1950. By the Atlantic economy, we mean those countries that experienced industrialization first and are now members of the OECD: the nations of western Europe, southern Europe, North America, and Australasia. By convergence, we mean the process by which poorer countries have grown faster than richer countries, so that the economic distance between them has diminished, most of it having disappeared a half-century later. By unconditional convergence, we mean that poor countries tended to catch up with the rich. (Later, we use the term *conditional convergence,* which is relevant when poor countries have not actually caught up with the rich but would have exhibited some catching up had it not been for offsetting disadvantages.)

What explains this late-twentieth-century convergence? Theoretical work is certainly plentiful, although this has usually been couched in terms of closed economy growth theory, rather than open economy trade theory, which we feel is more relevant. First-generation growth models implied unconditional or conditional convergence (Solow 1956; see Mankiw, Romer, and Weil 1992 for an augmented version). Second-generation growth models qualified these predictions: divergence became theoretically possible by taking into account increasing returns, learning by doing, externalities, schooling, and skills (Arrow 1962; Romer 1986, 1989; Lucas 1988, 1990; Barro and Sala-i-Martin 1995).

Empirical research on late-twentieth-century convergence has come on in a rush. All of it has relied heavily on the post–World War II International Comparisons Project (ICP) data gathered in the series of Penn World Table publications (e.g., Summers and Heston 1991). Early on, economists found that as the sample expanded from the OECD to the rest of the world, conditional convergence became more apparent than unconditional convergence (Dowrick and Nguyen 1989). Strong catch-up forces were at work everywhere, but many poor countries in the Third World exhibited catching up only when the researcher controlled for the fact that they were hampered by high population growth, low public savings rates, and human capital shortfalls (Barro 1991; Durlauf and Johnson 1992; Barro and Sala-i-Martin 1992; Mankiw, Romer, and Weil 1992). Thus, conditional controls are important if truly comprehensive convergence is to be uncovered even today.

Empirical applications of these conditional convergence models have advanced to such sophistication that they have been able to isolate the roles of openness, regulation, property rights, demography, natural resources, and even democracy (Barro 1996; Sachs and Warner 1995a, 1995b; Bloom and Williamson 1997; Williamson 1997b). For the most part, however, these models have been applied to only a tiny portion of history, the years since 1970. What about the vast stretch of history before?

Historical work has also proliferated, led by the pioneering contributions of Moses Abramovitz (1986) and William Baumol (1986), each building on the long-run macroeconomic data collected by Angus Maddison (1982, 1989, 1991, 1995). Abramovitz related the observed catching up of postwar Europe on the United States to Veblen's "leader handicap" theory and Gerschenkron's (1962) "advantages of backwardness" theory: a country with lower productivity can exploit the technological gap with respect to the leader, import or imitate best-practice technology, and, hence, raise labor productivity and living standards. The leader has no gap to exploit, its productivity increases are limited by the rate at which newly discovered technology is applied to production, and so its growth is slower. The more backward the country is, the bigger the technological gap and the faster the potential catch-up or convergence. Abramovitz found GDP per worker dispersion to have diminished over the past century or so, although convergence was particularly rapid in the post–World War II period.

Abramovitz noted the distinction between convergence and technological catch-up since capital-deepening forces make it possible for the latter to be neither a necessary nor a sufficient condition for the former. Furthermore, he noted that technological catch-up would be self-limiting since it would decline to zero as the productivity gap diminished. Abramovitz also contrasted convergence measured by dispersion levels, now called σ-convergence, with convergence measured by the extent to which poor countries grow faster than rich, now called β-convergence (Barro and Sala-i-Martin 1992, 1995).

Is Convergence a Recent Phenomenon?

Most economists take an ahistorical position when writing about convergence in the late twentieth century. So it is that Robert Barro and Gregory Mankiw and their collaborators (Barro and Sala-i-Martin 1992,

1995; Mankiw, Romer, and Weil 1992) ignore pre–World War II or even
pre-1970 experience, focusing instead on the past two or three decades.
The implicit assumption seems to be that the data for this kind of analysis are absent prior to the 1960s, or that the experience was irrelevant,
or, even worse, that there could not possibly have been any convergence in pre–World War II history. Some even make the explicit assumption that it was only with the emergence of global institutions
after Bretton Woods that convergence was possible, although even that
historic 1944 accord was hostile to globally open capital markets (Helleiner 1994a, 1994b). The few economists who look at a longer sweep
of history often ignore the rich historical information embedded in
their time series: William Baumol (1986) explored convergence over the
century following 1870, but even this pioneer ignored all the decades in
between (an oversight partially repaired in Baumol, Blackman, and
Wolff 1989). And when Barro and Xavier Sala-i-Martin (1992) look at
convergence between U.S. states since 1870, they too ignore the remarkable variance in convergence performance: there was none up to the
1930s, and all the convergence occurred thereafter (Williamson 1980a).
Furthermore, it is rare for any economist looking at the experience since
1970 to ask how much of a region's or a country's growth performance
is explained by the explanatory variables thought to matter. Instead,
economists looking at the modern evidence use it solely for hypothesis
testing—for example, was there conditional catch-up, and was it faster
in more open economies? Historians demand more. They tend to look
for deviant behavior and then search for explanations—for example,
which countries did not catch up when and why, and did all countries
catching up do so for the same reasons?

How great is the historical variety in convergence experience? Were
the post–World War II years as unique as contemporary economists
often imply? Or were the interwar years a profound interruption to a
secular convergence that started in the previous century? If the latter
turns out to be the case, why the go, stop, go? And are there reasons
to expect another stop in the near future?

Convergence in the Past

If we intend to show that history has a great deal to say about convergence, we must first define what we mean by the phrase. So, convergence of what?

The critical bottom line for us is whether the gap between the average worker's living standard in rich and poor countries falls over time.

Convergence implies an erosion in this gap, at least in percentage terms. There appear to be two data sets that can be used to explore the issue over long time periods. GDP per capita or per worker-hour estimates offer one: Angus Maddison's data were originally published in 1982, now superseded by his 1991 book and by even more recent revisions (Maddison 1994, 1995). Real wages of the urban unskilled offer another: Jeffrey Williamson's data were originally published in 1995, now superseded by recent revisions in our collaboration (O'Rourke and Williamson 1997). We will have more to say about how to measure convergence in a moment.

What is the relevant history? Our interest has always been in what Simon Kuznets called modern economic growth, and that translates here into about 170 years, from the 1820s when the British industrial revolution really took off after the French Wars, to the 1990s when even the poorest parts of Asia seem to be part of it.

Convergence among whom? As the introduction suggests, our net will capture only members of the present OECD club with European origins (plus Argentina). True, much of the unconditional convergence since 1870 disappears when the net is widened to include Eastern Europe, and as we have seen for the post-1945 period, if it were widened still further to include the Third World, unconditional convergence would totally evaporate. Why the small net? Because we think the sources of convergence in the OECD club are themselves misunderstood, and it matters to get these facts straight before venturing outside the club.

Convergence of What?

Abramovitz, Baumol, and other economists writing about the late twentieth century all use GDP per capita or per worker-hour to measure convergence. This chapter favors instead purchasing-power-parity (PPP) adjusted real wage rates (typically urban unskilled).[1] Real wages are certainly the right measure if our interest is in the impact of globalization on labor markets. We are not suggesting that the real wage or standard of living data are necessarily superior to the GDP per capita or per worker-hour data for all questions involving the growth of nations. But we can think of four good reasons why we should look at factor prices—something we do throughout this book—in addition to GDP aggregates, which are all that macroeconomists look at when assessing growth and convergence.

First, the pre–World War I real wage data are possibly of better quality than the GDP data. They are available annually rather than only for benchmark years separated by a couple of decades, and they are available for a wider sample of economies. Of course, it may be that the nominal wage series chosen are not representative, and there may be problems with the consumer price indexes used to deflate them, as well as with the PPP adjustments made.[2] But these problems are surely smaller than those involved in trying to estimate nineteenth-century national incomes. For several countries around the European periphery, national accounts for the previous century are simply unavailable (e.g., Ireland), while for others existing series may well be unreliable. At the very least, using real wages allows us to expand our sample of countries, reducing the risk of sample selection bias identified by De Long (1988) and others.

Second, income distribution matters. Real people earn unskilled wages, or skill premiums, or profits or land rents, not that statistical artifact known as GDP per capita. Although GDP per worker-hour may be the right measure of aggregate productivity, the living standards of ordinary workers are better indicators of the economic well-being of a society.[3] It is in principle possible to design a tax and transfer system that could redistribute income between citizens, leaving all equally well off, but such a scheme is as yet merely of theoretical interest, and it must have seemed wildly utopian to late-nineteenth-century observers. In any case, macroeconomists are throwing away valuable information by averaging all incomes.

Third, economic change nearly always involves winners as well as losers, and this fact is crucial to the evolution of economic policy. Changes that might increase GDP per capita are often successfully resisted, and examining the behavior of factor prices is a necessary first step in understanding such political responses. Indeed, this is the direction taken in chapters 5, 6, 9, and 10.

Fourth, and possibly most important, focusing on wages and other factor prices helps us understand the sources of convergence. The open economy mechanisms that we argue were central in driving late-nineteenth-century convergence—trade, migration, and capital flows—operated directly on factor prices, and thus only indirectly on GDP per capita. By focusing on only GDP per capita, macroeconomists are likely to miss a large part of the story. They may even make inferences that are just plain wrong. Suppose, for example, that we want to know whether convergence is due to technological catch-up, globalization through trade, or globalization through mass migration. If the dominant force is technological catch-up, then it is possible that wage rates, land rents, and profit rates will all rise with GDP per capita and GDP per worker, albeit at different rates depending on some possible technological bias. If the dominant force is globalization through trade, then the standard Heckscher-Ohlin trade theory, discussed in chapter 4, predicts that wage-rental ratios will move in opposite directions in land-abundant and land-scarce economies and that factor prices will converge much faster than either GDP per capita or GDP per worker. If the dominant force is mass migration, and if, as was the case, the migrants tended to be young adults, then GDP per capita should rise faster than GDP per worker in immigrant countries, and wage rates should fall relative to land rents and profit rates. The opposite would be true in emigrant countries. By relying solely on GDP per worker or GDP per capita data, macroeconomists are missing a chance to discriminate between these and other competing explanations for convergence.

Divergence Shocks and Convergence Responses, 1830–1870

The Atlantic economy was perturbed by two profound shocks in the first half of the nineteenth century: early industrialization in Britain, eventually spreading to a few countries on the European continent, and resource "discovery" in the New World, triggered by sharply declining international transport costs (an issue explored at length in chapter 3). Tariff barriers were high prior to midcentury even in Britain (the Corn Laws were repealed only in 1846, with liberal trade reform following on the European continent a decade or two after); commodity trade was modest; migration across national borders was not yet "mass" (the famine-induced Irish flood of migrants was not released until the late 1840s); and capital markets were as yet underdeveloped and not quite global. The resultant divergence can be documented only starting in 1830, and even then the sample is relatively small (eight countries in 1830, rising to thirteen by 1869). Nonetheless, the limited evidence points to steep divergence trends during the first half of the nineteenth century.

Figure 2.1 documents real wage dispersion between 1830 and 1869. The summary statistic $C(N)$ plotted there (where N is the sample size) has been used extensively in the convergence debate, and it is our measure of σ-convergence.[4] Based on the eight Atlantic countries for which data are available (Brazil, France, Great Britain, Ireland, the Netherlands, Spain, Sweden, and the United States), $C(8)$ rises from 0.143 in 1830 to 0.402 in 1846, a near trebling in the index of real wage and

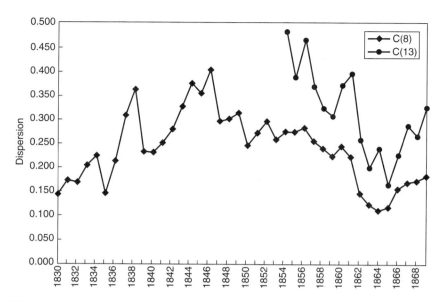

Figure 2.1
International real wage dispersion, 1830–1869. Source: Williamson (1995, table A2.1);
revised in O'Rourke and Williamson (1997).

living standard dispersion over the three decades. This global labor
market disequilibrium was driven primarily by a wage boom in the
United States and a wage slump in Spain and the Netherlands (Williamson 1995, appendix table A2.1; revised in O'Rourke and Williamson 1997). Relative to the European leader of the pack (Britain), Ireland
and France held their own, while Sweden lost some ground. Industrial
revolutionary events in Europe certainly contributed to this divergence
phase up to the mid-1840s, but the sharp rise in $C(8)$ is due primarily
to New World success: the United States increased its real wage advantage over England from 45 percent in 1830 to 89 percent in 1846.[5] This
is a surprising finding given that the British standard of living debate
points to wage improvement during these decades as unambiguous
evidence supporting the optimists' position (Lindert and Williamson
1983; Lindert 1994). Apparently real wage gains in England were far
less significant than they were in the United States. The British standard of living debate has never noticed this fact, nor, for that matter,
have the American "exceptionalists" made very much of the impressive U.S. relative wage performance.[6]

Although we do not have similar real wage data this early in the
century for, say, Canada or Australia, the American evidence certainly

suggests that the global labor market disequilibrium was being driven primarily by rising wage gaps between Europe and the English-speaking New World. Does it follow that there were no Gerschenkron-like industrial leader and latecomer-follower dynamics that augmented wage gaps in Europe? No. We must remember an inherent selectivity bias underlying this small sample of six European economies: it excludes many poorly documented latecomers. The dispersion within Europe is likely to have risen far more than these figures suggest. Thus, the sharp divergence in the Atlantic economy measured here understates the true magnitude of that event.

Figure 2.1 suggests a secular turning point somewhere between 1846—based on the smaller but longer sample underlying $C(8)$—and 1854—based on the larger but shorter sample underlying $C(13)$. Since convergence persisted for the next six decades or so, the mid-nineteenth century appears to date the start of modern convergence in the Atlantic economy. True, a good share of the real wage convergence between 1854 and 1865 can be explained by the well-known collapse of American wages during the Civil War (DeCanio and Mokyr 1977; Williamson 1974a), but the early convergence was more general than this exogenous and country-specific event would imply. After all, the otherwise impressive American postbellum real wage recovery in the late 1860s and 1870s (Williamson 1974a; Goldin and Lewis 1975) never led to the high wages relative to England achieved at the peak in 1854–1856 (105 percent). Furthermore, relative wages also fell in Australia after 1854, suggesting that it was an event common to more of the New World than simply North America. The results were mixed in Europe. Although Sweden gained a lot of ground on England between the mid-1850s and 1869, none of the other European countries in our Atlantic sample did (with the possible exception of Belgium), and France, Norway, and Spain lost ground. Once again it appears that the convergence from midcentury to 1869 was driven primarily by the erosion of the gap between Europe and the New World.

Three morals have emerged from our look at Atlantic labor markets over the four decades between 1830 and 1869. First, there was a very sharp divergence in real wages and living standards up to midcentury. Second, convergence in the Atlantic economy started shortly after midcentury. True, the Atlantic sample was still small around midcentury, but it rose to seventeen by 1870 (including five New World countries) so we should be more certain about convergence trends starting then. This date is commonly used by economic historians in describing other events anyway, and "late nineteenth century" typically refers to the years between 1870 and World War I. Third, σ-divergence and σ-convergence was driven by the behavior of wage gaps between Europe and the New World, not just by the behavior of wage gaps within Europe.

Late Nineteenth-Century Convergence

Economists are taught that really important shocks to any market are followed, with a lag, by transitions to new equilibria or new steady states, unless, of course, these are halted by state intervention. One might view late-nineteenth-century convergence as one such transition, caused by globally integrating commodity, labor, and capital markets around the Atlantic economy, one in which the state took a broadly liberal policy stance.

The Argentineans call the transition from 1870 to 1913 the *"belle époque,"* North Americans refer to it as their "gilded age" of industrial take-off to world dominance, the English dub it their "great Victorian boom" carried on a wave of high imperialism, but most economists are taught to view it as a liberal era of free trade under the gold standard.[7] If the two decades prior to 1870 are included, it involved the most extensive real wage and living standard convergence the Atlantic economy has ever seen, including the better-known convergence of the post–World War II era. However, most of the convergence was completed by the turn of the century, and the "speed" per decade was not as fast as that recorded during the post–World War II epoch (Crafts and Toniolo 1996); nevertheless, it was an impressive convergence.

As figure 2.2 shows, the striking convergence that started in mid-century continued up to around 1900, after which the decline in $C(17)$ ceased.[8] In fact, $C(17)$ dropped by more than a third over the three decades from 1870 to 1900 (falling from 0.313 to 0.200), and $C(13)$ fell by almost three-fifths over the sixty years following 1854. Our summary measure of real wage differences across countries can be decomposed into three parts: dispersion within the New World, dispersion within Europe, and dispersion between Europe and the New World, the last measured by the average wage gap between the two. When these three components are computed, the results are striking and repeat those for earlier in the century (Williamson 1996). First, throughout the period 1870–1913, the average wage gap between Europe and the New World accounts for about 60 percent of the real wage variance across these

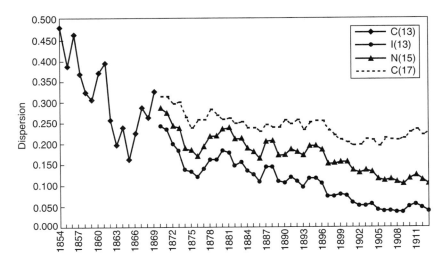

Figure 2.2
International real wage dispersion, 1854–1913. Source: Williamson (1995, table A2.1); revised in O'Rourke and Williamson (1997).

seventeen countries. The remainder, 40 percent, is explained by the variance within Europe and the New World. Furthermore, real wage variance within the New World accounts for more of the total variance than does real wage variance within Europe. All of this implies that real wage variance among our late-nineteenth-century European countries was a very modest part of real wage variance in the Atlantic economy as a whole (although we have already confessed that the absence of poor eastern European nations from the sample probably accounts for much of this result). Second, about 60 percent of the convergence between 1870 and 1900 is explained by the collapse in the wage gap between Europe and the New World.

Late-nineteenth-century convergence was not limited to real wages and labor markets. Figure 2.3 shows that GDP per capita converged as well. However, real wage convergence was a lot faster than GDP per capita or GDP per worker-hour convergence, and the globalization arguments that follow offer some reasons why.

Convergence was ubiquitous in the late-nineteenth-century Atlantic economy, but it was mostly a story about labor-abundant Europe with lower workers' living standards catching up with the labor-scarce New World with higher workers' living standards, and of Argentina and Canada catching up with Australia and the United States. It was less a

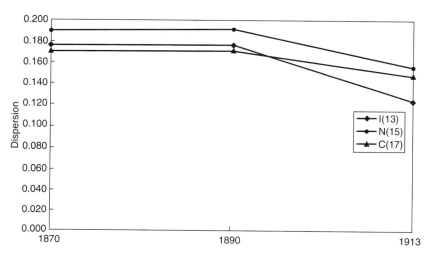

Figure 2.3
International per capita GDP dispersion, 1870–1913. Source: Maddison (1995).

story about European industrial latecomers catching up with European industrial leaders. Convergence did take place within Europe, but it was a more modest affair in the aggregate since spectacular catching-up successes on the Continent were offset by some equally spectacular failures. This European experience deserves a closer look.

Given the great debate about Britain's loss of industrial leadership, there is a tendency to look for evidence of, say, German catch-up on the leader. In spite of the enormous outpouring of literature on Britain's loss of leadership to America and Germany, this is definitely the wrong place to look if the purpose is to understand European convergence or the lack of it. Germany was certainly not one of the poorer countries in the Atlantic economy, and America even less so. The switch in roles among these big three—Britain, Germany, and the United States—involved an exchange of leadership among the leaders, an interesting event, but marginal to the issue at hand. What mattered far more was the behavior of the poorer agricultural European countries relative to the richer industrial ones, and the latter group included Belgium, France, and Germany, not just Britain.

Before we proceed with our narrative, let us first define the European sample. Table 2.1 reports real wages, GDP per head, and GDP per worker-hour for fifteen European countries and five New World countries in 1870 and 1913. How did these countries compare in 1870? The

Table 2.1
Living Standards and Productivity, 1870–1913

Country	Real wages (GB 1905 = 100)		GDP per capita (1990 US$)		GDP per worker-hour (1990 US$)	
	1870 (1)	1913 (2)	1870 (3)	1913 (4)	1870 (5)	1913 (6)
European periphery						
Austria	NA	NA	1,875	3,488	1.39	2.93
Denmark	36	102	1,927	3,764	1.51	3.40
Finland	NA	NA	1,107	2,050	0.84	1.81
Ireland	49	90	NA	NA	NA	NA
Italy	26	55	1,467	2,507	1.03	2.09
Norway	32	93	1,303	2,275	1.09	2.19
Portugal	18	24	1,085	1,354	NA	NA
Spain	30	39	1,376	2,255	NA	NA
Sweden	28	98	1,664	3,096	1.22	2.58
Average	31	72	1,476	2,599	1.18	2.50
European industrial core						
Belgium	60	94	2,640	4,130	2.12	3.60
France	50	66	1,858	3,452	1.36	2.85
Germany	58	92	1,913	3,833	1.58	3.50
Great Britain	67	98	3,263	5,032	2.61	4.40
Netherlands	57	78	2,640	3,950	2.33	4.01
Switzerland	NA	NA	2,172	4,207	1.75	3.25
Average	58	86	2,414	4,101	1.96	3.60
Europe	43	77	1,878	3,242	1.57	3.05
New World						
Argentina	61	92	1,311	3,797	NA	NA
Australia	127	128	3,801	5,505	3.32	5.28
Brazil	39	87	740	839	NA	NA
Canada	99	219	1,620	4,213	1.61	4.21
United States	115	169	2,457	5,307	2.26	5.12
Average	88	139	1,986	3,932	2.40	4.87

Source: Wage data are those underlying O'Rourke and Williamson (1997). GDP per capita and per worker-hour from Maddison (1995).
Note: British GDP per capita and per worker-hour figures include Ireland. All averages are unweighted.

three indexes reveal similar rankings, but they imply different gaps between these countries. As predicted, there were bigger gaps between real wages than between GDP per capita and GDP per worker-hour aggregates. Within Europe, the rich industrial core countries had levels of GDP per head 64 percent higher than the poor agricultural periphery. Their real wages were 87 percent higher than those of the periphery. Alternatively, real wages in the periphery were 47 percent below the industrial core average, and GDP per head was 39 percent below. Austria and Denmark seem to have been on the margin between core and periphery; without them, the periphery GDP per head would have been 45 percent below the industrial core average, not 39 percent below. Nonetheless, we throw Austria and Denmark in with the periphery countries. Thus, the nine members of the European periphery are Austria, Denmark, Finland, Ireland, Italy, Norway, Portugal, Spain, and Sweden. Note again that the sample excludes east and southeast Europe simply because the historical data are inadequate for those regions. Still, the countries were relatively poor. Paul Bairoch's (1976, table 6, p. 286) guesstimates suggest that none of them had levels of GDP per head that were even half that of the core—for example, Bulgaria's was 42.3 percent of the core; Greece's was 48.1 percent, Romania's was 40.4 percent; Russia's was 48.1 percent; and Serbia's was 44.2 percent. Thus, with the exception of Portugal, we ignore the poorest part of Europe. We hope that as better historical data emerge from east and southeast Europe, they will confirm the assertions that follow.

Let us start the narrative with the success up north—the spectacular Scandinavian catch-up on the leaders. Consistent with qualitative accounts, the evidence in table 2.2 confirms that Sweden and Denmark tended to outperform Norway and Finland, but not by much. While real wages show Sweden growing considerably faster than Norway, GDP per capita growth and GDP per worker-hour growth reveal only modest differences between the two fastest and the two slowest. Rapid growth seems to have been common to all four Nordic countries.

Real wages in Scandinavia grew at rates almost three times those prevailing in the European industrial core; Swedish workers enjoyed real wage growth about 2.7 times that of British workers; Danish workers enjoyed real wage growth about 2.6 times that of German workers; and Norwegian workers enjoyed real wage growth about 3.8 times that of Dutch workers. In fact, no other country in our European sample underwent real wage growth even close to that of Sweden, Denmark, or Norway.

Table 2.2
Relative Economic Performance of the European Periphery in the Late Nineteenth Century, Growth per Annum (%)

Country	(1) Real wage per urban worker, 1870–1913	(2) Wage-rental ratio, 1870–1910	(3) Real GDP per capita, 1870–1913	(4) Real GDP per worker-hour, 1870–1913
European periphery				
Denmark	2.63	2.85	1.57	1.91
Finland	NA	NA	1.44	1.80
Norway	2.43	NA	1.30	1.64
Sweden	2.73	2.45	1.45	1.76
Scandinavia	2.60	2.65	1.44	1.77
Italy	1.74	NA	1.28	1.33
Portugal	0.37	NA	0.69	1.10
Spain	0.44	−0.43	1.11	1.52
Mediterranean basin				
With Italy	0.85	−0.43	1.03	1.32
Without Italy	0.41	−0.43	0.90	1.31
Austria	NA	NA	1.45	1.75
Ireland	1.79	4.39	NA	NA
Other periphery	1.79	4.39	1.45	1.75
Periphery	1.73	2.32	1.29	1.60
European industrial core				
Belgium	0.92	NA	1.05	1.24
France	0.91	1.80	1.45	1.74
Germany	1.02	0.87	1.63	1.87
Great Britain	1.03	2.54	1.01	1.22
Netherlands	0.64	NA	0.94	1.27
Switzerland	NA	NA	1.55	1.45
Industrial core	0.90	1.74	1.27	1.46
Europe	1.39	2.07	1.28	1.54
New World				
Argentina	1.74	−4.06	2.50	NA
Australia	0.14	−3.30	0.87	1.08
Brazil	1.43	NA	0.29	NA
Canada	1.65	NA	2.25	2.26
United States	1.04	−1.72	1.81	1.92
New World	1.20	−3.03	1.54	1.76

Sources and notes: All averages are unweighted, and are calculated from unrounded numbers. Wage data are those underlying O'Rourke and Williamson (1997); growth rates are calculated from log-linear regressions, 1870–1913 (raw wage data are annual). Wage-rental ratio data from O'Rourke and Williamson (1997, table 2). GDP per capita and per worker-hour growth rates calculated from table 2.1, except for Italy, Portugal, and Spain, which are taken from O'Rourke and Williamson (1997, table 2) and are based on the data in Bardini, Carreras, and Lains (1995). British GDP per capita and per worker-hour figures include Ireland.

Table 2.2 also documents trends in the wage-rental ratio. It tells us how the unskilled worker's wage behaved relative to farm rents or farm land values per acre. Although not an indicator of income growth per se, such relative factor price movements will be an important analytical component of the open economy hypotheses we will be exploring. While the ratio of wage rates per worker to farm land values per acre fell everywhere in the New World, it rose everywhere in Europe (with the exception of Spain). These events reflect the invasion of grains from the New World (and Russia), which lowered farm rents and land values in Europe and raised them in the American Midwest, the Australian outback, the Argentine pampas, and, we assume but do not document, the Ukraine. While the Scandinavian wage-rental ratio seems to have tracked the British ratio very closely (2.65 versus 2.54 percent per annum growth), the ratio rose half again faster in Scandinavia than in the European core (2.65 versus 1.74 percent per annum).

Consistent with the predictions of conventional trade theory (see below), product per worker-hour documents a less spectacular Scandinavian catch-up than factor prices, but even these data confirm an impressive growth performance compared with the European industrial core (1.77 versus 1.46 percent per annum). Consistent with the fact that Scandinavian emigrants were economically active, the superiority of Scandinavian GDP per capita growth over that of the industrial core (1.44 versus 1.27 percent per annum) is smaller than that of real wages or GDP per worker-hour, but it is still superior.

Scandinavia outperformed the rest of Europe (and probably the rest of the world) in the late nineteenth century. Of that there can be no doubt. These countries were overachievers even by catching-up standards. What about the rest of the periphery?

Based on Maddison's data, Austria seems to have done about as well as Scandinavia: GDP per capita and GDP per worker-hour grew almost exactly as fast (1.45 versus 1.44 and 1.75 versus 1.77). In contrast, although Ireland certainly obeyed the laws of convergence, it was no overachiever. Irish real wages grew twice as fast as they did in the industrial core (1.79 versus 0.9 percent per annum), but they grew little faster than the periphery average, and they recorded less than three-quarters of the Scandinavian growth rate. On the other hand, the Irish wage-rental ratio rose faster.

The western Mediterranean basin did very badly. Gabriel Tortella (1994) has recently surveyed performance in the basin, so we can be brief. The Iberian peninsula fell far behind the growth rates recorded in the rest of the periphery. Real wages crawled upward at about 0.4 percent a year in Iberia, while they surged five and a half times as quickly elsewhere around the periphery. Like so many Third World countries during the second great globalization boom since 1970, Spain and Portugal seem to have missed out on the first great globalization boom, as did Egypt, Turkey, and Serbia at the other end of the Mediterranean basin (Williamson 1998a). While the wage-rental ratio soared at 3.23 percent a year elsewhere around the periphery, it fell by 0.43 percent a year in Iberia. The same wide gap appears for GDP per capita growth—0.9 percent per annum in Iberia and 1.42 percent per annum elsewhere around the periphery. Maddison's real GDP per worker-hour data also confirm a poor Iberian performance, but the gap is not quite so great, as open economy arguments would predict: 1.31 percent per annum in Iberia (slower than in the core, confirming Iberian "fallback") and 1.7 percent per annum around the rest of the periphery. Italy did somewhat better, but even it fell slightly below the average for the periphery, except for real wages. The importance of the Iberian failure to overall convergence in the Atlantic economy can be seen in figure 2.2. The convergence from 1854 to 1913 is steeper when the Iberians are removed (I-13 versus N-15: see later).

Let us now return to the average wage gap between Europe and the New World, the variable that accounted for so much of the convergence over the half-century. Four countries illustrate the process best: Ireland and Sweden (with heavy emigrations from the late 1840s onward), the United States (with heavy immigrations from the late 1840s onward), and Britain (the industrial leader, but losing its dominant grip). In 1856, unskilled real wages in urban Sweden were only 49 percent of British wages; in 1913 they were at parity, an impressive doubling in Sweden's wage relative over the fifty-seven years. Sweden's real wages rose from 24 to 58 percent of the U.S. wage over the same period. In 1852, and shortly after the famine, unskilled real wages in urban Ireland were only 61 percent of British wages, a figure that had changed hardly at all over the previous three decades. Real wages in Ireland started a dramatic convergence on Britain during the 1850s (and, notably, in the absence of any Irish industrialization)[9] so that they were 73 percent of British wages by 1870 and 92 percent by 1913. Ireland was transformed over this period of convergence from a desperately poor, poverty-stricken, peasant economy that had served as a source of cheap labor for booming cities in Britain and North America, to an economy at the start of the twentieth century that boasted wages close to those prevailing across the Irish Sea (and came to exceed British wages in the 1920s [O'Rourke 1994a]). Irish convergence on the booming U.S. economy was less dramatic, but convergence there was: Irish real wages increased from 43 to 53 percent of U.S. real wages between 1855 and 1913.

These patterns were sufficiently ubiquitous to have produced real wage and standard of living convergence in the Atlantic economy over the half-century or more prior to World War I. But as we have suggested, there were some deviant countries and periods that failed to conform to secular convergence patterns. It might be useful to cite them again.

First, the experience in the English-speaking New World varied. Australia experienced a steady erosion in its real wage position over the whole period of convergence (McLean and Pincus 1983)—from 148 to 90 percent above the British real wage between 1854 and 1870, to 47 percent above in 1890 and to just 31 percent above in 1913. But the other New World countries enjoyed a partial resurrection in their real wage advantage late in the regime. This was especially true of North America. Relative to Britain, real wages in the United States were 106 percent higher in 1855, 72 percent higher in 1870, 44 percent higher in 1880, but 72 percent higher in 1913 (after a great industrialization boom that pushed America into world leadership). Real wages in Canada were 48 percent higher than in Britain in 1870, 55 percent higher in 1880, but 123 percent higher in 1913 (after the great wheat boom and railroad expansion of which so much is made by Canadian economic historians).[10] In short, both Canada and the United States bucked the convergence tide after the mid-1890s. This result is consistent with North America's emerging industrial dominance about that time (Wright 1990), and it makes America's successful defense of its economic leadership for so long thereafter all the more impressive. North America's stubborn unwillingness to allow others to catch up matters to overall measures of convergence in the Atlantic economy. The σ-convergence from 1854 to 1913 in figure 2.2 is much greater when the North American experience is removed (the series labeled N-15 versus C-17).

Second, the Latin experience was very different on both sides of the Atlantic. We have already seen that Iberia fell further behind the core during the late nineteenth century. That is, when both the poor performance of Portugal and Spain and the good performance of Canada and the United States are removed, convergence is faster (the series I-13 in figure 2.2) than when just the two North American countries are removed (the series N-15 in figure 2.2). Meanwhile, through dramatic booms and busts, Argentina increased its real wage advantage over Spain and Italy, the source of the vast majority of its immigrants. Argentina improved its real wage position even relative to Britain, from 76 percent in 1864 to 94 percent in 1913, and its real wages actually exceeded Britain's in 1888, 1893, 1899, 1900, 1904, and 1912 (an achievement that Argentineans view with nostalgia: Cortes-Conde 1979). Thus, Argentina, and presumably its neighbors Chile and Uruguay, offer a Latin exception to the more general rule that European wages were catching up with New World wages in the late nineteenth century: the low-wage but resource-abundant southern cone was catching up to high-wage and industrial Britain.

What a Difference Factor Prices Make

What do we make of the fact that the two most prominent contributors to the historical convergence literature, Moses Abramovitz and William Baumol, make so little of these nineteenth-century convergence forces that seem to be so pronounced in the real wage data used here? In Abramovitz's words, "The rate of convergence . . . showed marked strength only during the first quarter-century following World War II," and "in the years of relative peace before 1913 . . . the process [of convergence] left a weak mark on the record" (1986, 385, 395). Of course, Abramovitz and Baumol looked at GDP per capita or GDP per worker-hour, while we use PPP-adjusted real wage rates. We have already seen how the convergence behavior of these three measures differed in the past, real wages and other factor prices converging far faster than the GDP aggregates. Now consider three reasons why this was so.

First, GDP per worker-hour is nothing more than a sum of per unit factor returns weighted by factor endowments per worker-hour. Factor price convergence does not imply that all factor prices in the rich country fall relative to those in the poor country. Some rise. Suppose the initially rich countries are land abundant and labor scarce, while the initially poor countries are land scarce and labor abundant. While factor price convergence implies that low wages in poor countries catch up to high wages in the rich countries, it also implies that low land rents in rich countries catch up to high land rents in poor countries. A similar argument applies to the premium on skills and schooling. Thus, theory suggests that wage convergence is likely to be more dramatic than GDP per worker-hour convergence and that relative factor price convergence (e.g., wage-rental ratio convergence) is likely to be more dramatic again. The historical facts from the globalization boom prior to World War I seem to be consistent with theory.

Second, the deflators for GDP and wage rates will always differ. In a world of very incomplete commodity price equalization, the difference may matter, especially since laborers heavily consume wage goods that are expensive to move internationally (for example, dwelling space and foodstuffs are a very big share of their total expenditures), more heavily than do white-collar employees, big landowners, and successful capitalists. The truth of this statement is easier to defend the further back in history we look. In the late nineteenth century, declining transport costs edged the global economy closer to commodity price equalization, especially in the grain market, but also for butter, cheese, and meats (see chapter 3). The commodity price gaps between countries that eroded most were foodstuffs, not finished manufactures. Thus, the worker's cost of living converged more dramatically across labor markets than did the implicit GDP price deflator, helping real wages converge faster than GDP per worker-hour and, hence, faster than labor productivity.

Third, the labor force participation rate can differ greatly between countries and over time in an environment of migration and differential rates of population growth, driving a wedge between per capita and per worker indexes. If the forces of early demographic transition (declining infant mortality but persistent high fertility) are strongest for richer countries, causing population growth to exceed labor force growth by more in richer countries, then per capita convergence will be faster than per worker convergence. If the forces of mass migration dominate instead, then the opposite will be true since migrants were disproportionately young adult males. That is, if mass migration dominates, it will serve to raise labor force participation rates in rich immigrating countries and lower them in poor emigrating countries, causing per capita convergence to be slower than per worker (and per worker-hour) convergence.

Do any of these considerations imply that the real wage data overstate GDP per worker-hour convergence? Absolutely, but it is equally true that the GDP per worker-hour data understate real wage convergence. Factor prices, average productivity, and per capita income *should* exhibit different convergence properties. We rely on factor prices since they matter far more in provoking the policy responses discussed later in this book.

Adding the Rest of the World

The literature on recent convergence makes much of the fact that while unconditional convergence has taken place in the Atlantic economy since the 1950s, conditional growth models are required when the convergence net is extended to capture the Third World. The same is true of the nineteenth century: European unconditional convergence prior to 1914 was limited mainly to the Atlantic economy as we have defined it. Using Bairoch's guesstimates (1976, table 6), there is absolutely no evidence of convergence when central, south, and east European countries like Austria-Hungary, Bulgaria, Greece, and Russia are added. The same point could be made even more forcefully if China, Egypt, India, Turkey, and the rest of Asia and the Middle East were added to the analysis (Williamson 1998a, 1998b).

This chapter has a limited goal: to motivate a book that will have something to say about the sources of convergence within the Atlantic economy prior to the Great War. We leave the additional (and perhaps tougher) question about when and why new members join the convergence club for another book.

When Convergence Stopped

North America's leap to industrial dominance after the 1890s by itself would have slowed convergence in the Atlantic economy. Already relatively rich due to abundant resources and scarce labor, it got even richer due to industrialization. But secular convergence stopped for other reasons too.

Between 1914 and 1934, real wage dispersion did not fall at all, implying that the secular convergence that had been at work since the middle of the nineteenth century stopped completely during these two decades. Following 1934, real wage gaps in the Atlantic economy widened so much that measures of global labor market (dis)integration retreated all the way back to the levels of the late 1870s.

The world wars and the interwar decades offer nothing but contrasts to the secular convergence of real wages and living standards initiated in the mid-nineteenth-century Atlantic economy. As figure 2.4 confirms, the convergence ceased between 1914 and 1937. The cessation of real wage convergence documented here offers a very different characterization from that found in *Productivity and American Leadership*. When Baumol and his associates plot the coefficient of variation (based

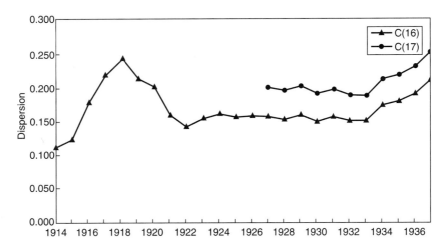

Figure 2.4
International real wage dispersion, 1914–1937. Source: Williamson (1995, table A2.1); revised in O'Rourke and Williamson (1997).

on Maddison's GDP data) beyond 1913 and up to the mid-1930s, convergence continues its long-run decline initiated in 1870.[11] Indeed, they state that convergence "has proceeded steadily, with the exception of a brief but sharp fallback during and after World War II" (Baumol, Blackman, and Wolff 1989, 92). The real wage data suggest the contrary: long-run convergence ceased between 1914 and 1937. And figure 2.5 shows that Maddison's revised GDP per capita data (unavailable to Abramovitz or to Baumol and his collaborators) also implies that secular convergence slowed sharply after 1913 and pretty much stopped after 1929.

The interwar cessation of convergence could not have been due to the Great Depression alone, since there is no evidence of real wage convergence during the 1920s either. Furthermore, after World War I overall trends in real wage dispersion were dominated by wage events in Europe, not the average real wage gap between Europe and the New World that was so important for convergence prior to World War I.

Real wage divergence took place after 1934 and up through World War II, and it took place everywhere: within Europe, within the New World, and between the two. A large share of that divergence was driven by the spectacular surge in real wages in the United States,[12] but it was at work everywhere. The divergence during the dismal decade 1935–1945 was so spectacular that all of the convergence gains

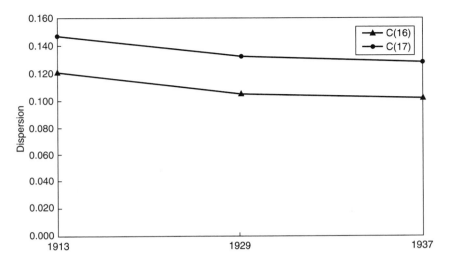

Figure 2.5
International per capita GDP dispersion, 1914–1937. Source: Maddison (1995).

up to the start of World War I were lost by the end of World War II. Note, too, that divergence rose during the late 1930s at a rate almost as steep as during the war years. Since our real wage rates do not take account of unemployment, and since unemployment rates in the United States in 1934 were higher than elsewhere, the surge in American unemployment-adjusted real wages from 1934 on would be even greater and the measured divergence greater as well.

How much of the wartime and interwar cessation in convergence can be explained by the breakdown of international commodity and factor markets?

The correlation is certainly apparent. After the passage of the Quota Acts in the 1920s, the United States would never again have an open immigration policy, and Argentina, Australia, Brazil, and Canada followed suit. International migrations between members of the Atlantic economy, and between members and nonmembers, dropped from a massive flood to a modest trickle, not to become a public issue again until the 1980s when nonmembers from Asia, Africa, and Latin America began to send emigrants (legal and illegal) in large numbers to the Atlantic economy. Governments intervened in capital markets, restricting the movement of financial capital across their borders. This hostility toward global capital markets was even manifested at Bretton Woods. The enormous flow of private capital from western Europe (led by Britain) to the Americas, to eastern Europe, and to Europe's colonies dried up, not to recover until the 1970s. Commodity trade was choked off by tariffs, quotas, preferential agreements, and exchange rate intervention, a protectionist shift that was to take decades to erase after World War II.

Is the correlation spurious? If we can show that convergence in the late nineteenth century was driven largely or even significantly by open economy forces in Atlantic commodity and factor markets, then it would invite the inference that the disintegration of the Atlantic economy between 1914 and 1950 had a great deal to do with the cessation of secular convergence that started in the middle of the previous century.

Searching for Causes and Assessing the Consequences

One way or another, the rest of this book speaks to this issue. What form did global integration take from the mid-nineteenth century to World War I? What exactly was its impact on labor markets in the Atlantic economy? Did contemporaries recognize the impact? Did these globalization events produce a policy backlash?

3   Transport Revolutions and Commodity Market Integration

Globalization has become a familiar catch-phrase, common to newspapers, television, and daily conversation. While there is much that is new about late-twentieth-century globalization and the world economy, the novelty can be exaggerated. To be sure, GATT (General Agreement on Tariffs and Trade) rounds have made impressive postwar progress in cutting tariff barriers, but similar progress was made in the move toward free trade between Waterloo and 1861 (when the United States raised Civil War tariffs) or the late 1870s and 1880s (when France and Germany adopted protection in the face of cheap New World grain). Furthermore, although transport costs have certainly declined since 1945, they probably fell even more sharply during the nineteenth century as steamships linked continents, canals eliminated long journeys around them, and railroads penetrated their interiors. In addition, exports may account for a growing share of world GDP today, but these shares also increased during the late nineteenth century.

So far, the similarities between the globalizing world economy after World War II and before World War I are far more striking than the differences. As we shall see, the main difference is this: *all* of the commodity market integration in the Atlantic economy after the 1860s was due to the fall in transport costs between markets, and *none* was due to more liberal trade policy. In contrast, most of the commodity market integration after the 1950s was (we suspect) due to more liberal trade policy.

Table 3.1 uses Angus Maddison's (1991) data to document the evolving share of exports in GDP for sixteen OECD countries between 1870 and 1987. The overall picture conforms with the periodization suggested in chapter 2: the average export share increased in the late nineteenth century (from 5.9 percent in 1870 to 8.2 percent in 1913), declined during the interwar period (to 5.2 percent in 1950, lower than the 1870

Table 3.1
Trade Shares, 1870–1987 (merchandise exports as percentage of GDP, 1985 prices)

Country	1870	1913	1950	1973	1987
Australia	6.3	10.9	7.8	9.5	12.4
Austria	9.0	13.9	4.0	12.6	20.0
Belgium	7.0	17.5	13.4	40.3	52.5
Canada	12.8	12.9	13.0	19.9	23.8
Denmark	6.6	10.1	9.3	18.2	25.8
Finland	10.5	17.0	12.7	20.5	23.0
France	3.4	6.0	5.6	11.2	14.3
Germany	7.4	12.2	4.4	17.2	23.7
Italy	3.3	3.6	2.6	9.0	11.5
Japan	0.2	2.1	2.0	6.8	10.6
Netherlands	14.6	14.5	10.2	34.1	40.9
Norway	9.3	14.6	13.5	27.4	34.0
Sweden	8.0	12.0	12.2	23.1	27.0
Switzerland	10.4	22.3	9.8	21.3	28.9
United Kingdom	10.3	14.7	9.5	11.5	15.3
United States	2.8	4.1	3.3	5.8	6.3
Total[a]	5.9	8.2	5.2	10.3	12.8

Source: Calculated from Maddison (1991, appendix tables F.6, A.2, A.3).
[a] Average over all sixteen countries, weighted by country GDP.

figure), and increased again after World War II (to 12.8 percent in 1987). This measure of globalization suggests that much of the post-1950 period was spent recouping the losses of Europe's "second Thirty Years War." Indeed, 1913 export shares were still unattained as late as 1973 in Australia, Austria, Switzerland, and the United Kingdom.

True, this measure of globalization oversimplifies. Dividing by GDP obscures the fact that export volumes increased far more than trade shares. Furthermore, true globalization forces could be hidden by the fact that consumers may have spent a growing share of their incomes on services and other goods that were not traded internationally. Under those conditions, trade might even be expected to fall as a percentage of GDP had there been no decline in transport costs. Thus, even constant trade shares might be consistent with international commodity market integration.

Trade volumes are determined by far more than the forces of international commodity market integration alone, as figure 3.1 illustrates. The figure assumes a two-country world, home and abroad (denoted by

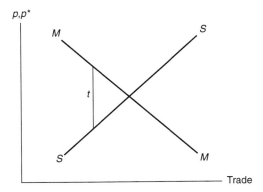

Figure 3.1
Trade and transport costs.

an asterisk), and examines the market for a good imported by the home country. *MM* is the home import demand function (that is, demand minus supply), and it varies inversely with the home market price (p). *SS* is the foreign export supply function (supply minus demand), which depends positively on the price abroad (p^*). In the absence of transport costs and trade barriers, international commodity markets would be perfectly integrated: prices would be the same at home and abroad, determined by the intersection of the two schedules. Transport costs and protection drive a wedge (t) between export and import prices: higher tariffs or transport costs increase the wedge, and lower tariffs and transport costs reduce it. Commodity market integration as we define it is represented by a decline in the wedge. Falling transport costs or trade barriers lead to falling import prices, rising export prices, and an increase in trade volumes. This is the rationale for using the export share in GDP as a proxy for globalization and international commodity market integration.

Yet figure 3.1 also shows that trade volumes can increase for reasons completely unrelated to commodity market integration and decline for reasons completely unrelated to commodity market disintegration. After all, outward shifts in either import demand (*MM*) or export supply (*SS*) can also lead to trade expansion. Such shifts could be driven by a variety of factors that might serve to raise the demand for importables and augment export capacity relative to the rest of the economy. For a New World country, these might include frontier settlement or rapid technological change in the export sector—neither of which is necessarily related to international commodity market integration. Inward shifts are also possible. For the same New World economy, these might include rapid technological change in the import-competing sector or a shift in demand toward nontradables—neither of which is related to market integration. Thus, trade shares depend on many factors completely independent of international commodity market integration.

The volume of trade is therefore an unsatisfactory index of commodity market integration. It is the cost of moving goods between markets that counts. The cost has two parts: that due to transport (including such factors as insurance) and that due to trade barriers (such as tariffs). The price spread between markets is driven by changes in these costs. Documenting the evolution of tariff barriers or transport costs is certainly useful, but economists have tended to look at the behavior of price and quantity in the markets of trading partners in order to assess changes in integration and globalization. At least four tests have been used: convergence in absolute price levels between pairs of markets; a reduction in the spatial variation of prices, as measured by some measure of dispersion; an increase in the correlation between prices quoted in different markets; and finally, an increase in regional output variance, which will occur as specialization takes place in response to market integration.

There are potential problems with each measure of market integration. If the prices being compared do not refer to goods of identical quality, then movements in quality differentials will affect the dispersion of prices. The correlation of prices between markets does not just depend on how integrated markets are, but also on other forces shifting demand and supply curves. Correlations between prices can be explained by "shared shocks," events that hit every market at the same time (such as industrial crises, wars, or famines) but may have nothing to do with market integration. If trade is driven by economies of scale rather than comparative advantage, then market integration need not lead to countries specializing into and out of particular industries but rather to increases in intraindustry trade.

In our own work, we have tended to focus on price gaps between pairs of markets, taking care to ensure that the products being compared are identical, or at least closely comparable. Nevertheless, this chapter will report several types of market integration evidence for the century prior to World War I. We start by describing the key transport innovations and trade policy changes that drove those patterns of integration.

Transportation Innovations and the Amazing Decline in International Transport Costs

Prior to the railway era, transportation was by either road or water, with water being the cheaper option by far. Investment in river and harbor improvements increased briskly, and the construction of canals overwhelmed the construction of turnpikes after the mid–eighteenth century. British navigable waterways quadrupled between 1750 and 1820 (Cameron 1989, 172), and canals offered a transport option 50 to 75 percent cheaper than roads (Girard 1966, 223). On the European Continent, French canal construction boomed, while the Congress of Vienna recognized freedom of navigation on the Rhine (Girard 1966, 224). In the United States, construction of the Erie Canal between 1817 and 1825 reduced the cost of transport between Buffalo and New York City by 85 percent, and cut the journey time from twenty-one to eight days. The rates between Baltimore and Cincinnati fell by 58 percent from 1821 to 1860, and by 92 percent between Louisville and New Orleans from 1816 to 1860. It took fifty-two days to ship a load of freight from Cincinnati to New York City by wagon and riverboat in 1817, but only six days in 1852 (Slaughter 1995, 6). Productivity in the U.S. internal transport sector probably rose at about 4.7 percent per annum in the four decades or so before the Civil War (Williamson and Lindert 1980), and Matthew Slaughter estimates that as a result, regional price differentials fell from as high as 100 percent to as low as 10 percent (Slaughter 1995, 13).

Steamships were the most important nineteenth-century contribution to shipping technology. The *Claremont* made its debut on the Hudson in 1807; a steamer had made the journey up the Mississippi as far as Louisville by 1815; British steamers had traveled up the Seine to Paris by 1816. In the first half of the century, steamships were mainly used on important rivers, the Great Lakes, and inland seas such as the Baltic and the Mediterranean. A regular transatlantic steam service was inaugurated in 1838, but until 1860 steamers mainly carried high-value goods similar to those carried by airplanes today, like passengers, mail, and gourmet food (Cameron 1989, 206).[1]

A series of innovations in subsequent decades helped make steamships more efficient: the screw propeller, the compound engine, steel hulls, bigger size, and shorter turn-around time in port. A particularly important development was the opening of the Suez Canal on November 17, 1869. Far Eastern trade was still dominated by sail, but the Suez

Table 3.2
Railway Mileage, 1850–1910

Country	1850	1870	1890	1910
Austria-Hungary	954	5,949	16,489	26,834
Australia	—	953	9,524	17,429
Argentina	—	637	5,434	17,381
Canada	66	2,617	13,368	26,462
China	—	—	80	5,092
France	1,714	11,142	22,911	30,643
Germany	3,637	11,729	25,411	36,152
India	—	4,771	16,401	32,099
Italy	265	3,825	8,163	10,573
Japan	—	—	1,139	5,130
Mexico	—	215	6,037	15,350
Russia (in Europe)	310	7,098	18,059	34,990
United Kingdom	6,621	15,537	20,073	23,387
United States	9,021	52,922	116,703	249,902

Source: Hurd (1975, appendix 2, 278).

Canal helped change all that (Fletcher 1958). In the absence of sufficient coaling stations around the coast, the trip around Africa by steamer required carrying too much coal. The compound engine reduced fuel requirements, and the Suez Canal made it possible to pick up coal at Gibraltar, Malta, and Port Said, in addition to halving the distance from London to Bombay. Not only did the Suez Canal make it possible for steamships to compete on Asian routes, but it was of no use to sailing ships, which would have to be towed for the roughly one-hundred-mile journey. Before 1869, steam tonnage had never exceeded sail tonnage in British shipyards; in 1870, steam tonnage was over twice as great as sail, and sail tonnage exceeded steam in only two years after that date (Fletcher 1958, 560).

The other major nineteenth-century development in transportation was the railroad. The Liverpool-Manchester line opened in 1830; early continental emulators included Belgium, France, and Germany. Table 3.2 indicates the phenomenal growth in railway mileage during the late nineteenth century, particularly in the United States, where trains would play a major role in creating a truly national market. Indeed, the railroad was in many ways to the United States what the 1992 Single Market program was to the European Union. Alfred Chandler (1977) has shown how the single U.S. market facilitated the creation of pan-American companies, foreshadowing the European merger wave of the 1990s; and just as Brussels is today appropriating powers to regulate companies operating throughout the European Union, so too was there a move to federal regulation in the late-nineteenth-century United States, and for similar reasons (McCraw 1984).

Refrigeration was another technological innovation with major trade implications. Mechanical refrigeration was developed between 1834 and 1861, and by 1870 chilled beef was being transported from the United States to Europe (Mokyr 1990, 141). In 1876, the first refrigerated ship, the *Frigorifique*, sailed from Argentina to France carrying frozen beef. By the 1880s, South American meat, Australian meat, and New Zealand butter were all being exported in large quantities to Europe (Mokyr 1990; Ó Gráda 1994a, 169). Not only did railways and steamships mean that European farmers were faced with overseas competition in the grain market, but refrigeration also deprived them of the natural protection that distance had always provided local meat and dairy producers. The consequences for European farmers of this overseas competition would be profound (O'Rourke 1997a; chapter 6 below).

What was the impact of these transport innovations on the cost of moving goods between markets? The title of this subsection uses the word *amazing* advisedly, because the decline in international transport costs after midcentury was enormous, and it ushered in a new era. When economists look at this period, they tend to ignore this fact and focus instead on tariffs and trade. This is a mistake. It turns out that tariffs in the Atlantic economy did *not* fall from the 1870s to World War I; the globalization that took place in the late nineteenth century cannot be ascribed to more liberal trade policy. Instead, it was falling transport costs that provoked globalization. Indeed, rising tariffs were mainly a defensive response to the competitive winds of market integration as transport costs declined: "artificial oceans" being substituted for the real thing (Bairoch 1989, 55–58). Of this, more later.

The impact of these productivity improvements on transport costs around the Atlantic economy can be seen in figure 3.2. What is labeled North's index (North 1958) accelerates its fall after the 1830s, and what is labeled the British index (Harley 1988) is fairly stable up to midcentury before undergoing the same big fall. The North freight rate index among American export routes dropped by more than 41 percent in real terms between 1870 and 1910. The British index fell by about 70 percent, again in real terms, between 1840 and 1910. These two indexes

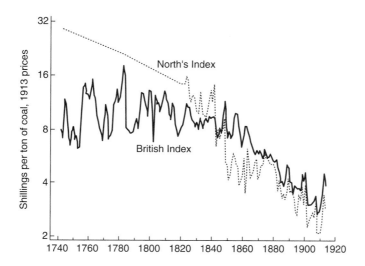

Figure 3.2
Freight rate indexes, 1741–1913. Source: Harley (1988, figure 1), nominal rates deflated by UK GNP deflator.

imply a steady decline in Atlantic economy transport costs of about 1.5 percent per annum, or a total of 45 percentage points up to 1913, a big number indeed. There is another way to get a comparative sense of the magnitude of this decline. The World Bank reports that tariffs on manufactures entering developed country markets fell from 40 percent in the late 1940s to 7 percent in the late 1970s, a 33 percentage point decline over thirty years (Wood 1994, 173). While impressive, this spectacular postwar return to "free trade" from interwar autarky is still smaller than the 45 percentage point fall in trade barriers between 1870 and 1913 due to transport improvements.

European Trade Policy: From Mercantilism to Free Trade

For much of the nineteenth century, these globalizing technological developments in transportation were reinforced by a simultaneous liberalization of trade policy, just as has been the case since the 1950s. This move toward liberal trade policy in the Atlantic economy can be dated from the dismantling of the severe restrictions imposed during the Napoleonic Wars. It was only after about five decades that a retrenchment began in earnest. The retreat started in the 1870s and 1880s when trade policy began to respond to globalization backlash at home, and many countries began to use tariffs as a defense against the competitive exposure brought about by railways, steamships, and declining transport costs. This globalization backlash will be explored in chapter 6.

The wars that raged between 1792 and 1815 brought an end to the strong outward orientation of much of late eighteenth-century Europe. In a classic article, François Crouzet (1964) drew attention to the disruptive effects of these wars on continental industry. From 1807 to 1813, the Continent was subjected to a sea blockade by the British Royal Navy: shipbuilding, rope-making, sailmaking, sugar refining, and the linen industry all suffered. Industrial activity shifted from the Atlantic seaboard to the interior, as import-substituting industries such as cotton textiles flourished behind the protection from British competition afforded by war. The gains to interior regions such as Alsace were mirrored by the population loss in coastal cities such as Amsterdam, Bordeaux, and Marseilles. Naturally, continental industries that had prospered under these wartime circumstances were unlikely to favor peacetime moves toward free trade; indeed, Crouzet suggests that the inward-looking nature of such industries was to persist well into the second half of the twentieth century, helping to explain contrasting British and continental attitudes toward protection as late as the 1960s (Crouzet 1964, 588).

Paul Bairoch (1989, 7) has described European trade policy after Waterloo as "an ocean of protectionism surrounding a few liberal islands." Prohibitions of manufactured imports were "numerous" in Austria-Hungary, France, Russia, Spain, and Sweden. In Britain, protection was symbolized by the Corn Laws. War had protected British agriculture from traditional competitors (like Prussia), and British landlords were determined to hold on to their wartime gains. The Corn Law of 1815 allowed grains to be imported and warehoused at any time, but imported wheat could not be sold in the domestic market until the domestic price rose to 80 shillings (s) per quarter (Williamson 1990b). Wheat prices had risen to 74s and 6 pence (74s/4d) in 1814, but were only 52s/10d in January 1816. The act meant that domestic markets were closed to foreign grain for most of the seven years following 1816.

Gradually the demand for postwar trade liberalization in Britain grew, partly under the influence of economists like David Ricardo. The proglobalization movement applied to both commodity and factor markets. Skilled workers were allowed to emigrate in 1825, an option that had not been available to them since 1719. A new Corn Law Act in 1828 abandoned import prohibitions for grains, replacing them with a sliding-scale tariff that varied inversely with the domestic price of grain. Various tariffs were reduced again in 1833. Robert Peel allowed the export of machinery in 1842 (banned since 1774), abolished the export tax on wool, and reduced protection on grains and other goods still further. Tariffs were again reduced in 1845. Britain finally made the decisive move toward free trade by repealing the Corn Laws in 1846. Chapter 5 will discuss the causes and consequences of this historic proglobalization evolution in detail, but note that 1846 did not mark some discontinuous switch in the British policy regime: rather, repeal was preceded by three decades in which restrictions on trade and factor mobility were gradually dismantled. Indeed, ad valorem tariff equivalents on grains fell from about 70 percent over 1815–1827, to about 50 percent over 1828–1841, and to about 7 percent over 1842–1845, *before* repeal in 1846 (Williamson 1990b, table 1, 128).

The British example was followed by the rest of Europe, but much more slowly: "Before 1860 only a few small Continental countries, representing only 4% of Europe's population, had adopted a truly liberal trade policy. These were the Netherlands, Denmark, Portugal and Switzerland, to which we may add Sweden and Belgium (but only from 1856–7 onwards), and even these maintained some degree of protection" (Bairoch 1993, 22). However powerful was Ricardo's economic rhetoric favoring free trade, it overcame protectionist interests only very slowly, and at first only in small countries, which had the most to gain from trade.

Continental trade policy and attitudes toward globalization may have changed only very slowly, but when they did change, they did so in a rush. The Cobden Chevalier treaty between France and the United Kingdom was not signed until January 23, 1860, but, though delayed, the signature heralded a decisive shift toward European free trade. The treaty abolished all French import prohibitions, replacing them with ad valorem duties not to exceed 30 percent. Britain reduced wine tariffs by more than 80 percent, admitted many French products duty free, and abolished the export duty on coal. Most important, perhaps, the treaty's use of the most-favored-nation (MFN) clause established the principle of nondiscrimination as a cornerstone of European commercial practice. The clause stipulated that each country would automatically extend to the other any trade concessions granted to third parties. MFN clauses were inserted into the many bilateral trade treaties that followed in the ensuing years, ensuring that bilateral concessions were generalized to all. France and Belgium signed a treaty in 1861; a Franco-

Prussian treaty was signed in 1862; Italy entered the "network of Cobden-Chevalier treaties" in 1863 (Bairoch 1989, 40); Switzerland in 1864; Sweden, Norway, Spain, the Netherlands, and the Hanseatic towns in 1865; and Austria in 1866. By 1877, less than two decades after the Cobden Chevalier treaty and three decades after British repeal, Germany "had virtually become a free trade country" (Bairoch 1989, 41). Average duties on manufactured products had declined to 9 to 12 percent on the European Continent, a far cry from the 50 percent British tariffs, and "numerous" prohibitions elsewhere, of the immediate post-Waterloo era (Bairoch 1989, table 3, 6; table 5, 42).

What explains this burst of trade liberalization on the Continent after such a long commitment to autarky? In particular, why the French conversion to free trade? Charles Kindleberger argued that free trade ideas were crucial: "Manchester and the English political economists persuaded Britain, which persuaded Europe" (1975, 51). The fact that Napoleon III moved to free trade by signing a commercial treaty, bypassing a protectionist Parliament, has been seen by some as evidence in favor of this view: "A group of theorists succeeded in introducing free trade into France, and thus indirectly to the rest of the Continent, against the will of most of those in charge of the different sectors of the economy. The minority in favor of free trade were strongly supported by Napoleon III, who had been converted to free trade during his long stays in Great Britain and who saw the political implications of this treaty" (Bairoch 1993, 23).

Others have argued that British hegemony was responsible for the rise in late-nineteenth-century liberalism, just as U.S. hegemony was responsible for the late-twentieth-century move toward free trade. In this view, dominant economic powers have both the incentive and the ability to maintain an open world trading system; protection between the world wars in this century can be explained in part by the absence of a single hegemon; and as we move today from a hegemonic U.S.-centered system to a multipolared world, the implications of the theory for the start of the next century are both obvious and alarming.[2] This position, however, has been ably debunked by McKeown (1983), at least in the late-nineteenth-century context. Britain may have deployed military forces overseas, but it did not use gunboat diplomacy to open markets in continental Europe. Nor did Britain use economic power to accomplish this, since its commitment to free trade was absolute and unilateral. The moves to free trade by France and the Zollverein were not due to British pressure; the latter decision, for instance, was due to the Prussian desire to keep protectionist Austria out of the German customs union (McKeown 1983, 87), thus consolidating Prussian political influence within the trade bloc. McKeown's coup de grace was to pose the following question: Surely Britain was as dominant in 1815 as in 1846 or 1860, if not more so, so why did Europe not move to free trade sooner?

Other authors have instead emphasized economic interests. Kindleberger (1975) himself argued that vested interests favored liberalization in some continental countries; for example, Prussian landowners favored free trade as long as Prussia remained a net grain exporter. More recently, Ronald Rogowski (1989) has used the Stolper-Samuelson theorem to erect a powerful argument in favor of the interest-based view of trade policy formation (see chapter 6). To take another recent example, John Nye (1991) argued that the French move toward free trade was in part due to the fact that the demand for its exports was becoming more elastic over time, implying that the national interest required lower tariffs. Chapter 5 provides our own detailed description of the political economy forces pushing for British liberalization in the 1840s.

So much for the proglobalization trend. What about the retreat starting in the 1860s with the United States? As will be discussed in chapter 6, northern import-competing industries' demands for protection had been a central issue in congressional debate ever since Alexander Hamilton (1791) crafted late-eighteenth-century infant industry arguments for young America. The end of the Napoleonic Wars meant that Britain was now free to flood American markets with cheap British manufactures, and the transport revolution served to reinforce the winds of competition: northern industry's wounds were salved with moderate tariffs before the Civil War. The financial burden of the Civil War induced the northern Federal government to increase tariffs substantially as a revenue device, and Civil War tariffs stuck at high levels long after the war ended in 1865 with the defeat of the export-oriented, free-trading South. In continental Europe, the shift away from free trade can be dated from the late 1870s in response to the invasion of cheap American and Russian grain. As a result, tariffs on agricultural and manufactured goods were reintroduced or increased. Whether rising continental protection actually overturned the impact of declining transport costs or simply muted it will be discussed at length in chapter 6. Having done so, that chapter then uses similar argument to those employed in chapter 5, but this time to explain the retreat from liberalization on the Continent in the last few decades of the nineteenth century.

National Market Integration: The United States, Russia, India, and Germany

So far, this chapter has focused mainly on the price gaps and barriers to trade between national markets, but declining transport costs within national markets were just as important, for both the development of national economies and the world economy. After all, the American wheat that flooded Europe in the 1870s and 1880s did not originate on the East Coast but rather in the Midwest. The eastern states were themselves major grain importers during this period, and they had to adjust structurally to the flood of grains too (Williamson 1974c; Harley 1980). The transport costs separating American grain producers from their European consumers included rail costs within the United States, as well as transatlantic shipping costs. Similarly, grain shipments from Russia, India, and other exporting regions relied on rail transport from interior village to coastal port.

If anything, transport costs between the American Midwest and East Coast fell even more dramatically than transatlantic transport costs during the late nineteenth century. Drawing on American sources, the British Board of Trade published in 1903 an annual series of transport costs for the wheat trade between Chicago, New York, and Liverpool. It cost 6s/11d to ship a quarter of wheat by lake and rail from Chicago to New York in 1868. The cost using rail alone was 10s/2d. The cost of shipping a quarter of wheat from New York to Liverpool by steamer was 4s/7½d.[3] In 1902, these costs had fallen to 1s/11d, 2s/11d, and 11½d, respectively. The percentage decline in transatlantic costs may have been greater, but in absolute terms it was the technical improvements on American railways that did most of the work in reducing price gaps between producer and consumer,[4] and the Board of Trade example ignores the significant additional cost of getting the grain from an Iowa or a Wisconsin farm to the Chicago railhead (Williamson 1974c, 187–190, 277–284). In any case, regional price convergence within the United States was dramatic. The wheat price spread between New York City and Iowa fell from 69 to 19 percent from 1870 to 1910, and from 52 to 10 percent between New York City and Wisconsin (Williamson 1974c, 259).

Matthew Slaughter (1995) has documented price convergence within the United States for an even earlier period, the antebellum years between 1820 and 1860, when the arrival of the canals and railroads served to slash transport costs. Using price data for ten commodities (five foodstuffs and five manufactures), Slaughter finds powerful evidence of price convergence across regions. Interregional price ratios converged toward one at a rate of about 1 percent per year, while absolute price gaps converged toward zero at a rate of about 4 percent per year. These price convergence rates are comparable to the experience between 1870 and World War I.

Jacob Metzer (1974) has provided similar evidence for Russia, where railway construction took off after the mid-1860s. He finds a clear decline in St. Petersburg–Odessa price gaps for wheat and rye, starting in the 1870s; bilateral grain price differentials declined for a wider sample of nine markets between 1893 and 1913. Corresponding to this price convergence was a growing regional dispersion of wheat and rye production, as regions specialized. Metzer also documents the growing commercialization of Russian agriculture. Between 1878 and 1885, almost 29 percent of the grain produced in European Russia was shipped out of the point of production, by either rail or water. That export share, already big by the early 1880s, had risen to more than 42 percent by 1906–1910.

Prior to the introduction of the railroad, price differentials across India's various regions and districts were extremely large, and local famines were common: "In the 1860s, the prices of grain in some districts were eight to ten times higher than the prices in others" (Hurd 1975, 265–266). Things began to change rapidly after the 1860s. By 1910, only the United States, Russia, and Germany had more railway mileage than India. John Hurd (1975) has documented the predictable consequences for Indian food grain prices, as internal transport costs were reduced by about 80 percent. The coefficient of variation of wheat and rice prices across districts fell from over 40 percent in 1870 to well below 20 percent in the decade before World War I; moreover, the coefficient of variation was consistently higher among India's districts without railways than among districts with railways.

Market integration increased within Germany as more and more members joined the Zollverein and stepped behind a common tariff wall. Prussia (1818) and Bavaria (1834) were among the earliest and biggest members. By 1834, the Zollverein encompassed six German states, accounting for 77.5 percent of the total 1850 German population;

by 1841, it encompassed eleven, accounting for 86.7 percent of the 1850 German population. But figure 3.3 clearly indicates that market integration also increased substantially within Germany after political unification in 1871: the ratio of Bavarian to Prussian grain prices was far more volatile before 1871 than after, and oat and rye prices were close to parity by the mid-1870s. Similar forces were at work in other European countries, as Betrand Roehner (1994) has shown for French wheat markets.

The bottom line is that the evolution of a global economy had to compete with the rise of large and integrated home markets. An older literature, taught to think in static terms, would have called globalization trade creation and internal market integration trade diversion. The facts of the late nineteenth century were that both national and international markets were becoming better integrated, and for much the same reasons. If internal market integration grew faster, it was because transport costs fell more dramatically there and because there were no rising tariff barriers to offset the fall.

Transport Costs, Tariffs, and Price Convergence in the Atlantic Economy

What was the impact of changing transport costs and tariffs on transatlantic price gaps in the late nineteenth century? Did they produce significant commodity price convergence between national markets? They certainly did, even though the rise in tariffs after the 1870s and 1880s tried hard to offset the bigger collapse in transport costs.[5]

Trend estimates based on Harley's (1980) annual data show that Liverpool wheat prices exceeded Chicago prices by 57.6 percent in 1870, 17.8 percent in 1895, and 15.6 percent in 1913. Both the Liverpool–New York and New York–Chicago price gaps declined (figure 3.4), which is consistent with the evidence on freight rates offered earlier. Moreover, these estimates understate the size of the price convergence because they ignore the collapse in price gaps between midwestern farm gates and Chicago markets.

Was the experience in Anglo-American wheat markets repeated for other foodstuffs? The second biggest tradable foodstuff consisted of meat and animal fats, such as beef, pork, mutton, and butter. Figure 3.5 plots London-Cincinnati price differentials for bacon. Although there was no convergence across the 1870s, there was convergence after 1879–1880. Indeed, the price convergence after 1895 was even more

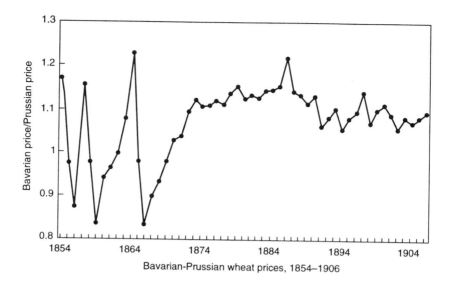

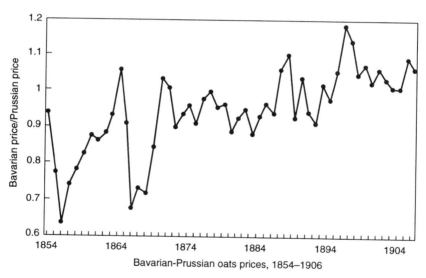

Figure 3.3
Intra-German grain price differentials, 1854–1906. Source: O'Rourke (1997a).

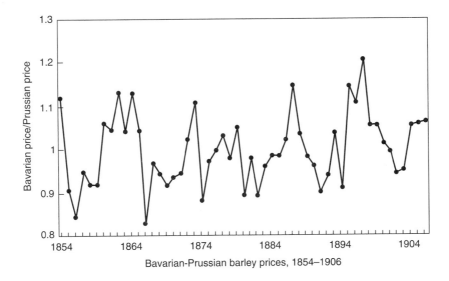

Bavarian-Prussian barley prices, 1854–1906

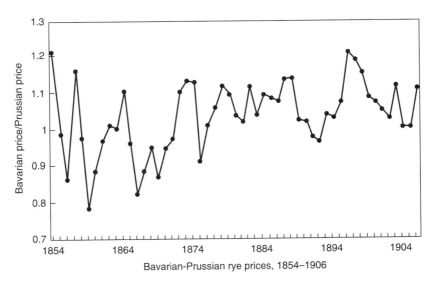

Bavarian-Prussian rye prices, 1854–1906

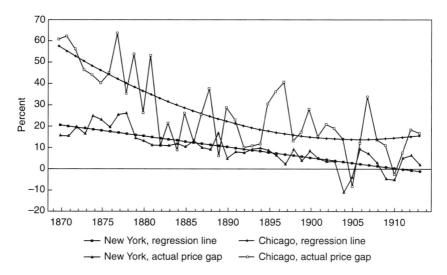

Figure 3.4
Wheat price differentials: British Price–U.S. Price (percent of U.S. price). Source: Taken
from data underlying O'Rourke and Williamson (1994).

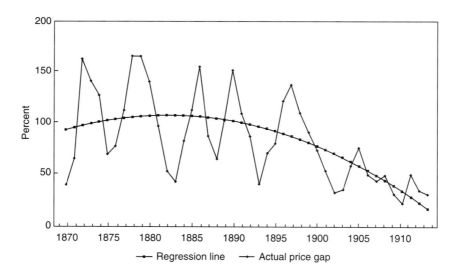

Figure 3.5
Meat price differentials: British Price–U.S. Price (percent of U.S. price). Source: Taken
from data underlying O'Rourke and Williamson (1994).

dramatic for meat than it was for wheat: price gaps were 92.5 percent in 1870, over 100 in 1880, 92.3 in 1895, and 17.9 in 1913.[6] The delay in price convergence for meat, butter, and cheese has an easy explanation: it required the advances in refrigeration made toward the end of the century.

Anglo-American price data are also available for many other nonagricultural commodities (O'Rourke and Williamson 1994). The Boston-Manchester cotton textile price gap fell from 13.7 percent in 1870 to −3.6 percent in 1913; the Philadelphia-London iron bar price gap fell from 75 to 20.6 percent, while the pig iron price gap fell from 85.2 to 19.3 percent and the copper price gap fell from 32.7 to almost zero; the Boston-London hides price gap fell from 27.7 to 8.7 percent, and the wool price gap fell from 59.1 to 27.9 percent. Commodity price convergence can also be documented for coal, tin, and coffee.[7]

International transport costs were also declining within Europe. O'Rourke and Williamson (1995a) documented as much for the Anglo-Swedish case. The price gap for vegetable products fell from about 55 percent (higher in Britain) in 1870 to about 18 percent in 1910; that for animal products fell from about 40 percent (higher in Britain) to almost zero; and the price gap for forestry products fell from more than 145 percent (higher in Britain) to a little over 70 percent. There was, however, only modest Anglo-Swedish price convergence for manufactures produced for the Swedish home market behind tariff barriers, such as wheat flour and cotton yarn.[8]

O'Rourke (1997a) explored international grain price convergence for a broader sample of countries. Figure 3.6 documents strong Anglo-Scandinavian price convergence for oats and barley, two goods exported by Scandinavia and imported by Britain. Denmark was a free trader throughout this period, and one might therefore expect to see Danish price convergence on the United States equal to that of Britain. Figure 3.7 does indeed show that there was Danish-U.S. grain price convergence throughout the period, but it was weaker than in the Anglo-American case (figure 3.8): indeed, the Danish-U.S. barley price gap actually increased. This does not reflect absence of market integration: rather, it illustrates the dangers of naively comparing prices between markets without thinking spatially. Declining transport costs were increasing American *and* Danish grain prices relative to British prices during this period, giving the erroneous impression of the absence of significant Danish-U.S. commodity market integration, especially for barley (which Denmark exported throughout). Finally, price

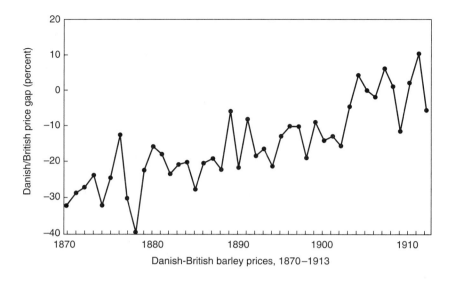

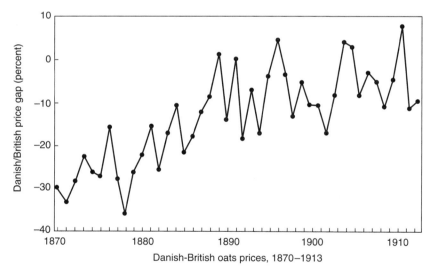

Figure 3.6
Anglo-Scandinavian grain price gaps, 1870–1913. Source: O'Rourke (1997a).

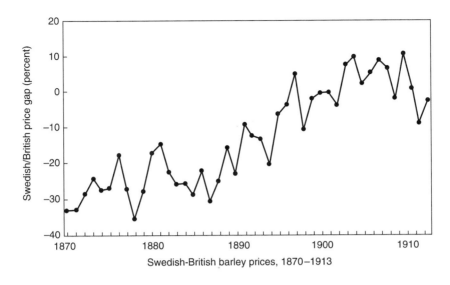

Swedish-British barley prices, 1870–1913

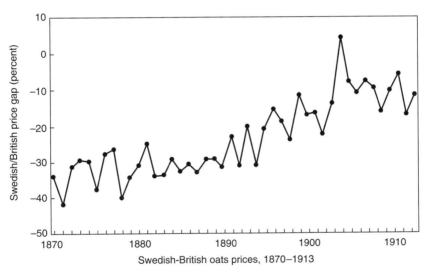

Swedish-British oats prices, 1870–1913

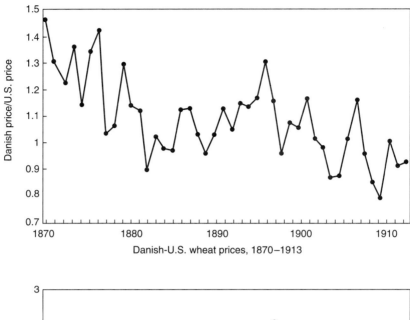

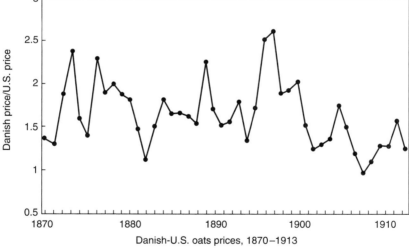

Figure 3.7
Danish-U.S. grain price differentials, 1870–1913. Source: O'Rourke (1997a).

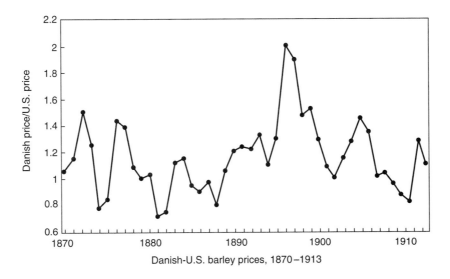

Danish-U.S. barley prices, 1870–1913

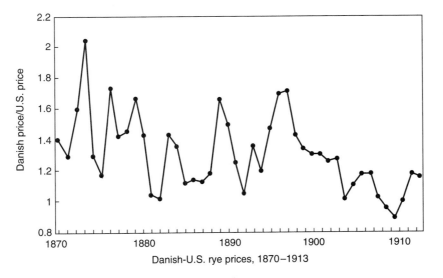

Danish-U.S. rye prices, 1870–1913

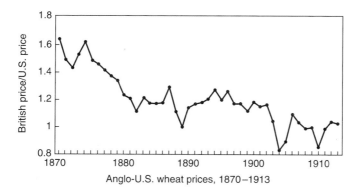

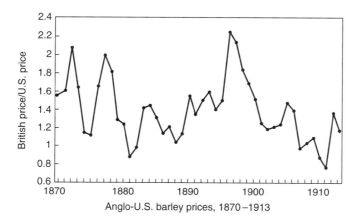

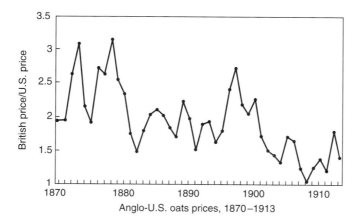

Figure 3.8
Anglo-U.S. grain price differentials, 1870–1913. Source: O'Rourke (1997a). Note: Grain prices are from an alternative source to those used in figure 3.4.

convergence reached as far as the Ukraine. The wheat price gaps between Odessa and Liverpool of about 40 percent in 1870 had almost evaporated by 1906 (O'Rourke 1997a), and a recent paper by Barry Goodwin and Thomas Grennes (1998) uses time-series econometric evidence to argue that the Liverpool and Odessa grain markets were, if anything, more tightly integrated than the English and New York markets.

Asia and the World Economy: Breaking Down the Tyranny of Distance

What about the rest of the world? What about that part of the periphery most distant from the Atlantic economy core: Asia? In a book entitled *The Tyranny of Distance* (1966), Geoffrey Blainey showed how distance shaped Australian history. Distance had the same impact on the rest of Asia until late in the nineteenth century, isolating Asia from Europe, where the industrial revolution was unfolding. Late in the nineteenth century, transport innovations changed all that.[9]

We have already seen that there was impressive commodity price convergence within India, as railroad mileage increased by more than six times between 1870 and 1910 (Hurd 1975, 266). Transport cost declines from interior to port and from port to Europe also ensured that Asian economies became more integrated into world markets. Price gaps between Britain and Asia were driven down by the completion of the Suez Canal, the switch from sail to steam, and other productivity advances on long-distance sea-lanes. The cotton price spread between Liverpool and Bombay fell from 57 percent in 1873 to 20 percent in 1913, and the jute price spread between London and Calcutta fell from 35 to 4 percent (Collins 1996, table 4). The same events were taking place even farther east, involving Burma and Java. The freight rates on sugar between Java and Amsterdam fell by 50 to 60 percent between 1870 and World War I (Yasuba 1978, graph 2). They fell by about 65 percent on rice shipments between Burma and Britain (Yasuba 1978, graph 2). Indeed, the rice price spread between London and Rangoon fell from 93 to 26 percent in the four decades prior to 1913 (Collins 1996, table 4). These events had a profound impact on the creation of an Asian market for wheat and rice and, even more, on the creation of a truly global market for grains (Latham and Neal 1983; Brandt 1985, 1993; Kang and Cha 1996).

China and Japan were also involved in these events. The freight rate on coal (relative to its export price) between Nagasaki and Shanghai fell by 76 percent between 1880 and 1910, and it has been estimated that the total factor productivity growth rate on Japan's tramp freighter routes serving Asia stood at 2.5 percent per annum in the thirty years between 1879 and 1909 (Yasuba 1978, tables 1, 5).

This commodity price convergence generated a trade boom between 1870 and 1913 in Asia, just as it did in the Atlantic economy. Export shares in GDP (constant price, Maddison 1995, 190, 237) almost doubled in India (3 to 5.7 percent); they more than doubled in Indonesia (1 to 2.2 percent) and more than tripled in Thailand (2.1 to 6.7 percent). But perhaps the greatest nineteenth-century "globalization shock" in Asia did not involve transport revolutions at all. Under the persuasion of American gunships, Japan switched from virtual autarky to free trade in 1858. It is hard to imagine a more dramatic switch from closed to open trade policy, even by the standards of the late-twentieth-century Asian Miracle, riding on exports and openness (IBRD 1995; ADB 1997). In the subsequent fifteen years, Japan's foreign trade rose seventy times, from almost nil to 7 percent of national income (Huber 1971). The prices of (labor-intensive) exportables soared, rising toward world market levels; the prices of (land and machine-intensive) importables slumped, falling toward world market levels. One researcher estimates that Japan's terms of trade rose by a factor of 3.5 between 1858 and the early 1870s (Huber 1971); another thinks the rise was even bigger—a factor of 4.9 between 1857 and 1875 (Yasuba 1996, 548). Whichever estimate one accepts, this combination of declining transport costs and a dramatic switch to free trade created powerful globalization forces in Japan. Other Asian nations followed this liberal path, most forced to do so by colonial dominance or gunboat diplomacy. China signed a treaty in 1842 opening its ports to trade and adopting a 5 percent ad valorem tariff limit. Thailand adopted a 3 percent tariff limit in 1855. Korea emerged from its autarkic "Hermit Kingdom" about the same time, integrating with Japan long before colonial status became formalized in 1910. India went the way of British free trade in 1846, and Indonesia mimicked Dutch liberalism. In short, sharply declining transport costs in Asia did not have to contend with rising tariff barriers, as was the case in Europe and the United States. Asian commitment to globalization started more than a century ago.

Conclusions

This chapter has documented an impressive increase in the extent of commodity market integration in the Atlantic economy as the late nineteenth century unfolded. Sharply declining transport costs brought distant national markets much closer together than at any other time before. International and intercontinental trade flourished, regions and countries increased commodity specialization, and formerly self-sufficient peasants in Russia, farmers in Kansas, and artisans in Japan were brought into intimate contact with the world economy. Much of the rest of the book will explore the economic and political implications of this enormous globalization shock.

4

Were Heckscher and Ohlin Right?

The dramatic decline in transport costs across the late nineteenth century led to a trade boom and commodity price convergence across countries. Shortly after World War I, two Swedish economists looked back on the episode and thought they could discern other, more subtle consequences of the transport revolution. Both Eli Heckscher, an economic historian, and Bertil Ohlin, a young trade theorist, argued that commodity price convergence had important income distribution effects within both the Old and New Worlds: they argued that commodity price convergence implied factor price convergence. They began by exploring the determinants of specialization and trade patterns:

Australia has a small population and an abundant supply of land, much of it not very fertile. Land is consequently cheap and wages high, in relation to most other countries. It would therefore seem profitable to produce goods requiring large areas of less fertile land but relatively little labour. Such is the case, for example, in wool production. . . . Similarly, regions well endowed with technically trained labor and capital will specialize in industrial production. . . . Exports from one region to the other will on the whole consist of goods that are intensive in those factors with which this region is abundantly endowed and the prices of which are therefore low. . . . In short, commodities that embody large quantities of particularly scarce factors are imported, and commodities intensive in relatively abundant factors are exported. . . . Australia exchanges wool and wheat for industrial products since the former embody much land and little labour while the opposite is true of industrial products. Australian land is thus exchanged for European labor. (Ohlin 1924, in Flam and Flanders 1991, 90)

Then they held that the level of trade integration helped determine factor prices in both regions:

If, for example, Australia produced its own industrial products rather than importing them from Europe and America in exchange for agricultural products,

then, on the one hand, the demand for labor would be greater and wages consequently higher, and on the other the demand for land, and therefore rent, lower
than at present. At the same time, in Europe the scarcity of land would be greater
and that of labor less than at present if the countries of Europe were constrained
to produce for themselves all their agricultural products instead of importing
some of them from abroad. Thus trade increases the price of land in Australia
and lowers it in Europe, while tending to keep wages down in Australia and
up in Europe. The tendency, in other words, is to approach an equalization
of the prices of productive factors. (Ohlin 1924, in Flam and Flanders 1991,
91–92)

Although Ohlin was talking about factor price convergence, this
statement marks the birth of the factor proportions approach and the
factor price equalization theorem that continue to dominate trade theory to this day.[1] They still inform public debate, as the ongoing controversy about the causes of rising inequality in the OECD testifies. Is
commodity market integration between the industrialized North and
the developing South leading to an increase in wage inequality in rich,
skill-abundant countries by forcing down the prices of goods intensive
in unskilled labor, which can be more efficiently produced in the Third
World? Is commodity market integration leading to wage equality in
the Third World? Adrian Wood (1994) has made the Heckscher-Ohlin
argument most forcefully, although others disagree (e.g., Lawrence
and Slaughter 1993; Krugman and Lawrence 1994). Given the intensity
of the current debate, discussed in chapter 9, it is of obvious relevance
to ask whether declining transport costs had a significant impact on
income distribution in the late nineteenth century, the period that motivated Heckscher and Ohlin in the first place.

There are good reasons for political scientists to be interested in this
question as well. The influx of cheap American and Ukrainian grain
into Europe has provided political theorists with a canonical example
of a common shock affecting many countries but provoking different
political responses in each. (Chapter 6 examines these political responses in detail.) Implicit in the work of authors such as Gourevitch
(1986) and Rogowski (1989) is the assumption that cheap grain did tilt
the distribution of income away from European landowners, as
Heckscher and Ohlin predicted. Indeed, Rogowski goes on to erect a
broad-ranging theory of political coalition formation in the past two
centuries based on the insights of Heckscher-Ohlin trade theory. Again,
the question naturally arises: Did late-nineteenth-century commodity
market integration in fact have the implications for factor prices and
income distribution assumed by Rogowski and others?

So, were Heckscher and Ohlin right?

Income Distribution in the Late-Nineteenth-Century Atlantic Economy

First, the behavior of factor prices in both the Old and New Worlds must be documented for the late nineteenth century. Is it the case that the big winners then were New World land and European labor, while the big losers were European land and New World labor? Were Heckscher-Ohlin forces strong enough to leave their mark on nineteenth-century history? After all, these are predictions from a static trade theory that assumes that commodity market integration was the only shock affecting the world economy at this time. Nothing could be further from the truth. This was a period of dramatic industrialization, technical change, and demographic revolutions, forces that also must have had their impact on real wages, farm rents, and income distribution more generally. In particular, economic growth meant that wages across the present-day OECD were rising rapidly: American (and Australian) labor certainly did not lose in absolute terms. In an expanding world like this, the Heckscher-Ohlin prediction becomes a counterfactual one: commodity market integration meant that European real wages grew more rapidly than they otherwise would, and it meant that New World real wages grew less rapidly than they otherwise would. Clearly, factor price trends cannot by themselves tell us whether these counterfactual predictions were fulfilled.

There are, however, four questions that we can sensibly ask of the data. First, was there real wage convergence across the Greater Atlantic economy in the late nineteenth century? Did European real wages converge on higher real wages in the New World, and did real wages along the backward European periphery converge on the higher wages in industrial leaders like Britain, France, and Germany? Second, did land rents converge internationally? Did cheap and abundant New World land become less so compared with expensive and scarce European land? Third, did land rents move in absolute terms as predicted by Heckscher and Ohlin? Did European rents fall, and did New World rents rise? And fourth, was there relative factor price convergence? Did the ratio of wages to rents rise in Europe and fall in the New World, as Heckscher and Ohlin predicted?

Chapter 2 examined the first question using PPP-adjusted real wages, and the answer favored the Heckscher-Ohlin thesis. There *was* real wage convergence within the OECD club during the late nineteenth century, and the bulk of this convergence was accounted for by convergence between the Old and New Worlds.

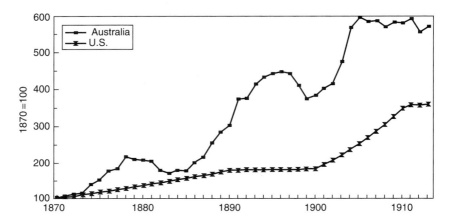

Figure 4.1
Real land prices, 1870–1913, New World. Source: Land price data underlying O'Rourke, Taylor, and Williamson (1996). Land prices are deflated by country-specific consumer prices.

What we need to answer the second and third questions are price data for land of comparable quality across countries. Alas, such data are unavailable, a point that Heckscher himself appreciated (Flam and Flanders 1991, 48). Nevertheless, if we make the plausible assumptions that Old World quality-adjusted land was initially more expensive than New World quality-adjusted land and that land rents moved like land prices, then land rent convergence during this period is a certainty. Figures 4.1 to 4.3 show that between 1870 and 1910, real land price increases in Australia (over 400 percent) and the United States (over 250 percent) were enormous, far greater than the biggest real land price increases in this sample of European countries (Denmark, where land prices increased by 45 percent between 1870–1873 and 1910–1913). Moreover, in three European countries—Britain, France, and Sweden—land prices fell, in Britain by over 50 percent.[2] Land prices in the New World certainly increased relative to those in the Old World, as Heckscher and Ohlin predicted.

The figures also show that European land rents and land prices did not always decline in absolute terms as Heckscher and Ohlin predicted. In particular, they increased in Denmark and were fairly stable in Germany. However, much of the Danish land price increase took place in the early 1870s, before cheap grain really made its presence felt in the European market. More important, Danish agriculture was famously progressive during this period, while German protection largely

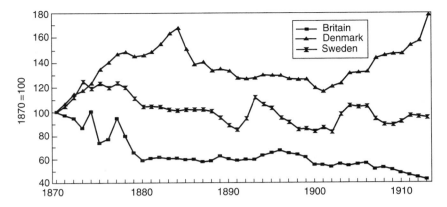

Figure 4.2
Real land prices, 1870–1913, free-trading Old World. Source: Land price data underlying
O'Rourke, Taylor, and Williamson (1996). Land prices are deflated by country-specific
consumer prices.

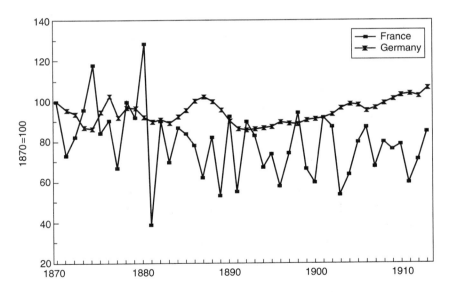

Figure 4.3
Real land prices, 1870–1913, protectionist Old World. Source: Land price data underlying
O'Rourke, Taylor, and Williamson (1996). Land prices are deflated by country-specific
consumer prices.

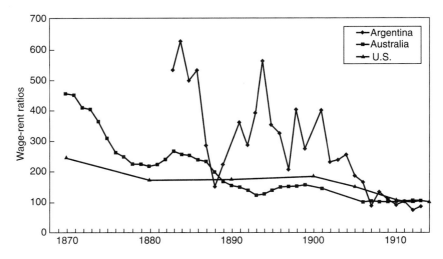

Figure 4.4
New World wage-rent ratio, 1870–1914 (1911 = 100).

shielded farmers from the impact of cheap grain (chapter 6). In an environment where many changes were taking place at once, absolute factor prices did not always move in the way predicted by the theory, but the theory does remarkably well just the same.

It is the fourth question that is really central to any test of Heckscher-Ohlin trade theory, especially in the context of a growing economy, and especially since the theory relies so heavily on relative factor endowments and relative factor prices. Figures 4.4 to 4.6 supply the answers. The figures trace the evolution of the ratio of wages to land prices for three groups of countries: three New World countries—Argentina, Australia, and the United States; four European free traders—Denmark, Great Britain, Ireland, and Sweden; and three European protectionists—France, Germany, and Spain. Relative factor price convergence certainly characterized the period from 1870 to 1913. In the New World, the wage-rental ratio plunged. By 1910, the Australian ratio had fallen to one-quarter of its 1870 level, the Argentine ratio had fallen to one-fifth of its mid-1880 level, and the U.S. ratio had fallen to half of its 1870 level. In Europe, the ratio boomed: the British ratio in 1910 had increased by a factor of 2.7 over its 1870 level, while the Irish ratio had increased even more, by a factor of 5.6. The Swedish ratio had increased by a factor of 2.6, and the Danish ratio by a factor of 3.1. This increase was less pronounced in protectionist economies: the ratio

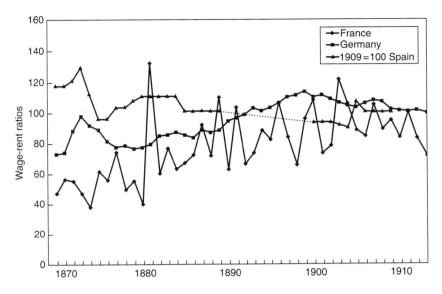

Figure 4.5
Protected Old World, wage-rent ratios, 1870–1913 (1911 = 100, except Spain, 1909 = 100).

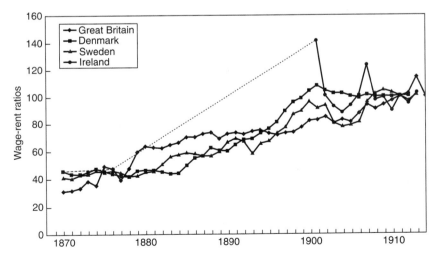

Figure 4.6
Free-trade Old World, wage-rent ratios, 1870–1914 (1911 = 100).

increased by a factor of 2.0 in France, 1.4 in Germany, and not at all in Spain.[3]

What factor price evidence we have seems to offer a priori support for the Heckscher-Ohlin analysis of trade and income distribution in the late nineteenth century. Real wages grew everywhere, but they grew faster in labor-abundant Europe compared with the labor-scarce frontier. Rents surged in the land-abundant New World and plunged in land-scarce, free-trading Britain, while remaining relatively stable on the European Continent, which either protected its agriculture or made profound structural changes in farming practice. And the wage-rental ratio increased dramatically in Europe, especially in free-trading countries, while declining equally dramatically in the frontier economies of the New World.

Correlation is not causation, however. Just as rising inequality in the OECD today may plausibly be attributed to technical change rather than globalization, so there may have been other forces at work affecting nineteenth-century income distribution independent of any trade-induced price shocks. Mass migration should have, and did, contribute to international real wage convergence during this period (chapter 8). Technical change should have, and did, save on labor and use land at the frontier, while it should have, and did, save on land and use labor in Europe (O'Rourke, Taylor, and Williamson 1996). We need to disentangle the impact of these and other forces affecting income distribution in the late nineteenth century, and this requires some theory. To make the connection between the commodity price trends documented in chapter 3 and the factor price trends just outlined, we have to make the theoretical links between the two explicit and test whether these links operated during the late nineteenth century. The rest of the chapter will attempt to do precisely this.

Trade and Income Distribution in the Late-Nineteenth-Century Atlantic Economy

Methodological Issues

The controversy in the 1990s about the relationship between North-South trade and rising OECD inequality illustrates how difficult it is to isolate the impact of globalization on income distribution. Several methodological issues raised in that debate need to be repeated here, and the appendix deals with some of these at greater length.

Theory makes it clear that the way trade affects factor prices is by changing commodity prices; it is these prices that provide the signal to domestic agents to shift economic resources, leading some sectors to contract and others to expand. "Explaining" changes in factor prices and income distribution by linking these to changes in trade volumes or import penetration rates is not particularly meaningful since these trade flows are themselves determined by worldwide supply and demand.[4] It is the commodity prices that matter.

Furthermore, exploring the impact of terms of trade shocks on absolute and relative factor prices makes sense only in the context of general equilibrium models, that is, models that simultaneously explore the behavior of all relevant commodity and factor markets, rather than focusing on one market in isolation from the rest of the economy. The Heckscher-Ohlin theory relies on price signals to trigger the expansion of some sectors and the contraction of others, leading to a reallocation of resources between sectors and an altered balance of supply and demand for particular factors of production. It asserts that price shocks affecting one sector can have an impact on wages, profits, and rents throughout the economy, in nontraded as well as in traded sectors. Relating wages to import penetration rates on an industry-by-industry basis, as some labor economists have done, makes no sense if labor is mobile between sectors, and is certainly not a test of the Heckscher-Ohlin theory (Revenga 1992). That theory posits a link between all traded goods prices and economy-wide factor prices. The appropriate unit of observation for econometric tests of the theory is thus the economy, not the industry.

There are two empirical strategies for testing the Heckscher-Ohlin hypothesis that make methodological sense to us. First, we can build detailed general equilibrium models of particular economies, fitted to historical data (i.e., calibrated) for a particular year, and then impose trade-related price shocks on these models, holding all other relevant factors constant. This computable general equilibrium (CGE) approach, which allows for the full set of influences felt throughout the domestic economy, is certainly not new to economists; CGE models have become common in the development, trade, and public finance literatures.[5] Economic historians have also been finding many useful applications for CGE models since the early 1970s, and the appendix provides a brief introduction to the methodology. Second, we can use far simpler general equilibrium models to derive reduced-form relationships between factor prices, and income distribution, on the one hand, and endowments, technology, and traded goods prices, on the other. We can then estimate these relationships econometrically, where the relevant sample is a group of countries, measured at different points over time. Or we can do both. We do both in what follows.

Factor Endowments and Trade in the Late Nineteenth Century

First, readers familiar with the "new trade theory" of the 1980s may be wondering whether the basic assumption underlying the Heckscher-Ohlin analysis of trade and income distribution was valid in the late nineteenth century: that is, was trade driven by factor endowments during this period? Ever since Wassily Leontief (1953) found that U.S. imports were more capital intensive than U.S. exports shortly after World War II, simple versions of the Heckscher-Ohlin model have been under attack. More recently, theorists such as Elhanan Helpman and Paul Krugman (1985) have shown that it is possible to build formal general equilibrium trade models incorporating increasing returns to scale and imperfect competition, which can better account for such phenomena as intraindustry trade than can traditional factor endowment models.[6]

We contend, however, that the factor endowment model fares extremely well when applied to the late nineteenth century, the period that motivated Heckscher and Ohlin in the first place.[7] Two recent and influential papers by economic historians have analyzed the determinants of comparative advantage in British and American manufacturing in the late nineteenth century. Nick Crafts and Mark Thomas (1986) find support for the Heckscher-Ohlin hypothesis, since endowments explain the pattern of trade in British manufacturing between 1910 and 1935, as well as the United States in 1909. Gavin Wright (1990) finds the same in accounting for the evolution of U.S. trade patterns between 1879 and 1940, an account that Richard Nelson and Wright (1992) have recently extended. Antoni Estevadeordal (1997) has found even more support for the Heckscher-Ohlin model based on a large sample of eighteen countries around 1913. For thirty-seven of forty-six sectors, he finds that net trade by country is well explained by endowments and distance from markets.[8] Finally, it seems relevant to note that William Whitney (1968) found no evidence of a Leontief paradox in the U.S. 1899 data.

Anglo-American Factor Price Convergence

Thus encouraged, let us begin by examining the impact of trade on income distribution in the canonical Old World and New World countries: Britain and the United States.[9] Commodity price gaps between those two economies declined dramatically between 1870 and 1913, not just for wheat, but also for meat, iron, and a wide range of other manufactured goods. How can we assess the impact of these price shocks on the two economies?

One approach is to simulate the impact of these shocks using simple CGE models of the two economies. The basic metaphor driving the exercise is that Britain exported manufactures and imported foodstuffs, while the reverse was true for the United States. Thus, the simplest models capable of capturing Heckscher-Ohlin effects will have at least two sectors in each economy, agriculture and manufacturing. Land, labor, and capital are assumed to produce food, while manufacturing uses labor, capital, and various intermediate inputs.

Both models are calibrated so as to reflect accurately the structures of these two economies in 1870. They must therefore be made at least a bit more complicated, since not all economic activity can be classified as agricultural or manufacturing. A minimum concession to reality is to acknowledge that there were large nontraded service sectors in both economies; in addition, U.S. industrial crops like cotton are modeled separately from the rest of agriculture (and are again produced with land, labor, and capital).[10]

The next step is to translate the changes in individual commodity price gaps, documented in chapter 3, into aggregate price shocks affecting the two economies. In the absence of any other shocks affecting prices, these declining commodity price gaps would have lowered British agricultural prices by 17.6 percent and U.S. manufacturing prices by 19.4 percent between 1870 and 1913. They would have raised U.S. agricultural prices by 14.9 percent and British manufacturing prices by 10.9 percent.[11]

Simulation suggests that these commodity price shocks should by themselves have had a large impact on British and American income distribution.[12] They should have raised British wages by 20 percent. This is an extremely large number since it implies that over four-tenths of British real wage growth over this period was generated by the trade-creating decline in transport costs. The results also suggest that commodity price shocks should by themselves have led British land rents to decline by over one-half. This is also an extremely large number that accounts for virtually all of the decline in British rents actually observed. Britain was a smaller economy than the United States and more open to trade, so it is not surprising that the results suggest a larger role for Heckscher-Ohlin forces in Britain than in America. The simulations indicate that commodity market integration left American wages almost unchanged, and while it boosted rents by 12 percent, this accounted for only one-twentieth of the increase in U.S. rents.

Overall, these results strongly support the Heckscher-Ohlin thesis that trade had an important impact on factor prices and income distribution during the late nineteenth century. On its own, it produced an increase in the British wage-rental ratio of 152 percent, over half of the total British increase, and it led to the U.S. wage-rental ratio's falling by 11 percent, almost a fifth of the total U.S. decline. Anglo-American commodity price convergence was indeed a powerful force for factor price convergence between the two countries, although it had by far the larger impact on British wages and rents.

Heckscher-Ohlin Theory and Sweden

The available evidence thus suggests that commodity market integration had a powerful impact on factor prices and income distribution in Britain. Did it have a similar effect in Sweden, home to Eli Heckscher and Bertil Ohlin? Chapter 3 documented Anglo-Swedish commodity price convergence for most products of importance to the Swedish economy of that time. This was particularly true for vegetable products such as grain and potatoes, animal products such as meat and butter, and hewn timber. Anglo-Swedish price gaps fell only modestly for Swedish home-market-oriented industries, such as wheat flour and cotton yarn; surprisingly, they did not fall at all for Swedish export-oriented industries, such as mining, metals, and wood products.

When the price shocks implied by these declining price gaps are imposed on a model of the Swedish economy in 1870, we find that commodity market integration had only a modest impact on Swedish income distribution (O'Rourke and Williamson 1995a). Anglo-Swedish commodity price convergence boosted real Swedish urban wages by only 2 percent; commodity price convergence in relation to the United States boosted Swedish urban wages by 6 percent, only about a third as much as in Britain.[13] These relatively modest impacts reflect three

Swedish-specific features: the failure of the labor-intensive export industries' prices to converge upward on British prices, Swedish protection, and a Swedish history of grain exporting. This history meant that, as in Denmark (chapter 3), initially low Swedish grain prices were converging upward on initially high British prices; since American prices were doing the same, U.S.-Swedish price gaps for these products converged hardly at all (O'Rourke 1997a). Commodity market integration *did* increase Swedish real wages, as Heckscher and Ohlin would have predicted. Moreover, it also lowered Swedish rents, at least in grain-growing areas, and by as much as 40 percent, according to the simulations. Nevertheless, the impact was less dramatic than in the British case.

These Swedish results remind us that globalization will have different effects on different countries depending on their exposure to trade, resource endowments, trade patterns, and policy responses. Thus, we have been given no warrant to assume that Anglo-American experience is the lesson from history to take to the current debates about North-South trade and inequality. We need more evidence to choose between the Anglo-American and Anglo-Swedish lessons.

Factor Price Convergence: An Econometric Test

The previous section suggested that commodity market integration may have had different effects in different countries.[14] However, building country-specific models, calibrating them to available national accounts data, and calculating the country-specific price shocks associated with declining transport costs is time-consuming business. An alternative approach is possible: explore the determinants of relative factor prices for a large number of countries using econometric techniques. The econometrics can be performed for seven countries between 1875 and 1914: Australia, Britain, Denmark, France, Germany, Sweden, and the United States (O'Rourke, Taylor, and Williamson 1996).

Figure 4.7 offers a simple graphical representation of the sector-specific factors model of trade, which motivates the econometrics.[15] As with the British CGE model, there are two traded sectors, agriculture and manufacturing. Food is produced with labor and land, while manufactures are produced with labor and capital. Labor is assumed to be fully mobile between sectors.[16] The economy's labor endowment is given by the horizontal distance between O_F and O_M, with agricultural

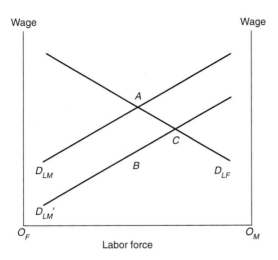

Figure 4.7
Specific factors model.

labor being measured from O_F and manufacturing labor being measured from O_M. Labor demand curves in agriculture and manufacturing are given by the curves D_{LF} and D_{LM}, respectively. The initial equilibrium is at A.

What determines the wage-rental ratio in this model? Consider first a decline in manufacturing prices. The demand for labor curve in manufacturing shifts down to D_{LM}', with the vertical distance AB reflecting the price decline. The economy adjusts to a new equilibrium, C, in which employment and output in manufacturing are lower than originally, while employment and output in agriculture are higher. Nominal wages are now lower, which implies lower labor costs for landowners, whose output price has remained unchanged; rents therefore increase. A decline in manufactured goods prices therefore leads to a decline in the wage-rental ratio. An increase in agricultural prices has the same effect; more generally, increases in the price of agricultural goods relative to manufactured goods should lower the wage-rental ratio, with the size of this impact of relative prices on the wage-rental ratio varying from country to country.

If the economy's endowment of labor falls, the horizontal axis of the graph gets narrower, with O_F and O_M moving closer together. Nominal wages will clearly increase, and this naturally implies a loss for landlords and capitalists; the wage-rental ratio increases. If the supply of land increases, the price of land naturally falls. With more land, agricultural labor becomes more productive, and the agricultural labor demand curve shifts out, raising nominal wages: the wage-rental ratio increases. More generally, increases in the land-labor ratio should increase the wage-rental ratio.

If the capital stock increases, more labor is demanded in manufacturing, and wages increase. This reduces agricultural rents, and the economy-wide wage-rental ratio rises. More generally, the economy-wide capital-labor ratio should be positively associated with the wage-rental ratio.

Finally, the technology used in the two sectors will influence wages and rents, and therefore the wage-rental ratio. Habakkuk (1962), Hayami and Ruttan (1971), and David (1975) all suggested that technological change may have differed in important respects in the Old and New Worlds. Poor, labor-abundant economies should have searched for and found new techniques that economized on land and used labor intensively; rich, land-abundant economies should have adopted labor-saving and land-using technologies. If this induced-innovation hypothesis is correct, then innovation should have lowered the demand for labor and increased the demand for land in the New World, thus reducing wage-rental ratios, while increasing labor demand, lowering the demand for land, and thus increasing wage-rental ratios in Europe.

Table 4.1 reports the results when wage-rental ratios in the seven countries, over the eight five-year periods between 1875 and 1914, are regressed on relative prices, land-labor and capital-labor ratios, and the economy-wide level of technology (i.e., the Solow residual).[17] The regressions were run separately for the Old World and New World samples, and the coefficient on the relative price variable was allowed to vary by country. As expected, the results show the capital-labor and land-labor ratios having a positive effect on wage-rental ratios. There is also strong support for the induced-innovation hypothesis, with the coefficient on the Solow residual being negative in the New World sample and positive in the Old World sample. However, it is the impact of commodity prices on relative factor prices that is at issue here, and the results are broadly supportive of Heckscher and Ohlin. The ratio of agricultural to manufacturing prices has the expected negative effect on wage-rental ratios for five of our seven countries, the exceptions being Australia and Denmark. Moreover, the Danish case was special, with Denmark switching from grain production to intensive grain-consuming animal husbandry, based partly on stall-feeding grain to

Table 4.1
Determinants of the Wage-Rental Ratio in the Old and New Worlds, 1875–1914

Regression sample	(1) ALL	(2) NEWWORLD	(3) OLDWORLD
LANDLAB	1.09**	1.16**	0.77**
	(6.88)	(11.39)	(3.53)
CAPLAB	1.26**	1.19**	0.83**
	(5.37)	(3.43)	(3.17)
PROD	0.71**	−0.85**	1.05**
	(3.66)	(3.60)	(8.79)
AUS×PAPM	0.76	0.58	—
	(1.20)	(1.21)	
USA×PAPM	−6.09**	−1.94*	—
	(10.66)	(2.08)	
FRA×PAPM	−4.78**	—	−4.74**
	(7.17)		(8.79)
GER×PAPM	−0.93*	—	−0.91*
	(1.82)		(1.76)
GBR×PAPM	−1.64**	—	−1.26**
	(3.68)		(3.28)
DEN×PAPM	1.19	—	0.14
	(0.92)		(0.14)
SWE×PAPM	−0.45	—	−0.63**
	(1.42)		(2.15)
R^2	0.834	0.936	0.879
Standard error of estimate	0.12	0.10	0.10
Number of observations	56	16	40
Degrees of freedom	39	9	27
Durbin-Watson	2.10	2.60	1.83
Restrictions	$p = 0.00$**	$p = 0.02$**	$p = 0.00$**
Cointegration tests			
Durbin-Watson	$p < 0.01$**	$p < 0.01$**	$p < 0.01$**
Dickey-Fuller (0 lags): Z_{DF}	−51.43**	−19.02**	−38.07**
Phillips-Perron (4 lags): Z_{PP}	−43.45**	−14.74**	−34.43**
Bayes: t^2	56.19	24.27	51.27
F-test, {column 1} vs. {columns 2,3}: $F(3,36) = 7.91$, $p = 0.00$.			

* Significant in one-tailed test at 5 percent level.
** Significant in one-tailed test at 1 percent level.
Source: O'Rourke, Taylor, and Williamson (1996, table 3).
Note: Dependent variable is WGRENT. Estimation: panel OLS with fixed effects (variables have country mean removed prior to regression). Absolute t-statistics in parentheses. Restrictions is the test that the PAPM coefficients are equal across countries. Durbin-Watson cointegration test follows Sargan-Bhargava testing for DW = 0. Dickey-Fuller and Phillips-Perron test for unit root in the residuals and include a constant term but no trend. All regressions and tests are implemented using the RATS econometrics software. NEWWORLD = (AUS, USA); OLDWORLD = (FRA, GER, GBR, DEN, SWE).

cattle, and partly on organizational and technological innovation (chapter 6).

The results can be used to decompose wage-rental trends in the seven countries, showing how much can be explained by trends in each of the exogenous variables (O'Rourke, Taylor, and Williamson 1996, table 4, 514). This step should, of course, be critical to both economists and historians. We are not just interested in hypothesis testing. We want to know what mattered most. For Anglo-America, almost half of the observed wage-rental ratio convergence can be attributed to movements in relative goods prices, that is, to commodity price convergence. However, the econometric exercise shows that commodity price convergence had little or no impact on wage-rental ratio convergence elsewhere in the Atlantic economy. For Australia the share explained was only 6 percent, for Denmark it was even smaller, and for the rest the sign is wrong since protection meant that the relative price of food to manufactured goods rose rather than fell on the Continent (chapter 6). Nevertheless, about a quarter of the observed wage-rental ratio convergence for the seven countries as a whole (comparing the New World with the Old World) can be ascribed to commodity price convergence.

The econometrics suggest that trade had a predictable impact on relative factor prices and income distribution along Heckscher-Ohlin lines. Not surprisingly, trade had the greatest impact where it was relatively free and trading partners were "open"; countries that imposed protection may have been able to insulate themselves from these global forces.

Chapter 6 examines European protection during this period in much greater detail, and chapter 9 explores the impact of both trade and mass migration on inequality among all members of the Greater Atlantic economy.

Trade and Income Distribution in Nineteenth-Century Asia

What about the rest of the world, especially that part of the periphery most distant from the Atlantic economy core: Asia?

Chapter 3 showed that the revolutionary decline in transport costs across the nineteenth century certainly had its counterpart in Asia. Price gaps between Europe and Asia were driven down by the completion of the Suez Canal, the switch from sail to steam, and other productivity advances on long-distance sea-lanes. Most dramatically, Japan switched from virtual autarky to free trade in 1858. Between 1858 and the early 1870s, prices of labor-intensive exportables soared, rising toward world market levels, while prices of land and machine-intensive importables slumped, falling toward world market levels. Heckscher-Ohlin thinking would predict that the abundant factor (labor) would have flourished, while the scarce factor (land) would have languished over the fifteen years. Did they?

The available factor price evidence for Japan in midcentury is limited—we have nothing on land rents or land values—but what we have certainly seems to confirm Heckscher and Ohlin. Based on the work of Smith (1973) and Hanley and Yamamura (1977), Angus Maddison (1995, 196) conjectures that GDP per capita increased by only 5 percent between 1820 and 1870. Assume that all of that increase took place between 1850 and 1870—an unlikely event. J. Richard Huber (1971) estimates that the real wage for unskilled workers in Osaka and Tokyo increased by 67 percent in this period. According to these estimates, the abundant factor's price increased by 59 percent relative to average incomes in Japan. And under plausible assumptions,[18] this implies that land rents fell by 80 percent. (If some of the GDP per capita growth between 1820 and 1870 took place before 1850, then land rents fell by even more.) Thus, the wage-rental ratio rose by over 700 percent, from 1.0 to 1.67/0.20.

These are only informed guesses, of course, but we have the real thing for the Punjab, where land was relatively abundant and agricultural exports to Europe boomed after the 1860s and early 1870s. Here we would expect the wage-rental ratio to fall—not rise, as was true of land-scarce Japan—and fall it did: between 1873 and 1906, the wage-rental ratio in the Punjab fell by 68 percent (Collins 1996, table 2, based on Mukerji 1969, 545).

The factor price convergence theorem seems to have been alive and well in late-nineteenth-century Asia too.

Conclusions

Heckscher and Ohlin were right. Commodity market integration led to factor price convergence in the late nineteenth century. Declining transport costs had a particularly large impact on land rents, in both food-importing regions such as Europe and Japan, where they declined, and in food-exporting regions like the New World and the Punjab, where they increased. Commodity market integration also had the potential to increase real wages in labor-abundant economies, although this was more true of Britain than of the other economies examined.

There are several lessons here. First, countries differ in terms of their endowment, economic structure, and consumption patterns, and thus the effects of common shocks may vary across economies, even within a similar region. Commodity market integration in general increased real wages in Britain more than in Sweden. Similarly, we will see that cheap grain had different effects on European real wages, depending on whether the economy in question was Britain or some continental power (chapters 5 and 6). This suggests that researchers interested in the impact of North-South trade on OECD inequality should be wary of generalizing from the experience of a particular economy (e.g., the United States) to other wealthy nations. Trade will have a bigger impact on factor prices in some economies than in others.

Second, the most consistent results across countries related to land rents. This should come as no surprise. While agricultural land could be, and was, switched between alternative agricultural activities, it was specific to agriculture as a whole, and was thus extremely vulnerable to shocks affecting that sector. Capital and labor could move between town and country, but land could not. When agricultural prices fell, exit was not an option for landowners, and agricultural interests gave voice to a strong demand for protection. How this demand for protection was dealt with in Britain and on the European continent is the subject of the following two chapters.

The Politics of Free Trade: Repeal of the Corn Laws

In the 1940s, the United States was at the center of a series of international agreements that symbolized and underpinned the liberal postwar international order. One hundred years previously, the industrial leader of that day unilaterally signaled the dawn of a new liberal international order by moving toward free trade. The United Kingdom's repeal of the Corn Laws in 1846 remains the symbol of that era, which also saw a profound convergence of living standards in the half-century that followed. Robert Peel's decision split his party and ruined his own career, since it came after more than a decade of fierce political debate during which he and the Tories had advocated continued protection. Why did Peel repeal? What were the consequences of his decision for income distribution, national welfare, and global convergence?

Causes of Repeal

The French Wars had predictable effects on the British economy. Agricultural prices in Britain, a net food importer, soared, and with them land rents in a country where landholdings were highly concentrated and landed interests had disproportionate political power. The Corn Law Act of 1815 was a postwar attempt to maintain high grain prices by prohibiting imports when domestic prices fell below a certain level. These prohibitions were replaced in 1828 with a sliding scale of tariffs, varying inversely with the domestic price.

The ensuing debate between supporters of the tariff and the Anti–Corn Law League—led by Richard Cobden and based in Manchester where manufacturing interests were located—was an explicit clash between rural and urban interests, with the Tories supporting the former and the Whigs the latter. The paradox of Peel, a Tory, introducing free trade has been frequently analyzed, with two positions emerging.

The first position has it that the growing power of the cities, symbolized by the Reform Act of 1832, made repeal inevitable. This political economy view believes that interest groups were crucial: "Economists exert a minor and scarcely detectable influence on the societies in which they live. . . . If Cobden had spoken only Yiddish, and with a stammer, and Peel had been a narrow, stupid man, England would have moved toward free trade in grain as its agricultural classes declined and its manufacturing and commercial classes grew" (Stigler 1982, cited in Irwin 1989, 41). Others view Peel's conversion to free trade as a classic vindication of Keynes's contention that "the ideas of economists and political philosophers, both when they are right and when they are wrong, are more powerful than is commonly understood. Indeed the world is ruled by little else" (Keynes 1936, 383). The second position cites repeal as a triumph for classical political economy: ideas and ideology were crucial.

Douglas Irwin (1989) has recently argued that both interpretations are incorrect. Ideas were indeed crucial, but it was Peel's gradual awareness that political economy was wrong, not his conversion to political economy, that mattered. Based on Peel's parliamentary speeches, his memoirs, and his private papers, Irwin traces the evolution of Peel's thought on the tariff controversy. Peel showed himself familiar with economic theory but highly skeptical of "the harsh, cold blooded economist, regarding money as the only element of national happiness" (cited in Irwin 1989, 45). Peel understood that free trade was efficient, but he also knew that it might cause considerable distress. Moreover, economic theorists continually disagreed among themselves: "The very heads of Colonel Torrens's chapters are enough to fill with dismay the bewildered inquirer after truth. These are literally these: 'Erroneous views of Adam Smith respecting the value of Corn,' 'Erroneous doctrine of the French economists respecting the value of raw produce,' 'Errors of Mr Ricardo and his followers on the subject of rent,' 'Error of Mr Malthus respecting the nature of rent,' 'Refutation of the doctrines of Mr Malthus respecting the wages of labour' " (cited in Irwin 1989, 45).

What caused Peel to change his mind on tariffs? The key lies in the stagnation of English living standards during the Napoleonic Wars. Only after 1815 or so did real wages start their sustained rise (Lindert and Williamson 1983; Williamson 1985, chapter 2; Lindert 1994). The assumption that real wages were fixed in the long run must have seemed sensible to Malthus and Ricardo, who were formulating their models between 1790 and 1815. One consequence of this classical constant real wage assumption was that free trade could have no long-run impact on workers' living standards. Cheap imported food would merely lead to a decline in the nominal wage, with the real wage remaining constant. So why adopt free trade? The answer could be only that the decline in the nominal wage would benefit urban interests. The prices of their products would rise under free trade, or at least not fall. Thus, with the drop in nominal wages, their profits and their investment would rise, and economic growth would accelerate.

By the 1840s, however, classical pessimism concerning long-run wage stability was becoming impossible to reconcile with the facts. A recently computed British real wage index stands at 41 in 1750–1755, 34 in 1790–1795, 35 in 1810–1815, but 66 in 1840–1845 (Crafts and Mills 1994, table 1). Irwin argues that Peel gradually became convinced that classical wage theory was incorrect and that expensive food might indeed be hurting workers: "Writers upon political economy have already said, that the ultimate tendency of wages is to accommodate itself to the price of food. I must say that I do not believe it" (cited in Irwin 1989, 55). As a paternalist Tory, Peel began to see this as a powerful argument for free trade.

Debate over the Distributional Consequences of Repeal

Was the converted Peel correct in believing that repeal would benefit workers? If so, did this mean that manufacturers would not gain? After all, cheap food meant low nominal wages and high profits to Ricardo. If nominal wages did not fall at all, where would be the benefit for Cobden's urban capitalists?

Simple trade theory suggests that both workers and capitalists could gain from repeal, but that workers might lose. Figure 5.1, like figure 4.7, shows the market for labor in an economy producing two goods, food (F) and manufactures (M). The horizontal axis represents the total supply of labor; D_{LF} shows the agricultural demand for labor, measured from O_F, while D_{LM} shows the manufacturing demand for labor, measured from O_M. Initially the economy is in equilibrium at A, with wages equal to w_0 and a labor allocation of L_0. Let food tariffs be abolished, and assume that the world prices of both commodities are fixed; the agricultural demand for labor schedule shifts downward by the amount of the price decline (AB), reflecting the decline in the value of labor's marginal product at all levels of employment. The economy

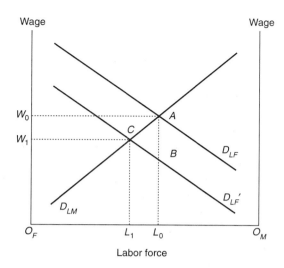

Figure 5.1
Impact of repeal.

moves to a new equilibrium at C, with nominal wages w_1 and labor allocation L_1. Manufacturing expands and farming contracts, as labor migrates to the cities. Nominal wages fall, as agricultural labor demand falls, but food prices fall by more (that is, w_0-w_1 is much smaller than A-B). The impact of repeal on workers is ambiguous in theory; it all depends on the ability of manufacturing to absorb the rural emigrants (the elasticity of D_{LM}) and on the importance of food in workers' budgets. They will gain if food is a large component of the consumption basket, but they could lose otherwise. Urban profits rise since nominal wages fall. Land rents decline since farm prices drop by more than do farm wages.

Was Peel right? Did workers benefit from the cheap food that repeal represented, or did declining agricultural employment depress nominal wages so much that workers actually lost? When Joseph Chamberlain was agitating for tariffs in the early twentieth century, he stressed the latter effect. Speaking of the decline in agricultural employment that had taken place since repeal, he asked:

What has become of this one million persons? The oldest, for whom there was no change of employers, have gone to the workhouse. Others have broken up their homes, have gone to foreign countries, and have contributed to their prosperity, when they might have remained to contribute to ours. Many of them have migrated to the towns, and what have they done there? Crowded the courts and alleys of our great cities, lowered the standard of health and strength of the people, and flooded the market with a surplus of underpaid labour. (cited in Eversley 1907, 268)

Who was right about the effects of free trade on labor, Peel or Chamberlain? Did capitalists gain and landlords lose? Were the distributional effects of repeal large or small? Were the political actors of the time right to expend so much intellectual and emotional energy on the tariff issue, or was repeal no big deal?

The Effect of Repeal on Prices

Surprisingly, grain prices did not fall sharply after 1846. Rather, they oscillated around fairly high levels until the 1870s, when they started a dramatic decline. This observation has led some traditional historians to conclude that "the Laws appear to have made little difference to British grain prices; the ability of contemporaries to understand their own affairs is discredited, and the whole Corn Law controversy is made to seem pointless and 'much ado about nothing'" (Fairlie 1965, 562). Their argument ignores, of course, all the offsetting events that by chance followed in the wake of repeal—the Crimean War, the American Civil War, a booming world population, the spread of the industrial revolution—events that would have driven British grain prices to far higher levels in the absence of repeal. Traditional historians have offered two other arguments to establish the supposed irrelevance of the Corn Laws. The first assumes that Britain was self-sufficient in food, while the second assumes that there was no European grain surplus waiting to spill onto British markets.[1]

The first argument is logically flawed. Figure 5.2 depicts the market for British grain. The world price is OA, so if the country adopts free trade, imports are DE. If the country imposes a specific tariff of AB, the domestic price is increased to OB, and imports are reduced to FG. If the tariff is pushed up as high as AC, imports are eliminated and the British price is determined by the intersection of domestic demand and supply. Self-sufficiency, as evidenced by an absence of imports, is clearly no proof that protection was irrelevant since self-sufficiency may itself be a product of protection.

The second argument is also logically flawed. It is based on the testimony of William Jacobs, comptroller of the corn returns in the 1820s, who returned from a trip to the Continent to report seeing no European

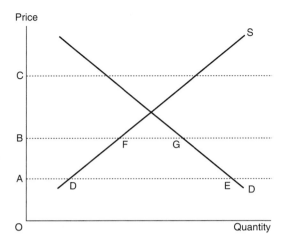

Figure 5.2
Tariffs and British grain prices.

grain glut at the time. But the absence of swelling stockpiles simply
implied that continental grain prices cleared continental grain markets.
A potential European grain glut was another matter entirely. The grain
price evidence certainly is consistent with a potential continental glut:
between 1828 and 1841 grain prices were on average 45 percent lower
in Prussia, 45 percent lower in Trieste, and 57 percent lower in Odessa
than they were in England. Furthermore, these price gaps far exceeded
transport costs (Fairlie 1969, 92–93, and 1965, appendix, 574). Interpre-
tation of these price gaps depends on whether we believe that the English and continental grain markets were well integrated. If they were,
then English prices equaled world prices (inclusive of transport costs)
plus the tariff; lower tariffs would automatically imply lower English
grain prices. Moreover, the fact that prices did not fall in England after
1846 is not evidence that repeal was irrelevant, but that countervailing
forces were pushing up world prices. In the absence of repeal, English
grain prices in the decades after 1846 would have been even higher
than they actually were.

Were English and continental grain markets well integrated? Two
pieces of evidence suggest that they were. A simple test of market integration is to ask whether British prices in fact equaled world prices,
plus transport costs, plus the tariff. Table 5.1 gives the Prussian, and
what we take to be the world, wheat price between 1829 and 1841, as
well as an estimate of the world price inclusive of transport costs plus

Table 5.1
International Wheat Market, 1829–1841

Year	Prussian price	Estimated British price	Actual British price	Imports
1829	35/7	66	66/3	1,364
1830	34/0	65	64/8	1,701
1831	42/1	68	66/4	1,492
1832	34/6	66	58/8	325
1833	24/11	60	52/11	82
1834	23/6	60	46/2	65
1835	24/6	61	39/4	23
1836	23/4	60	48/6	25
1837	25/5	61	55/10	244
1838	33/1	65	64/7	1,834
1839	40/2	68	70/8	2,591
1840	37/6	67	66/4	2,390
1841	35/2	66	64/4	2,620

Source: O'Rourke (1994b, table 2, 125).
Note: Prices are in shillings per quarter and imports in quarters. Estimated British (domestic) price assumes market integration and transport cost of 10 shillings per quarter.

the tariff. The estimated and the actual British wheat prices are strikingly similar, except in years when imports were particularly low. The evidence is clearly consistent with the analysis of figure 5.2, with imports being excluded for the years 1832–1837.

Williamson (1990b) performed a more sophisticated test of market integration, regressing English on Prussian wheat prices over the period 1815–1861. The result was the following equation (t statistics in parentheses):

$$p_e = 10.22 + 0.91p_p + 25.09D15 + 18.60D28$$
$$(0.93) \quad (9.58) \quad (2.99) \quad (3.39)$$
$$+ 8.47D42 + 0.07t, R^2 = 0.76$$
$$(1.87) \quad (0.27)$$

(5.1)

where p_e and p_p are English and Prussian wheat prices, respectively; t is a time variable; and $D15$, $D28$, and $D42$ are dummy variables reflecting the Corn Law regimes of 1815–1827, 1828–1841, and 1842–1845, respectively. The coefficient on Prussian prices is highly significant and not much less than one (where a fully integrated market would have a coefficient of one); the coefficients on the dummy variables decline over time, reflecting the retreat from protection over the three regimes; and the intercept, an indirect estimate of transport costs (10.22s per quarter), is close to Fairlie's direct estimate (7.5s per quarter). The regression thus strongly supports the view that British and continental grain markets were well integrated. Repeal therefore must have lowered grain prices below what they otherwise would have been.

Williamson (1990b, 128) estimates that the Corn Laws in the 1830s were equivalent to a 54 percent ad valorem tariff on grain imports, significant protection indeed. What would the retention of protection have implied for grain prices in the decades following 1846? O'Rourke (1994b) provided an estimate of how much higher grain prices would have been in the absence of repeal than they actually were, using the analysis of figure 5.2. We know what world prices, inclusive of transport costs, actually were over the period, as well as what the corresponding sliding scale tariffs would have been; this information, together with actual imports and elasticities of demand and supply, suffices to generate a counterfactual "no repeal" grain price series. Figure 5.3 graphs actual and counterfactual wheat prices over the period 1847–1876; in all but eight of the thirty years, wheat prices would have been over 20 percent higher than they actually were.

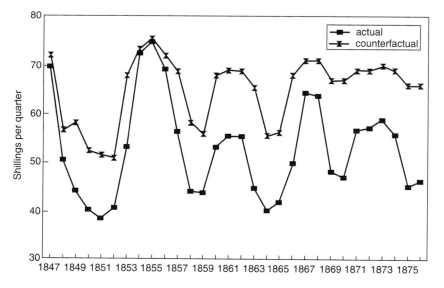

Figure 5.3
"No Repeal" wheat prices in England and Wales, 1847–1876. Source: O'Rourke (1994b).

Distributional Consequences of Repeal in the 1830s

The Corn Law debate was not merely an exercise in symbolic politics since agricultural landlords and manufacturing capitalists were debating a policy that had profound implications for British agricultural prices. Did these prices have a significant impact on income distribution? Indeed, how would income distribution have been different in the 1830s had repeal occurred then rather than a decade or so later?

This counterfactual experiment amounts to removing all tariffs, but what mattered most was the removal of the grain tariff of 54 percent.[2] The effects of such a reform have been examined in the context of a CGE model of the 1841 British economy (Williamson 1990b). The model distinguished between tillage and pasture within agriculture, and between manufacturing, services, and mining within the urban sector. We start where Ricardo did, assuming that Britain was "small" in world markets and that the British terms of trade were fixed by world market conditions. As expected, early repeal would have caused agricultural employment to fall sharply, by 21 percent. It also would have lowered nominal wages, but only slightly, implying very elastic labor absorption in the cities and towns. The cost of living, on the other hand, would have fallen by 25 percent, implying an increase in real unskilled wages of 23 percent. The Anti–Corn Law League's emphasis on the "food tax" aspect of the tariff seems fully justified. Landlords in grain-producing areas (especially in the south and east of England) would have been badly hit: grain rents would have fallen by 49 percent. Non-grain rents (on pasture, in the north and west of England) would have fallen by only 6.5 percent. Manufacturing profits would have increased by 22 percent, implying the possibility of a significant expansion in investment, as Ricardo would have predicted. It would appear that contemporary observers understood well what the stakes involved in repeal were.

Like Ricardo, we have ignored a possible terms of trade twist to this tale. Robert Torrens (1844) maintained that Britain was such a large player on world manufactured goods markets that the Corn Law raised world manufacturing prices. It did so by attracting British resources into agriculture and out of industry, hence reducing British manufacturing output and export supply. These events served to raise prices of manufactured goods in world markets, thus improving Britain's terms of trade and augmenting Britain's national income. If this analysis was valid, repeal would have lowered world manufacturing prices, as British agriculture contracted, British manufacturing expanded, and British exports flooded world markets. Furthermore, repeal could have increased world raw materials prices as British manufacturing demanded more imported industrial intermediate inputs like cotton.[3] Manufacturing profits would have increased by less under Torren's large country assumption than under the Ricardian small country assumption. Indeed, if manufacturing prices fell by enough, manufacturing profits might actually have fallen.

If world prices of manufactured goods and raw materials are assumed to be endogenous, very different results are generated by the same tariff shocks. Indeed, suppose foreign elasticities of demand and supply were very low.[4] The impact of early repeal on grain rents would still have been significant and negative: they would have fallen by 42 percent. Early repeal would also still have increased unskilled real wages, although they would have increased by less (12 percent). The surprising result is that if Britain had been sufficiently large in world markets for manufactures and raw materials, manufacturing profits could actually have *declined* (by 22 percent), and the boom in manufacturing output and employment would have evaporated. The big difference between the "small" country and the "large" country view of Britain in the 1830s is that in the former case, British capitalists paid most of the subsidy to British landlords under the Corn Laws, while in the latter case foreigners paid most of the subsidy.

Landlords in grain-growing areas were clearly right to oppose repeal, and workers were right to support it. Peel was right about the impact of free trade on real wages, and Chamberlain was wrong. Whether the urban manufacturers who dominated the Anti–Corn Law League were correct in their assessment of their own interest depends, however, on what one assumes about international trade elasticities. Guided by Irwin's (1988) econometric evidence, we tend to favor the Torrens view, but only for the first half of the nineteenth century. Britain may have been a "large" country in manufacturing prior to 1846, but it had become a "small" country by the 1870s after so many other countries had copied the first industrial revolution and were flooding world markets with manufactures. Thus, repeal might have lowered profits initially, but in the long run free trade in grain must have had the expected positive effect on capitalists' incomes.

Repeal and the Changing Structure of British Agriculture

What was the impact of repeal on British agriculture? Looking at time trends always invites the post hoc ergo propter hoc criticism, but it would be nice even so to examine British agricultural statistics before and after repeal. Unfortunately, reliable agricultural data became available only after the 1880s. Such estimates as we do have tell a plausible story, however: agriculture held steady or advanced slightly until the 1870s; it declined shortly thereafter with the onset of the agricultural depression; and it recovered slightly in the decade before World War I. Feinstein's index of agricultural output stands at 101 in 1862, 105 in 1878, 101 in 1896, 98 in 1905, and 100 in 1913.[5] Thus, it was only with the onset of the grain invasion that agriculture actually went into retreat, and only then did British agricultural interests really miss protection (although they would have done even better in the 1850s and 1860s if tariffs had still been in place).

Repeal left a much bigger imprint on the mix of agricultural output than on its overall level. Tillage lost ground to animal husbandry, whose output was less tradable, especially before the advent of refrigerated shipping in the 1880s and 1890s. Animal products rose from 58.6 percent of British agricultural output in 1870–1876 to 71.5 percent in 1904–1910, and the share of grains fell from 25.5 to 13 percent over the same period (Ó Gráda 1994a, table 6.3). Within dairying, nontraded milk gained at the expense of traded butter and cheese (ibid., 151–152).

Repeal, the Terms of Trade, and National Income

The links between free trade and prosperity seemed obvious to many late-nineteenth-century observers. Although growth slowed after the turn of the century and Britain was eventually overtaken in many fields by German and American competitors, Britain's aggregate growth performance from repeal to World War I was unprecedented (for Britain). Indeed, Britain surpassed that performance only during the "Golden Age" of 1950–1973 (Floud 1994, table 1.4). The late nineteenth century was a period of extraordinary technological progress, booming trade, and globalization, an age symbolized by the excitement of *Around the World in Eighty Days*.

Surely this global prosperity owed much to the free trade stance taken by the country at its center, the United Kingdom. Yet any undergraduate textbook will suggest that free trade may not have been an optimal strategy for an economy as dominant as Britain. Recall the argument that Robert Torrens made in 1844: when a large country imposes a tariff, it might obtain "in exchange for the produce of a given quantity of her labor, the produce of a greater quantity of foreign labour"—that is, it might improve its terms of trade (cited in Irwin 1988, 1145). Conversely, repeal may have spurred British manufacturing exports and raw materials imports to such an extent that the terms of trade loss might have outweighed any allocative gains associated with trade liberalization.

Donald McCloskey (1980) was the first economic historian to put empirical content into this view, arguing that repeal probably reduced British national income, although not by much. The extent of the terms of trade loss depends on trade elasticities (the smaller the elasticities, the greater the loss), and the elasticities that have recently been estimated for the years 1820–1846 (Irwin 1988) imply that the move to free trade may have reduced British economic welfare by about 2 percent. However, if foreign trade liberalization can be viewed as a response to British liberalization, then free trade on balance may have increased British welfare, although only marginally (Irwin 1988, 1158–1160). If one believes that those trade elasticities were far higher in the 1870s than they were in the 1830s or 1840s, then there is further reason to believe that repeal eventually raised British national income.

It is difficult to know how seriously to take these static terms of trade arguments. Dynamic forces may have mattered much more. Since manufacturing seems to have recorded higher total factor productivity growth rates than agriculture, it follows that anything that led Britain to transfer resources from agriculture to industry would have been good for economy-wide growth—a dynamic force emphasized by some new-growth theorists. In addition, if industrial capitalists had higher marginal savings rates than landlords and if repeal raised profits, then economy-wide accumulation got a boost from repeal, a growth mechanism emphasized by classical economists like David Ricardo.[6]

In fact, the UK terms of trade did not deteriorate in the late nineteenth century, but rather improved (Imlah 1958, cited in Edelstein 1994, 193). Chapter 3 argued that transport and infrastructural investments overseas were an important reason for this, making food and raw materials cheaper at home. Since these investments, funded largely by British capital, were intimately linked with booming trade in wheat and raw materials, it is unlikely that they would have been made with the same enthusiasm had Britain been protecting agriculture. Any attempt to model even the static welfare effects of Britain's move to free trade will thus have to accommodate the international mobility of both labor (chapters 7 and 8) and capital (chapters 11 and 12), as well as the presence of an endogenous land frontier in the New World (chapter 13).

The Impact of Repeal on Ireland

Although English landlords and capitalists seem to get all the attention in the debate over repeal, we must remember that other parts of the United Kingdom common market were equally affected, if not so vociferously represented. Ireland is a good case in point.

The famine ensured that, if nothing else, Irish agriculture would be better documented than its British counterpart, and indeed official Irish agricultural statistics are available from the late 1840s. In addition, good estimates of prefamine output have been computed by Peter Solar (1987) and Cormac Ó Gráda (1993). This evidence argues that the adjustment of Irish agriculture in the sixty years after repeal was dramatic, especially its composition. Tillage excluding potatoes dropped from 32.6 percent of output in 1840–1845 to only 8.9 percent in 1908; animal or pasture products surged from 45.2 to 86.6 percent of output over the same period; and the percentage of agricultural land in pasture increased from 63.5 to 84.2 percent.[7] The Emerald Isle was a lot greener in the second half of the nineteenth century.

Not all of this shift away from tillage can be attributed to repeal. Tillage was a labor-intensive activity, and as Ireland's population fell, due to the famine of 1845–1849 and the lure of foreign labor markets, it was natural that tillage output would decline in the face of rising labor scarcity. This is precisely what the classic Rybczynski theorem would predict,[8] and we have already seen how Irish wages caught up to the leaders in the late nineteenth century, making Irish labor more expensive over time and tillage less attractive. As always in economic history, there were many other forces at work in postfamine Ireland, which makes it difficult to distinguish the independent influence of repeal. In fact, the decline in tillage can be largely explained by the famine and its aftermath (O'Rourke 1991, 1994c), but might Britain's move to free trade also have had some impact?

This was certainly the view of contemporary observers of the Irish economy. To them, the changing structure of Irish agriculture could be explained by the relative price consequences of free trade. For example, between the late 1850s and 1876, grain prices increased by 14.6 percent, while animal product prices rose almost twice as much, by 30.7 percent (O'Rourke 1991, table 7, 422). This relative price shift favoring animal products implied an incentive to switch from tillage to pasture. Furthermore, since pasture was less labor intensive than tillage, the switch could help explain the 19 percent decline in agricultural employment over the same period. Rather than depopulation explaining the decline of tillage, the decline of tillage was held responsible for depopulation, with the repeal of the Corn Laws being the prime mover in this chain of events. So goes the argument. Thus, the distinguished classical economist, John Elliot Cairnes, wrote that "the famine of 1846 is commonly taken as the turning-point in the industrial history of Ireland. In fact it has proved so, because the famine precipitated free trade; but it is not less true that free trade would of itself have entailed, though without the frightful aggravations incident to the sudden failure of a people's food, all the consequences of a permanent kind which we trace to that calamity" (Cairnes 1873, 136). Karl Marx joined Cairnes in arguing this view. Writing on the effects of repeal, Marx commented that "this event alone was sufficient to give a great impulse to the conversion of Irish arable land into pasture, to the concentration of farms, and to the eviction of small-scale cultivators. . . . The Irishman, banished by the sheep and the ox, reappears on the other side of the ocean as a Fenian" (Marx 1977, 870).

In the locus classicus of Irish nationalist economic history, George O'Brien (1921, 197) went so far as to denounce repeal as "another calculated aid" to the depopulation of Ireland. Finally, Bertil Ohlin (1933, 367–368) thought that "the sudden surge of emigration, which in six years reduced the Irish population by 20 percent, was partly the result of the British free-trade policy."

How may we distinguish between the view that repeal was a major spur to Irish emigration (a price shock, lowering labor demand), and the alternative hypothesis, which sees emigration as being due to overseas pull factors (a wage shock, lowering labor supply), each view implying very different causes of the changing structure of Irish agriculture? As is so often the case, prices offer the answer—in this case, the price of Irish agricultural labor. The Cairnes-Marx argument that free trade pushed Irish labor off the land implies that wages should have remained stagnant or even declined. The alternative pull hypothesis implies that wages should have increased as Irish labor was pulled off the land. We have already seen that Irish urban wages started a dramatic increase in the wake of the famine (chapter 2), and the same was true of agricultural wages (O'Rourke 1989). Between the 1850s and 1870s, for example, nominal agricultural wages rose by 29 percent (O'Rourke 1991, table 7, 422).

Postfamine emigration is thus primarily explained by pull rather than by push factors. Moreover, CGE analysis suggests that agricultural price shocks were increasing labor demand rather than reducing it between the 1850s and the 1870s (O'Rourke 1991). Repeal may have lowered the relative price of labor-intensive grains, but all agricultural prices rose during the period, ensuring buoyant agricultural employment. Does this mean that Cairnes and Marx were wrong in arguing that repeal lowered Irish employment? Not necessarily, since grain prices would have been almost 15 percent higher in the mid–1870s than they actually were in the absence of repeal (O'Rourke 1994b, 131), and thus agricultural labor demand would have been even higher still. CGE simulations indicate that had repeal not occurred, Irish tillage output would have remained about constant between the 1850s and 1870s rather than declining by 25 percent. Agricultural employment would have declined by 10 percent rather than by 19 percent, implying an extra 100,000 jobs (at least) in the Irish countryside (O'Rourke 1994b, 130–133).

The Bottom Line: Repeal, Convergence, and Politics

Even if it is assumed that Britain was a very large country facing extremely inelastic trade elasticities, repeal still had a substantial positive impact on real unskilled wages, increasing them by 12 percent. If repeal had occurred in 1830, sixteen years earlier, the Anglo-American wage gap would have been 30 percent rather than 45 percent, as was in fact the case.[9] Free trade did make a substantial contribution to Anglo-American living standards convergence in the mid-nineteenth century and to convergence in the Atlantic economy if these effects can be generalized.

Repeal had its greatest effect after the 1870s, when the grain invasion had its full impact. Protection would have helped insulate the British economy from the dramatic commodity market integration that was then taking place. As it was, British agriculture was left exposed when the onslaught came, and the effect on landlords was dramatic: rents plunged in real terms by more than 50 percent, a decline almost fully explained by commodity market integration (chapter 4). In Kindleberger's words: "By 1886 [the landlords'] relative position had begun to slip. No action was taken to halt the decline in farm prices or to assist the farming community. The dominant group in society—the rising industrial class—was content to have cheaper food and cheaper labor. Rents fell, young men left the farm for the town, lands planted to crops shrank rapidly. The response to the decline in the world price of wheat was to complete the liquidation of agriculture as the most powerful economic force in Britain" (Kindleberger 1951, 32–33).

The political impact may have been even greater in Ireland, an important member of the United Kingdom common market. Contrary to popular belief, Irish tenant farmers did not pay market (or "rack") rents to landlords, but a rent that was below market and very rarely adjusted (Solow 1971; Guinnane and Miller 1996). Tenant rights—the capitalized discrepancy between market and actual rents—were in fact bought and sold. Agricultural prosperity and sticky rents implied a boom in the value of tenant-right in the quarter-century prior to the mid–1870s. With the collapse in agricultural prices, however, sticky rents hurt tenants, and those who had borrowed heavily to buy into tenant rights were badly hurt. The agricultural depression helped bring about widespread agitation and rent strikes—the so-called land wars of 1879–1882 and 1887–1890. Government responded with land reform and loans to tenants to help them buy out their tenancies, and eventually (in the 1920s) it made land purchase compulsory. Thus, "by the 1970s hardly one quarter of the mansion houses of the 1870s were lived in by descendants of nineteenth-century landed families" (Vaughan 1984, 39). The grain invasion, and ultimately the repeal of the Corn Laws, was one force accounting for the decline and eventual disappearance of the Irish landlord.

6   Globalization Backlash: Tariff Responses

Chapter 3 documented a profound decline in late-nineteenth-century transport costs.[1] The impact of the railroad and the steamship was reinforced by political developments after 1860 as European economies moved rapidly toward free trade. The world was becoming a much smaller place, and to an observer in 1875, it must have seemed as if it was going to get a lot smaller. Yet nothing is inevitable. History shows that globalization can plant the seeds of its own destruction. Those seeds were planted in the 1870s, sprouted in the 1880s, grew vigorously around the turn of the century, and then came to full flower in the dark years between the two world wars.

To be sure, once invented, technological developments are hard to undo.[2] However, political responses to technological change can mute or even overturn the economic effects of that change, and nowhere is this more true than in the field of international economic relations. The three or four decades prior to 1914 offer several examples of globalization backlash, and understanding what caused them may provide useful lessons for today's policymakers anxious to avoid the mistakes of the past.

A major theme of this book is that globalization can have profound implications for the distribution of income. These distribution effects can, in turn, create a political backlash. Three key events triggered this response in the late-nineteenth-century Atlantic economy. The major event in Europe was the invasion of cheap New World and Ukrainian grain, which threatened to reduce agricultural incomes. There were two major events that mattered in the New World: mass migration from Europe, which threatened to lower workers' living standards, and the competition that European manufactured exports gave to New World infant industries. There were four political responses to these three events: (1) the continental European response, which typically involved imposing tariffs on the New World's agricultural exports; (2) the British, Irish, and Danish response, which meant holding firm to free trade in agricultural goods; and, in the New World, (3) a gradual escalation in immigration restrictions and (4) the creation of high tariffs protecting manufacturers. These four political responses have left scars that remain visible today.

This chapter looks at the causes of rising protection in the Atlantic economy. We focus on agricultural protection in Europe, although we also examine the links between European tariffs on foodstuffs and manufactured goods and briefly explore some of the debates surrounding protection in the major New World economy, the United States. Chapter 10 deals with the causes of immigration restrictions in the New World.

The Key Issue: Common Challenge, Varying Responses

We have seen how the land-abundant economies in the New World became increasingly integrated with the labor-abundant economies of Europe in the last decades of the nineteenth century. We have also seen that there is broad support for the Heckscher-Ohlin prediction that European land should have suffered, both in absolute terms and relative to labor. Not surprisingly, agricultural interests lobbied for protection. Landowners were successful in some countries, such as France and Germany, and tariffs were introduced. These tariffs can be viewed as the precursors of today's European Common Agricultural Policy (Tracy 1989). In other countries, like the United Kingdom and Denmark, authorities stuck to their free trade guns, forcing agriculture to adapt or decline.

What explains the differing European political responses to the grain invasion? This has become a canonical question in the comparative political economy literature, and this chapter attempts to advance that debate by distinguishing between the size of the shock, its distributional impact, and, only then, the response. The traditional literature typically deals just with the response. We begin, however, by presenting a sketch of the development of trade policy in western Europe in the half-century leading up to the Great War.

Trade Policy in Late-Nineteenth-Century Europe

The evolution of European trade policy between 1860 and 1913 is well known.[3] Chapter 3 reported how the Franco-British trade agreement of 1860 initiated a wave of commercial treaties involving all the main western European powers. The inclusion of the most-favored-nation (MFN) clause in these treaties ensured that concessions were rapidly generalized, and free trade quickly spread across Europe. This "liberal interlude," as Bairoch calls it, was short-lived. The turning point came in the late 1870s and 1880s, when the impact of cheap New World and Russian grain began to make itself felt in European markets. Real British land rents fell by over 50 percent between 1870 and 1913. Chapter 4 presented evidence confirming that globalization probably accounts for almost all of this decline. More important, the observers of that time reached the same conclusion without the aid of any CGE model. With land rents under pressure, a political reaction was inevitable where landlords and farmers wielded political power.

The German turning point came in 1879, when Bismarck protected both agriculture and industry. In 1870 he had spoken of a new German empire forged with blood and iron; a decade later his critics were to complain of an empire of iron and rye. The specific tariffs started low, amounting to only 6 percent ad valorem on wheat and 8 percent on other cereals. They were raised in 1885 and again in 1887, reaching the equivalent of about 33 percent ad valorem on wheat and 47 percent on rye. Tariffs were briefly reduced under Caprivi in 1891–1894, but were raised again in 1902 after a decade of violent controversy between protectionists and free traders (Barkin 1970). The former were represented by the Bund der Landwirte, founded in 1893, and supported by large Prussian landowners and Junkers.

Substantial changes were made to the French tariff during the 1880s, with the duty on wheat reaching the equivalent of 22 percent in 1887. Even so, the protectionist breakthrough is commonly taken to be 1892 when the *Méline* tariff was adopted. Not only did the tariff sharply increase the duty on wheat, but it also reimposed duties on a wide range of raw materials.[4] Tariffs were specific, but were equivalent to ad valorem rates of 10 to 15 percent for agricultural commodities and over 25 percent for industrial goods. As in Germany, both French agriculture and French industry received protection, even though it was cheap grain that triggered the return to protectionism. In 1894, the duty on wheat was further increased to 7 francs per 100 kilograms. Since the domestic price was 22 francs per kilogram, this implied an ad valorem rate of 32 percent.

Many of the smaller European countries can be slotted into this continental pattern of liberalization, followed by globalization backlash. Johan August Gripenstedt had already begun to liberalize Swedish trade in the 1850s when Sweden entered the web of bilateral treaties signed in the wake of Cobden-Chevalier (Heckscher 1954, 237–238). Protection for Swedish agriculture was reimposed in 1888, and industrial protection was increased in 1892. Italy had been a free trader in the wake of unification, but shortly after it introduced moderate tariffs in 1878, followed by rather more severe tariffs in 1887. The latter led to a trade war with France, which lasted until 1892.

Liberalization was both shorter and less dramatic in Spain. Prohibitions were abolished in 1869 and replaced with tariffs of 30 to 35 percent; although the intention was to reduce these to 15 percent by 1881, they were not reduced in 1875 as had been planned, and were actually increased in 1877. Some duties were relaxed in 1882, but 1892 saw a return to very severe protection for cotton textiles, iron and steel, and cereals. Bairoch (1989) portrays Portuguese trade policy as being fairly liberal until the adoption of a strict protectionist tariff in 1892. In contrast, Lains (1992) sees no liberalism in his evidence that Portuguese manufacturing enjoyed tariffs of more than 20 percent between 1843 and 1913.

Other small countries were more liberal in the wake of the grain invasion, having also moved toward free trade in the 1860s and 1870s. It was only in 1895, when Sweden unilaterally abrogated the Swedish-Norwegian free trade treaty of 1827, that protectionist sentiment in Norway increased, and duties on machine imports and meat were introduced. There was a more significant shift toward protection in 1905 when tariffs on grains were introduced and those already imposed on animal produce were raised still higher. Denmark adhered to agricultural free trade throughout, switching from a net grain exporter to a net grain importer (feed for its booming animal husbandry).[5] The Netherlands followed a similar path, maintaining free trade throughout the period. Dutch farmers also adopted improved techniques and developed a strong export trade in animal products, fruit, and vegetables (Tracy 1989, 23). Both Belgium and Switzerland maintained free, or nearly free, grain imports, although they did impose some duties on animal products, as well as moderate duties on manufactured goods.

The United Kingdom was alone among the larger European countries in maintaining free trade. It did so despite some domestic dissension. The Fair Trade League, which existed from 1881 to 1891, demanded retaliatory duties against countries imposing tariffs on British manufactures, but with no success. The real challenge to free trade came at the end of the century, when Joseph Chamberlain, the Colonial Secretary, proposed that the British Empire become a preferential trading area. His speech in Birmingham in 1903 marked the beginning of an intense debate on trade policy. It lasted until 1906, when a sweeping victory for the free-trade Liberals settled the issue, at least until the interwar years.

Table 6.1 summarizes such information as we have regarding tariff levels in twelve western European economies in the decades prior to World War I. The data come in several forms. There are Bairoch's (1989) estimates of tariffs on wheat. There are several average tariffs, computed using a variety of weights, for both manufacturing and the economy as a whole. There are also the estimates of sectoral and overall protection calculated by Estevadeordal (1997) using Leamer's (1988) methodology. Estevadeordal estimated a model predicting trade flows for eighteen countries in 1913. He then constructed two measures of openness based on the difference between countries' actual and predicted trade intensities. Table 6.1 indicates where countries ranked among Estevadeordal's eighteen nations in terms of their openness (the most open being ranked 1 and the least open being ranked 18).

Although the table contains two Scandinavian surprises,[6] it certainly confirms the overall picture of liberal policies in the Netherlands, Britain, and Denmark, of protection in France and Germany, and of severe protection in Iberia.

The Impact of Protection: Evidence from the Grain Market

Before embarking on a discussion of why western European responses to the grain invasion varied so much, it is worth pausing to ask whether late-nineteenth-century tariffs were high enough to matter. Did they severely impede the integration of international commodity markets, or was their impact swamped by those declining transport costs documented in chapter 3? Did they serve only to signal that a more severe interwar globalization backlash was yet to come?

The grain market is a good place to look for the answer to these questions, since the grain invasion was such an important cause of

Table 6.1
European Tariffs, 1875–1913

Manufacturing

Country	1875 (percent)	1913 (1) (percent)	1913 (2) (percent)	1913 (3) (rank)	1913 (4) (rank)
Belgium	9–10	9	9	11	11
Denmark	15–20	14	NA	16	14
France	12–15	20	21	12	12
Germany	4–6	13	13	6	3
Italy	8–10	18	20	15	17
Norway	2–4	NA	NA	8	8
Portugal	20–25	NA	NA	14	13
Spain	15–20	41	34	18	18
Sweden	3–5	20	25	5	6
Switzerland	4–6	9	8	3	7
Netherlands	3–5	4	NA	1	1
United Kingdom	0	0	0	4	5

Agriculture

Country	Wheat, 1913 (percent)	All agriculture, 1913 (1) (rank)	All agriculture, 1913 (2) (rank)
Belgium	0	8	7
Denmark	0	1	1
France	38	10	12
Germany	36	6	6
Italy	40	12	16
Norway	4	16	13
Portugal	Prohibitive	18	18
Spain	43	14	17
Sweden	28	7	8
Switzerland	2	17	14
Netherlands	0	3	3
United Kingdom	0	4	2

Overall

Country	Overall, 1913 (1) (percent)	Overall, 1913 (2) (percent)	Overall, 1913 (3) (percent)	Overall, 1913 (4) (rank)	Overall, 1913 (5) (rank)
Belgium	15.8	6	14	10	10
Denmark	5.8	9	NA	2	4
France	8.7	18	24	14	14
Germany	7.9	12	17	8	8
Italy	9.7	17	25	16	17
Norway	11.4	NA	NA	11	12
Portugal	23.7	NA	NA	17	15
Spain	14.3	33	37	18	18

Table 6.1 (continued)

Overall

Country	Overall, 1913 (1) (percent)	Overall, 1913 (2) (percent)	Overall, 1913 (3) (percent)	Overall, 1913 (4) (rank)	Overall, 1913 (5) (rank)
Sweden	9	16	28	7	7
Switzerland	4.4	7	11	9	9
Netherlands	0.4	3	NA	1	1
United Kingdom	5.6	0	0	3	3

Source: O'Rourke and Williamson (1997, table 8, 178–179).
Note: Manufacturing 1875: average levels of duties on manufactured products in 1875, from Bairoch (1989, table 5, 42).
Manufacturing 1913 (1): League of Nations estimate, as reported in Bairoch (1989, table 9, 76).
Manufacturing 1913 (2): Liepmann (1938) estimate, as reported in Bairoch (1989, table 9, 76).
Manufacturing 1913 (3): Rank among eighteen countries (1 = least protectionist, 18 = most protectionist), based on the adjusted trade intensity ratios in Estevadeordal (1997, table 6, 104).
Manufacturing 1913 (4): Rank among eighteen countries (1 = least protectionist, 18 = most protectionist), based on the adjusted trade intensity ratios in Estevadeordal (1997, table 6, 105).
Wheat 1913: Levels of duties on wheat, calculated by Bairoch (1989, table 9, 76).
Agriculture 1913 (1): Rank among eighteen countries (1 = least protectionist, 18 = most protectionist), based on the adjusted trade intensity ratios in Estevadeordal (1997, table 6, 104).
Agriculture 1913 (2): Rank among eighteen countries (1 = least protectionist, 18 = most protectionist), based on the adjusted trade intensity ratios in Estevadeordal (1997, table 6, 105).
Overall 1913 (1): Import duties as percentage of special total imports (1909–1913), calculated by Bairoch (1989, table 9, 76).
Overall 1913 (2): League of Nations estimate, as reported in Bairoch (1989, table 9, 76).
Overall 1913 (3): Liepmann (1938) estimate, as reported in Bairoch (1989, table 9, 76).
Overall 1913 (4): Rank among eighteen countries (1 = least protectionist, 18 = most protectionist), based on the adjusted trade intensity ratios in Estevadeordal (1997, table 8, 107).
Overall 1913 (5): Rank among eighteen countries (1 = least protectionist, 18 = most protectionist), based on the adjusted trade intensity ratios in Estevadeordal (1997, table 8, 107).

Table 6.2
European Cereal Protection, 1909–1913 (ad valorem equivalents, in percent)

	France	Germany	Sweden
Wheat	38.1	37.2	32.0
Barley	21.0	35.5	42.2
Oats	16.9	45.1	0.0
Rye	20.6	42.9	39.9
Weighted geometric average	26.6	40.0	0.0
Weighted arithmetic average	28.4	40.1	24.0

Source: O'Rourke (1997a, table 2, 783).

continental protection. Table 6.2 gives average tariffs during the five-year period 1909–1913 for the main grains in Germany, France, and Sweden.[7] The figures confirm what qualitative histories stress: the disproportionately high protection given to wheat in France, and rye (and oats) in Germany,[8] as well as the higher average level of protection in Germany than in France or Sweden. As a traditional oats exporter, Sweden did not impose tariffs on imports of that grain.

Recall that chapter 3 documented an enormous decline in the Anglo-American grain price gap, with Liverpool wheat prices exceeding Chicago wheat prices by 57.6 percent in 1870 but only 15.6 percent in 1913. Were French and German tariffs high enough to overturn these globalization forces?

First, we need to be convinced that continental tariffs did in fact increase continental grain prices. This issue was raised in chapter 5, where we encountered arguments made by traditional British historians, who doubted that the Corn Laws raised British grain prices in the 1820s and 1830s. Here it is raised again by a traditional historian discussing Germany fifty years later. Karl Hardach claimed that east German grain prices were *not* increased as a result of tariff protection in the 1880s (Hardach 1967). He argued that Prussian landlords exported almost half their output. Furthermore, he argued that market segmentation between grain-exporting east Germany and grain-importing west Germany ensured that higher western prices did not translate into higher eastern prices. The evidence presented in chapter 3 should suffice to cast considerable doubt on the assertion. After all, Bavarian and Prussian grain prices were very similar, particularly after unification (see figure 3.3). Indeed, Webb (1982) found a very tight correlation between east and west German grain prices, a further contradiction of Hardach's assertions. Webb also reported that the gap between the Prussian and the world grain price was well explained by German grain tariffs. In short, the evidence shows convincingly that continental tariffs were effective in raising grain prices.

More recently, O'Rourke (1997a) compared grain prices in protected continental markets with world prices (i.e., prices in free-trading economies such as Britain and Denmark). These intra-European price gaps were then compared with tariff levels in protectionist countries. If tariffs were effective in raising grain prices (and grain markets were well integrated internationally), then domestic prices should have equaled world prices plus the tariff. French and Bavarian grain prices were compared with British prices, and Prussian and Swedish prices were compared with Danish prices. Figure 6.1 shows that there was a very tight correlation between continental wheat prices and wheat tariffs. Throughout the late nineteenth century, Swedish and Prussian wheat prices exceeded Danish wheat prices by the amount of the two countries' tariffs, while Franco-British and Bavarian-British price gaps mirrored exactly the evolution of French and German tariffs. It seems clear that wheat tariffs were binding; that is, domestic wheat prices were raised above world prices by the amount of the tariff.

Tariffs raised domestic prices, but were they high enough to insulate continental economies from the globalizing impact of steamship and railroad? Table 6.3 supplies the answers. It reports grain price gaps in 1870 and 1913 between eight locations: Bavaria, Britain, Denmark, France, Prussia, Russia (Odessa), Sweden, and the United States (Chicago). For the sake of comparison, the table begins with Anglo-American price gaps for wheat, oats, and barley.[9] Even if the U.S. and European grain prices are not fully comparable, the trends in these price gaps should be reliable, and they are unmistakable.[10] The Anglo-American wheat price gap fell from 54 percent in 1870 to nothing in 1913; the barley price gap declined from 46 percent to 11 percent over the same period; and the oats price gap collapsed from 138 percent to 28 percent. Since Britain maintained a free trade stance, these Anglo-American gap trends should offer an excellent global commodity integration yardstick by which to judge the impact of globalization backlash on the Continent.

Part B, which reports the behavior of U.S.-Scandinavian grain price gaps, supports the assertion that tariffs seriously muted globalization effects on the Continent. As we saw in chapter 3, Danish-U.S. price gaps did not decline by as much as did Anglo-American price gaps.

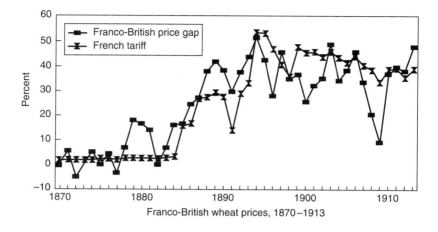

Franco-British wheat prices, 1870–1913

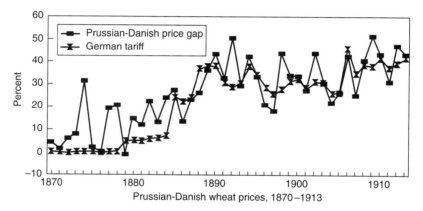

Prussian-Danish wheat prices, 1870–1913

Figure 6.1, above and opposite
Tariffs and domestic prices: wheat, 1870–1913. Source: O'Rourke (1997a).

This was due to the fact that as a traditional exporter of barley and other grains, Danish grain prices were converging upward on British prices. Since American and Danish grain prices were converging on British grain prices from below, it should not be surprising to learn that the Danish-U.S. barley price gap actually increased between 1870 and 1913. What was true of Denmark was even more true of Sweden, since the latter imposed tariffs on wheat, barley, and rye. Thus, while the Danish-American rye price gap was all but eliminated, the Swedish-U.S. price gap was reduced by only a third; and while the Danish-American wheat price gap was eliminated, the Swedish-American price gap remained unchanged over the period.

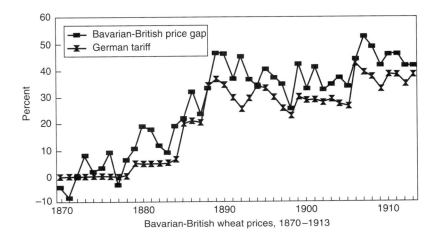

Bavarian-British wheat prices, 1870–1913

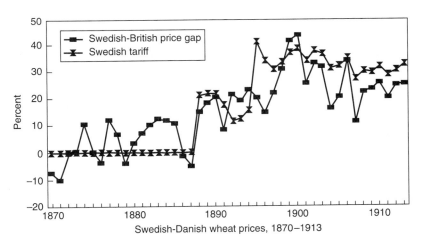

Swedish-Danish wheat prices, 1870–1913

France and Germany also succeeded in insulating themselves to a considerable extent from the impact of transatlantic transport cost declines (part C). The Franco-American wheat price gap fell by only a third; the Bavarian-American wheat price gap fell by less than a sixth; the Bavarian-American rye price gap fell by little more than a quarter; finally, Bavarian oat prices, Bavarian barley prices, and French barley prices all moved even further away from American levels.

In short, average Bavarian cereal prices cannot have moved much closer to American prices during the period, while French and Swedish cereal prices converged only modestly on American prices. In contrast, British and Danish cereal prices converged strongly on American

Table 6.3
International Grain Price Spreads, 1870 and 1913 (in percent)

Grain	Countries	1870	1913
A. Transatlantic price gaps			
Wheat	Britain–United States	54.1	−0.8
Barley	Britain–United States	45.9	10.9
Oats	Britain–United States	138	28.1
B. U.S.-Scandinavian price gaps			
Wheat	Denmark–United States	28.9	−4.6
Barley	Denmark–United States	0.4	11.4
Oats	Denmark–United States	60.1	19.4
Rye	Denmark–United States	44.7	5.3
Wheat	Sweden–United States	18.7	17.3
Barley	Sweden–United States	−6	17.6
Oats	Sweden–United States	53.4	22.3
Rye	Sweden–United States	39.2	26.1
C. Continental European–U.S. price gaps			
Wheat	France–United States	43.8	29.3
Barley	France–United States	6.1	15.4
Oats	France–United States	118	61
Rye	France–United States	61.1	16.9
Wheat	Bavaria–United States	44	37.1
Barley	Bavaria–United States	5.4	43.6
Oats	Bavaria–United States	82.6	106.3
Rye	Bavaria–United States	66.5	48.5
D. Western European–Odessa price gaps			
Wheat	Britain–Odessa	37.9	6.5
Wheat	Denmark–Odessa	15.7	4.9
Wheat	Sweden–Odessa	9.4	35.9
Wheat	France–Odessa	28	48.8
Wheat	Bavaria–Odessa	25.3	43.8
E. Intra-European price gaps			
Wheat	Britain–France	5.8	−23.5
Wheat	Denmark–France	−11.2	−26.2
Wheat	Sweden–France	−17.1	−9.2
Wheat	Bavaria–France	0.6	7.1

Source: O'Rourke (1997a, table 1, 782).
Note: Predicted values from regressions of price gaps on time and time squared. Underlying price data as described in O'Rourke (1997a, appendix 1).

prices. This contrast between the two free-trading Old World countries (Britain and Denmark) and the three protectionist Old World countries (Germany, France, and Sweden) is further born out when wheat prices in these five western European countries are compared with Odessa prices (part D). There was clear commodity price convergence in the British and Danish cases, while wheat prices *diverged* between Odessa and Sweden, Bavaria and France. Indeed, by 1913 British prices were closer to Odessa prices than were Swedish, French, or Bavarian prices, whereas the opposite had been true in 1870.

Continental protection muted or overturned price convergence between western Europe and the United States and Russian granaries, and it also hindered commodity market integration within western Europe. Part E makes the point by focusing on wheat price gaps between France and other European countries. With the exception of Sweden-France, price gaps actually increased on the Continent over the period. To summarize, there is absolutely no evidence of grain market integration on the Continent during the forty years prior to the Great War. An era in which the Old and New Worlds became much more economically integrated with each other was also an era in which grain markets within Continental Europe became more balkanized. Globalization was not a universal phenomenon, even during the comparatively liberal late nineteenth century. Tariff hikes were big enough to matter. Explaining the evolution of European trade policy is thus well worth the effort.

Contemporary Debates

The two-sector specific-factors model considered in the previous chapter suggests that cheap grain should have lowered rents, raised profits, and had an ambiguous effect on real wages, lowering nominal wages as well as food prices. The model predicts a conflict between protectionist landowners and free-trading capitalists, with the interests of workers being a priori indeterminate.[11] Reality was somewhat more complex, of course, with cleavages typically emerging within both agriculture and industry. While the specific-factors model is useful in understanding these disputes, it must be extended to three or more sectors to be effective, each with their own specific factor.

A constant feature of the period is the dispute between (typically large) grain-producing farms and (typically small) grain-using farms

engaged in animal husbandry. Tariffs on grain might benefit grain producers, but they could hurt smallholders by making their feed more
expensive. Indeed, Alexander Gerschenkron (1943) claimed that southern German peasants were hurt by tariffs on rye. (Rye was particularly
important to the Junkers, which is why it was so heavily protected.)
That peasants supported the Junkers was for Gerschenkron merely evidence that they had been duped. Webb (1982) disagreed, arguing
instead that tariff protection on animal products, as well as health regu-
lations, ensured that German animal producers benefited from protection as well.

Swedish agricultural protection was preceded by a vigorous debate
between these two groups (Kuuse 1971, 40–44), but the large grain-
growing landlords were better represented politically, and so won the
argument. However, smallholders were compensated later, at least in
part, by duties on pig meat. The Swedish experience thus closely parallels that of Germany. By contrast, Norway lacked a strong aristocracy,
which may explain why grain tariffs were so long in coming. When
they were finally introduced in 1905, they were accompanied by higher
tariffs on animal products, reflecting smallholder interests. The size
distribution of landholdings and the importance of grain growing thus
emerge as central (and perhaps interdependent) determinants of European trade policy during the period.

Another division emerged in countries like France and Italy, this
time between protectionist grain growers and free-trading cultivators
of Mediterranean products, notably wine. French viticulturers and silk
growers were strongly opposed to protection; it took the phylloxera
epidemic of the 1870s and 1880s to undermine their support for free
trade (Caron 1979, 110). Similarly, while Italy imposed heavy tariffs on
grain imports, Prime Minister Giovanni Giolitti was willing to reduce
manufacturing tariffs in order to secure markets for Italian wines, citrus
fruits, and other Mediterranean exports (Coppa 1970).

Within the manufacturing sector, tariffs that helped one industry
could damage another, depending on downstream use. The German
iron industry provides a good example. Tariffs on crude iron benefited
large, vertically integrated firms in cartelized segments of the industry,
but hurt smaller firms that purchased iron, like those that produced
cast-iron goods (Webb 1977). Another good example is offered by Italian iron and steel tariffs, which, according to many experts, inhibited
the development of the Italian engineering industry (Gerschenkron

1962, 82; Toniolo 1977). A diverse range of French export-oriented industries (Parisian luxury goods and the Lyonnais silk industry, to name
but two) favored free trade, while import-competing cotton textiles,
metallurgy, and mining favored protection (Smith 1980, chapters 2
and 3).

These disputes within agriculture and within industry can help explain Bismarck's marriage of iron and rye, which otherwise seems
paradoxical. In a two-sector specific-factors model, the interests of agriculture and industry are opposed. In a multisector model, it would be
quite possible for owners of two or more specific factors (grain growers
and heavy industrialists) to combine and benefit at the expense of politically weaker groups, owning other specific factors (light industry capitalists and smallholder peasants).

Agricultural interests and organized labor produced another cleav-
age in Germany. While in theory labor could lose from cheap grain—
employment effects exceeding the effects of cheap food—in practice
continental socialist groups tended to support free trade.[12] Social Dem-
ocrats in Germany and socialist parties in Italy, Switzerland, and Belgium all took the view that cheap food was welcome. The British
Labour party adopted a free trade position in 1904, to which it adhered
for thirty years. And while an active intellectual debate took place in
Germany between advocates of protection like Adolf Wagner and free
trade liberals like Max Weber and Luigi Brentano, the major opposition
to the agrarians came from socialists. Indeed, Brentano and others
made much of the bread tax that grain tariffs imposed on urban workers (Tracy 1989, 92–94). European labor's position around the turn of
the century is certainly consistent with the results of chapter 5 dealing
with the repeal of the Corn Laws a half-century earlier.

Advocates of protection argued not only on the basis of self-interest.
In Germany, Adolf Wagner and others also objected to the allocative
and distributional consequences of the grain invasion. In particular,
cityward migration was seen by many as socially undesirable—overur-
banization was a concern in Europe then, as it is today in the Third
World (Williamson 1990a)—and it was obvious to all that the grain
invasion was hastening the process. Agricultural protection would
help slow this undesirable trend, and thus was viewed as a welcome
force.

The debate was rather different in Britain. Jagdish Bhagwati and
Douglas Irwin (1987) have pointed to the many striking similarities

between the arguments deployed by late-nineteenth-century British protectionists and late-twentieth-century American protectionists. Both countries previously had been committed to free trade; both had seen their international market shares eroded by upstart rivals (in Britain's case, Germany and the United States; in America's case, Japan and newly industrial Third World countries). The "diminished giant" syndrome, and a sense that foreigners were unfairly resorting to protection, reduced support for a policy of unilateral free trade in both cases. In the late nineteenth century, Lord Randolph Churchill called for foreign markets to be opened, like oysters, with a strong clasp knife (Bhagwati and Irwin 1987, 113); in the late twentieth century, U.S. trade representative Carla Hill wielded a crowbar in her efforts to achieve "fair trade."

In their attempts to secure a level playing field, fair traders eventually made common cause with imperialists such as Joseph Chamberlain, colonial secretary from 1895 and anxious to promote closer ties among the peoples of the empire (Irwin 1994). Colonies such as Australia and Canada imposed infant-industry protection to shield local manufacturing from European (including British) competition, but sought preferential access for their agricultural exports to the open British market. Chamberlain's imperial preference scheme would have given the colonies duty-free (and therefore preferential) access to the British market by imposing moderate agricultural and industrial tariffs in Britain; at the same time, the colonies would have increased their tariffs on nonempire products. Imperialists saw this as a way to promote better relations with the colonies, while protectionists saw it as a way to reintroduce wholesale protection. Economists like Alfred Marshall responded with the usual academic objections to protection, while the Liberal party appealed to the working classes' fear of food taxes. Both argued that education and retraining, not tariffs, was the solution to flagging competitiveness at home (Irwin 1994), an amazingly close parallel to American policy debate in the 1990s.

On the European Continent, it was the distributional consequences of globalization that led to calls for protection. In Britain, it was the process of international convergence associated with globalization that led to calls for protection: British incomes were growing strongly, but their relative income was slipping. Globalization backlash seemed to be on the rise in both cases. Why did it produce such different outcomes in Britain and on the Continent?

Explaining Trade Policies: The Historical Debate

Was the laissez-faire doctrine less securely established on the Continent where liberalism was comparatively recent, and where Friedrich List and others had always provided a powerful interventionist counterweight? Or can the different policy outcomes be explained by the differing balance of power of various interest groups?

Political scientists have produced several comparative studies that favor an interest group explanation. In Gourevitch's account, "highly concentrated industrial producers with strong and intense preferences, who occupy strategic positions in the economy, seem to win out everywhere, whatever the institutions, parties, and ideology of the particular country" (1986, 120). Gourevitch thus based his account on a sector-by-sector analysis of who favored free trade or protection. British financiers and specialist manufacturers, German junkers and heavy industrialists, French farmers and Swedish landowners were all crucial to their respective economies and obtained the results they sought. Ronald Rogowski's (1989) explanation is more parsimonious, being class based rather than sector based. Rogowski focuses on the balance of power between land, labor, and capital. Using familiar Heckscher-Ohlin logic, he argues that scarce factors should favor protection, and abundant factors should favor free trade. European labor was abundant and therefore in favor of free trade (i.e., cheap food), while European land was scarce and therefore protectionist. Capital was in favor of free trade in capital-abundant Britain but was protectionist on the Continent, where accumulation had not yet advanced as far. Rogowski argues that this contrast explains the differing British and continental responses to the grain invasion: workers and capitalists provided a winning coalition in Britain, while landowners and capitalists provided a winning coalition elsewhere in Europe. His model thus predicts that both agriculture and industry should have benefited from protection on the Continent, which fits the facts better than the predictions of the simple two-sector specific-factors model. Furthermore, Rogowski's model predicts that the German protectionist coalition of Junker and heavy industrialist should have started to fray as soon as Germany became relatively capital abundant and capital-intensive industries became capable of competing on international markets. Indeed, capital-intensive industries such as chemicals and electrical equipment seceded from the protectionist Centralverband deutscher Industrieller in

1895, to found a more free-trading lobby group of their own (Rogowski 1989, 40).

Ironically, while political scientists have often turned to economics to provide interest-based explanations of the differing responses to the grain invasion, at least one prominent economist, Charles Kindleberger (1951, 42), has argued that "the decisive factors do not appear to lie in the field of economics at all, but in that of sociology." The argument is illustrated most clearly by the Danish switch from grain production to grain consumption, and its export of high-quality animal products. The switch involved the rapid introduction of new technologies such as the cream separator, as well as institutional innovations, notably the cooperative, which allowed large numbers of small farmers jointly to reap the economies of scale associated with new technology, marketing, and quality control. The result was that Danish agriculture flourished in the absence of protection.

Kindleberger explains this superior Danish adaptation to the grain invasion in part by Denmark's greater "group cohesion." Prussia had seized Schleswig in 1864, leading to intense Danish soul searching. The folk high schools, which brought together farmers from differing regions to improve literacy, further heightened the sense of national solidarity. Social cohesion, high levels of education, and the prevalence of medium-sized farms all facilitated the spread of dairy cooperatives, which in turn were needed to introduce new agricultural technologies: "In general, then... the flexibility of a society in devising institutions to accomplish its purposes under changing conditions is a function of its social cohesion, which, in turn, depends upon its internal social mobility, system of communications, and set of values" (Kindleberger 1951, 45).

The evolution of trade policy is almost certainly more complicated than can be captured in any one model. Sectoral interests may play the key role in some circumstances and class interests in others (Verdier 1994). Nor should economists reject the relevance of ideological or sociological factors. But is it really the case, as all these authors implicitly assume, that the grain invasion represented an identical shock to which European states responded differently? Or did the shock itself vary?

The Grain Invasion: Comparative Perspectives

There are two reasons why the grain invasion could not have implied the same shock everywhere in western Europe. First, each country had a different economic structure, and so identical price shocks would

Table 6.4
Grain Production, 1871 (shares of total grain production, in percent)

	Britain	France	Germany	Sweden	Denmark
Wheat	48.3	50.1	34.4	7.5	10.1
Barley	28.0	9.8	12.9	22.2	33.5
Oats	23.5	27.6	5.6	39.6	31.0
Rye	0.2	12.6	47.1	30.7	25.4

Source: O'Rourke (1997a, appendix 5).
Note: Danish figures for 1875. Percentage totals do not always add up to 100 due to rounding.

have had different effects on wages, profits, and rents. Second, the price shocks associated with globalization in the international grain market were not identical everywhere. These two considerations can help explain why Britain and Denmark did not resort to agricultural protection in the wake of the grain invasion, while France, Germany, and Sweden did.

Consider the second reason first. Transatlantic integration may have been lowering European grain prices, but intra-European integration was raising grain prices in traditional grain-exporting countries such as Denmark. In addition, wheat, whose price was most affected by the grain invasion, accounted for an unusually small share of Danish grain production, while barley, a Danish export good throughout the period, accounted for an unusually large share (table 6.4). The result was that while average real cereal prices fell by 29 percent in Britain between 1870 and 1913, they fell by only 10 percent in Denmark over the same period (O'Rourke 1997a, appendix 5). In contrast, French and German grain prices would have declined by 34 percent under free trade, and Swedish prices would have declined by 27 percent.

If the grain invasion lowered grain prices by less in Denmark than in the rest of Europe, then the grain invasion lowered Danish rents by less as well. O'Rourke (1997a) estimates an elasticity of real land prices with respect to real grain prices of about a half.[13] This implies that while the cost to French, German, and Swedish landowners of maintaining free trade in the face of the grain invasion was a reduction in land values of about 15 percent, cheap grain lowered Danish land values by only 4 or 5 percent.[14] Moreover, globalization also raised the prices of Danish animal products exported to the British market. Refrigerated shipping started eroding transatlantic meat price gaps from only the 1890s onward, so Danish exports of bacon and dairy products would

Table 6.5
Economic Structure, 1871

	Britain	France	Sweden
A. Sectoral output shares within agriculture (percent)			
Pasture	56.5	40.7	27.8
Grain	27.2	23.7	39.4
Nongrains	16.3	35.6	32.8
B. Sectoral output shares (percent)			
Agriculture	19.2	40.7	36.9
Manufacturing	44.6	38.5	30.3
Services	36.2	20.8	32.8
C. Sectoral value-added shares (percent)			
Agriculture	14.9	35.9	40.1
Manufacturing	39.8	38.2	11.4
Services	45.4	25.9	48.5
D. Share of labor force in agriculture (percent)	22.6	50.5	67.6
E. Net grain imports/production (percent)	54.7	4.3	13.9

Source: O'Rourke (1997a).
Note: Percentage totals do not always add up to 100 due to rounding.

have been largely immune from New World competition for much of the late nineteenth century. In short, the net impact of globalization on Danish land values might well have been positive, not negative. Armed with this new evidence, the Danish decision not to protect agriculture seems less surprising.

Identical price shocks can also have very different effects on each country's income distribution. After all, agriculture was relatively small in countries like Britain, an industrial leader. Britain was also more capital abundant, another attribute of industrial leadership. Table 6.5 gives some key statistics for late nineteenth-century Britain, Sweden, and France. O'Rourke (1997a) constructed CGE models for these countries and used them to explore what would have happened if each country had experienced the 29 percent decline in real grain prices that Britain absorbed. As expected, the same shock had different distributional implications: average rents would have declined by 4 percent in France, 9 percent in Britain, and 14 percent in Sweden, reflecting the differing shares of grain in total agricultural production (part A of table 6.5). The experiment yielded another important difference: cheap grain increased British real wages, but, in the absence of tariffs, it would have reduced French real wages (by between 3 and 4 percent), while

Swedish real wages would have been pretty much unaffected. This difference can be easily interpreted in the context of the sector-specific factors model and the data in table 6.5. Cheap grain lowered workers' cost of living, but reduced the demand for agricultural labor, and hence nominal wages. Only 23 percent of the British labor force worked in agriculture in 1871, while the corresponding figure for France was 51 percent.[15] A negative shock to agricultural labor demand would thus have had a much bigger impact on French nominal wages, while the impact on workers' cost of living would have been the same.

The economics helps explain why Britain maintained free trade while the Continent protected agriculture. Agriculture in 1900 was a lot less important to the more mature industrial British economy than to the more agrarian continental economies. Not only did this imply that cheap grain was better for British than for continental workers, it also meant that agricultural interests had less political clout in Britain than in France or Germany.

European Trade Policy: Conclusions

Britain and Denmark appear to have been special cases: the structure of their economies ensured that the grain invasion would have a less profound political impact there than in other European countries. To this day, Britain remains more committed to agricultural free trade than either France or Germany. A great deal of the variation in European trade policy a century ago can be explained by appealing to such factors as the impact of globalization on grain prices and land values, and the impact of cheap food on real wages. These depended in turn on such factors as the role of grain production within agriculture and the share of agriculture in the overall economy. The size distribution of landholdings may also have been important in explaining contrasts between Denmark and Norway, on the one hand, and Sweden and Germany, on the other. Countries that had a comparative advantage in producing goods immune from extra-European competition, such as Denmark and the Netherlands, were also in a better position to maintain free trade.

The most common European response to globalization was to protect agriculture. Declining transport costs typically provoked offsetting tariff policies—designed to compensate those whose interests were damaged by steamship and railroad—rather than structural adjustment policies like education and retraining, designed to make the transition faster and smoother. Successful Danish and Dutch responses to the grain invasion still retain an interest for today's OECD policymakers, coping with Third World industrial competition and Common Agricultural Policy reform.

The Politics of New World Protection

Landowners were protectionist in land-scarce Europe, while capitalists supported free trade. Things were very different in the New World. Owners of abundant and cheap land favored free trade, so they could export food and raw materials to the markets of Europe. Manufacturers, on the other hand, sought protection from capital-abundant Britain and the rest of the European core, which were exporting cheap industrial goods.

This rural-urban conflict took on an important regional dimension in the United States, the most important New World economy.[16] Initially the primary aim of protection was to provide the new federal government with tariff revenue. This continued to be the case even after Alexander Hamilton's (1791) *Report on Manufactures* recommended protection on infant industry grounds. The Embargo Act of 1807 was an important turning point. Finding itself embroiled in Franco-British attempts to prevent each other from trading, even with neutrals, the United States banned trade with both countries. The result was a dramatic reduction in trade, with the United States developing a range of manufacturing industries producing goods previously imported from Europe (Frankel 1982). As was the case in France (chapter 3), these wartime industries would form an important interest group lobbying for protection in the years ahead.

Mid-Atlantic states such as Pennsylvania were particularly successful in developing import-competing industries, and they would become strong advocates of protection. As manufacturing made progress in New England, states such as Connecticut and Rhode Island began to favor protection too (Taussig 1888, 72). The South exported raw cotton, tobacco, and other agricultural commodities. It had no significant industry of its own, and it stayed firmly in the free trade camp. The middle and western states combined with New England manufacturers[17] to obtain protection for manufactures in 1824 against southern objections. A similar coalition was able to pass the even more protectionist 1828 "Act of Abominations." It was declared null and void by South Carolina in 1832, and that state threatened to withdraw from the Union

(Ashley 1905, 171–172). The Compromise Act of 1833 defused the regional tension, bringing about a phased reduction in tariffs that persisted until 1860 (barring 1842–1846). Nonetheless, the tariff question was one of the issues that persistently aggravated North-South relations in the decades before the Civil War. To southern spokesmen, the tariff was nothing more than a device to redistribute wealth from South to North and from planters to capitalists.

What about labor, the third classical factor of production, so important in the British debates over the Corn Laws? Initially, free traders had pointed to high wages "as an insuperable obstacle to the successful establishment of manufactures" (Taussig 1888, 65), while protectionists "felt called on to explain away the difference of wages; they endeavored to show that this difference was not so great as was commonly supposed, and that, so far as it existed, it afforded no good reason against adopting protection" (ibid.). Around 1840, protectionists began to change their tune; they now accepted that American wages were relatively high and argued that "high duties were necessary to shut out the competition of the ill-paid laborers of Europe, and to maintain the high wages of the laborers of the United States" (Taussig 1888, 66), a striking echo of today's trade and inequality debate (chapter 9).[18] Opponents of protection dissented. The free-trade Secretary of the Treasury Robert Walker wrote in December 1845 that

an appeal has been made to the poor by the friends of protection, on the ground that it augments the wages of labor. In reply it is contended that the wages of labor have not augmented since the tariff of 1842, and that in some cases they have diminished. . . . A protective tariff is a question regarding the enhancement of the profits of capital. That is its object, and not to augment the wages of labor, which would reduce those profits. It is a question of percentage, and is to decide whether money vested in our manufactures shall by special legislation yield a profit of 10, 20, or 30 per cent., or whether it shall remain satisfied with a dividend equal to that accruing from the same capital invested in agriculture, commerce, or navigation. (cited in Ashley 1905, 186)

The two-sector specific-factors model supports Secretary Walker's view. According to that model, the U.S. antebellum tariff hurt landowners and benefited capitalists, thus helping the North at the South's expense, but the impact on wages could have gone either way. In any case, were the magnitudes large or small? And is the specific-factors model the right way to view the American tariff debate?

Lloyd Metzler (1949) offered one way to defeat Secretary Walker's rgument for free trade. The United States was clearly a large player in world cotton markets around midcentury.[19] The antebellum tariff, by reducing U.S. supplies of cotton and other raw materials, drove up their world price and thus reduced the world price of manufactures relative to cotton. Metzler argued that this world market effect might have been strong enough to outweigh the direct effect of the tariff. In this case, it would have hurt northern manufacturers and helped southern planters and slaveholders.

The Metzler possibility was addressed by Clayne Pope (1972) in one of the first papers to apply CGE methods to economic history. Pope's most striking finding was that tariffs on cotton textiles might have increased the incomes of planters and slaveholders by raising sufficiently the world price of raw cotton. Was the South therefore wrong to oppose protection for cotton textile industries? More recent analysis suggests not: both John James (1978) and Knick Harley (1992a), incorporating greater disaggregation and flexibility in their models, found that eliminating tariffs would have boosted the incomes of southern planters and slaveholders and hurt northern capitalists. The impact of tariffs on labor is, however, less clear. James finds that the tariff made labor slightly better off, while Harley finds that labor was made slightly worse off. This empirical ambiguity corresponds to the theoretical ambiguity discussed earlier in this and the previous chapter.

A key reason for Harley's results was his dismissal of the presumption that the tariff had important terms of trade effects. The United States was a dominant cotton producer before the American Civil War, but only a marginal producer of foodstuffs. Eliminating the tariff would have led to a massive expansion of food exports, which would not provoke a decline in world prices, and to a modest expansion in cotton exports, which would. Food exports would have dominated. It thus appears that the Metzler paradox did not apply and that Secretary Walker emerges victorious: the tariff hurt agriculture and benefited industry, just as contemporary debates suggested. Viewed in this light, the northern victory in the Civil War had predictable consequences for subsequent tariff policy. Tariffs were raised during the war for revenue purposes, but Republican domination of Congress would ensure that they remained exceptionally high for a very long time thereafter.

The United States was not the only late-nineteenth-century New World country to adopt a protectionist policy. Canada also protected manufacturing, especially after 1878 when the Conservatives were elected on a platform aiming "to select for higher rates of duty those [goods] that are manufactured or can be manufactured in the country."[20] In Australia, the Victoria tariff bill of 1865 allowed for maximum ad valorem tariffs of 10 percent, but by 1893, after a succession of tariff increases, the maximum rates stood at 45 percent (Siriwardana 1991, 47). The first federal tariff of 1902 represented a compromise between protectionist Victoria and the other more liberal colonies, but protection was greatly strengthened in 1906 and 1908 (Bairoch 1989, 146–147), and it proved to be remarkably enduring. The advocates of Victorian protection argued that tariffs would boost labor demand, and thus increase employment, real wages, or some combination of the two. This argument was restated in the famous 1929 Brigden Report, which became known as the "Australian case for protection." Debate over the report attracted the best economists in the world and became the intellectual predecessor of the Stolper-Samuelson theorem (Irwin 1996a, chap. 11).[21]

While the third quarter of the nineteenth century saw an easing of protection in Latin America, tariffs rose again in the final quarter. Argentina increased tariffs from the 1870s onward (Bairoch 1989, 150–151). By 1913, average tariffs were almost 35 percent in Uruguay, almost 40 percent in Brazil, and over 45 percent in Venezuela (Bulmer-Thomas 1994, 142). It appears that the highest tariff barriers were in the New World, not Europe. The tariffs were directed toward manufactures, and they served to favor scarce urban labor and capital while penalizing abundant land.

Conclusions

There was a powerful and comprehensive globalization backlash on the European Continent prior to World War I, and it was even more dramatic in the New World. As such, there was plenty of precedent for the globalization implosion that took place between the wars.

Mass Migrations: Why They Moved

About 60 million Europeans set sail for the resource-abundant and labor-scarce New World in the century following 1820.[1] Three-fifths went to the United States. Earlier migration from resource-scarce and labor-abundant Europe had been a mere trickle. The only comparable intercontinental migration had been that of black slaves from Africa to the Americas and the Caribbean: 8 million or so had made the journey by 1820 (Eltis 1983, 252). Indeed, it was not until the 1840s that annual (free) European migration to the Americas exceeded (coerced) African migration, and it was not until the 1880s that the cumulative European migration exceeded that of the African (Eltis 1983, 255). Until well into the nineteenth century, the cost of the move was too great for most potential migrants, and, except under slavery and indentured servitude, it was impossible to secure financing for the move (Galenson 1984; Grubb 1994). Declining time and financial costs of passage, augmented family resources generated by economic development at home, and financial help from previous pioneer emigrants' remittances would all serve to change these conditions as the century progressed.

European intercontinental emigration averaged about 300,000 per annum in the first three decades after 1846, the figures more than doubled in the next two decades, and after the turn of the century, they rose to over a million per annum (Hatton and Williamson 1998, figure 1.1). The European sources also underwent dramatic change. The dominant emigration stream in the first half of the century was from the United Kingdom, followed by Germany. A rising tide of Scandinavian and other northwest European emigrants joined these streams by mid-century. Southern and eastern Europeans followed in the 1880s. This new emigrant stream accounted for most of the rising emigrant totals in the late nineteenth century. It came first from Italy, Spain, and

Portugal, but after the 1890s it swelled to include Austria-Hungary, Russia, and Poland.

The overwhelming majority of these Europeans arrived as immigrants in the Americas. Although the United States was the dominant destination, there were significant flows to South America after the mid–1880s, led by Argentina and Brazil, and to Canada after the turn of the century. A small but persistent stream also linked the United Kingdom to Australia, New Zealand, and South Africa.

Very important migrations also took place within Europe. To take one example, more than half of all Italian emigrants in the 1890s went to European destinations, chiefly to France and Germany. To take another example, a large westward migration of Poles to eastern Germany filled vacancies created by the westward migration of Germans to the Ruhr (Barkin 1970, 160–161; Hussain and Tribe 1981, 51–53; Kitchen 1978, 200–202). Significant migrations also took place within the New World, especially those from Canada across the border. Indeed, some have argued that up to 1900, Canadian emigration to the United States completely offset Canadian immigration from Europe (McInnis 1994).

These mass migrations refer mainly to gross rather than net flows. The distinction is unimportant for most of the nineteenth century since the cost of return migration was simply too high. However, the distinction becomes increasingly important as the upward trend in emigration is partially offset by an even steeper rise in return migration late in the century. U.S. authorities estimated that between 1890 and 1914, return migration was 30 percent of the gross inflow. It varied greatly by nationality; the proportion was nearly half among Italians and Spaniards, but only 5 percent among Russians, and even lower for the Irish and Scandinavians. Similarly, the return migration rate was much higher from some New World countries than others. Between 1857 and 1924, return migration from Argentina (Italians and Spaniards) was 47 percent of the Argentine gross inflow. The high return migration rate among Italians represented a growing trend toward temporary, often seasonal migration, so much so that eventually they would be called "birds of passage" (Bailey 1912).

If the only purpose of this chapter were to explain why so many Europeans left for the labor-scarce New World in an era when state policy was but a modest barrier, the chapter would be short. To quote Nobel laureate Robert Lucas:

The eighteenth and nineteenth century histories of the Americas [and] Australia [show] the ability of even simple neo-classical models to account for important economic events. If we . . . treat labor as the mobile factor and land as immobile, we obtain a model that predicts exactly the immigration flows that occurred and for exactly the reason—factor price differentials—that motivated these historical flows. Though this simple deterministic model abstracts from considerations of risk and many other elements that surely played a role in actual migration decisions, this abstraction is evidently not a fatal one. (Lucas 1988, 6)

But this chapter deals with many more questions than the critical one raised by Lucas. Why did emigration rates vary so much across countries? They ranged from a massive 50 or more per thousand per decade from countries like Ireland and Norway to a mere 2 per thousand from France (table 7.1). Why the variety in trends? The Austro-Hungarian, Italian, and Portuguese rates trend upward after the 1880s while the Danish, German, and Swedish rates trend downward. The biggest challenge facing economists, however, is this: Why were emigration rates often lowest from the poorest countries, whose populations would have gained most from the move? Why were emigration rates often lowest for the poorest regions within a given country? Why were emigration rates often lowest among the poorest laborers within those poor regions? Why did emigration rates so often rise from low levels as successful economic development took place at home? After all, conventional theory would suggest that successful development at home would make the move overseas less, not more, attractive. What economic hypotheses can be offered to account for these counterintuitive historical events? Can the variety in European emigration rates be explained by a common economic framework, or do the explanations lie instead with each country's idiosyncratic culture, well outside economics?

Who Were the Emigrants?

Economic forces could have been central to the move only if those who migrated were for the most part directly involved in the labor market, and thus responsive to wages and employment opportunities in sending and receiving areas. Furthermore, economic explanations for the mass migrations are likely to look more promising if the composition of the migrant streams was similar across countries and cultures. So, who were the emigrants?

Table 7.1
Migration Rates by Decade (per 1,000 mean population)

Country	1851–1860	1861–1870	1871–1880	1881–1890	1891–1900	1901–1910
European emigration rates						
Austria-Hungary			2.9	10.6	16.1	47.6
Belgium				8.6	3.5	6.1
British Isles	58.0	51.8	50.4	70.2	43.8	65.3
Denmark			20.6	39.4	22.3	28.2
Finland				13.2	23.2	54.5
France	1.1	1.2	1.5	3.1	1.3	1.4
Germany			14.7	28.7	10.1	4.5
Ireland			66.1	141.7	88.5	69.8
Italy			10.5	33.6	50.2	107.7
Netherlands	5.0	5.9	4.6	12.3	5.0	5.1
Norway	24.2	57.6	47.3	95.2	44.9	83.3
Portugal		19.0	28.9	38.0	50.8	56.9
Spain				36.2	43.8	56.6
Sweden	4.6	30.5	23.5	70.1	41.2	42.0
Switzerland			13.0	32.0	14.1	13.9
New World immigration rates						
Argentina	38.5	99.1	117.0	221.7	163.9	291.8
Brazil			20.4	41.1	72.3	33.8
Canada	99.2	83.2	54.8	78.4	48.8	167.6
Cuba						118.4
United States	92.8	64.9	54.6	85.8	53.0	102.0

Source: Hatton and Williamson (1998, table 2.1) based on Ferenczi and Willcox (1929, 200–201).

The emigrants in 1800 were certainly different from those in 1900. Early-nineteenth-century migrant streams were often led by farmers and rural artisans, traveling in family groups, intent on acquiring land and settling permanently at the New World frontier. While many still had rural roots in the late nineteenth century, the emigrants from any given country were increasingly drawn from urban areas and non-agricultural occupations. Thus, emigrants from Britain in the 1830s, a country that had already undergone a half-century of industrialization, were mainly from nonfarm occupations. This industrialization-induced trend within emigrant countries was overwhelmed by the shift from old emigrant regions—the industrial leaders—to new emigrant regions—the industrial followers. Thus, the increasing importance of less industrial eastern and southern Europe as an emigrant source served to raise the emigrant proportion from rural Europe and lowered their average skills and literacy (Lindert 1978, 243; Hatton and Williamson 1998, chapter 7).

By the late nineteenth century, migrants were typically young adults. An enormous 76 percent of the immigrants entering the United States between 1868 and 1910 were between the ages of fifteen and forty—this during a period when the total U.S. population share between fifteen and forty was only about 42 percent. Thus, the migrants carried very high labor force participation rates to the New World. The migrant flow was also dominated by males: they accounted for 64 percent of all U.S. immigrants between 1851 and 1913, and for more than three-quarters of the emigrants from Spain and Italy. Emigrants tended to be single and emigrated as individuals rather than in families, although a significant minority were young couples with small children. In short, the migrants carried both very high labor force participation rates and very low dependency burdens with them to the New World.

The typical migrant was unskilled. No doubt this was in part simply due to the fact that he was young, but it also reflected his limited schooling and training in skilled trades. And as the source of the European emigrant shifted east and south, he became even less schooled and less skilled (Hatton and Williamson 1998, chapters 7, 8). Instead, he increasingly became an illiterate peasant who had spent hardly any time away from his village roots. In the language of the U.S. immigration debate prior to the imposition of the quotas, or the U.S. immigration debate of the 1990s, the emigrants diminished in "quality" as the century progressed.

Although the quality of the migrants may have declined, it appears that those who emigrated had more to gain from the move than the population as a whole, and they were likely to be more responsive to labor market conditions. Many moved to escape religious or political persecution, and others did so in convict chains, but most moved to escape European poverty. And most moved under their own initiative, without government pressure, assistance or "guest worker" permission.[2] As the technology of transport and communication improved, the costs and uncertainty of migration fell, and overseas migration came within reach of an increasing share of the European population for whom the move offered the most gain. European famine and revolution may have pushed the first great mass migration in the 1840s, but it was the underlying economic fundamentals that made each subsequent surge bigger than the previous one up to World War I.

All of these facts reinforce the premise that labor market conditions at home and abroad must have been paramount to the migration decision, and increasingly so as the late nineteenth century wore on.

Determinants of Emigration

In his pioneering paper published almost four decades ago, Richard Easterlin (1961) examined the relationship between European emigration and population growth. If emigration was a true vent for surplus population, he argued, then countries with higher rates of natural increase should have exhibited higher emigration rates, ceteris paribus. Easterlin viewed the rate of natural increase twenty years earlier as a proxy for the current rate of additions to the labor force: thus, "relatively high additions to the labor market would be expected . . . to result in labor market slack . . . , and . . . to relatively higher emigration" (1961, 332). Easterlin argued that past demographic events had an indirect influence on present emigration through labor supply. If so, then they would be better captured by an index of current labor market conditions, such as the real wage, reflecting the net impact of both labor supply (reflecting previous baby booms) and demand.

There is, however, another way to interpret Easterlin's correlation. If differences in natural increase were driven chiefly by variations in births and infant mortality, then it could act as a proxy for the share of the population who, twenty or twenty-five years later, were young adults. Since this age cohort had a much higher propensity to emigrate than those older or younger, one might observe higher emigration rates associated with faster lagged natural increase even if real wage gaps between home and abroad remained unchanged. This would imply a direct demographic impact on emigration, quite distinct from the indirect effect felt through labor markets that Easterlin stressed. And since rising fertility rates and falling infant mortality rates are associated with early industrialization, rising emigration rates might possibly be correlated with rising real wages at home if the influence of these demographic variables was sufficiently powerful.

No adequate measure of internationally comparable real wage rates was available to Easterlin when he was writing, and he had to make do with Mulhall's crude estimates of per capita income. Crippled by lack of adequate data, this important debate lay dormant for about two decades. The real wage database described in chapter 2 (Williamson 1995) makes it possible to breath new life into the debate. These data have three principal advantages over the data available to Easterlin. First, they offer an income measure far more relevant to the decision facing potential migrants. The wage rates were taken from unskilled male urban occupations (such as those in the building trades) that were ubiquitous in all countries, and they were deflated by PPP-adjusted cost of living estimates. Second, since these real wage indexes are comparable across time and between countries, the country time series can now be pooled to form a panel, something earlier emigration studies were unable to do. Third, since comparable real wage estimates for major immigrant New World countries are also now available, wage gaps between sending and receiving countries can be constructed to index the gains from migration.

The rows labeled A in table 7.2 report the absolute real wage indexed on Britain (1905 = 100). The rows labeled B report the home real wage as a percentage of that in the relevant destination countries. In most cases the destination real wage is a weighted average of the most important receiving countries, including, where relevant, other European countries. The weights are based on the distribution of emigrant flows in the 1890s. The main exception is Spain, where the destination wage is represented by Argentina alone.

Row A indicates that real wages were rising strongly everywhere. As we pointed out in chapter 2, some countries, like Denmark, Ireland, Norway, and Sweden, were doing especially well, while others, like Belgium, France, and Spain, were not. If we compared real wages with emigration rates, the expected negative relationship would be weak since, with the exception of Ireland, there is no comprehensive

Table 7.2
Internationally Comparable Wage Rates and Wage Ratios

Country		1850–1859	1860–1869	1870–1879	1880–1889	1890–1899	1900–1913
Belgium	A	45.5	52.8	64.2	73.9	85.6	86.9
	B	—	118.2	110.7	109.0	115.9	109.9
Denmark	A	—	—	41.0	52.6	70.6	94.2
	B	—	—	34.6	40.1	47.9	56.8
France	A	44.3	46.2	52.0	60.4	65.1	71.2
	B	—	—	45.6	45.4	38.3	42.9
Germany	A	52.5	55.4	62.3	68.5	78.1	85.9
	B	—	—	54.1	53.4	53.9	52.7
Great Britain	A	59.4	59.0	70.3	83.5	99.4	98.2
	B	—	—	59.6	63.0	66.0	59.4
Ireland	A	44.4	43.6	51.7	64.5	87.3	90.9
	B	—	—	45.4	50.0	60.2	56.2
Italy	A	—	—	26.2	34.2	37.4	46.4
	B	—	—	37.8	42.6	40.7	45.5
Netherlands	A	45.7	48.9	62.8	79.9	88.1	77.8
	B	—	52.5	53.0	60.9	59.8	46.9
Norway	A	27.2	30.7	40.1	45.8	67.5	83.8
	B	26.0	32.9	25.0	34.9	45.8	50.5
Portugal	A	18.8	19.6	20.1	27.4	23.3	24.6
	B	—	36.2	33.7	36.1	25.1	23.9
Spain	A	30.4	28.0	27.6	25.5	26.8	30.4
	B	—	56.3	52.1	36.6	30.9	31.7
Sweden	A	24.2	34.6	39.0	51.1	70.7	92.2
	B	—	—	36.7	43.2	52.3	59.9

Source: Based on data in Williamson (1995), revised in O'Rourke and Williamson (1997).
Note: A = real wage rate, Great Britain 1905 = 100; B = real wage ratio, home to receiving countries.

evidence of a downward trend in emigration rates. There is at best only a very weak negative correlation between home wages and emigration. Rising real wages at home did not appear to diminish emigration in the late nineteenth century.

A better measure of the overseas migration incentive is the real wage gap between home and destination. Except for Belgium, home wages were substantially below destination wages (row B, table 7.2). Chapter 2 showed that real wages among the current OECD countries converged in the late nineteenth century, and most of that convergence was driven by the gradual erosion in the real wage gap favoring the New World. For some, the convergence was dramatic, a finding confirmed in row B of table 7.2. Between the 1870s and the early twentieth century, Danish real wages rose from about 35 percent to about 57 percent of the United States (the principal destination), a very impressive catch-up over only about three decades. Sweden's real wage catch-up on the United States was even more dramatic—from about 33 to about 56 percent.[3] But the catch-up was most spectacular in Norway, from 25 to about 51 percent over the same three decades. Ireland sent its emigrants to North America, Australia, and Britain, and Irish real wages also enjoyed rapid convergence on real wages in those destinations—from 45 to 56 percent. Dutch convergence on its major destination, the United States, was a little less impressive—and there was some backsliding from 1900 to 1913—but Dutch relative real wages rose from 53 in the 1870s to 60 percent in the 1890s. Similarly, Italian real wages relative to France, Germany, the United States, and Argentina rose from 38 to 46 percent between the 1870s and 1900–1913. The European industrial leaders—Britain, France, and Germany–did not join the convergence; Spain underwent a dramatic collapse in home relative to destination wages, from 56 percent in the 1860s to 32 percent in 1900–1913; Portuguese relative wages also collapsed, from 36 percent in the 1860s to 24 percent in 1900–1913. Despite these (important) exceptions, real wage convergence between emigrant and immigrant countries characterized the period, a trend chiefly driven by the convergence of Europe on New World wages.

An inverse correlation between emigration and the wage ratio (home to foreign) is clearly revealed in the raw data for cases like Ireland and Norway. Indeed, that inverse correlation has been confirmed for Ireland, and most of the secular fall in the Irish emigration rate after the famine has been successfully explained by appealing to the declining wage gap between home and abroad (and other measures of

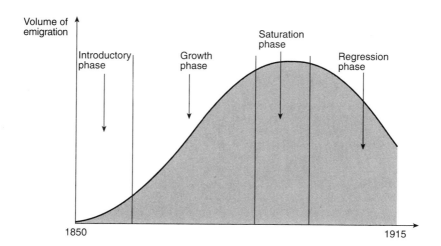

Figure 7.1
Stylized pattern of European late nineteenth century emigration. Source: Akerman (1976: 25).

relative labor market performance, including living standards and poverty indicators: Hatton and Williamson 1993). Previous studies of other emigrating countries also support this view (Wilkinson 1970). However, over the full intertemporal cross section, the inverse correlation between the wage ratio and the emigration rate is still modest. The weak correlation implies that a more comprehensive model is needed to account for late-nineteenth-century European emigration to the New World.

As the introduction to this chapter pointed out, a central stylized fact makes it clear that real wage gaps will not suffice by themselves. During the course of modern economic growth in Europe, country emigration rates rose steeply at first from very low levels, the rise then began to slow, emigration rates reached a peak, and subsequently they fell off. This stylized fact has emerged from studies of both the time series of aggregate emigration for a number of countries (Akerman 1976) and of regional emigration rates within countries (Gould 1979). It has also been used to make predictions about the future of Mexican immigration into America (Massey 1988). The stylized fact as represented by Sweden is reproduced in figure 7.1. Several explanations have been offered for its shape, but Hatton and Williamson (1994b; 1998, chapter 2) use figure 7.2 to capture the time path, where movements along some downward-sloping home country emigration func-

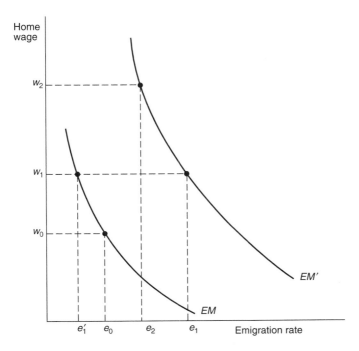

Figure 7.2
Stylized emigration responses. Source: Hatton and Williamson (1998, figure 3.1).

tion (EM) are isolated from shifts in that function. In preindustrial episodes, we observe low emigration rates (e_0) and low wages (w_0). Industrialization and other events then serve both to raise the emigration function to EM' and real wages to w_1. The former dominates in this example since emigration rates have risen to e_1; in the absence of the shift in EM, emigration rates would have fallen to e_1'. In later stages of development, EM is taken to be stable so that further improvements in real wages at home, to w_2, cut back emigration rates to e_2. Thus, the stylized facts of figure 7.1 are reproduced in figure 7.2. What, then, might account for the rightward shifts in EM during early industrialization and its stability thereafter?

The first explanation appeals to the costs of migration. Although there is a strong incentive to flee preindustrial poverty and rural subsistence, the costs may be prohibitive for most workers. After all, the potential migrant cannot get loans for the move, and his income is too close to subsistence to make it possible to accumulate the necessary savings. Thus, enormous wage gaps between an industrializing, resource-rich New World and a backward, resource-poor Old World can be quite consistent with low emigration rates. As industrialization takes place in the home country, real wages rise and the supply constraint on emigration is gradually released. More and more potential emigrants can now finance the move, and, in contrast with conventional theory, the home wage and emigration are positively correlated. As industrialization continues, the backlog of potential migrants is slowly exhausted as more and more workers find it possible to finance the move. When the migration cost constraint is no longer binding, further increases in the real wage cause the emigration rate to decline from the peak. This argument has recently been used to explain the surge in Italian emigration in the late nineteenth century (Faini and Venturini 1994a).

According to this view, emigration histories should pass through two regimes: the first emigrant supply constrained, and the second emigrant demand constrained. The emigrant-supply-constrained regime is consistent with the rising emigration and rising home wages implied by figure 7.1, and it can also be made consistent with the downward-sloping EM function in figure 7.2 by appealing to rightward shifts in that function induced by wage increases. At some point, home wages are high enough that financial constraints are no longer binding: further increases in the home wage now reduce the emigration rate as the economy moves up a more stable EM function, and emigration experience enters regime 2. Although this tale of regime switch is plausible, we should remember that it takes no account of changing employment conditions overseas. The Old World has to begin catching up with the New at some stage on the emigration upswing if the emigration rate is ever to decline from its peak after the regime switch.

There is general agreement that many potential emigrants from subsistence economies were too poor to move, and were thus income constrained. But was the constraint eased by rising income at home, as suggested above, or by other forces, like rising remittances from abroad?

Ó Gráda and O'Rourke (1997) argue that poverty traps prevented the poorest in Ireland from emigrating during the famine of the late 1840s. To cite just one piece of evidence, the ratio of emigration to deaths was higher in richer counties than in poorer counties during that crisis. Those poverty traps would be overcome after the famine, even though Ireland did not industrialize: chain migration provided the key in Ireland and was important in other emigrant countries as well. The idea is that rightward shifts in the EM function can also be driven by the remittances of previous (now prosperous) emigrants who finance the moves of impecunious latecomers. As the stock of emigrants abroad increases, so too do their remittances home, and thus the current emigration rate rises even though the home wage is increasing. The same previous migrants can also supply room and board for the new immigrant as he starts his job search. This influence continues as long as potential emigrants find their move financially constrained.

There is certainly a lot of evidence relating to chain migration and the impact of friends and relatives abroad. The influence of letters containing information about prospects in destination countries is well documented, and such information is likely to have reinforced the decision to emigrate. Furthermore, there is abundant evidence that current emigrants' cost of passage was financed by previous emigrants. This evidence takes the form of large emigrant remittances and frequent use of prepaid tickets. Those traveling on prepaid tickets accounted for 30 percent of Finnish emigrants between 1891 and 1914, 50 percent of Swedish emigrants in the 1880s, 40 percent of Norwegian emigrants in the 1870s, and about 25 percent of Danish emigrants between 1881 and 1895 (Kero 1991, 191; Hvidt 1975, 129). Such evidence clearly argues for the case that past emigration encourages present emigration— what economists call *persistence* or *path dependence,* and what historians call the *friends and relatives effect.*

Persistence is typically captured by the lagged dependent variable in time-series studies. This is often the most significant variable in regressions explaining emigration rates, and some analysts have interpreted the result as evidence of chain migration (Gould 1979, 658). However, it might also be interpreted as evidence of the adaptive formation of expectations (Hatton 1995). In any case, one would expect the friends and relatives effect to operate through the stock of all previous migrants, not just the previous year's flow, even though recent emigrants sent letters and remittances home more frequently than did those who emigrated much earlier.

The important historical point is that persistence is likely to matter in accounting for the variety in late-nineteenth-century European emigration experience. Events in the past, like famines and revolutions, are likely to have a potent influence on emigration in the present, even after those events have disappeared from the memory of current generations. Low French emigration in the 1890s may have had its source in the revolution-induced land reforms a century before, just as high

Irish emigration in the 1890s may have had its source in the potato famine a half-century before. Persistence and path dependence also imply that labor markets in the Atlantic economy were becoming integrated through time, an evolution toward truly global labor markets that must have been reinforced by the decline in transport costs.

A second explanation for rightward shifts in EM appeals to a process of diffusion. Gould (1980b) illustrated the process by reference to the experience of latecomers to mass migration, such as Italy and Hungary, where the within-country regional variance in emigration rates diminished over time. Regions with low initial emigration rates converged on the earlier emigrating regions, causing the aggregate emigration rate to increase. It is not clear from these facts alone, however, what mechanism was driving the diffusion process. If some interregional convergence of wage rates within the home country was at work, with backward rural regions catching up with more advanced urban regions, then the process would be consistent with the cost-of-migration arguments outlined above. Some have suggested that the diffusion process depended instead on the diffusion of information, but in this case, other arguments would have to be invoked to get the process started and to cause it to diminish after the initial surge.

Finally, what about the influence of industrialization and structural transformation? In many qualitative accounts of European emigration, the key factor is economic development at home—not just rising wages but the whole set of changes that accompany industrialization and alter attitudes toward emigration. The importance of industrialization in raising labor mobility has also recently been stressed by Massey (1988). European industrialization involved, above all, reduced attachment to the land and a rise in wage labor. For that reason alone, agrarian countries ought to have had lower emigration rates. The combination of more commercialized agriculture, more consolidated landholdings, diminished smallholdings, the erosion of common rights, and relatively high and rising wages in the booming cities all served to produce a rural exodus (Williamson 1990a). The rise of overseas emigration was correlated with the growth of internal migration and can be seen as part of the same phenomenon (Baines 1985). To the extent that migrants from rural areas in Europe became urban workers in the New World (or in other European countries), it was simply a rural-urban movement across international boundaries (Thomas 1972).

These, then, are the major contending explanations offered for the nineteenth-century mass migrations.

The Econometric Facts

Theory is one thing; fact is another. Hatton and Williamson (1994b; 1998, chapter 3) have recently supplied some fact by incorporating the hypotheses discussed above in an econometric model, which they then applied to the late-nineteenth-century European emigration experience. Five key explanatory variables were introduced in their analysis: the real wage gap between the home country and foreign destinations; a demographic variable for lagged natural increase; the level of industrialization, measured by the share of the labor force in agriculture; the stock of previous migrants living abroad; and the dependent variable lagged one decade.

To repeat, the wage gap is the real urban unskilled wage rate in the home country relative to a weighted average of those real wages at the relevant destination (table 7.2). The destination wage varied across emigrant countries to the extent that destinations differed, and different destinations reflected linguistic and cultural preferences as well as overt discrimination. In any case, there was segmentation among different migration streams.[4] The real wage gap measures the expected income gain from emigration. As we argued above, it is possible that the home wage by itself might also matter if potential migrants were constrained by low incomes. It is an empirical issue as to whether this constraint was released most by real income improvements at home, a decline in migration costs, remittances from those who had already made the move, or in-kind support (room and board during job search abroad) from the same source. As we shall see, the evidence will point to the last two sources, and not the first.

Following Easterlin (1961), the rate of natural increase lagged two decades captures the demographic effect. However, since we have already controlled for the indirect influence of demographic gluts on home labor supply and labor markets by including the wage gap, the lagged natural increase should now be interpreted, in contrast with Easterlin, as reflecting a glut in the size of the prime emigration age group two decades later, a direct demographic influence. Since emigration was more worthwhile in present value terms to young adults, this composition effect should have served to raise the emigration rate for any given wage gap.

The migrant stock variable is intended to capture the friends and relatives effect associated with the assistance of previous emigrants through better information, prepaid tickets, and lower costs of job search. But it may also reflect the broader impact of the attractiveness of migrating to an immigrant community with the same language, culture, and ethnic background. The lagged dependent variable is also included to test whether chain migration was driven by recent emigrants rather than by the total emigrant stock abroad.

Finally, the share of the male labor force in agriculture, a time trend, and a set of country-specific dummy variables are also included. The share of the male labor force in agriculture is an inverse proxy for the level of industrialization, the expectation being that agrarian societies had lower mobility and emigration rates. The time trend is introduced to capture whatever influence the decline in the overall costs of migration, due to faster passage and falling passenger fares, might have had. To the extent that country-specific effects are significant, then the list of forces determining European emigration is incomplete and must be augmented by other factors peculiar to individual countries.

Annual migration flows speak to decisions about when to move (Hatton 1995; Hatton and Williamson 1998, chapters 4–6). Decade averages speak to the issue of why to make a long-distance move at all; that is, they are driven by the long-run fundamentals of economic growth and demographic change. Hatton and Williamson used decade averages, and their econometric results strongly support a number of the hypotheses developed earlier in this chapter.

The only significant country dummies were those for Italy and Spain, combined into one Latin dummy, and Belgium. Latin and Belgian emigration rates were higher than international wage gaps suggest should have been the case. None of the other country dummies were significant. Thus, the observed low emigration rates from France and the high emigration rates from Ireland were not due to some deviant behavior in these countries, but rather to differences in the economic and demographic fundamentals dictating those emigration experiences.[5]

Although the time trend took a positive coefficient as expected, it was not significant. Thus, while the greater part of the variation across countries and through time can be explained by underlying market and demographic fundamentals, declining migrant transport costs does not appear to be one of them, at least in the late nineteenth century.

The real wage gap between source and destination countries had a powerful influence on emigration rates, and in the direction that conventional theory predicts: the higher the real wage was at home, the lower the emigration rate. This result confirms the downward-sloping emigration function in figure 7.2.

The paradox of rising emigration coinciding with the convergence between Old World and New World wage rates is largely explained by demographic and industrialization forces that induced rightward shifts in the emigration function. Hatton and Williamson tested the competing hypothesis that an inverted U-shaped emigration life cycle might arise from the growth of home wages alone: as the home wage first rises, the financial constraint is released and the emigration rate rises, but later, as the home wage continues to rise and the wage gap closes, emigration begins to fall. The hypothesis was rejected: it was relative, not absolute, home wages that drove emigration from Europe in the late nineteenth century. This evidence does not imply that poverty traps were unimportant in constraining emigration. They were, but rising wages at home did not play an important role in relaxing those constraints. Rather, it was remittances from increasing numbers of pioneer emigrants abroad that played the major role in relaxing the constraint.

The rate of natural increase was important, just as Easterlin suggested, but its influence was felt directly on emigration, not simply indirectly through an induced glut in home labor supply and a consequent fall in home wage rates. That is, the indirect effect that Easterlin stressed is already present in the wage variable, but additional direct demographic effects are significant and large. The twenty-year generational lag implies that the impact was felt only in the long run, but the rise in the rate of natural increase was sufficiently pronounced on the upswing of the European demographic transition to have had a big impact on the mass migrations. It appears that these demographic forces accounted for much of the intercountry variation in emigration rates, as well as movements in emigration rates through time.

The impact of the share of the labor force in agriculture was not significant. Although industrialization (a fall in the agricultural share) may have raised labor mobility, to the extent that it also raised the rural wage relative to the urban wage, it reduced emigration. The former effect dominated, although the latter must have served to mute the impact.

What about persistence? The lagged dependent variable has an estimated coefficient of 0.4, suggesting that the effects of a once-and-for-all shock such as a famine should have died out almost completely after three decades. But the influence of past emigration (occurring through the emigrant stock) had a much longer-lasting effect. Furthermore, the emigrant stock effect was very powerful; for every

1,000 previous emigrants still living, 20 more were pulled abroad each year.

A good illustration of how important this stock effect was in practice comes from the Irish postfamine experience. In fact, the coefficient on the emigrant stock was twice as big for Ireland as for Europe as a whole (Hatton and Williamson 1993). A coefficient of this size implies that the famine emigration of 1 million could have boosted the Irish postfamine emigration rate by as much as six per thousand annually, and this is in fact exactly the amount by which average postfamine emigration rates exceeded prefamine rates (thirteen versus seven: see O'Rourke 1995a). The famine made a crucial contribution to high Irish emigration rates long after the late 1840s and early 1850s. In the words of Roy Geary, "The great exodus of 1847–1854, in placing vast Irish population across the Atlantic and the Irish Sea which created a powerful magnetic field in which millions of Irish were irresistibly drawn from their native country in subsequent decades, was the fount and origin of Irish emigration and depopulation. . . . [The famine made] migration part of the ordinary life of nearly every family in Ireland . . . thus making Irish labour the most mobile in the world and the most free to pursue its best market" (1935–1936, 25, 31). History matters.

We need to add a final word to this summary of the econometric facts dealing with the determinants of the mass migrations before World War I. We have said nothing so far about migration policy. There are, of course, unexplained residuals in the regressions we have summarized, and policy may well help account for some of those. The problem, however, is getting good measures of the subsidies and restrictions that played a role, sometimes a powerful role, even in this "age of free migration." We save this issue for chapter 10, where we explore migration policy backlash.

The Stylized Facts of European Emigration

Can this model of emigration account for the emigration life cycle stylized in figure 7.1? What role did each of these variables play in contributing to the observed European mass migration life cycle? Hatton and Williamson offer answers by multiplying the estimated coefficients associated with each explanatory variable by the changes in the variables themselves. The changing contribution of each variable is shown in

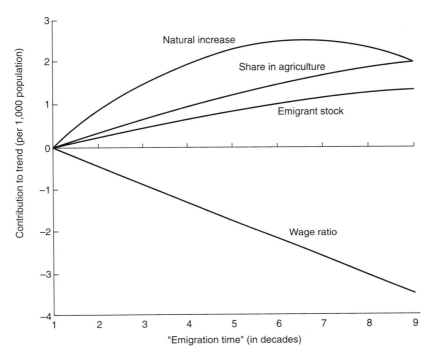

Figure 7.3
Factors in the emigration cycle. Source: Hatton and Williamson (1998, figure 3.3).

figure 7.3, where each is normalized to zero in the first decade of the emigration cycle.

The long-run contribution of direct demographic events rises up to decade 6, when it contributes about two per thousand per annum to emigration compared to decade 1. This was clearly an important source of the upswing in emigration, but it gradually weakened as these countries passed through their demographic transitions. It was assisted by the weaker effects of industrialization. These effects appear gradually to have raised emigration at a declining rate throughout the emigration cycle, to an extent amounting to almost 1 per thousand per annum by decade 9. These two forces were enhanced by the cumulative effect of the stock of emigrants abroad. This rose strongly through the first six decades of emigration time, peaking in decade 9 with a contribution of over 1 per thousand per annum to the annual emigration rate. Of course, this effect was itself the product of economic and demographic fundamentals acting on emigration and reaching far back in time.

These three variables together jointly implied a trend rising strongly at first, but then flattening out and reaching a peak in the eighth decade of emigration time. At the peak, the total contribution of these variables to emigration, compared with the starting decade, was 4.2 per thousand per annum. Had there been no other forces at work, the predicted emigration profile would have been very different to the actual emigration trends, illustrated in figure 7.1. The difference lies in the strong negative influence of the real wage gap between labor markets. As figure 7.3 shows, the impact of changes in the home-to-destination wage ratio was to reduce emigration by over 3 per thousand per annum by decade nine of emigration time.

It might be helpful to summarize our argument thus far. First, the ratio of home-to-destination wages had a significant negative impact on emigration. While consistent with conventional theory, earlier studies, constrained by lack of comparative data on real wages, had been unable to isolate this effect adequately. Second, the rate of natural increase lagged twenty years had a powerful effect on emigration rates, just as Richard Easterlin forcibly argued some time ago. This demographic effect stimulated emigration directly by raising the share of the population in the prime emigration age group, rather than only indirectly by lowering the domestic wage, raising unemployment, or both. Third, there is strong evidence of persistence in these mass migrations. Both the emigration rate in the previous decade and the stock of previous emigrants living abroad served to pull many more migrants abroad, and the impact was powerful. Finally, emigration did increase as the proportion of the labor force in agriculture fell, but this effect was never very strong. Thus, there is only weak support for the argument that industrialization led to increased labor mobility.

The emigration life cycle identified for so many European countries can be explained by demographic trends, industrialization, real wage convergence, and chain migration. High rates of natural increase, rapid industrialization, and a growing stock of previous emigrants abroad dominated the upswing of the emigration cycle. Thus, early industrialization and its associated demographic effects bred European emigration in the late nineteenth century, much as has been observed for Mexico, Central America, the Middle East, and Asia since the 1950s. But European real wages were catching up with New World real wages from midcentury to World War I, and this convergence served to lower emigration rates. When the forces of demographic transition eased and industrialization slowed, the forces of convergence began to dominate, aided by the weakening pull of the stock of previous emigrants as their numbers abroad leveled out. When the forces of the demographic transition reversed, they joined the forces of wage convergence, causing emigration rates to fall sharply, even before World War I and the quotas of the 1920s.

Were the Latins Different?

The Latin countries—Italy, Portugal, and Spain—were industrial latecomers on the European periphery. They also experienced mass emigration late in the nineteenth century. The fact that they joined the mass migrations late, that they were poor by western European standards, and that so many went to Latin America has generated a number of debates on both sides of the Atlantic. The debates imply that the Latins were different. Were they?

Certainly Sir Arthur Lewis thought so. Indeed, he thought that his model of development (Lewis 1954) with immigrant-augmented elastic labor supplies applied to Latin America in the late nineteenth century (Lewis 1978), and many Latin American scholars agree. Carlos Diaz-Alejandro wrote that the labor supply in Argentina before 1930 was "perfectly elastic at the going wage (plus some differential) in the industrial centers of Italy and Spain" (1970, 21–22). Nathaniel Leff believes the same was true of Brazil and that elastic labor supplies can account for stable wages in São Paulo and Santos from the 1880s onward (Leff 1992, 6). If the elastic labor supply thesis is correct, then late-nineteenth-century Latin emigration should have been far more responsive to wage gaps between home and abroad than the early emigration from northwest Europe.

If Latin emigration was more responsive to wage gaps between home and abroad, why were the wage gaps between southern and northern Europe so big? Urban real wages for the unskilled in Italy and Spain were far below those in the United States, Argentina, and Germany in 1870, but Italy at least caught up a bit with those destination regions by 1890. Between 1890 and 1913, however, these two countries underwent quite different real wage experiences. The wage gap between Italy and destination countries fell (Italian economic success), while it rose for Spain (Spanish economic failure). In the 1870s, Italian wages were only 22 percent of those in the United States, 49 percent of those in Argentina, and 42 percent of those in Germany. In the decade prior to World War I, the Italian figures were 28, 48, and 54 percent, respectively, evidence of strong catching up. Spanish wages in the 1870s were only 23 percent of those in the United States and 52 percent of those in Argentina. In the decade prior to World War I, the Spanish figures were 18 and 32 percent, revealing a serious fallback. Portuguese experience was much like that of Spain. These expanding Iberian wage gaps seem to be inconsistent with elastic emigration responses and contrast with catching up elsewhere.

Why did so few Latins go north? Did this reflect language affinity and cultural preference, or discrimination in labor markets, or both? Alternatively, were emigrants from southern Italy, Spain, and Portugal better equipped to meet the demands of coffee plantations in São Paulo and Santos, or of the estates in the Argentine pampas, or of the streets in Buenos Aires and Rio de Janeiro, than the needs of European and North American industrial labor markets?

Why the Latin emigration delay? Since the poorest had the most to gain by a move to higher living standards, one would have expected the Latins to have left earlier than the Germans or the British. When they finally did leave en masse, why were the Iberian rates so low compared with the peak rates that other economies reached when passing through their emigration cycle? These questions implicitly suggest either that Latin migrants behaved differently or that the Latin economic and demographic environment was different.

The econometric model estimated by Hatton and Williamson shows that the Latin countries *were* different, but only in one sense: holding everything else constant, emigration rates from late-nineteenth-century Italy and Spain were significantly higher than they were in northwestern Europe. The finding could, however, be spurious. Recall that the return migration rate was far higher in the Latin countries, especially Italy. This could be due to the fact that lower transportation costs made temporary migration more feasible toward the end of our period, when the Latins started migrating in earnest. It follows that the gross emigration rates used in the regression exaggerate net emigration rates for Mediterranean countries far more than for the rest of Europe: the relatively high gross migration rates for the Latin latecomers (controlling for economic fundamentals) might disappear if we had really good net migration data. Alas, we do not.

Was the delay in Latin emigration due to differences in Latin behavior, or was the Latin environment different? Hatton and Williamson show that Latin emigration was not uniquely constrained by poverty. Recall the argument that potential emigrants in the poorest European countries were so income constrained by their poverty that they could not afford the move. Poverty was greater in Iberia and Italy, and thus the constraint was more binding. Blanca Sanchez-Alonso (1995, 257, 265) has shown that when controlling for other influences, Spanish provinces with low agricultural wages had low emigration rates in 1888–1890 and 1911–1913. However, note that the initial existence of such poverty traps cannot help account for the eventual acceleration in Spanish emigration, since economic failure in Iberia (Molinas and Prados 1989) did not produce any significant wage increase. In Italy, by contrast, both wage increases at home (Faini and Venturini 1994a, 1994b) and, especially, remittances from abroad helped release the constraint on emigration. Furthermore, Sanchez-Alonso (1998) has stressed the role that policy played in creating an even poorer emigration environment in Spain. While the rest of the world stuck with the gold standard, Spain depreciated the peseta (and raised tariffs on cereals) so that Spanish agriculture could compete with foreign imports in the domestic market. Depreciation (and tariffs) reduced imports, but depreciation also served to increase the costs of migration, raising ticket prices and reducing the value of Spanish savings overseas. In short, (lower) trade and (lower) emigration were complements.[6] It was environment, not behavior, that made the Latins different.

Is it true that Latin migration supplies to the New World were more elastic than was true of the rest of Europe? The hypothesis is soundly rejected (Hatton and Williamson 1994a; 1998, chapter 3): Latin emigrants were no more responsive to wage gaps between home and abroad than was true of other European emigrants, including the English. It is simply not true that the Latin economies in the late nineteenth century had more elastic emigrant labor supplies than the rest of Europe. This revisionist finding is consistent with Alan Taylor's (1994) research, which shows that Argentina's immigration was no more responsive to wage gaps than was Australia's. These findings seem to damage the arguments of Sir Arthur Lewis (1978) and Carlos Diaz-Alejandro (1970) that Latin American development took place in an environment of uniquely elastic labor supplies.

If the Latin emigrants seem to have responded to their economic and demographic environment pretty much as the rest of Europe did, it was the environment that they left behind that was different. Table 7.3 explores this proposition by replicating the analysis of figure 7.3 for the three Mediterranean countries, Britain, and Sweden. That is, the table multiplies the estimated coefficients from the emigrant regression

Table 7.3
Sources of Changing Emigration Rates, 1890s–1900s

	(1)	(2)	(3)	(4)	(5)
	Predicted			Due to:	
	change in	Lagged			
	emigration	natural	Agricultural	Real wage	Migrant
Country	rate	increase	share	ratio	stock
Italy	0.350	1.305	0.079	−1.304	0.270
Spain	2.803	−0.340	0.711	2.102	0.330
Portugal	2.526	1.663	0.082	0.512	0.269
Sweden	−0.845	−0.140	0.619	−1.579	0.255
Great Britain	0.110	−0.500	0.181	0.633	−0.204

Sources: Hatton and Williamson (1998, table 3.5).
Note: The predicted values in column 1 refer to the change in gross emigration rates between 1890–1899 and 1900–1913; they are derived by summing the four entries in columns 2–5. The $\hat{\beta}_x$ used in columns 2–5 refer to estimated coefficients from the emigration regression equation, evaluated at their long-run values. The ΔX refer to changes in each explanatory variable between 1890–1899 and 1900–1913.

equation by the change in the right-hand-side variable of interest. The multiplication yields a figure that tells us just how much of the predicted rise in decadal emigration rates between, say, 1890–1899 and 1900–1913 (the sum of columns 2–5) can be explained by changes in each explanatory variable.

The typical northern European patterns are illustrated by Sweden, which was on the downside of its emigration cycle after the 1890s, having reached peak emigration rates earlier (table 7.1). The decline in the predicted gross emigration rate for Sweden, −0.845, is explained entirely by two forces: the decline in the rate of natural increase two decades previously (−0.140) and the spectacular catching up of real wages (−1.579), the other two forces tending to have offsetting but weaker effects.

Table 7.3 shows that very different economic and demographic forces were at work in the latecomer Latin countries. True, a boom in the natural rate of population increase two decades earlier was a powerful force serving to push up emigration rates in Italy and Portugal, experience on the upswing of the demographic transition that was replicated in the rest of Europe earlier in the century. These are by far the most powerful forces accounting for the surge in Italian and Portuguese emigration rates after the 1890s. Spain, however, is an exception: two decades earlier, rates of natural increase were falling, not rising, a fact well appreciated by demographic historians (Moreda 1987). If emigrant-inducing demographic forces were absent in Spain after the 1890s, why the rise in Spanish emigration rates? The answer seems to lie largely with economic failure at home. The wage gap between Spain and destination countries widened at the end of the century (table 7.2), and this event explains almost all of the surge in Spanish emigration. The same was true of Portugal, although the failure at home was not nearly as great. In contrast, Italian wages were catching up with those in destination countries—Argentina, Germany, and the United States—and that wage success muted the surge in Italian emigration by partially offsetting those powerful emigrant-inducing demographic forces.

For all three Latin countries, there were additional underlying fundamentals that they shared and served to contribute to the surge in emigration: modest rates of industrialization and rising migrant populations abroad. Nonetheless, what really made the Latin countries different after the 1890s was the delayed demographic transition and the economic failure in Portugal and Spain.

Latin economic failure helps account for the surge of emigration after the 1890s. Oddly enough, the same is true of Britain. British emigration rose to a peak in the 1880s, falling thereafter, thus obeying an emigration life cycle that was repeated by so many other countries in nineteenth-century Europe. However, British emigration departed from this emigration life cycle pattern after the 1890s: the emigration rate *rose* rather than continuing its fall. What made Britain different after the 1890s? Exactly the same forces that made Spain and Portugal different: relative economic failure at home.

A European Model of Mass Emigration Emerges

The forces underlying the European mass migrations are now much clearer. In the early phases of emigration and modern development, the positive impact of the demographic transition, industrialization, and the increasing number of previous emigrants abroad outweighed the negative impact of real wage catch-up. Thus, although European real wages were slowly catching up on real wages in more labor-scarce destinations, emigration rates surged. But as demographic transition forces petered out, as the rate of industrialization slowed, and as the emigrant stock abroad began to level out, real wage convergence between labor markets at home and abroad increasingly dominated events. The continued fall in the wage gap between home and destination areas finally caused emigration rates to drop off. This fall accelerated on the downswing as direct demographic forces now joined these long-run labor market effects, that is, as the young adult cohort—the cohort most responsive to labor market forces—declined in relative importance. Our guess is that these forces would have stemmed the European mass migration tide soon after World War I, making the American quotas and the disappearance of immigrant subsidies in Argentina, Australia, Brazil, Canada, and elsewhere overseas at least partially redundant.

This story about the evolution of a truly global labor market in the nineteenth-century Atlantic economy is only half told. Chapter 8 adds the second half: an assessment of the impact of the mass migrations on real wage convergence itself.

Mass Migrations: Impact on Labor Markets, Home and Abroad

The mass emigrations within Europe and between it and the New World overseas surely had a significant impact on labor markets at home, raising real wages, improving living standards, and eroding poverty.[1] And just as surely, the mass migrations must also have had a significant impact on labor markets abroad. Compared with a counterfactual world without them, the arrival of new immigrants reduced real wages, raised poverty incidence, and lowered living standards for the previous immigrants and unskilled native-born workers with whom the new arrivals competed. Thus, mass migration was a force tending to create economic convergence among the participating countries, living standards in the poor emigrant countries being pushed up closer to living standards in rich immigrant countries. Not all countries participated, some participated more than others, and some experienced other events that offset the migration forces, but the underlying tendencies must have been pervasive. Now we want to give these qualitative assertions some quantitative muscle.

This chapter starts by offering that muscle for two important emigrating countries that exhibited impressive catch-up: Ireland and Sweden. It then explores the same issue for the biggest immigrant labor market of them all: the United States. What about all the rest? How big was the impact of the mass migrations on the Atlantic economy as a whole? The remainder of the chapter identifies the contribution of the mass migrations to convergence, and the magnitudes are very large. The estimated contribution is so large, in fact, that its impact on convergence must have been partially offset by a variety of countervailing forces: independent disequilibrating forces of technical change (faster in some rich countries, like the United States and Canada); and dependent offsetting forces of capital accumulation (international capital chasing after the migrants or native capital accumulation stimulated by the presence of immigrants), natural resource exploitation (land settlement by migrants or by natives whom the migrants displaced in settled areas), trade (migrant labor favoring the expansion of laborintensive activities in rich countries), or productivity gains (migrantlabor-induced scale economies). While these partial offsets must have been many and subtle, and may indeed have been interrelated (chapter 13), this chapter can report that the mass migrations made an unambiguous and profound contribution to economic convergence and global labor market integration prior to World War I.

A Solution to Problems at Home?

European emigration generated no shortage of political debate and moral judgment. Some Irish postfamine commentators, for example, viewed the emigrant flood as the result of Ireland's failure to industrialize and thus its inability to create enough good jobs (Ó Gráda 1994b, chap. 13). Others saw the flood in even more negative terms, as one more *cause* of industrial failure. One worry was that these emigrations drained the home country of the best and the brightest, jeopardizing the future.[2] A Mr. O'Brien reported to the 1893 Royal Commission on Agricultural Labour that "there is a very general opinion, and, probably, a perfectly well-founded opinion entertained by the employers of labour in this district that the labourers are now . . . [not] as efficient as formerly . . . owing to the circumstance that the best, youngest, and most competent are those who have emigrated; the old and immature remaining behind" (BPP 1893–1894, 35). As we will see in chapter 12, such emigrant self-selection might help explain Ireland's inability to attract foreign capital, despite its low wages (Mokyr 1991; O'Rourke 1992).

Another argument was that Ireland failed to industrialize because its home market was too small; once too small, scale economies were hard to achieve, Irish manufacturing lost its competitive edge, and industrial job creation faltered; emigrants fled the stagnant Irish labor market; and the market grew even smaller. Such commentary would imply that a dismal path-dependent historical process was at work that ensured Irish industrial failure (Ó Gráda 1994b, 342–347). Of course, this argument seems at first sight to ignore the fact that there was an enormous British market close by, which Ireland could and did exploit by trade. However, Paul Krugman (1991b) has constructed a model in which transport costs between markets ensure that domestic market size matters for industries' location decisions, and Karl Whelan (1995), in an unpublished paper, has applied this model to nineteenth-century Ireland, arguing that the famine of the 1840s, and its associated emigration, could have spurred subsequent deindustrialization by reducing the domestic rural market for Irish manufactured goods.[3]

There is some evidence from prefamine Ireland that emigration may have implied a loss to the economy, providing other nations with "instant adults" reared at the nation's expense (Neal and Uselding 1972; Mokyr and Ó Gráda 1982), and some evidence that the better educated and more highly skilled were those who left (Nicholas and Shergold 1987).[4] However, although postfamine Ireland certainly experienced industrial failure, it did undergo an impressive catch-up on both Britain and America. Economics as old as Adam Smith can explain why: emigration made labor more scarce in Ireland, thus raising real wages and living standards at home, both in absolute terms and relative to immigrant nations. This kind of Smithian economics exploits diminishing returns: given land, capital, technology, and resources, more labor means lower labor productivity, real wages, and living standards; less labor means higher labor productivity, real wages, and living standards. While the movers may have been able to escape to higher wages abroad, the now-scarcer stayers found conditions improving at home.

Swedish commentators also viewed emigration as a sign of failure. Surely, they seem to have said, it is a poor economy that cannot generate enough good jobs to keep young Swedes at home. The Swedes left in especially large numbers in the 1880s, and the debate became most intense right about that time—and this in spite of the fact that Sweden and the rest of Scandinavia was in the midst of the most impressive European catch-up by far, a catch-up that, in contrast with Ireland, seemed to be carried by vigorous industrialization (O'Rourke and Williamson 1995a; 1995c; 1997). In 1882, Knut Wicksell, a young theorist and neo-Malthusian, wrote a popular essay that argued the Smithian case: emigration would eventually solve the pauper problem that blighted labor-abundant and land-scarce Swedish agriculture and thus was a good thing to be tolerated, perhaps even stimulated (Wicksell 1882, cited in Karlstrom 1985, 155).

What *was* the impact of mass emigration on the home country? The literature is loud on assertion but quiet on evidence, even though more than a century has passed since Wicksell's essay appeared. We will deal with Wicksell's Sweden in a moment, but first we turn to O'Brien's Ireland, where, after all, the European mass migrations started.

The Impact on Labor Markets at Home: Ireland

Estimates of Irish national income for the late nineteenth century are sketchy, but Cormac Ó Gráda (1994b, 242, 379) uses what we have to guess that Irish national income grew at about 0.7 percent per annum between 1845 and 1913.[5] Per capita income grew more than twice as fast, at 1.6 percent per annum. That is not a typographical error: per capita income grew a lot faster than did total income since the Irish population fell over the period. Per capita income growth is somewhat slower if we skip over the famine—say, about 1.3 percent per annum. Irish income per capita rose from about two-fifths to about three-fifths that of Britain. Furthermore, the share of the population in poverty declined, and that of families living in low-quality housing (third and fourth class) dropped from 63 percent in 1861 to 29 percent fifty years later (Hatton and Williamson 1993).

Although gross national product (GNP) per capita and other indicators of well-being suggest significant improvement, real wages offer information more directly relevant in describing the labor market conditions that were driving emigrants abroad and in describing the market that had to adjust most to their departure. Figure 8.1 plots the real wage for Irish building and agricultural laborers. Three features stand out. First, the two indexes move quite closely together over the whole period, suggesting that the Irish unskilled labor market was fairly well integrated. The second feature is the substantial real wage growth that these series exhibit. Between 1855 and 1913, real wages more than doubled, an observation consistent with the available evidence on the growth of national income per capita. Third, most of the growth was concentrated in the period between 1860 and 1895.

The trends in Irish real wages can be compared with those in the major receiving countries, Britain and the United States, using the same PPP-adjusted wage rates presented in chapter 2. Figure 8.2 plots the ratios for building laborers: it shows no convergence before the famine, but substantial catch-up after. Irish wages rose from about 60 percent of British wages in the late 1840s and early 1850s to about 90 percent after the turn of the century; over the same period, they rose from about 40 percent to about 55 percent of American wages. Given that Ireland did not industrialize rapidly during the period and that the Irish population declined, it is tempting to conclude that labor force contraction was the main source of the convergence. This appeal to Smithian rea-

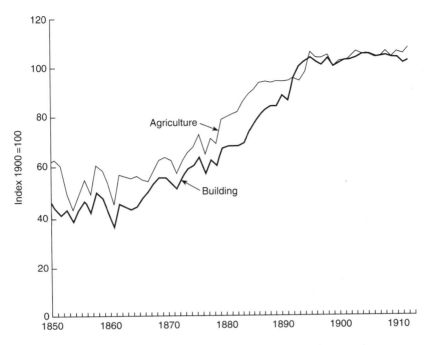

Figure 8.1
Irish real wages, 1850–1913. Source: Boyer, Hatton, and O'Rourke (1994, figure 9.1).

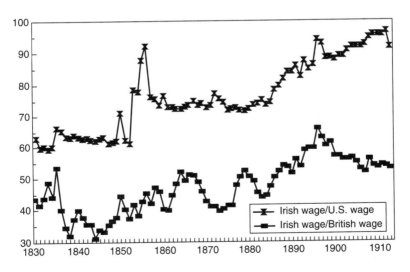

Figure 8.2
Irish urban wages relative to Britain and the United States, 1830–1913. Source: William-son (1995), revised in O'Rourke and Williamson (1997).

soning—an easing of pressure on the land—is certainly consistent with the relative rise in Irish wages and a decline in the rural labor surplus.

Most of the decline in the Irish population and labor force between the Great Famine and the Great War took place in rural areas and on the farm. Between 1851 and 1913 the rural population fell by over 2.6 million, a decline of almost one-half. Meanwhile, the population living in towns and cities rose by about a half-million, so the share living in urban areas more than doubled, jumping from 12 to 29 percent of the total. In fact, only two of the thirty-two Irish counties experienced a population increase over the six decades. These were the largely urban counties of Dublin and Antrim.

To summarize, economic conditions facing Irish laborers improved dramatically in the half-century following the famine, not only in absolute terms but relative to Britain and the United States. These facts are certainly supportive of the hypothesis that the real wage in postfamine Ireland was being driven by the labor force and thus that the wage was intimately tied to emigration. Although supportive, the hypothesis needs reinforcement. After all, the economics is very simple and population is unlikely to be a perfect proxy for the labor force. We need to estimate the impact of emigration on the labor force, and we need a more complete model to measure its effects.

Enormous labor force shocks such as the Irish exodus can best be assessed by a general equilibrium approach, which allows for the full set of influences felt throughout the domestic economy. What follows relies on a CGE model of the Irish economy in 1907–1908, designed to assess the effects of postfamine emigration on Irish real wages and living standards (Boyer, Hatton, and O'Rourke 1994). A similar model will be applied to Sweden later in this chapter.

How much of the postfamine rise in real wages was due to emigration? To get the answer, Boyer, Hatton, and O'Rourke (1994) estimated how much higher the 1907–1908 Irish labor force would have been in a world of no emigration from 1851 onward. They then used the 1907–1908 model to calculate what wages would have been in this counterfactual no-emigration world. This gave them an estimate of the independent impact of postfamine Irish emigration on labor markets at home. Their model is capable of dealing with the fundamental insight of Eli Heckscher and Bertil Ohlin that trade can be a partial substitute for factor mobility between countries (chapter 13). The Irish model allows trade to have an offsetting impact on real wages, just as Heckscher and Ohlin insisted: changes in labor scarcity induced by movements abroad will change trade patterns (Ireland will shift into less labor-intensive exports) and output mix (producing less labor-intensive products). Those changes in economic activity and trade will tend to diminish (but not eliminate) the impact of rising labor scarcity on real wages. Heckscher and Ohlin would be happy on that score.

But what about world capital markets? Can't capital flows serve as a substitute for labor migration by moving in the opposite direction? If emigration had been only a trickle from a labor-surplus area like Ireland, wouldn't capital have flooded in to exploit the cheap labor? Since Irish emigration was actually a flood, shouldn't capital have retreated from the now more expensive labor market area? Cormac Ó Gráda (1994b, chapters 12–14) makes a persuasive case that capital was mobile over Irish borders prior to the Great War. But exactly how mobile? We do not know, so Boyer, Hatton, and O'Rourke offer two cases: one where the rental rate on capital is taken as exogenous, implying that small Ireland could have borrowed (or loaned) as much additional capital as it wished from (to) world capital markets (e.g., London) without influencing world interest rates;[6] and one where Ireland had to go it alone and thus could not have borrowed (or loaned) any additional capital from (to) foreign markets.

In the internationally immobile capital case, Boyer, Hatton, and O'Rourke estimated that the real wage in agriculture was 19 to 41 percent higher as a result of emigration, and the nonfarm wage was 23 to 52 percent higher. Per capita GNP rose by between 15 and 33 percent due to emigration. Thus, wages rose by more than per capita income due to emigration. This result certainly confirms who gained and who lost from emigration. Workers gain, since increasing labor scarcity raises wages. Landlords lost, since increasing labor scarcity cut into their rents: rents were reduced by 33 to 55 percent due to emigration. Capitalists lost, since increasing labor scarcity cut into their profits: rates of return on capital were reduced by 28 to 45 percent.

Suppose instead that capital is viewed as having been completely mobile over Irish borders. What then? All of the effects of emigration just discussed would have been somewhat smaller, although still big. In the absence of emigration, more labor and lower wages would have attracted more foreign capital (or kept more Irish capital at home); more foreign capital would have meant better-equipped Irish workers than in the immobile capital case; and thus the glut of workers in the counterfactual world without emigration would have been at least partially offset by more capital.[7] Under the mobile capital case, both farm and nonfarm wages increase by 6 to 12 percent as a result of emigration, not the 19 to 52 percent seen in the immobile capital case. The average of all of these emigration-induced wage increases is about 21 percent.

These figures imply that postfamine Irish emigration may have accounted for as much as half of the real wage growth and over one-quarter of the per capita GNP growth observed. It also explains a large share of Irish catch-up on the leaders abroad: emigration can account for a third of Irish convergence on Britain and the United States even if capital is assumed mobile.

Irish emigration by itself made a powerful contribution to Irish real wage and living standards convergence on Britain and the United States. What happens when U.S. immigration is added to the story? Later in this chapter, we will find that immigration after 1870 made the 1910 U.S. population around 17 percent bigger than it otherwise would have been and the 1910 labor force around 24 percent bigger. As we shall see, immigration lowered U.S. unskilled urban real wages by between 8 and 15 percent, which implies that *all* of the postfamine Irish convergence on the United States was due to mass migration.[8] The same was not true for Irish convergence on Britain since Britain recorded high emigration rates too. In the absence of emigration, British wages would have been between 5 and 7 percent lower (Taylor and Williamson 1997, table 4, 40; O'Rourke, Williamson, and Hatton 1994, table 10.1, 209). Thus, allowing for the impact of migration on the two leaders strengthens migration's contribution to Irish real wage convergence on the United States but weakens it on Britain.

The Impact on Labor Markets at Home: Sweden

Ireland, Scandinavia, and even Italy underwent catch-up from the Great Famine to the Great War. The performance of the Scandinavian countries was particularly impressive: per capita income, real wages, and average labor productivity grew faster in Denmark, Norway, Sweden, and even Finland than in the rest of northwestern Europe (tables 2.1, 2.2, and 7.2). Thus, the gap between the Scandinavian latecomers and Britain narrowed considerably. To offer just two examples, between 1870 and 1913, Swedish labor productivity rose from 47 to 59 percent of British levels; between 1870 and 1910, Danish unskilled urban real wages rose from 54 to 106 percent of real wages in Britain. Indeed, real wages in Scandinavia even rose relative to fast-growing America: Norwegian urban unskilled real wages rose from 28 to 49 percent of those in the United States, and Swedish real wages rose from 31 to 59 percent.[9]

This rapid Scandinavian catch-up is now well documented, but it was also apparent to Swedish economists writing in the middle or at the end of the period—like Knut Wicksell, Eli Heckscher, and Bertil Ohlin. The amazing aspect of the literature on the Scandinavian catch-up is that until recently no one tried to assess its sources. There has been no shortage of assertion, of course, ranging from schooling advantages, favorable price shocks, the right natural resource endowment, trade creation, mass emigration, and elastic foreign capital inflows. The two of us recently put some empirical content into those assertions (O'Rourke and Williamson 1995a, 1995c).

What contribution did Scandinavian emigration make? As we pointed out at the start of this chapter, Knut Wicksell asserted a century ago that emigration would solve the pauper problem that blighted Swedish agriculture. His proemigration agitation was followed by other voices in the 1890s, including Adrian Molin and Gustav Sundbarg. Tests of Wicksell's assertion were very slow in coming, despite the intensity of the debate on the economic impact of the late-nineteenth-century mass migrations.

There are two questions one can pose of the Swedish migrations. How much of Swedish real wage and labor productivity growth can be ascribed to emigration, the out-migrations having created more labor scarcity at home? And how much of the Swedish catch-up can be assigned more generally to mass migration—both the emigration from poor Sweden and the immigration (of Swedes and non-Swedes) into the rich New World, like the United States (where most of the Swedes and the rest of the Scandinavian emigrants went)? What about Swedish catch-up on Britain, itself an emigrant country? Our primary interest is in the last two catching-up questions, but as we saw in the Irish analysis, each of these questions employs the same methodology to get answers: estimate the labor force in a counterfactual no-migration environment for both the rich and poor country; with the counterfactual labor force estimate in hand, assess the impact of the altered labor force on living standards and productivity by the application of some model of the rich and poor economies; finally, compute the share of the measured living standards and productivity catch-up explained by the mass migrations.

Irish experience has illustrated how a CGE model can be applied to the problem, but a pioneering application by Urban Karlstrom (1985) did the same for Sweden more than a decade ago. Although Karlstrom did not make the calculation himself, his results imply that the mass migrations might have accounted for about a quarter of the impressive contraction of the American-Swedish wage gap between 1870 and 1910 (O'Rourke, Williamson, and Hatton 1994). Karlstrom's pioneering work stimulated the construction of an improved Swedish CGE model in an effort to sharpen our answers to Wicksell's question (O'Rourke and Williamson 1995a).

Did emigration have a big impact on the labor force at home? Scandinavian emigration rates reached their peak in the 1880s, and at that time they were among the highest in Europe, exceeded only by Ireland and the rest of the United Kingdom. The rate for the decade was 95.2 per thousand of the population in Norway, 70.1 per thousand in Sweden, and 39.4 per thousand in Denmark (table 7.1). Sweden lay in the middle of the Scandinavian range. Emigration went through booms and busts, but by 1910 the Danish population was 11 percent below what it would have been in the absence of the emigrations over the four decades following 1870, the Swedish population was 15 percent lower, and the Norwegian population 19 percent lower (table 8.1). Since emigration favored young adults with high labor force participation rates, the impact on the home labor force was even bigger than on the home population. The bottom line is that the Swedish labor force was about 20 percent smaller in 1910 than it would have been in the absence of emigration. Thus, the influence of emigration on Sweden (and the rest of Scandinavia) was not trivial.

O'Rourke and Williamson (1995a, appendix 2) report the cumulative impact of Swedish emigration between 1870 and 1910 on Swedish real wages in 1910. In contrast with the Irish analysis, we do not explore the mobile capital case here. Capital inflows into Sweden over these four decades were very large in spite of the Swedish emigration; it is hard to imagine that they would have been even larger in the absence of emigration, so we ignore the possibility. The bottom line in terms of labor market impact is this: emigration between 1870 and 1910 served to raise urban wages in Sweden by 12.3 percent above what they would have been in its absence. Urban unskilled wages in Sweden actually increased by 190 percent over the four decades,[10] so the 12.3 percent looks small by comparison. Granted, Wicksell was talking about agricultural poverty, but the impact of emigration on farm wages was still "only" 11.8 percent, hardly enough to

Table 8.1
Summary Data: Net Migration Rates and Cumulative Impact, 1870–1910

	Persons		Labor force		Impact of migration		
	Adjusted net migration rate, 1870–1910	Adjusted cumulative population impact, 1910	Adjusted net migration rate, 1870–1910	Adjusted cumulative labor force impact, 1910	On real wages (actual versus counterfactual), 1870–1910	On GDP/capita (actual versus counterfactual), 1870–1910	On GDP/worker (actual versus counterfactual), 1870–1910
Argentina	11.74	60%	15.50	86%	–21.5%	–8.2%	–21.0%
Australia	6.61	30	8.73	42	–14.6	–6.8	–14.4
Belgium	1.67	7	2.20	9	–4.4	–3.1	–5.1
Brazil	0.74	3	0.98	4	–2.3	–0.5	–1.5
Canada	6.92	32	9.14	44	–15.6	–7.6	–15.5
Denmark	–2.78	–11	–3.67	–14	7.6	3.7	7.4
France	–0.10	0	–0.13	–1	1.4	0.2	0.3
Germany	–0.73	–3	–0.96	–4	2.4	1.3	2.2
Great Britain	–2.25	–9	–2.97	–11	5.6	2.8	5.8
Ireland	–11.24	–36	–14.84	–45	31.9	NA	NA
Italy	–9.25	–31	–12.21	–39	28.2	14.2	28.6
Netherlands	–0.59	–2	–0.78	–3	2.7	1.1	1.9
Norway	–5.25	–19	–6.93	–24	9.7	3.1	10.4
Portugal	–1.06	–4	–1.40	–5	4.3	0.0	0.0
Spain	–1.16	–5	–1.53	–6	5.9	0.0	0.0
Sweden	–4.20	–15	–5.55	–20	7.5	2.5	8.2
United States	4.03	17	5.31	24	–8.1	–3.3	–8.1
New World	6.01	29%	7.93	40%	–12.4%	–5.3%	–12.1%
Old World	–3.08	–11	–4.06	–13	8.6	2.3	5.4

Source: Taylor and Williamson (1997, tables 1, 3, 4).
Note: Migration rates per thousand per annum. Minus denotes emigration. Taylor and Williamson calculated the difference between real wages, GDP per capita, and GDP per worker in a counterfactual (no-migration) scenario with their actual levels; here we report the difference between actual and counterfactual levels.

confirm Wicksell's optimism that emigration would solve the pauper problem in Swedish agriculture. Other events mattered far more, it seems.

What about as a share of the catch-up with Britain or the United States? Simulations suggest that the impact of mass migration on the rapidly contracting wage gap between Britain and Sweden was small, accounting for perhaps a twelfth of the catch-up. The reason for the small contribution is clear: Britain recorded an emigration rate not too far below that of Sweden (and the rest of Scandinavia). Once again, Wicksell seems to have been wrong: emigration did not make a significant contribution to Anglo-Swedish catch-up. But what about Swedish catch-up with the United States, the country that absorbed 98 percent of the Swedish overseas emigrants?[11] As we have already mentioned, and will see below, the immigration rate in the late-nineteenth-century United States was very large, and its cumulative impact from 1870 served to make urban wages between 8 and 15 percent lower there than they would have been without the immigration. The mass migration had a big impact on the rapidly contracting wage gap between the United States and Sweden, explaining between a quarter and two-fifths of the Swedish catch-up on the United States.

Absorbing the Immigrants: The Impact on American Labor Markets

The impact of the immigrants on American labor markets obsessed contemporary observers, and it was discussed at length in the famous Immigration Commission Report of 1911. Here we confront three questions that are just as relevant today as they were almost a century ago: Where did the immigrants find employment? Did they crowd out natives? Did the increased foreign-born presence significantly reduce native workers' wages?

On the issue of employment location, we can discriminate between two views. The first view is optimistic: it argues that the immigrants entered rapidly growing, high-wage employment, thereby easing short-run labor supply bottlenecks in leading industries. The second view is pessimistic: it argues that immigrants crowded in to slow-growing, low-wage employment in industries undergoing relative decline, thereby crowding out unskilled natives. These competing views can be examined by comparing the share of immigrants in a given occupation with employment growth in that occupation. If that share was high and rising in rapidly expanding industries and occupations, then immigrants could be regarded as the "shock troops" of structural change.[12] Hatton and Williamson (1998, chapter 8) examine the share of male immigrants in 106 occupations in 1900 and the change in that share between 1890 and 1900—the only pair of census years in which both the same occupational definitions and the share of immigrants are available.

Their evidence confirms that immigrants found employment more frequently in unskilled jobs compared with natives. New immigrant arrivals tended to be unskilled. More to the point, immigrants located in slow-growth sectors, not fast-growth sectors. In short, there is no evidence to support the view that the foreign-born dominated fast-growing occupations and sectors prior to World War I. Nor is there any evidence to support the view that immigrants flowed dispropor-tionately into high-growth sectors and occupations. In fact, the evi-dence suggests the contrary: immigrants flowed disproportionately into the slowest-growing occupations.

We have a ready explanation for these facts: given that occupational growth reflects shifting comparative advantage and that the United States was exploiting its comparative advantage in resource- and capital-intensive industries, it follows that fast-growing sectors should have generated buoyant demand growth for skilled labor (a comple-ment with capital) and sluggish demand growth for unskilled labor (a substitute for capital). Thus, unskilled immigrants *should* have flooded into unskilled labor-intensive industries and occupations where growth was slower. Indeed, these findings are consistent with those from the 1980s and 1990s, when the flood of new, less-skilled immi-grants into services and import-competing manufacturing has raised the same concern (Baumol, Blackman, and Wolff 1989; Borjas 1994) that New York's immigrant sweatshops did in the 1890s. The evidence from the 1890s also seems to confirm a mismatch between labor demand, which was shifting away from unskilled occupations (becoming more skilled), and booming immigrant labor supplies that were declining in quality (becoming less skilled). This had inequality implications then (Williamson and Lindert 1980; Williamson 1982; chapter 9) just as it does now (Goldin and Margo 1992; Borjas, Freeman, and Katz 1992). Immigration crowded out native unskilled workers (including south-ern blacks; B. Thomas 1972, 130–134, chapter 18; Collins 1997) and thus widened the gap between the working poor and the rest. In this sense, the 1911 Congress, reading the Immigration Commission Report, and today's Congress, reading gloomy news in the *Economist* on rising inequality, share the same concerns.

What we have said about occupations need not apply to regions. Surely immigrants moved into the most rapidly expanding states, thus easing excess demand in local labor markets. Once again Hatton and Williamson (1998, chapter 8) supply the answer: they examine the proportion of foreign-born in the total population across states for the intercensal periods 1880–1890, 1890–1900, and 1900–1910. Their results show that northeastern states whose populations grew rapidly experienced a significant rise in foreign-born density. This reflects the well-known fact that immigrants moved to the cities in the most rapidly growing states on the eastern seaboard. By contrast, however, the more rapid was the growth of a state's population in the West North Central or Mountain region, the more the foreign-born share fell. Thus, immigrants moved disproportionately into the most rapidly growing centers on the East Coast, but not elsewhere in the United States. These facts about regional growth raise a relevant question about push and pull. Did immigrants crowd out the natives in the fast-growing East Coast labor markets, thus pushing them West? Or did the westward movement of natives pull foreign immigrants into East Coast labor markets? When the spatial analysis takes proper account of labor demand conditions, it seems clear that immigrants were indeed crowding out unskilled natives on the urban East Coast (Hatton and Williamson 1998, table 8.5; Collins 1997).

Were immigrant and native workers complements or substitutes? If they were complements, then immigration could have raised the productivity and hence the wages of the more skilled native workers. As we will see in chapter 10, James Foreman-Peck (1992) recently estimated a translog production function for U.S. manufacturing in 1890, treating immigrant and native labor as separate factors of production. His results showed that these two types of labor were not complements: bigger immigrant labor supplies did not increase the marginal product of native labor.

The key immigrant absorption question, however, has always been whether today's unskilled immigrants lowered the wage rates and living standards of the natives and yesterday's immigrants with whom they competed. In one recent study, Claudia Goldin (1994) estimated the correlation between immigration and wage changes across cities between 1890 and 1915. She found that a one percentage point increase in the foreign-born population share reduced unskilled wage rates by about 1 to 1.5 percent. True, her objective was to identify local relative wage impacts rather than to infer the economy-wide effect of immigration. But local labor market studies almost certainly understate (or miss entirely) the economy-wide impact of immigration on wages. After all, immigration will lower wages in a local labor market only insofar as it increases the total supply of labor there. If there is instead completely offsetting native emigration, then a rise in the immigrant share in a city or region is consistent with no change in the size of the local labor force and no wage effect of immigration compared with other local labor markets in which natives relocate. But wages should fall in all locations (perhaps equally, perhaps not). These effects are not measured by local labor market studies if local labor markets are well connected.

Another way to examine the impact of immigration on the real wage is to estimate the wage adjustment mechanism from time-series data. By altering labor supply and unemployment in the short run, immigration should drive down the wage along some long-run Phillips curve. Hatton and Williamson (1998, table 8.6) estimate such a model on annual observations for 1890–1913. The long-run solution to their estimated model suggests that, holding output constant, an increase in the labor force by 1 percent lowered the real wage in the long run by 0.4 or 0.5 percent. Based on the stock of foreign-born and their children enumerated in the 1910 census, immigration after 1890 accounted for about 12 percent of the 1910 labor force and immigration after 1870 accounted for about 27 percent of the 1910 labor force.[13] These magnitudes suggest that the real wage would have been 5 to 6 percent higher in the absence of immigration after 1890 and 11 to 14 percent higher in the absence of immigration after 1870.

These time-series results are consistent with those based on CGE models. For example, the first effort to apply computable general equilibrium techniques to the late-nineteenth-century United States estimated that immigration after 1870 lowered real wages in 1910 by 11 percent (Williamson 1974c, 387), almost identical to the time-series estimate.[14] More recently, we implemented two other CGE experiments, one jointly with Timothy Hatton, using alternative estimates of the impact of migration on the U.S. labor force. In the first, we found that a 21 percent increase in the U.S. labor force due to immigration lowered real wages there by 15 percent (O'Rourke and Williamson 1995d, appendix 6). In the second, we found that real wages would have been 9 percent higher in the absence of immigration, assuming that the U.S.

labor force would have been 27 percent lower, and allowing capital to chase after labor (O'Rourke, Williamson, and Hatton 1994, table 10.1, 209).[15]

The Impact on the Atlantic Economy

Real wages and living standards converged among the currently industrialized OECD countries between 1870 and World War I. The convergence was driven primarily by the erosion of the average wage gap between the New World and the Old, but many poor European countries caught up, at least in part, with the industrial leaders. How much of this convergence was due to mass migration? How much was due to other forces like trade-induced factor price convergence, resource accumulation, and productivity advance? So far, we have used the experience of one immigrant country—the United States—and two emigrant countries—Ireland and Sweden—to illustrate the potential impact of mass migrations on Atlantic labor market convergence between the 1860s and World War I. What about the rest of the Atlantic economy?[16]

Table 7.1 reports late-nineteenth-century net migration rates for five New World and fifteen Old World countries. Table 8.1 assesses the labor force impact of these migrations on each country in 1910. The impact varied greatly: Argentina's labor force was augmented most by immigration (86 percent), Brazil's the least (4 percent), and the United States' in between (24 percent), the latter below the New World average of 40 percent; Ireland's labor force was diminished most by emigration (45 percent), France and the Netherlands the least (1 and 3 percent), and Britain in between (11 percent), at just a little below the Old World average of 13 percent. These, then, are the Atlantic economy mass migrations whose labor market impact we wish to assess.

Like the CGE analysis earlier in this chapter, what follows exploits the counterfactual. However, the model Taylor and Williamson used, though much simpler, was estimated econometrically. As before, the purpose is to assess the role of migration in accounting for convergence, here measured by the decline in dispersion between 1870 and 1910. Overall, real wage dispersion declined by 28 percent over the period, GDP per capita dispersion by 18 percent, and GDP per worker dispersion by 29 percent (Taylor and Williamson 1997, table 3, 36). What contribution did international migration make to that measured

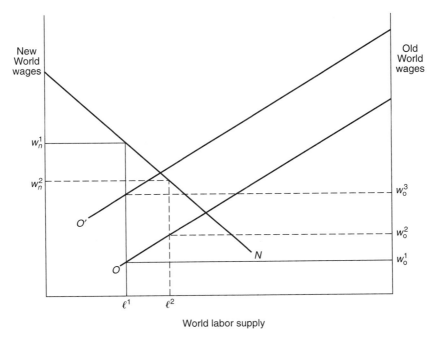

Figure 8.3
Allocating labor supplies between the New and Old Worlds.

convergence? To answer the question, we ask another: What would have been the measured convergence between 1870 and 1910 had there been no (net) migration?

The standard way of dealing with this question on the blackboard is illustrated by figure 8.3, and we simplify the answer by looking at only the wage gap between New World and Old World labor markets. New World wages and labor's marginal product are on the left-hand side and Old World wages and labor's marginal product on the right-hand side. The world labor supply is measured along the horizontal axis. An equilibrium distribution of labor occurs at the intersection of the two derived labor demand schedules (O and N). Instead, we start at l^1 where labor is scarce in the New World, and thus where the wage gap between the two regions is very large, $w_n^1 - w_o^1$. If mass migrations redistribute labor toward the New World, say to l^2, the wage gap collapses to $w_n^2 - w_o^2$, and all the observed convergence would be attributable to migration. However, the same kind of convergence could have been achieved by a relative demand shift: a shift in O to O', an event driven perhaps by relative price shocks favoring labor in the Old World or by faster accumulation and technological change there. The no-migration counterfactual invokes the ceteris paribus assumption: we adjust population and the labor force according to the average net migration (and labor force participation) rate observed during the period, and assume that technology, capital stocks, prices, and all else remain constant. Such assumptions impart an upward bias to the measured impact of mass migration, but let us see whether the magnitudes for the Atlantic economy as a whole are large enough to warrant further debate over bias.

Migration affects long-run equilibrium output and wages to the extent that it influences aggregate labor supply. Taylor and Williamson estimated labor demand elasticities econometrically, and used these results to assess the wage impact of changing labor supply by country. They also estimated the impact of migration on GDP per capita and per worker, which required information on labor's share of income. The last three columns of table 8.1 present the results (Taylor and Williamson 1997, tables 3, 4).

The results certainly accord with intuition. The mass migrations lowered wages and labor productivity by a lot in the New World and raised them by a lot in the Old; they typically (but not always) lowered income per capita marginally in the New World and typically (but not always) increased income per capita marginally in the Old World. Not surprisingly, the biggest impact is reported for those countries that experienced the biggest migrations: emigration raised Irish wages by 32 percent, Italian by 28 percent, and Norwegian by 10 percent; and immigration lowered Argentine wages by 21 percent, Australian by 15 percent, Canadian by 16 percent, and American by 8 percent.[17]

This partial equilibrium assessment of migration's impact is higher than a general equilibrium assessment would be. After all, it ignores trade responses and changes in output mix, both of which would have muted the impact of migration, and it also ignores global capital market responses, although this latter shortcoming will be repaired in a moment. Whether an overstatement or not,[18] table 8.1 certainly lends strong support to the hypothesis that mass migration made an important contribution to late-nineteenth-century convergence. Taylor and Williamson calculate that in the absence of the mass migrations, real wage dispersion would have increased by 7 percent rather than decreased by 28 percent, as it did in fact. GDP per worker dispersion would have decreased by only 9 percent rather than by 29 percent, as it did in fact. GDP per capita dispersion would also have decreased by only 9 percent rather than by 18 percent, as it did in fact. Wage gaps between New World and Old in fact declined from 108 to 85 percent, but in the absence of the mass migrations they would have risen to 128 percent in 1910.

Pairwise comparisons are also easily constructed using table 8.1 and the wage data presented in chapter 2. Wage gaps between many Old World countries and the United States fell dramatically as a result of mass migration. Without Irish emigration (some of whom went to America) and U.S. immigration (some of whom were Irish), the American-Irish wage gap would have risen by 33 percentage points (from 135 to 168 percent), while in fact it fell by 48 (from 135 to 87 percent); without Italian emigration (a large share of whom went to America) and U.S. immigration (many of whom were Italian), the American-Italian wage gap would have risen by 32 percentage points, while in fact it fell by 102; without British emigration and Australian immigration, the Australian-British wage gap would have fallen by only 14 percentage points, while in fact it fell by 48; and without Italian emigration and Argentine immigration, the Argentine-Italian wage gap would have risen by 75 percentage points, while in fact it fell by 45. Furthermore, the mass migrations to the New World had an impact on economic convergence within the Old World. Without the Norwegian emigration flood and the German emigration trickle, the German-Norwegian wage gap would have fallen by 63 percentage points, while in fact it fell by 71; and without the fact that Irish emigration exceeded British emigration by far, the British-Irish wage gap would have fallen by only 7 percentage points, while in fact it fell by 33. Although the impact of mass migration within the Old World was much smaller than between the Old and New Worlds, remember the caveat that migrations within Europe were underenumerated.

The results in table 8.1 suggest that more than all (125 percent) of the real wage convergence between 1870 and 1910 (log measure of dispersion) was attributable to migration and about two-thirds (69 percent) of the GDP per worker convergence. In contrast, perhaps half (50 percent) of the GDP per capita convergence might have been due to migration.

The contribution of mass migration to convergence in the full sample and in the New and Old Worlds differs, the latter being smaller. Indeed, in the cases of GDP per capita and per worker, New World convergence would have been greater in the absence of mass migration. While those two cases may at first appear bizarre, the fact that the

Atlantic labor market was segmented can account for it. Immigrant flows were not efficiently distributed everywhere, since barriers to entry limited destination choices for many southern Europeans, a point central to discussions of Latin migration experience in chapter 7 and invoked as an important determinant of Argentine economic performance (Diaz-Alejandro 1970; Taylor 1992b, 1994a; Hatton and Williamson 1998, chapters 2, 3, 6, 10). Thus migrants did not always obey some simple market-wage calculus; kept out of the best high-wage destinations or having alternative cultural preferences, many went to the "wrong" countries. The South-South flows from Italy, Spain, and Portugal to Brazil and Argentina were a strong force for local (Latin), not global, convergence. Furthermore, while barriers to exit were virtually absent in most of the Old World, policy (like assisted passage) still played a part in violating any simple market-wage calculus.[19] However, the small contribution of migration to convergence within the Old World and within the New illustrates our opening point: the major contribution of mass migration to late-nineteenth-century convergence was the enormous movement of about 60 million Europeans to the New World.

The relative insensitivity of GDP per capita convergence to migration is a result of countervailing effects inherent in the algebra. For real wages or GDP per worker, high migrant-to-population ratios of labor force participation rates amplify the impact of migration, but with GDP per capita, the impact is muted. Why? In the former two cases, migration has a bigger impact on the labor force, GDP and wages, the bigger is the labor content of the migrations. In the case of GDP per capita, things are less clear. For example, with emigration, population outflow generally offsets diminishing returns in production for a net positive impact on output per capita; but selectivity ensures that emigration will take away a disproportionate share of the labor force, increasing dependency rates and reducing output per capita. The latter effect was important in the late-nineteenth-century Atlantic economy (Taylor and Williamson 1997), so muted GDP per capita effects are no surprise. Based on table 8.1, four decades of migration never lowered New World GDP per capita by more than 8 percent anywhere in the New World, and by as little as 3 percent in the United States, in contrast with per worker impacts of 21 and 8 percent, respectively. This labor-supply compensation effect operated in addition to the usual human capital transfer influences invoked to describe the net benefit to the United States of the millions received before World War I (Uselding

1971; Neal and Uselding 1972). Similar reasoning applies to the Old World: Swedish emigration after 1870 may have raised wages in 1910 by about 8 percent, but it served to raise GDP per capita by only 3 percent.

Qualifying the Bottom Line

The previous section argued that mass migration accounted for 125 percent of the real wage convergence observed in the Atlantic economy between 1870 and 1910. Haven't we overexplained late-nineteenth-century convergence? Perhaps, but remember that there were other powerful proconvergence and anticonvergence forces at work. Consider capital accumulation. We know that capital accumulation was faster in the New World, so much so that the rate of capital deepening was faster in the United States than in any of its competitors (Wright 1990; Wolff 1991), and the same was probably true of other rich New World countries. There is evidence therefore that the mass migrations may have been at least partially offset by capital accumulation, and a large part of that capital widening was being carried by international capital flows that reached magnitudes unsurpassed before or since (Edelstein 1982; Zevin 1992; Taylor 1996a; chapter 11). The evidence on the role of global capital market responses to migration is very tentative, but Taylor and Williamson (1997) make exactly this kind of adjustment to the results reported in table 8.1. They implement the zero-net-migration counterfactual in a model where the labor supply shocks generate capital inflows or outflows in order to maintain a constant rate of return on capital in each country. The capital-chasing-labor offsets are very large. Whereas mass migration explained 125 percent of the observed real wage convergence using the model without capital-chasing-labor, it explains about 70 percent of the convergence using the model with capital-chasing-labor, leaving approximately 30 percent to other forces. The findings for labor productivity are similar.

In theory, the forces of late-nineteenth-century convergence could have included commodity price convergence and trade expansion, technological catch-up, and human capital accumulation, but in fact mass migration was the central force. Capital flows were mainly an anticonvergence force (Scandinavia being an outstanding exception), in that they raised wages and labor productivity in the resource-abundant New World, while lowering them in the resource-scarce Old World (chapter 12). Furthermore, relatively little of the late-nineteenth-century convergence is likely to have been the result of technological catch-up or human capital accumulation (chapter 14), the central elements of modern convergence models.

These results offer a new perspective on the convergence debate, one relevant for both economic historians and macroeconomists. The convergence power of free migration, when it is tolerated, can be substantial given the late-nineteenth-century evidence. Convergence explanations based on technological or accumulation catch-up in closed economy models miss this point. The millions on the move in the late nineteenth century did not.

9   Globalization, Relative Factor Price Convergence, and Inequality

The Atlantic economy has witnessed three regimes since the mid-nineteenth century: the late-nineteenth-century *belle époque*, the dark middle ages between 1914 and 1950, and the late-twentieth-century renaissance.[1] The first and last epochs were ones of convergence (poor countries catching up on rich) and globalization (trade booms, mass migration, and huge capital flows). The middle ages were ones of de-globalization and divergence. Thus, the history of the Atlantic economy offers an unambiguous positive correlation between globalization on the one hand and convergence on the other. This book argues that the correlation is causal; the concluding chapter will show how globalization—in the form of mass migration and trade—played *the* critical role in contributing to convergence.

Since contemporary economists are now hotly debating the impact of these same globalization forces on wage inequality in the OECD, the recently liberalized Latin American regimes, and the open Asian tigers, it seems relevant to ask whether similar distributional forces might have been at work during the late nineteenth century. Distributional issues were raised very early in this book when exploring the question, "Were Heckscher and Ohlin right?" However, the search for the answer looked only to factor prices, and often for only a small subset of the Atlantic economy. Here we will augment the sample and explore more comprehensive inequality measures. Chapter 8 reviewed a literature, almost a century old, that argues that immigration hurt American labor and accounted for much of the poor real wage performance and rising inequality from the 1890s to World War I, so much so that a labor-sympathetic Congress passed immigration quotas. Chapter 6 cited a literature even older, which argues that a New World grain invasion eroded land rents in Europe, so much so that landowner-dominated continental parliaments raised tariffs to help protect them from the impact of globalization. But until very recently (Williamson 1997a), nowhere in this historical literature had anyone used late-nineteenth-century evidence to test three contentious hypotheses similar to those that Adrian Wood (1994) has explored for the late twentieth century:

HYPOTHESIS 1: Inequality rose in resource-rich, labor-scarce New World countries like Argentina, Australia, Canada, and, most important, the United States. Inequality fell in resource-poor, labor-abundant agrarian countries around the Old World periphery like Italy, the Iberian Peninsula, Ireland, and Scandinavia. Inequality was more stable for the European industrial leaders like Britain, France, Germany, and the Lowlands, all of which fell somewhere in the middle of the endowment range between the rich New World and poor Old World.

If the first hypothesis survives the test, then a second follows:

HYPOTHESIS 2: These inequality patterns can be explained largely by globalization.

If the second hypothesis survives the test, then a third follows:

HYPOTHESIS 3: These globalization-induced inequality trends help explain the retreat from globalization during the dark ages between 1914 and 1950.

The next two sections review the theory and tie historical debate about the first globalization boom in the late nineteenth century to current debate about the second globalization boom in the late twentieth century. There is a striking similarity between the two debates, just as there is a striking similarity between the debates over the impact of immigration on the American labor market in the 1890s and the 1980s. This chapter explores the extent to which the late-nineteenth-century and interwar Atlantic economy experiences confirm the first two of these three hypotheses. As we shall see, both hypotheses 1 and 2 survive the test of history, although international migration (and its absence) mattered far more than trade (and its absence).

Many contemporary observers held the view that globalization had increased inequality in the rich nations before the interwar age of autarky. However, a century ago this view could have been based only on anecdotes and strong priors. New facts now appear to offer support for those strong priors. Furthermore, they also appear to support hypothesis 3: that globalization-induced inequality contributed to the deglobalization and autarkic policies that dominated between 1914 and 1950. Indeed, during this dark age of trade suppression and binding migration quotas, the old globalization-inequality connection completely disappeared. It took the globalization renaissance after the 1960s to renew this old inequality debate. But we are getting ahead of our story here, since chapter 10 will be devoted entirely to globalization backlash as it influenced immigration policy in the New World.

Globalization and Inequality: The Late-Twentieth-Century Debate

After 1973, and especially in the 1980s, the United States experienced a dismal real wage performance for the less skilled, mostly due to declining productivity growth coupled with increasing wage inequality between skills. The ratio of weekly wages of the top decile to those of the lowest decile increased from 2.9 in 1963 to 4.4 in 1989 (Kosters 1994; Freeman 1995). This rising inequality was manifested primarily by increasing wage premiums for workers with advanced schooling and age-related skills. The same inequality trends were apparent elsewhere in the OECD (Smeeding and Coder 1995), but they were steeper in the United States. What makes this recent rise in inequality especially striking is that it was preceded by four decades of sharply falling inequality between 1929 and the late 1960s. These inequality developments also coincided with globalization, after four decades of relative isolation. Trade shares in the United States increased from 12 percent of GNP in 1970 to 25 percent in 1990 (Lawrence and Slaughter 1993), while the share of output exported from low-income countries rose from 8 percent in 1965 to 18 percent in 1990 (Richardson 1995, 34). Rates of U.S. immigration have risen, while the "quality" of the new immigrants has fallen (Borjas 1994). The inequality developments also coincided with a shift in U.S. spending patterns that resulted in large trade deficits. Given the similar timing of these events, economists have quite naturally devoted a lot of energy to exploring the links between trade and immigration, on the one hand, and wage inequality, on the other.

The standard Heckscher-Ohlin trade model makes unambiguous predictions about these issues. Every country exports those products that use its abundant and cheap factors of production intensively. Thus, a trade boom induced by either declining tariffs or transport costs will cause exports and the demand for the cheap factor to boom.

Globalization in poor countries should favor unskilled labor and disfavor skilled labor (in the rhetoric of the modern debate, call these countries "South"); globalization in rich countries should favor skilled labor and disfavor unskilled labor (call these countries "North"). Robert Lawrence and Matthew Slaughter (1993) asked whether the standard Heckscher-Ohlin trade model can explain rising U.S. wage inequality and determined that there is little evidence to support this view. Instead, the authors concluded that technological change was the key source of rising wage inequality. Hot debate ensued.

This strand of the debate stressed the evolution of labor demand by skill, ignoring the potential influence of supply. George Borjas (1994) and his collaborators (Borjas, Freeman, and Katz 1992) took a different approach, emphasizing instead how trade and immigration served to augment U.S. labor supply. In order to do this, they first estimated the implicit labor supply embodied in trade flows. Imports embody labor, thus serving to augment the effective domestic labor supply. And exports imply a decrease in the effective domestic labor supply. In this way, the huge U.S. trade deficit of the 1980s implied an increase in the U.S. labor supply, and since most of the imports were in goods that used unskilled labor relatively intensively, it also implied an increasing ratio of unskilled to skilled effective labor supplies. In addition, there was a shift in the national origin of immigrants from the 1960s to the 1980s: an increasing proportion of immigrants were from less developed nations (e.g., Mexico and Asia) and were thus more unskilled. A far higher fraction of immigrants were relatively unskilled just when immigration levels increased. It follows that both trade and immigration increased the supply of unskilled workers relative to skilled workers in the 1980s.

These relative supply shifts give us the desired qualitative result; that is, they imply increased wage inequality between skill types. The quantitative result, at least in Borjas's hands, also seems big. Borjas estimates that 15 to 25 percent of the relative wage decline of high school to college graduates is due to trade and immigration. He also estimates that 30 to 50 percent of the decline in the relative wage of high school dropouts to all other workers is due to these same globalization forces—one-third due to trade and two-thirds to immigration. Migration was the more important globalization force producing U.S. inequality trends in the 1980s, according to Borjas. We shall see that it was far more important in the late nineteenth century and, furthermore, that it was ubiquitous across practically all countries involved in the globalization experience.

Thus far, we have been talking about only one country, the United States, perhaps because this is where rising inequality and immigration have been greatest. But the question is not simply why the United States and even Europe experienced a depressed relative demand for low-skilled labor in the 1980s and 1990s (Freeman 1995, 19), but whether the same factors were stimulating the relative demand for low-skill labor in the poor Third World. This is where Adrian Wood (1994, chapter 6; 1995) entered the debate. Wood was one of the first economists to examine inequality trends systematically across countries, including the poor South.

Wood distinguishes three skill types: uneducated workers, labor with basic education, and the highly educated. The poor South is richly endowed with uneducated labor, but the supply of labor with basic skills is growing fast. The rich North is abundant in highly educated labor, with a slow-growing supply of labor with basic skills. Wood assumes that capital is fairly mobile and technology is freely available. As the South improves its skills through the expansion of basic education and as trade barriers fall, it produces more manufactures that require only basic skills, whereas the North produces more of high-skill goods. The tendency toward relative factor price convergence raises the wage of workers with a basic education in the South (relative to that of high-skilled workers) and lowers it in the North, producing, ceteris paribus, rising inequality in the North.[2] Wood concludes that the decline in the relative wage of less-skilled northern workers is due to the elimination of trade barriers and increasing relative abundance of southern workers with a basic education.

Wood's research has been met with stiff critical resistance.[3] Since his book appeared, we have learned a lot more about the inequality and globalization connection in the Third World. The standard (two-factor) Stolper-Samuelson prediction would be that unskilled labor-abundant poor countries should undergo egalitarian trends in the face of globalization forces unless they are overwhelmed by inequality forces like industrial revolutionary labor-saving events on the upswing of some Kuznets curve (Kuznets 1955); and/or Mathusian gluts generated by the demographic transition, where falling infant mortality generates a rapid growth in new labor force entrants fifteen to twenty years later, glutting the bottom of the income pyramid where the impecunious young usually locate (Bloom and Williamson 1997; Higgins and Williamson 1998); and/or a shortfall in schooling supplies, which raises the premium on scarce skills. Just as we saw in chapter 4, a true test of the prediction would attempt to control for as many of these other forces as possible. A recent review by Donald Davis (1996) reports that the evidence contradicts Stolper-Samuelson, and a study of seven countries in Latin America and East Asia shows that wage inequality typically did not fall after trade liberalization; rather it rose (Robbins 1996). Wood himself has recently argued that while East Asia became more equal during the 1960s and 1970s as it opened to trade, the Latin American experience of the 1980s was the opposite (Wood 1997). According to Wood, the discrepancy is due to differences between the two decades rather than between the two regions—notably, the entry of China into world markets and the advent of new technology biased against the unskilled.

Such apparent anomalies have been strengthened by other studies, some of which have been rediscovered since Adrian Wood's book appeared. For example, about twenty years ago Anne Krueger (1978) studied ten developing countries covering the period through 1972, and her findings were not favorable to the simple predictions of standard trade theory. Her conclusions have been supported by Bourguignon and Morrisson (1991) and by recent work on the impact of Mexican liberalization on wage inequality (Feenstra and Hanson 1995; Feliciano 1995). However, none of these studies is very attentive to the simultaneous role of emigration from these developing countries.

The debate on the late-twentieth-century globalization and inequality connection is far from resolved. History never repeats itself, but perhaps some fresh evidence from an earlier globalization experience might help us find a resolution.

Globalization and Inequality: The Late-Nineteenth-Century Issues

Eli Heckscher and Bertil Ohlin argued that the commodity market integration documented in chapter 3 should have led to international factor price convergence. Chapter 4 showed that Heckscher and Ohlin were right: the late-nineteenth-century trade boom led to rising wage-rental ratios in Europe and falling wage-rental ratios in the New World. But what about trade and inequality more generally?

And what about mass migration? The poorest Old World countries tended to have the highest emigration rates, while the richest New

World countries tended to have the highest immigration rates. Chapter 7 showed that the correlation was not perfect, since potential emigrants from poor countries often found the cost of the move too high, and some New World countries restricted the inflow of migrants from the poor European periphery (or failed to subsidize them, while doing so for those from the European core). But the correlation between wages and migration rates was still very strong. Furthermore, the average impact of migration on labor supplies in both the sending and receiving regions was very big: the New World labor force was augmented by 40 percent, the European labor force was reduced by 13 percent, and the labor force of the emigrant countries around the European periphery was diminished by 22 percent (table 8.1). The impact of immigration on New World labor supplies was much bigger than that which the United States experienced in the 1980s. Chapter 8 reported one estimate that suggested that mass migration can explain about 70 percent of the real wage convergence in the late nineteenth century (Taylor and Williamson 1997). This estimate, in contrast with contemporary debate about the United States in the 1980s, includes the total impact on both rich receiving countries and poor sending countries. It is a statement about wage convergence between countries rather than about wage levels within countries.

Since the migrants tended to be unskilled, and increasingly so as the late nineteenth century unfolded (much like the late twentieth century), they served to flood labor markets at the bottom in the immigrant countries, thus lowering the unskilled wage relative to the skilled wage, white-collar incomes and land rents. Immigration implied rising inequality in labor-scarce, resource-rich countries. Emigration implied falling inequality in labor-abundant, resource-poor countries.

So much for plausible assertions. What were the facts?

The Inequality Facts, 1870–1913

Complete income distributions are unavailable between the mid-nineteenth century and World War I, except for a few countries and a few benchmark dates.[4] But even if they were available, it is not obvious that we would want them to test the impact of globalization. Like economists involved in the late-twentieth-century debate, our interest is in factor prices—unskilled wages, skilled wages, land rents, and profit rates—and in the structure of pay—the size of the average income gap between the upper and lower classes. As a test of globalization effects, these measures are more relevant than the number of income recipients within these classes. Indeed, if rising inequality was explained by more poor people who were all new immigrants, then the rising inequality would be far less interesting and certainly less dangerous politically. But suppose the immigrants also lowered the relative incomes of the poor native-born with whom new immigrants competed? Inequality trends of this sort are far more interesting *and* have more dangerous political implications. How, then, did the typical unskilled worker near the bottom of the distribution do relative to the typical landowner or capitalist near the top, or even relative to the typical skilled blue-collar worker and educated white-collar employee in the middle of the distribution? Late-twentieth-century debate has a fixation on wage inequality, but since land and landed interests were far more important to late-nineteenth-century inequality trends, they need to be added to our distribution inquiry.[5] We have two kinds of evidence available to document late-nineteenth-century inequality trends so defined: the ratio of the unskilled wage to farm rents per acre and the ratio of the unskilled wage to GDP per worker hour. Consider each in turn.

Recall the panel database used in chapter 4 to document wage-rental[6] ratio convergence among eleven late-nineteenth-century countries (O'Rourke, Taylor, and Williamson 1996): four New World countries plotted in figure 4.4 (Argentina, Australia, Canada, and the United States); four European free trade countries plotted in figure 4.5 (Denmark, Great Britain, Ireland, and Sweden); and three European protectionist countries plotted in figure 4.6 (France, Germany, and Spain). It might be helpful to repeat the findings in chapter 4 to help motivate the larger inequality issues raised here. Relative factor price convergence *did* characterize the four decades prior to World War I. The wage-rental ratio plunged in the New World, where it had been high initially. The Australian ratio had fallen to one-quarter of its 1870 level by 1910, the Argentine ratio had fallen to one-fifth of its mid–1880 level, and the U.S. ratio had fallen to half of its 1870 level. In Europe, the (initially low) wage-rental ratio surged up to World War I. The British ratio increased by a factor of 2.7 over its 1870 level, while the Irish ratio increased by a factor of 5.6, the Swedish ratio by a factor of 2.6, and the Danish ratio by a factor of 3.1. Not surprisingly, the surge was more pronounced in free trade than in protectionist countries: the ratio increased "only" by a factor of 2.0 in France, 1.4 in Germany, and not at all in Spain. Relative to the European free traders, the New World wage-rental ratio dropped by a factor of ten between 1870 and

1910; relative to the European protectionists, it dropped by a factor of four.

Since landowners tended to be near the top of the distribution,[7] this evidence is consistent with the hypothesis that inequality rose in the rich, labor-scarce New World, while inequality fell in poor, labor-abundant Europe. There is also some evidence that globalization mattered: European countries staying open absorbed the biggest distributional hit; those retreating behind tariff walls absorbed the smallest distributional hit.

So much for wage-rental ratios. What about the ratio of the unskilled worker's wage (w) to the returns on all factors per laborer—namely, GDP per worker hour (y)? Changes in the ratio w/y measure changes in the economic distance between the working poor near the bottom of the distribution and the average working adult in the middle of the distribution. It turns out that this statistic is highly correlated with more comprehensive inequality measures in the interwar period, when full income distribution data are far more abundant (Williamson 1997a, appendix table 3).

Figure 9.1 summarizes the wide variance across the fourteen countries in the sample. When the index is normalized by setting w/y

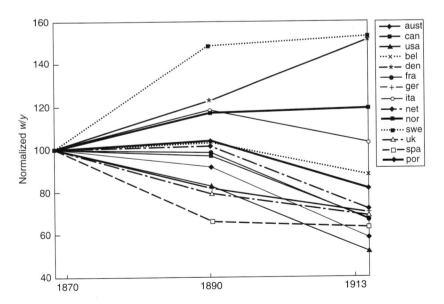

Figure 9.1
Normalized inequality levels, 1870–1913 (1870 = 100). Source: Williamson (1997, figure 5).

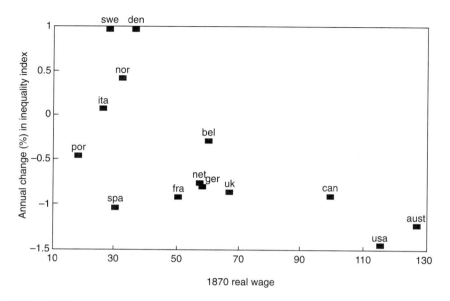

Figure 9.2
Initial real wage versus inequality trends, 1870–1913. Source: Williamson (1997, figure 6).

equal to 100 in 1870, we get the following: powerful Danish and Swedish equality trends establish the upper bound (the index rises from 100 to about 153 or 154), and powerful Australian and United States inequality trends establish the lower bound (the index falls from 100 to about 53 or 58). An alternative way to standardize these distributional trends is to compute the annual percentage change in the index relative to its 1870 base: the per annum rates of change range from +0.97 and +0.98 for Denmark and Sweden, to −1.22 and −1.45 for Australia and the United States. This measure of the annual rate of change in inequality is plotted against the 1870 real wage in figure 9.2, and it offers a stunning confirmation of Hypothesis 1: between 1870 and 1913, inequality rose dramatically in rich, land-abundant, labor-scarce New World countries like Australia and the United States; inequality fell dramatically in poor, land-scarce, labor-abundant, newly industrializing countries like Norway, Sweden, Denmark, and Italy; inequality was more stable in European industrial economies like Belgium, France, Germany, the Netherlands, and the United Kingdom; and inequality was also more stable in the poor European economies that failed to play the globalization game, like Portugal and Spain.

The key stylized fact that emerges from the globalizing late nineteenth century is that resource-rich, labor-scarce countries underwent rising inequality, and resource-poor, labor-abundant countries underwent falling inequality.

The Impact of Globalization on Inequality Trends, 1870–1913

The correlation in figure 9.2 is really quite amazing given the state of the literature on the Kuznets curve.[8] When Kuznets made his presidential address to the American Economic Association in 1955, he hypothesized that inequality should rise in early stages of modern development, reach a peak during what we have come to call the NIC (newly industrialized country) stage, and then fall therefter. Montek Ahluwalia (1976) and his World Bank colleagues offered two decades of post–World War II evidence that seemed to confirm the Kuznets curve. Since then, the thesis has taken a beating, most recently by a newly constructed late-twentieth-century database (Deiniger and Squire 1996). What is surprising about this literature, however, is that it treats a very complex problem so simply. There are a number of forces that can drive inequality in the long run, and we have listed some of them: globalization, demography, schooling, and technology. The technological forces that Kuznets thought were pushing his Kuznets curve cannot by themselves explain the trends in figure 9.2 since the Kuznets thesis argues that inequality should have been on the rise in newly industrializing but poor European countries and on the decline in richer, more mature industrial economies. The historical evidence plotted in figure 9.2 offers the opposite correlation.

It appears likely that one of these four forces, globalization, must be doing most of the work in accounting for these late-nineteenth-century Atlantic economy inequality trends. As we have seen, theory suggests that globalization should have increased inequality in rich countries and lowered it in poor countries. Theory is one thing, however, and fact is another. What is the trade and migration evidence that supports the (apparently plausible) globalization-inequality hypothesis?

We start with trade effects. We know that there was a retreat from trade liberalism from the 1860s or 1880s onward (chapter 6), and we know that the retreat in Europe included Italy, Portugal, Spain, France, and Germany. Protection in poor labor-abundant countries should raise the returns to their scarce factors, like land, relative to their abundant factors, like unskilled labor, thus creating inequality. In the presence of globalization forces, protection should at the very least mute the rise in unskilled labor's relative scarcity and thus stem the fall in inequality. The evidence seems to be roughly consistent with these predictions, supporting the inequality-trade connection. That is, the correlation between rising inequality and initial labor scarcity turns out to be better for 1870–1890—an environment of shared liberal trade policies—than for 1890–1913—an environment of rising protection on the Continent (Williamson 1997a). In addition, the slope on an estimated inequality–real-wage regression line is far steeper during 1890–1913 without the protected five (Italy, Portugal, Spain, France, and Germany) than with them. We saw the same contrast when comparing wage-rental ratio trends in figures 4.5 and 4.6.

We turn next to mass migration. Its impact on labor supplies in sending and receiving countries between 1870 and 1910 ranged from 40 percent for four New World immigrant countries (Argentina at 86 percent being the largest, followed in order by Canada, Australia, and the United States) to −22 percent for seven poor European peripheral emigrant countries (Ireland at −45 percent being the largest, followed in order by Italy, the three Scandinavian countries, Spain, and Portugal). We also know that migration's impact on the labor force was highly correlated with initial labor scarcity, although not perfectly (Hatton and Williamson 1997, chapter 3; chapter 7). Mass migration is therefore a prime candidate in accounting for the distribution trends we observe in the Atlantic economy. Figure 9.3 plots the result: where immigration had a large, positive impact on the labor force, inequality underwent a steep rise; where emigration had a large negative impact on the labor force, inequality underwent a steep fall.

Unfortunately, it is impossible to decompose globalization effects into trade and migration using this time-series information since the correlation among migration's impact, trade's impact, and initial labor scarcity is so high. Yet an effort has been made to finesse this problem by constructing a trade-globalization-impact variable as the interaction of initial labor scarcity and "openness" (Williamson 1997a). The former is proxied by dummies for the labor-scarce New World ($d1 = 1$: Australia, Canada, the United States), the labor-abundant European periphery ($d2 = 1$: Denmark, Italy, Norway, Sweden, Spain, Portugal), and the core European industrial leaders making up the remainder (Belgium,

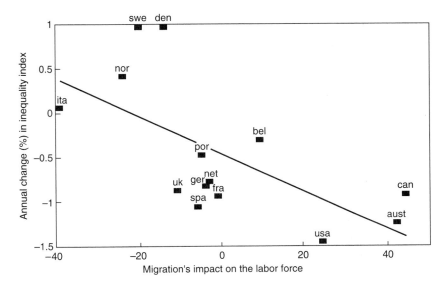

Figure 9.3
Inequality trends versus migration's impact on the labor force, 1870–1913. Source: Williamson (1997, figure 7).

France, Germany, the Netherlands, United Kingdom). Although it can be subjected to the same criticism we made of such proxies earlier in this book, openness is proxied by trade shares (*trade*). The per annum rate of change in the inequality index, here called *e*, is explained by ($R^2 = 0.72$, *t*-statistics in parentheses):

$$e = -52.07 - 0.31mig + 0.25trade + 0.55(d1 * trade) + 2.42(d2 * trade)$$
$$ (2.56) \quad\quad (1.00) \quad\quad\quad (0.36) \quad\quad\quad\quad (3.38)$$

where *mig* stands for the impact of net migration on labor supplies. The impact of mass migration is powerful, significant, and of the right sign: when immigration rates were big (+*mig* was big), *e* was small and inegalitarian trends were strong; when immigration rates were small (+*mig* was small), *e* was bigger and thus inegalitarian trends were weaker; when emigration rates were big (−*mig* was big), *e* was even bigger and thus egalitarian trends were strong. Moreover, chapter 8 showed that workers in rich countries did not lose just in relative terms as a result of immigration; they lost in absolute terms as well.

Around the European periphery, the more open economies had more egalitarian trends ([0.25 + 2.42] * *trade*)—bigger *trade* implying bigger *e*—just as Heckscher and Ohlin would have predicted. It

appears that the open, industrializing tigers of that time enjoyed be-
nign egalitarian trends, while those among them opting for autarky did
not. Furthermore, the coefficient 2.42 on ($d2 * trade$) passes conventional
significance tests. In the European industrial core, the effect was far
less powerful since the smaller coefficient 0.25 on trade does not pass
any significance test. It appears that open economy effects on income
distribution were ambiguous among the European industrial leaders
with moderate initial income levels.[9] Heckscher and Ohlin would have
predicted this result too. In the labor-scarce New World, however, the
more open economies also had more egalitarian trends ([0.25 + 0.55] $*$
$trade$), which is certainly not what Heckscher and Ohlin would have
predicted. The result is not statistically significant however.

Overall, we read this evidence as strong support for the impact of
mass migration on distribution trends: the effects were big everywhere
in the Atlantic economy where the migrations were big. The evidence
offers weak support, however, for the impact of trade on distribution
trends, except around the European periphery, where trade lowered
inequality. This econometric exercise was able to explain about two-
thirds of the variance in distributional trends across the late nineteenth
century. As we saw in chapter 4, the globalization-inequality connection has also been explored using the wage-rental data in figures 4.4
through 4.6 (O'Rourke, Taylor, and Williamson 1996). It turns out that
commodity price convergence and Heckscher-Ohlin (trade) effects accounted for about 30 percent of the fall in the New World wage-rental
ratio and for about 23 percent of its rise in the Old World (O'Rourke,
Taylor, and Williamson 1996, table 4, 514). Factor-saving technological
change appears to explain much of the remaining trends in the wage-
rental ratios, but not in the way Kuznets argued that it would. Instead,
it took the form of labor saving in the more labor-scarce New World
and labor using in the more labor-abundant Old World. These factor-
saving results should sit well with the emerging conventional wisdom among economists looking at OECD experience since the 1970s
(Aghion 1998).

The Inequality Facts, 1921–1938

Did citizens living through these events prior to World War I feel that
globalization accounted for these distributional trends? Did they mod-
ify their open and liberal policies in response? Did the policy switch
matter? Chapter 10 will establish the globalization backlash connection

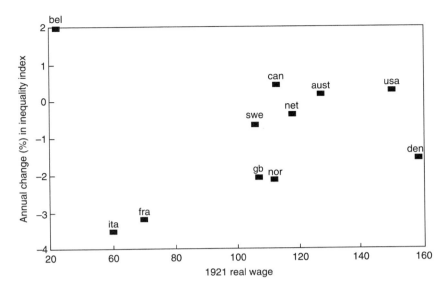

Figure 9.4
Initial real wage versus inequality trends, 1921–1938. Source: Williamson (1997, figure 9).

for New World immigration policy, but it might be useful to see whether inequality trends changed during the interwar period when quotas were imposed in immigrant countries, capital markets collapsed in the face of government intervention, and trade barriers soared to autarkic heights—that is, under conditions of deglobalization.

Chapter 2 documented that convergence ceased. It now turns out that the globalization-inequality connection was also broken. Figure 9.4 shows the correlation between inequality trends as measured by changes in w/y and a 1921 real wage measure of labor scarcity. The late-nineteenth-century inverse correlation has completely disappeared, replaced by a positive correlation. In the interwar period of deglobalization, the poorer countries underwent sharply increasing inequality while the richer countries underwent more moderate increases or, in four cases, egalitarian trends. This finding is consistent with the Stolper-Samuelson theorem: protection should raise demand for the scarce factor, thus improving the position of the unskilled in rich countries and contributing to egalitarian trends, while eroding the position of the unskilled in poor countries and contributing to inegalitarian trends. Whether it really was deglobalization that precipitated this dramatic switch in distribution trends has yet to be established with firmer evidence, but there seems to be no doubt about the switch itself: the pre-1913 egalitarian trends in Scandinavia and Italy disappeared and were replaced by post-1921 inequality trends; the pre-1913 inequality trends in the New World disappeared and were replaced by post-1921 egalitarian trends, which Arthur Burns (1954) called a "revolutionary leveling"; and the relatively stable pre-1913 distribution trends in industrial France and Germany were replaced by dramatic post-1921 inequality trends, consistent with the rise of fascism (Rogowski 1989, chapter 3).

Some Things Never Change

It appears that the late nineteenth and the late twentieth centuries shared more than globalization and convergence alone. In the late nineteenth century, inequality rose in rich countries and fell in poor countries. According to Wood, the same has been true of the late twentieth century, although the inequality evidence is fiercely debated. Furthermore, although Borjas and Wood seem to think that globalization accounted for something like a third to a half of the rise in inequality in America and other OECD countries since the 1970s, the late-nineteenth-century evidence suggests at least the same, and perhaps more. However, modern economists who favor an explanation of rising inequality coming from (unskilled) labor-saving technological change should note that it may have accounted for about two-fifths of the rising inequality in the New World. They should also note that labor-using technological change may have accounted for as much as half of the falling inequality in the Old World (O'Rourke, Taylor, and Williamson 1996, table 4, 514).

At least two events distinguish these two globalization epochs. First, falling inequality seems to have been significant and pervasive in the poor, industrial latecomers in our late-nineteenth-century Atlantic economy sample, like Denmark, Norway, Sweden, and Italy. This has not been universally true of late-twentieth-century Latin America and East Asia. Second, the econometric evidence suggests that mass migration, not trade, seems to have played the critical globalization role in the late nineteenth century. Except for the United States and perhaps West Germany, this does not seem to have been true of the late twentieth century, although no economist has yet assessed the impact of emigration on distributional trends in Turkey, Mexico, the Philippines, or other Third World countries where net out-migration has been significant over the past half century. We suspect that this and other sources of labor supply, like the demographic transition, matter a great deal—enough that they may offset trade globalization forces. Indeed, recent findings by Matthew Higgins and one of us (Higgins and Williamson 1998) suggest that, ceteris paribus, inequality rises when the share of the young in the total labor force rises.

Some things never change, and that fact implies a warning. Globalization and convergence ceased between 1913 and 1950. The inequality trends that globalization seems to have produced in the rich nations may have been partly responsible for the interwar retreat from globalization, which was also first introduced by the rich industrial nations. We also know that the globalization-inequality connection was broken between World War I and 1950. The rising inequality in the rich countries ceased exactly when labor migration was choked off by quotas, global capital markets collapsed, and the international community retreated behind high trade barriers. Are these interwar correlations spurious? The pre–World War I experience suggests not.

10 Globalization Backlash: Migration Policy Gets Restrictive

After the 1880s, there was a gradual closing of New World doors to immigrants.[1] The doors did not suddenly and without warning slam shut on American immigrants when the U.S. Congress overrode President Wilson's veto of the immigrant literacy test in February 1917 or when it passed the Emergency Quota Act of May 1921. Over the half-century prior to the Literacy Act, the United States had been imposing restrictions on what had been free immigration (contract labor laws, Chinese exclusion acts, excludable classes, head taxes, and so on). And the United States was hardly alone. Argentina, Australia, Brazil, and Canada enacted similar measures, although the timing was sometimes different, and the policies often took the form of an enormous drop in or even disappearance of large immigrant subsidies rather than of outright exclusion. Contrary to the conventional wisdom, there was not one big regime switch around World War I from free (and often subsidized) immigration to quotas, but rather an evolution toward more restrictive immigration policy in the New World. Attitudes changed slowly and over a number of decades rather than all at once.

What explains this evolution in immigration policy? A number of candidates have been nominated: increasing racism, xenophobia, widening ethnicity gaps between previous and current immigrants, more immigrants, lower-quality immigrants, the threat of even lower-quality immigrants, crowded-out native unskilled workers, rising inequality, greater awareness of that inequality by the powerful (informed by activist urban reformers), and greater voting power in the hands of those hurt most—the working poor. The goal of this chapter is to identify the fundamentals that might underlie changes in immigration policy, distinguish between the impact of these long-run fundamentals and the determinants of short-run timing, and clarify the differences between market and nonmarket influences. In addition, the chapter will have something to say about the extent to which policy waited for immigrants to have their impact on labor markets and the extent to which it tried instead to anticipate those impacts by responding to the immigrations themselves. Finally, we explore the impact of policies abroad on policies at home. Which countries were most sensitive to the immigration polices elsewhere in the New World, and to what extent did the biggest among them, the United States, set the pace for the rest?

Measuring Immigration Policy

The standard view of globalization history seems to be that there was an exogenous—and this is the key word—collapse of the world economy after 1914, a deglobalization implosion driven by two world wars, two periods of fragile peace, a great depression, and a cold war. The late twentieth century has marked a successful struggle to reconstruct the pre–World War I global economy. This view (e.g., Sachs and Warner 1995a) ignores the fact that tariffs on the European continent and in Latin America were on the rise prior to 1914[2] and that immigration policy was becoming more restrictive. To ignore this fact is to miss some evidence of significant globalization backlash.

How do we construct an index that can quantify immigration policy in the New World? We want an index that reflects political attitudes toward immigration, not one that attempts to measure the impact of such policies. Such an index could then be used to assess the extent to which "globalization backlash" was at work and, if so, to identify the form that it took. Two recent papers turned to the literature produced by political scientists to design a policy index that ranges over a scale of +5 to −5 (Timmer and Williamson 1996, 1998). A positive score denotes a proimmigration policy, typically including comprehensive subsidies for passage and support on arrival. A negative score denotes anti-immigration policy, typically an outright ban on some groups, quotas, head taxes, literacy tests, and discriminatory treatment after arrival. A zero denotes policy neutrality, or a wash between conflicting pro- and anti-immigration policies. It takes some doing to summarize these policies with a score for each year, but applied economists struggle with the same problem when trying to summarize just how "open" a country's trade policy is at any point in time (Anderson and Neary 1994; Sachs and Warner 1995a).

The policy indexes plotted in figure 10.1 are quite clear regarding the very long run. Except for the modest lapse in the 1870s, Britain maintained a fairly stable and strong policy of emigrant support, although that support certainly had a powerful pro-Empire bias. No such policy stability can be found in the New World. Despite universal openness to immigration in the 1860s, the doors to the New World were effectively closed by 1930. Argentina's index dropped from +4.5 in the late 1880s to −2.5 in the mid-1920s, a 7-point fall (out of a possible 10). Brazil's index underwent a similar decline, although it all came in a rush at the end of the period. Australia's index fell from +3 in the mid-1860s to −1 shortly after the turn of the century, and to −2 in 1930, for a 4- or 5-point fall. The index for the United States fell from 0 in the early 1860s to −5 by 1930, a 5-point fall. Canada's index fell from +2 in the mid-1870s to −4.5 by 1930, a 6.5-point fall. The policy evolution varied widely over those seven decades: Argentina and the United States exhibited a steady drift away from free immigration; Brazil remained open much longer, suddenly slamming the door shut in the 1920s; and Canada reversed the trend in the 1920s while Australia did it more than once over the period.

Although there are some cases of remarkable short-term variance, as in Australia between 1890 and 1930, strong policy persistence is more notable. Policy was slow to change, sometimes constant over a decade or more, even though there was often intensive political debate underlying that apparent quiescence. The best examples of this stability are Brazil over the three decades from 1890 to 1920, a period that ended in 1921 when immigration restrictions were imposed, and the United States from 1888 to 1916, a period that ended with the override of President Wilson's veto in 1917.

Given that policy was often slow to change, it is important to look for long-run fundamentals that were responsible for the evolution of policy and distinguish them from short-run influences on the timing of those changes. What might explain the evolution of immigration policy from the middle of the nineteenth century to the Great Depression?

Searching for Hypotheses on Immigration Policy

Immigration flows have always been sensitive to wage differentials and unemployment rates between countries, but the literature suggests that immigration policy has also been sensitive to labor market

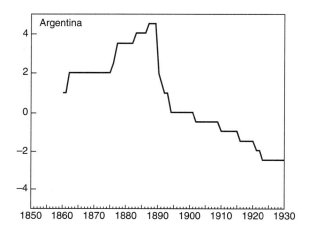

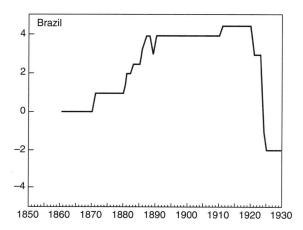

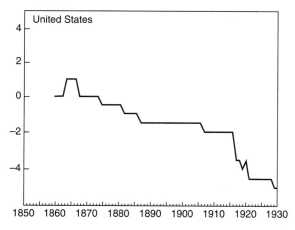

Figure 10.1
POLICY, an immigration policy index. Source: Timmer and Williamson (1998, figure 1).

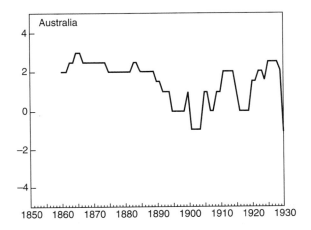

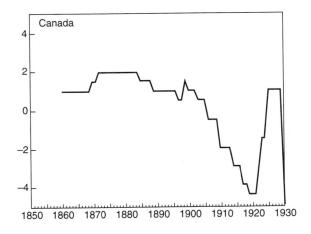

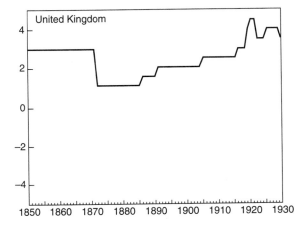

conditions.[3] For example, Claudia Goldin (1994) notes that there was a strong push for immigration restrictions in the United States in the late 1890s, a time of economic recession and high unemployment. At that time, however, the rate of immigration slowed dramatically, reaching a low in 1897, the same year that the first vote on immigration restriction was taken in the House of Representatives. Similarly, Australian inflows dropped sharply in the recession of the 1890s when attitudes toward immigrant subsidies hardened (Pope and Withers 1994). These events would seem to suggest that the impetus to restrict immigration was far more sensitive to labor market conditions than to immigration levels.

On the other hand, the ethnic composition of immigrants has always been a factor in the politics of restriction. Australia maintained a strict policy aimed at keeping the country one of British and Irish descent, and certainly not "yellow" (Pope and Withers 1994). The United States completely banned immigrants from China in 1882 and immigrants from all of Asia in 1917 (Green 1995). Increasing demands for restriction in the 1880s and 1900s paralleled an increase in the relative numbers of immigrants from southern, central, and eastern Europe—the so-called new immigrants. Partly due to these policies, the world labor market by 1890 was almost completely segmented into what economists today would call "North" and "South" (Lewis 1978; Taylor 1994a; Hatton and Williamson 1994b). What is difficult to sort out is whether these policies were a result of racism and xenophobia or whether ethnic origin merely served to signal, however imperfectly, the human capital content or "quality" of the immigrants (Foreman-Peck 1992).

In addition, any detailed investigation of immigration policy will require us to pay close attention to the influence of policy abroad. Did Latin America respond to changes in U.S. immigration policy? Did Australia and Canada respond to changes in British emigration policy?

We begin by surveying the limited literature that exists on these issues.

Three Models of Immigration Policy

As James Foreman-Peck (1992) notes, the two central questions for any model of immigration policy formation are: Who gains and who loses, and who decides the policy? There is a clear consensus regarding the first question. Wage earners lose with immigration, as the labor pool swells and wages sag. If the immigrants are mostly unskilled, then the unskilled native-born lose the most. Owners of other factors of production—land, capital, and perhaps even skills—gain to the extent that the more abundant unskilled labor supply makes these other factors more productive. Land rents go up as more labor is applied to a fixed acreage. Profits go up as more labor is applied to a given stock of capital. Skill premiums rise as more unskilled labor works with the same supply of skilled labor. Having said as much, two caveats deserve stress. Chapter 8 showed that most attempts to measure the impact of mass migration on wages prior to 1914 have found that they were pushed down by immigration. But one study, of Australia, found that wages actually increased with immigration, if only marginally (Pope and Withers 1994). This perverse Australian result could be explained if immigrants augmented labor demand enough to offset their impact on increased labor supply (for example, by working previously unsettled land or by inducing an accumulation response as capital from the home country chased after labor). If labor demand keeps pace with labor supply, it looks as though native labor is not hurt by immigration. The problem for us and the voters, however, is to distinguish between labor demand conditions that are dependent on the immigrants and those that are not. Under conditions of sagging wages, policy might still be used to keep out new immigrants—and even to send old immigrants home—even if their presence had nothing to do with the deteriorating labor market conditions.

Alternatively, suppose wages are sticky downward and unrelated to the size of the unemployment pool, perhaps for efficiency reasons or "fairness."[4] Immigration in this case will not have any effect on wages, but it will add to the number of unemployed, all the more so if new immigrants are last hired and first fired (Hatton and Williamson 1995; Collins 1997). No natives benefit: capitalists do not gain since wages do not fall; the unemployed native-born do not gain since no new jobs are created; and the unemployed may express their discontent by strikes and street violence. Eventually all sides might unite in favor of immigration restriction. Goldin (1994) suggests that this aligning of interests is exactly what happened in the United States during the 1890s.

On the other hand, what might be called guest worker effects should minimize the impact of an economic downturn on native-born unemployment, as recent (but now jobless) immigrants return home. That is, immigrants do voluntarily what a restrictive policy aims to do. Indeed, immigrants do it even better. A policy of immigrant exclusion can do no better than reduce the net inflow to zero. But voluntary return migration in bad times can drive up emigration rates to levels high enough to make net inflows negative during recessions. These guest worker effects were certainly present in the United States in the 1890s, but the return migration flows were never big enough to take a really big bite out of the high unemployment rates typical of that critical decade (Hatton and Williamson 1995).

These caveats aside, most discussions of the politics of immigration assume that the interests of capital and labor are divided. Foreman-Peck (1992) argues that landownership might have mattered too, especially in the late nineteenth century when agriculture was still a very big sector, and especially in the New World, the destination for so many European emigrants.[5] Foreman-Peck takes the following approach. Assume that individuals receive their incomes from one of the following three sources: wages, profits, or land rents. Depending on the franchise, the government maximizes a weighted objective function that includes rents, profits, and wages of native labor (but not immigrant labor). The critical question is whether immigrant and native labor are complements or substitutes in production. If they are substitutes, then immigration hurts native wages. Estimating a trans-log production function, Foreman-Peck concludes that they were substitutes in the late-nineteenth-century U.S. economy. Thus, the larger the weight that politicians attached to labor interests, the more restrictive the immigration policy; the larger the weights attached by politicians to capitalist or landlord interests, the more liberal the immigration policy. According to this reasoning, labor scarcity in the New World should have fostered immigration restrictions since labor scarcity and strong working-class political clout went together. The theory is not yet sufficiently precise to tell us whether it was absolute scarcity—real wages—or relative scarcity—inequality—that mattered more.

Foreman-Peck allows for the possibility of two types of immigrant labor: skilled and unskilled. It might be that skilled immigrant labor was a complement to domestic labor, whereas unskilled immigrant labor was a substitute. We would then expect to see a policy that encouraged immigration of skilled workers and discouraged unskilled ones. Foreman-Peck argues that this concern, rather than racism or xenophobia, was responsible for policies in the Americas that restricted Asian immigration and for policies in South Africa that restricted African immigration.

Although Foreman-Peck does not implement a formal empirical test, his discussion of Argentina, Britain, South Africa, and the United States indicates that some of the facts are consistent with his theory. For example, landed interests were largely in control of Argentina's policy, and the government offered generous immigration subsidies to attract farm laborers from the Mediterranean basin. In contrast, the United States had a more universal franchise, rejected subsidies, and gradually closed the door as the frontier itself was closed (by 1890, or so said the Census Commissioner at the time).

Goldin (1994) takes a different approach. Following a long tradition in American historiography that has focused on sectional interests, Goldin looks at regional splits and rural-urban differences in a way consistent with a median-voter model. She assumes that individual Senators and Congressmen pursued policies that favored their constituents, in proportion to the numbers represented by each urban, rural, and regional interest group. The passage of the immigrant literacy test, which was first attempted in 1897 and was finally successful in 1917, seems to have been the result of two (often opposing) forces: demographic changes and changes of heart. The changes of heart were many. Goldin suggests that for the first time, capitalists were aligned with labor in opposing immigration during the recessionary years of the 1890s when unemployment was high and wages sticky downward. In later years, faced with full employment and rising wages, capital would shift back to its more typical proimmigration stance. The South would shift to an anti-immigration stance, a change of heart probably motivated by the urge to protect its relative population share and voting clout in Congress. Finally, the northern Midwest, fairly proimmigration in the 1890s, would undergo an anti-immigration switch following World War I. Goldin argues that this was mostly a change of heart by older immigrant groups, pushed to patriotism by the war.

Where does demographic change enter the story? Goldin finds that the probability that a legislator would vote for immigration restrictions was strongly negatively related to the proportion of foreign-born in the district and was also negatively related to the level of urbanization. This relationship suggests that what we might now call family reunification effects were operating in the cities: a large stock of urban foreign-born voters created a political environment favorable to open immigration since the flows of new immigrants coming into the cities were likely to be from the same region as the stock, and the immigration must have involved some family, village, and kin reunification between the old and new foreign-born. Since cities were on the rise, proimmigration interests increasingly made themselves heard.

More important than either of these nonmarket forces, however, was the impact of increasing immigration on wages and the subsequent effect on votes. Especially after the turn of the century, Goldin finds a significant negative impact of immigration on wages, a result consistent with other historical studies we reviewed in chapter 8. The change in real wages is a significant explanatory variable in accounting for the congressional vote to override the presidential veto of the literacy test in 1915. The higher the growth in wages, the less likely was the Congressman to vote for an override (and thus for restriction).

These two findings—that wages influenced U.S. immigration policy and that immigrants influenced wages in U.S. labor markets—are useful in our comparative assessment of immigration policy in the New World. However, we require only that politicians and their constituents *believed* that immigration retarded wage advance. It appears that they did.

William Shughart, Robert Tollison, and Mwangi Kimenyi (1986) take a somewhat different approach. They look at shifting degrees of enforcement of immigration restrictions. Workers want high wages, and they pressure politicians to enforce immigration restrictions. Capitalists and landowners want lower wages, and they try to reduce enforcement. The model predicts that as the economy goes through business cycles, the ideal policy mix shifts, resulting in changes in the degree of enforcement against immigration. The authors test their model using data from the United States from 1900 to 1982, and the results are supportive of their theory. Even taking into account official changes in immigration policy, the size of the enforcement budget, and the party in the White House, the degree of enforcement is significantly, and negatively, related to real GNP. Unemployment and the real wage were also significant predictors of enforcement, but not so consistently as real GNP. Had Shughart, Tollison, and Kimenyi looked at U.S. policy toward indentured labor contracts prior to 1900, they would have seen the same correlation: harsh policy during slumps, soft policy during booms.

These are the only studies that offer empirical support for any theory of immigration policy. All three address the role of labor markets, but they limit their attention to the absolute gains and losses associated with some given immigration policy. What about relative gains and losses? What about inequality?

Income Distribution and the Politics of Immigration

Economists have recently awoken to the fact that migration can create more inequality in receiving countries. Certainly this has been true of recent experience in the United States (Borjas 1994), but the debate has spilled over to confront European immigration as well (Freeman 1995). Chapter 9 showed that the distributional impact of migration is confirmed for the late nineteenth century since inequality increased in receiving countries *and* decreased in sending countries. How would we expect policy to respond?

Citizens might vote in favor of immigration restrictions for other reasons than simply those derived from special interests. For example, rational and farsighted voters might consider the impact of immigration on future economic growth. If so, how would they assess it? Immigration induces falling wages and greater inequality, but does that inequality augment or inhibit economic growth? The traditional Smithian view held that the rising inequality would place relatively more income in the hands of those who save, thus raising the investment rate and growth. Modern political economists take a different view, arguing that if a country lets its poorest voters become too poor, richer voters might join poorer voters to pass distortionary redistributive policies that can slow growth (Alesina and Perotti 1994; Perotti 1996). What are the facts? Economists do not yet have a clear answer, especially for the years prior to the 1930s when government redistributive intervention was so modest. Citizens might vote for immigration restriction for other reasons too. For example, they may dislike, and fear the results of, the increased inequality around them, or the deterioration of the living standards of their unskilled neighbors.

Links to the Literature on Trade Policy

The literature on the political economy of migration policy is recent and small, whereas the literature on the political economy of trade policy is mature and large. Models of "endogenous tariffs" have flourished.

Who are the interest groups in trade theory? In the short run, when factors are assumed to be relatively immobile, protection of a given industry (like textiles or steel) will benefit both capital and labor in that sector. As local prices rise, the value marginal product of all factor inputs will rise, including wages and profits. In the long run, when capital and labor have had time to relocate, protection helps the scarce

factor (labor in rich countries) since the import-competing industries typically use more of the scarce factor. Most models of trade
policy take the short-run approach, focusing on the pressure from
specific industries, although some of the empirical tests focus on the
long-run importance of factor endowments (the most notable example
being Rogowski 1989). Stephen Magee, William Brock, and Leslie
Young (1989) present some evidence for the United States from 1900
to 1988 that exploits the median voter model; Howard Marvel and
Edward Ray (1983) provide empirical support for the pressure group
approach.

There is an obvious historical symmetry between trade and immigration policy (Wong 1983). While trade policy may seek to protect wages
by restricting imports made with cheap labor, immigration policy may
seek to protect wages by restricting growth of the labor pool. If free
trade is a partial substitute for free migration, closed trade and immigration policy should go hand in hand; if trade and migration are complements, then restricting either one may suffice. We shall have far
more to say about this issue in chapter 13.

This is only a small window on a very large literature, but it should
be large enough to see the obvious parallels between the literature on
endogenous tariffs and that on immigration policy. The important
point is that trade policy can easily undo what immigration policy has
done: thus, we expect consistency between them.

A Menu of Hypotheses

This brief review of the literature offers some promising explanations
for the New World retreat from open (and subsidized) immigration
policies to increasingly restrictive immigration policies, reaching a cre-
scendo with the quotas after World War I.

First, immigration policy might respond to either the quantity or the
quality of immigration, or both. Thus, the size of the immigrant flow
as a share of the native labor force is one obvious candidate for the
right-hand side of any regression explaining immigration policy, although the experience of the 1890s has already suggested that labor
market conditions might have mattered far more. The quality of the
immigrants is another candidate, measured in comparison with the native labor force. The vast majority of the immigrants came from and
entered unskilled jobs. Some had good health, high levels of literacy,
numeracy, on-the-job training, and considerable exposure to work dis-

cipline. Others did not. Quality and quantity are highly correlated prior to World War I. The switch of emigrant source from higher-wage to lower-wage areas of Europe coincided with the rise in immigration rates. It is likely that these two effects reinforced each other in their impact on policy.

Second, immigration policy might respond to labor market conditions. This likely possibility can be sharpened by distinguishing between short-run and long-run influences. Unemployment, wage growth, and other macroeconomic indicators should serve to isolate the role of business cycles, trade crises, world price shocks, and other short-run events that might influence the timing of immigration policy. Long-run labor market fundamentals should be captured by real unskilled wages—a measure of absolute performance—or by the behavior of unskilled wages relative to incomes of the average citizen—a measure of relative performance that we call WTOY. This measure of inequality was already used in chapter 9 (w/y), and it is scaled to 1900 = 100 on the right-hand side of each of the five graphs in figure 10.2.[6] It gauges the unskilled worker's economic performance against that of the average, and it is a measure that the politician and the voters could most easily see and understand. The use of these measures in our regression analysis does not require that immigration be the key force driving the living standards of the working poor in the New World. Both require only that the politicians and voters *believed* that immigration was a powerful influence on the living standards of the working poor. Whether it was the absolute or the relative performance that mattered is an empirical issue, but figure 10.2 suggests that WTOY, the inequality variable, is likely to do well everywhere but in Brazil, since the secular fall in WTOY is highly correlated with the retreat from open immigration policies.

Third, a lagged dependent variable should help identify just how slowly policy responds even to long-run labor market fundamentals, especially in democratic countries where debate over these issues, and (in some cases) the resolution of bicameral differences, takes time. This is illustrated very clearly by the United States in the period between the introduction of the Literacy Act in the 1890s and the override of President Wilson's veto in 1917. When the House of Representatives first voted in 1897, 86 percent of those voting favored the literacy test, and thus more restriction. Yet it took twenty more years to get the Senate to agree, to defeat the presidential veto, and to get the act on the books (Goldin 1994, table 7.1).

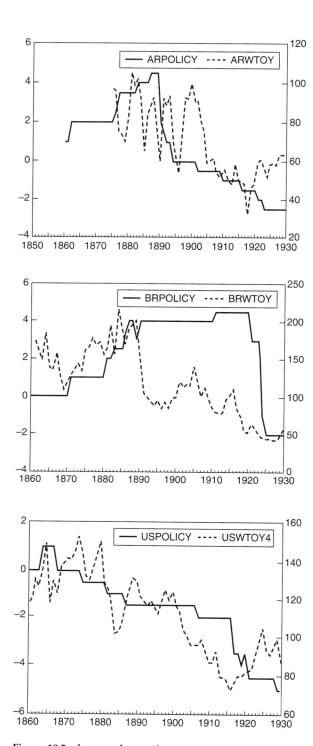

Figure 10.2, above and opposite
Inequality (WTOY) and immigration policy (POLICY) correlation. Sources: Figure 10.1
for POLICY. WTOY from data underlying Timmer and Williamson (1996).

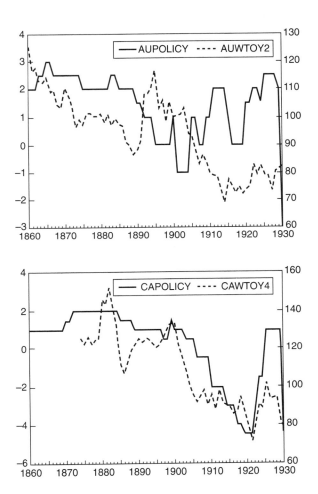

Fourth, a country's immigration policy may have been influenced by the immigration policies of other countries, either directly or indirectly. If the country anticipates the influence of immigration policies abroad on immigration inflows at home, the impact is direct. Since the labor market in the United States was so enormous relative to the rest of the New World, and since so many European emigrants went there,[7] it seems very unlikely that the United States paid much attention to the immigration policies being introduced elsewhere. This may have been true of Australia as well, to the extent that it was at least partially shielded from events in the United States by British Empire settlement policy, a policy of labor market segmentation. However, Argentina and Brazil must have paid close attention to the United States, since they could reasonably expect the marginal European emigrant (for example, the southern Italian) to be pulled from or pushed toward Latin America in response to less or more restrictive policy in the United States. Presumably authorities might have moderated those changes by mimicking U.S. policy before being confronted with the actual migrant response. It seems likely that the same might have been at least partially true of Canada, which in spite of British Empire settlement policy, had to accommodate that long, porous border with its big neighbor to the south.

Fifth, what nonmarket forces remain after these market forces have been allowed to have their impact? After controlling for immigrant quality, did racism have an independent influence? Did the resident population have less sympathy for free immigration if new immigrants were not of the same ethnic origin as the previous immigrants? Did the political response to market events change as the working poor found their political power increasing?

Some Evidence

The empirical literature on the determinants of immigration policy is very new, so that much of what follows is still speculative. But based on the work of Timmer and Williamson (1996, 1998), the main outlines are beginning to emerge. Table 10.1 gives a representative regression result, based on a panel data set of five-yearly observations between 1860 and 1930, for our five New World countries. Similar messages emerge from time-series regressions using data for individual countries, and several of the findings we report below rely on those results.

The most consistent effect is that immigration policy was slow to change; the coefficient on the lagged dependent variable is positive and significant. This was especially true of Brazil and the United States, but the result is driven by the 1888–1916 period in the United States (years of congressional debate that ended in the 1917 Immigration Act and the quotas that followed) and by the 1890–1920 period in Brazil (when heavily subsidized immigration, financed by fat export earnings generated by high coffee prices, was replaced by restriction, when export earnings contracted as coffee prices plunged). It is worth noting that the two countries that offer the strongest evidence of historical persistence also exhibit an episode containing an enormous switch in policy, from open to closed. Big policy switches often required long periods of debate. However, this was not always true, as can be seen by the

Table 10.1
Determinants of Immigration Policy, c. 1860–1930

Variable	Coefficient (t-statistic)
Lagged dependent variable: POLICY(−1)	0.809* (9.744)
Lagged ratio wage to GDP per worker: WTOY(−1)	0.015* (2.646)
Lagged real wage of the unskilled: WAGER(−1)	0.005 (0.637)
Unemployment rates: UNEMP	0.009 (1.242)
Trade share measure of "openness": [X + M]/Y	0.005 (0.800)
Lagged unskilled wage, immigrant origin: IMWAGE(−1)	−0.028*** (1.896)
Lagged immigrant supply threat: THREAT(−1)	−0.847** (2.573)
R^2	0.867
Adjusted R^2	0.839
SE of regression	0.911
Number of observations	56

Source: Timmer and Williamson (1996).
Note: The dependent variable is POLICY, the Timmer and Williamson migration policy index. POLICY measures liberal (+5) versus restrictive (−5) policies toward immigration. Unit of observation is half-decade. Estimated by fixed effects, although the fixed effects coefficients are excluded from the table.
* 1 percent significance level.
** 5 percent significance level.
*** 10 percent significance level.

enormous switch in Argentina's policy over only five years, 1889–1894, when the country was hard hit by world depression.

Measures of current macroeconomic conditions—like growth in real GDP per capita and unemployment rates—are predictably of little help in accounting for long-run policy changes. Despite a literature that supports their influence on short-run timing, only Australia offers any evidence that these factors contributed to long-run policy formation.

Did labor markets have a consistent influence on immigration policy? And if so, was it the absolute or relative income performance of the unskilled workers that mattered? It appears to have been both. Real wage growth mattered most in the United States, nominal wage growth mattered most in Australia, and real wage levels mattered most in Brazil. In all cases, poor wage performance was associated with more restrictive policy. What about inequality? The most consistently significant variable in the analysis reported by Timmer and Williamson is WTOY, the ratio of the unskilled wage to per capita income, or of income near the bottom of the distribution to income in the middle. Rising inequality was associated with increasingly restrictive immigration policy. It is well known that (new) immigrants tended to cluster at the bottom of the distribution, that they were unskilled, and that this was increasingly true as the late nineteenth century unfolded (Hatton and Williamson 1998; chapter 7). Regardless of what else is included in the regression equation, this measure of unskilled labor's relative economic position stands up as an important influence on policy. Rising relative unskilled labor scarcity encouraged more open immigration policies; declining relative unskilled labor scarcity encouraged more restrictive immigration policies.[8]

The evidence just summarized speaks to the indirect impact of immigration on policy by looking at absolute and relative wage performance in labor markets. What about the direct impact of immigration on policy? Perhaps the size and character of the current and expected future immigrant flow precipitated policy change, the latter serving to anticipate the labor market impact. Two variables might serve to measure these direct immigration effects. First, one might use a proxy for the quality, or human-capital content, of the immigrants (say, the real wage of unskilled urban workers in the source countries) and the change in that quality proxy. Second, one might measure immigrant quantity by the foreign-born population share. Rising immigrant quality tended to precipitate more open immigration policy in Australia, Canada, and the United States. More to the point, low and falling immigrant quality precipitated immigrant restriction, even after controlling for other forces.[9] To some extent, therefore, policy in these countries anticipated the impact of low-quality immigration on unskilled wages and moved to shut it down. In addition, Argentina seems to have looked to the north across the Río de la Plata to watch labor market events in Brazil, acting as if they knew that those events would divert immigrants to or from Argentina's borders. Thus, rising relative and absolute wages in Brazil tended to produce more open policy in Argentina. This result is consistent with the policy spillovers, which we will discuss in a moment.

The other measure of immigration's attributes—the difference in ethnic composition between the current immigration flow and the foreign population stock—seems to have had little bearing on policy. This is not the relationship the qualitative literature favors. According to that view, a rising gap between the ethnic origins of previous immigrants—who had become residents and probably voting citizens—and that of current immigrants would serve to erode commitments to free immigration. Timmer and Williamson find some weak Brazilian support for the view, but it does not appear anywhere else after they control for other influences.

To what extent was a change in a country's policy in part a reaction to policy changes abroad? As expected, the United States—the New World immigrant leader—was never responsive to competitors' policies. Nor, for that matter, was Canada, a surprising result that seems to confirm Canadian success in shielding its labor market from the eastern and southern European exodus to North America. For the other countries, policy abroad mattered a great deal. For Argentina, it was the combined impact of Australian, Canadian, and Brazilian policy that mattered, more restrictive policy abroad inducing more restrictive policy at home. Brazil tended to mimic the policies followed in Argentina and the United States, although it also exhibited a puzzling inverse response to policy change in Australia and Canada. Australia, in turn, tended to favor open immigration policies when the United Kingdom offered more generous subsidies to its emigrants and also, to some extent, when Canada adopted more open policies.

To summarize, although the size of the immigrant flow did not seem to have any consistent impact on New World policy up to 1930, its low and declining quality certainly did, provoking restriction. Racism or xenophobia do not seem to have been at work in driving the evolution of policy (which is not to deny that they existed). Rather, it was immigrant quality, labor market conditions, and policies abroad—especially those set by the economic leaders, Britain and the United States—that mattered most for policy. New World countries acted in a way that revealed an effort to defend the economic interests of unskilled labor.

How Big Were the Effects?

Using their econometric estimates, Timmer and Williamson (1997, table 5) report how much each variable contributed to closing the doors to immigrants. They identify for each country a period of major change toward more restrictive immigration policy. How much of the change was due to general economic conditions, indirect labor market effects, direct immigrant effects, and other factors?

When the Brazilian door slammed shut in the 1920s, almost 62 percent of the 6.5-point drop in the policy index was due to deteriorating labor market conditions, a good share of which was rising inequality. Labor market forces account for nearly two-thirds of this major policy switch from an open immigration policy with generous subsidies in 1917 to a restrictive policy with no subsidies in 1927.

Canada offers even stronger evidence in support of the view that labor markets mattered. During the prairie boom from 1899 to 1919, the policy index dropped 6 points. Two-thirds of this drop can be attributed to rising inequality over those two decades and another tenth or so to diminished immigrant quality.

Between 1888 and 1898, the policy index for Argentina fell by 4.5 points. Indirect labor market effects at home apparently made only a modest contribution to this big policy change. However, it could be argued that Argentina anticipated the likely labor market effects at home of labor market events in Brazil. Rising inequality and deteriorating wage growth in Brazil account for three-quarters of Argentina's policy switch. The increasing foreign-born presence in Argentina accounts for an additional quarter of the policy switch.

Between 1865 and 1885, the immigration policy index for the United States dropped by 2 points. Almost all of that drop can be attributed to labor market effects and the deteriorating relative income conditions of the unskilled. Direct immigrant effects mattered almost as much, captured here by declining quality (86 percent). We have no explanation for the big offsetting residual. In contrast with the powerful labor market effects apparent between 1865 and 1885, almost none of the 2.5-point drop between 1885 and 1917 can be assigned to labor market conditions. Thus, Goldin (1994) was right when she attributed much of the passage of the literacy test to nonmarket factors. That is, the residual is very large during this period, confirming the views of American historians who stress nonmarket forces. We should note, however, that deteriorating immigrant quality does account for four-tenths of the move toward restriction in the United States during the period. The estimated equations do not explain nearly as much of the Australian switch to more restrictive policy during the late 1920s. Along with the United States between 1865 and 1885, the Australian residual for the late 1920s is by far the largest (66 percent), and we have no explanation for it, except to argue that many of the variables may have already been influencing the political scene even though policy remained unchanged prior to 1926.

Conclusions

These results point to long-term influences driving immigration policy that are very different from the short-term influences about which so much has been written. Thus, while unemployment and macroinstability certainly influenced the timing of policy changes toward restriction, labor market fundamentals were the central forces driving policy in the long run. Furthermore, there is no compelling evidence that xenophobia or racism was driving immigration policy in the New World economies, once underlying economic variables are given their due.

Over the long haul, the New World countries tried to protect the economic position of unskilled workers. Labor became relatively more abundant when immigrants poured in, and governments sought to stop any absolute decline in the wages of the native unskilled with whom the immigrants competed, and often even in their wages relative to the average income recipient. The greater the perceived threat was to these wages from more immigrants, lower-quality immigrants, or both, the more restrictive policy became.

Immigration policy seems to have been influenced indirectly by conditions in the labor market and directly by immigration forces that, if left to run their course, would have had their impact on labor market conditions. Yet the switch to more restrictive policies was less a result of rising immigrant flows and foreign-born stocks and more the result of falling immigrant quality. Furthermore, immigration policy at home was often driven by immigration policy abroad, a correlation that suggests that countries tended to anticipate the likely impact of policies abroad on labor markets at home. And there were leaders and followers: the United States was a clear policy leader, showing no evidence of responding to policies adopted elsewhere; but the remaining immigrant-receiving countries were very sensitive to the leader's policies and the policies of their competitors.

The results of this chapter offer strong support for the third hypothesis proposed in chapter 9: that rising inequality can help account for the globalization backlash that started in the late nineteenth century and became so powerful in the interwar period. New World governments acted to reduce inequality, and thus gradually moved to insulate themselves from global market forces by restricting immigration.

Chapter 6 showed that U.S. and Australian protectionists also claimed to have the interests of labor at heart when arguing their case, and it showed that New World tariffs rose considerably prior to the Great War. But chapter 6 also showed that what is true for some countries need not be true for others. New World governments may have tried to reduce inequality, but many continental European governments were chiefly concerned with maintaining agricultural incomes, and to that end they raised tariffs, at the expense of increased inequality. If American and Australian policymakers had been more responsive to the interests of landowners, then those countries might have remained more open, as might have France and Germany had their governments cared more about inequality. Economic forces matter for policy, but so do the political institutions with which those forces interact.

The results here may offer some predictions for the outcome of the contemporary debates about immigration. The parallels are clear. Inequality has been on the rise in the OECD economies since the early 1970s, especially the gap between unskilled and skilled workers, just as it was in the New World economies of the late nineteenth century. Indeed, increases in the real income of the unskilled slowed dramatically after the early 1970s, and some economists argue that there has been little or no growth of unskilled real wages and incomes at all since then. We should therefore not be surprised by the renewed interest in reducing immigration over U.S. and European borders. Labor-scarce economies have been sensitive in the past to trends of greater inequality in their midst, using restrictive immigration policy to offset those trends. If history repeats itself, policies will become increasingly anti-immigrant in the future, at least as long as unskilled workers continue to lag behind other economic groups.

Forging and Breaking
Global Capital Markets

In 1995, a British merchant bank called Barings collapsed as a result of excessive speculation involving Japanese equity futures. To many observers, the crisis illustrated the new perils of a global capital market, fears further heightened by the Asian crisis of the late 1990s. Yet large-scale international capital flows are certainly not a phenomenon unique to the late twentieth century. Furthermore, many of today's debates surrounding international borrowing and lending have their counterparts in the decades before the Great War. The Latin American debt crisis of the 1980s was foreshadowed by the Argentine and Brazilian debt crises of the 1890s (Fishlow 1989). Nor do the similarities end there. In 1890, the same Barings faced insolvency and had to be bailed out by the Bank of England, having extended too many bad loans to the Argentine government.

International capital mobility has profound implications for economic growth in both theory and practice. It matters theoretically, because most theories of growth, from Ricardo to Solow to Romer, emphasize domestic savings as a key determinant of long-run growth. But international capital mobility breaks the link between domestic savings and domestic investment, making investment demand a far more important determinant of economic growth than domestic savings supply. It can matter hugely in practice, enabling poorer economies to invest and grow more rapidly than would otherwise have been the case (chapter 12). International capital mobility can lead to large shifts in the international location of production. It can stimulate or substitute for trade (chapter 13). And it can have profound implications for income distribution, the choice of exchange rate regime, and the conduct of macroeconomic policy.

The late nineteenth century saw international capital flows larger in scale than anything seen before or since. But large capital flows cannot by themselves tell us how integrated international markets are. It is the cost of doing business across national frontiers that matters, and the cost will be reflected in return differentials and other measures of market integration. We therefore begin this chapter with a review of the evidence on global capital market integration over the past 150 years. Are global capital markets really better integrated today than they were a century ago? How badly were they disintegrated and segmented by the turmoil of the interwar period? To what extent is the three-regime characterization offered in chapter 2 of this book—pre-1914 integration, interwar disintegration, and a post-1945 recouping of those interwar losses—supported by the evidence?

Having answered these questions, more arise. What explains the changing levels of capital mobility since 1850? Were there capital market equivalents to the railroad and the steamship that reduced the cost of lending overseas? To what extent was the classical gold standard responsible? Was there a capital market equivalent to the Smoot-Hawley tariff that can account for the interwar descent into autarky? Or was the breakdown of international capital markets largely an inevitable response to world depression?

The Evolution of Global Capital Markets Since 1850

Before the Great War: A Golden Age for World Capital Markets?

Capital exports from the center to the periphery were enormous in the late nineteenth century, as measured from the perspective of either lender or borrower. The City of London was at the center of this global capital market, and the British were doing a very large share of the capital exporting. The share of British wealth overseas in 1870 was already 17 percent, but it increased to 33 percent by 1913 (Edelstein 1982). Britain played the key role, but France, Germany, and other advanced European economies were involved too. For example, table 11.1 shows that German foreign investment amounted to almost a fifth of its total domestic savings in the 1880s, very big by the standards of the 1990s. France achieved even higher figures from the 1850s to the early 1870s, as well as during the late 1890s and late 1900s. With each surge in net foreign investment abroad, the British commitment to the global capital market rose: the ratio of net foreign investment abroad to total domestic savings was about 35 percent in the late 1860s and early 1870s, about 47 percent in the late 1880s, and about 53 percent in the years immediately prior to the Great War.

Table 11.1
Foreign Investment as Percentage of Domestic Savings (at current prices)

	United Kingdom	Germany	France
1850–1854	(12.3)	NA	(20.1)
1855–1859	(30.2)	NA	21.6
1860–1864	(21.5)	(1.4)	24.8
1865–1869	(32.2)	(3.4)	25.9
1870–1874	38.0	(7.3)	29.0
1875–1879	16.2	(13.1)	18.7
1880–1884	33.2	18.3	−1.1
1885–1889	46.5	19.3	11.3
1890–1894	35.3	12.6	10.0
1895–1899	20.7	11.5	23.0
1900–1904	11.2	9.0	16.1
1905–1909	42.7	7.6	22.0
1910–1913	53.3	7.3	12.5

Source: Jones and Obstfeld (1997). French numbers amended using Lévy-Leboyer and Bourguignon (1990).
Note: Numbers in parentheses are calculated using original current account data rather than the gold-adjusted data.

These net capital outflows were very unstable, as both table 11.1 and figure 11.1 document. Chapter 12 will discuss the causes of these long swings in foreign lending in some detail, but as a share of British GDP, net foreign investment rose from 1.3 percent at the 1862 trough to 7.7 percent at the 1872 peak, a 6 percentage point increase.[1] After falling to a trough in 1878 (less than 1 percent), it surged to 6.9 percent in 1888, and following the trough in 1902 (less than 1 percent), it surged again until 1911, this time to 8.7 percent of GDP. It is safe to say that no OECD country, including the United States, put up capital export numbers anything like that in 1980 or even 1990.[2] Western European late-nineteenth-century capital exports were enormous, even by the standards of the late twentieth century, when journalists make so much of a global capital market.

Foreign capital "dependence" was equally large at the receiving end. Alan Taylor (1992a, table 2) estimates that in 1913, foreigners owned almost half of the Argentine capital stock and a fifth of the Australian capital stock. Even the United States, whose domestic saving had taken on an increasing share of its investment requirements since the 1830s boom (Williamson 1964, 1979), registered high levels of foreign capital dependence toward the end of the century. Even though new capital

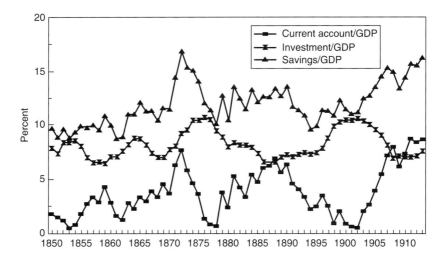

Figure 11.1
United Kingdom rates of saving, investment, and net foreign lending, 1850–1913. Source:
Jones and Obstfeld (1997). Note: Prior to 1869, gold-adjusted current account data are
not available, and "original" current account data are used.

inflows had diminished to a small share of GNP after the 1880s, the net
stock of foreign liabilities as a share of GNP was still about 26 percent in
1894 (Ufford 1984). This share was large even compared to some of the
Latin American countries that have had recent debt crises (and, it has
been argued by some, overborrowed): the 1980 figures were 22 percent
for Argentina, 19 percent for Brazil, and 30 percent for Mexico (IBRD
1983). Net inward foreign investment as a share of gross fixed capital
formation ranged from 10 to 20 percent among the major Third World
importers in the decade prior to 1984. The same statistic for the four
decades between 1870 and 1910 was 37 percent for Canada (Jones and
Obstfeld 1997), about 70 percent for Argentina,[3] and perhaps as much
as 75 percent for Mexico.

Although the data may have their flaws, it is absolutely clear that
those countries exporting and those countries importing capital a century ago were doing more of it than is true today. Not every capital-
scarce country was part of the club. Those without natural resources
to exploit were usually excluded. Table 11.2 summarizes the direction
of British overseas investment between 1907 and 1913. Two-thirds of
that investment headed for the New World (New World empire plus
the United States plus Latin America = 67 percent), and another 8 per-

Table 11.2
British Overseas Investment, 1907–1913

Area	Amount (£ million)	Share (%)
New World empire	319	28
Canada and Newfoundland	254	
Australasia	65	
United States	164	15
Latin America	268	24
Argentina	118	
Brazil	88	
Mexico	34	
Chile	28	
New World empire, United States, and Latin America		67
Other empire	163	14
China and Japan	50	4
Other empire, and China and Japan		18
Europe	49	4
Russia	46	4
Europe and Russia		8
Miscellaneous foreign	68	6
Total	1,127	100

Source: Taylor and Williamson (1994, table 1, 350).

cent headed for the granaries and other resource-intensive destinations of eastern Europe. If we ignore the miscellaneous category, then it appears that about eight-tenths of British foreign investment headed for regions where natural resources could be exploited, not necessarily where labor was cheap. Indeed, in the dominant New World destinations, labor was scarce, and immigrants entered in large numbers. Only two-tenths headed for Asia and the rest of the empire, where labor was more likely to be in surplus. There were some notable European exceptions, like the important role that French capital played in financing Swedish investment, but each exception can be matched by a counterexample, like the *lack* of British capital pouring in to Ireland or Spain (O'Rourke and Williamson 1997). We will have much more to say about these issues in chapter 12.

What form did British foreign investment take? First, it was portfolio investment, much like the private commercial capital export surge in the 1970s. That is, Britain purchased stocks and bonds—mainly the latter—issued in the City of London by some foreign interest. In 1913,

79 percent of the British investment in Latin America was of this form, and the figure was 85 percent for Australia and North America. Direct foreign investment was not common, although the modern multinational corporation did begin to emerge during this period. Most of the lending was being used for social overhead investment, as is true of the Third World today. About 70 percent went into railroads, harbor development, municipal sewage, telephones, and other social overhead investments. Railroads alone accounted for about 41 percent of the total in 1913 (Feis 1930, 27). The debt was issued largely by governments, as was also true of the Third World during most of the postwar years.

The Interwar Global Capital Market Collapse and the Postwar Recovery

The interwar period is not the main focus of this chapter, so we can be brief on these decades. The important point is that capital flows diminished in size during the 1920s, before the Great Depression, before World War II, and before the Cold War. The United States picked up some of the slack left by Britain's retreat from world capital markets after World War I, but not all (Eichengreen and Portes 1986). This is apparent in figure 11.2, which uses current account shares to document that most of the retreat from pre-1913 levels of international borrowing and lending took place prior to the Great Depression. There was also a shift from portfolio to direct investment. But the most important phenomenon was the collapse of European foreign investment in the New World by the 1920s. The literature has not dealt with this fact very well. How much of the decline in foreign investment in the New World, which accounted for about two-thirds of British capital exports prior to 1914, can be attributed to: the disappearance of the natural resource frontier, which caused conventional investment opportunities to dry up; the collapse in primary product prices, causing a further backward shift in investment demand at the periphery; political and war-related factors in Europe, which caused the pre-1914 capital surplus to evaporate; and policy intervention, which suppressed international capital flows, including going off the gold standard? To our knowledge, nobody has offered conclusive answers to these questions. Indeed, they are rarely posed.

Most of the limited capital flows that took place between 1945 and 1972 did so in the form of direct government and multinational institu-

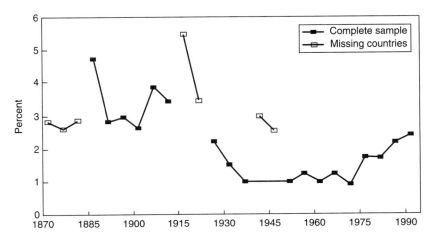

Figure 11.2
Extent of capital flows since 1870: mean absolute value of current account, fourteen countries, five-yearly averages (percent of GDP). Source: Based on Obstfeld and Taylor (1998). The gold-adjusted data in Jones and Obstfeld (1997) are used where possible; other data kindly supplied by Alan Taylor. Note: Countries are Argentina, Australia, Canada, Denmark, Finland, France, Germany, Italy, Japan, Norway, Spain, Sweden, United Kingdom, and United States. Data for first three periods exclude Japan and Argentina. French numbers amended using Lévy-Leboyer and Bourguignon (1990).

tional investment abroad. This fact raises another question that has yet to be answered. Did the interwar collapse of private portfolio investment markets pull in OECD governments and multinational institutions after 1945, or did their presence crowd out private portfolio investment?

Since 1972, a global capital market has tried to regain what it had achieved in 1913. But those modern economists who think that world capital flows over national borders are big today need only glance again at figure 11.2 to get things into proper historical perspective. The figure plots current account shares in GDP averaged over fourteen countries. That share, certainly on the rise since the early 1970s, is still only half of what it was in the late 1880s.

How Well Integrated Were Late-Nineteenth-Century Capital Markets?

The enormous magnitudes of late-nineteenth-century capital flows might be sufficient for some readers to conclude that there was indeed a well-integrated global capital market prior to the Great War, perhaps so well-integrated that most countries could have borrowed or lent as much as they liked at the going rate in world markets (risk adjusted to accommodate default possibilities). Other readers will need more evidence. As Alan Taylor reminded us recently, "The presence of flows is neither a necessary nor sufficient condition for market integration: a small autarkic country with capital scarcity no different from the 'world' market will exhibit no incipient flows upon opening itself to capital flows. Conversely, countries with substantial barriers to capital mobility may nonetheless experience capital flows . . . provided international rate-of-return differentials are sufficiently large" (Taylor 1996a, 2).

Earlier in this book we made the point that trade shares are a poor measure of global commodity market integration, so it should come as no surprise that we insist that capital flow shares may be a poor way to assess global capital market integration. Chapter 3 offered some ways to measure the extent of commodity market integration. As market integration progresses, price gaps and price dispersion should decline, price correlations between markets should increase, and the variance of outputs across markets should increase, reflecting specialization and comparative advantage. Precisely the same tests can be used to gauge capital market integration, although getting price data that are truly comparable across countries is, if anything, even more difficult for financial assets than for commodities (Neal 1985).

Larry Neal (1985, 1990) has provided ample evidence of well-integrated European capital markets as far back as the mid-eighteenth century, an integration that was disrupted by the wars of the Napoleonic era. The nineteenth century saw a recouping of those wartime losses and further integration gains. Indeed, James Lothian (1995) has presented data suggesting a very large increase in international capital market integration in the half-century or so prior to 1880. Maurice Obstfeld and Alan Taylor (1998) document the international dispersion of both real and nominal interest rates since the 1870s. Anglo-American nominal interest rate differentials were comparatively low and stable between 1870 and 1914.[4] They opened up during the war and into the early 1920s, narrowed in the late 1920s, and opened up again in the 1930s. They were narrower during the late 1950s and early 1960s, and again in the late 1980s. Based on Anglo-American nominal differentials, the overall picture is therefore one of interwar capital market disintegration, reversed only very recently. A similar picture emerged from Obstfeld and Taylor's evidence on real interest rates in a sample of ten Atlantic economy countries.[5] The standard deviation of real interest rates in these ten countries was 4.2 percent in the 1870s and 1880s and 3.4 percent between 1890 and 1913. It increased to 20.2 percent between 1919 and 1926, before narrowing to 6 percent from 1927 to 1931, and 6.5 percent from 1932 to 1939. The standard deviation remained at 6 percent in the late 1940s and 1950s, was only 1.6 percent from 1960 to 1973, increased to 3.7 percent between 1973 and 1989, and fell again to 1.7 percent from 1989 to 1996. Once again, the evidence points to the interwar period as the low point of international capital market integration. However, the real interest rate data suggest a much more rapid recouping of interwar losses in the post-1960 period than do the nominal data.[6]

Recently the most popular yardstick measuring the integration of international capital markets has, however, been quantity rather than price. It was first suggested by Martin Feldstein and Charles Horioka (1980), and their method is this: regress a country's domestic investment share in GDP on its domestic savings share. If the R^2 is high and the coefficient on the savings rate is close to unity, then this implies that domestic investment is constrained by domestic savings. If, on the contrary, the R^2 is low and the coefficient on the savings rate is close to zero, the conclusion is that domestic investment is independent of domestic savings, since foreign capital flows can take up the slack. The truth will, of course, lie somewhere in between, and thus the test is most effective in shedding light on the evolution of capital markets through time. Bayoumi (1989) performed this test for the pre-1914 period and found that the fit was poorer and the slope coefficient lower than for the modern period a century later, implying that the global capital market was better integrated a century ago. Robert Zevin (1992) added more countries and more periods, concluding the same. Critics have attacked the data and the sample (Eichengreen 1990), but the case now seems to have been clinched (Taylor 1996a; Obstfeld and Taylor 1998) by papers that use better national accounts data, more countries, and more of the tests that have become common since Feldstein and Horioka wrote.[7]

Figure 11.3 plots the results of the Feldstein and Horioka test from the 1870s to the 1980s (Taylor 1996a). It is hard to see any trend toward better integrated global capital markets in the Atlantic economy between 1870 and 1989. On the contrary, it appears that global capital markets were better integrated between 1870 and 1924 than they were between 1970 and 1989. Furthermore, there seem to be three

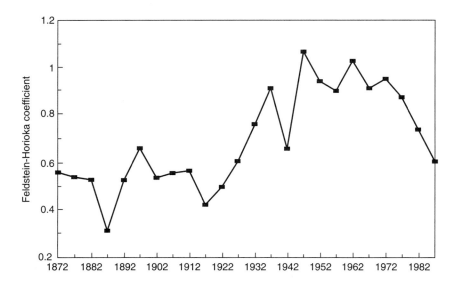

Figure 11.3
Feldstein-Horioka correlation in history. Note: The Feldstein-Horioka coefficient is the slope coefficient in a regression of investment shares on savings shares. Regressions are for a cross-section of countries in each five-year period. Source: Taylor (1996), revised 1997 version.

distinct regimes implied by figure 11.3: the pre–World War I regime of unrestrained capital mobility, the period of restrained capital immobility from the 1920s to the early 1970s, and the period of gradually increasing capital mobility since. Finally, there is some evidence that global capital market integration increased during booms (e.g., the 1880s) and diminished during busts (e.g., the 1890s and the 1930s).

We end this section with a brief reminder that capital market integration was taking place within as well as between countries during this period. Moshe Buchinsky and Ben Polak (1993) provide evidence that regional British capital markets were well integrated with the London market by the late eighteenth century, but in a larger economy such as the United States, it was during the late nineteenth century that really large integration gains were made. Lance Davis (1965) showed a substantial narrowing of U.S. regional interest rate differentials between 1870 and 1914, accompanied by a large transfer of capital out of the capital-abundant Northeast into the capital-scarce West. The reasons for this development will be discussed later in the chapter.

Direct Foreign Investment

International financial capital markets are no better integrated today than they were on the eve of World War I. However, direct foreign investment (DFI) may, on balance, make for better-integrated world capital markets today. Foreign affiliates of multinational corporations (MNCs) accounted for sales of $7 trillion in 1995, while the stock of foreign direct investment exceeded $3 trillion at the end of 1996.[8] None of this was true in 1913.

And yet the modern MNC did emerge in the decades prior to World War I, and it played a more important role in the pre-1914 era than is commonly assumed. Indeed, the stock of U.S. investment abroad amounted to $2.65 billion in 1914, or 7 percent of GNP. In 1966, when Americans were worrying about MNCs exporting jobs and Europeans fretted about *Le Défi Américain*,[9] the stock of U.S. direct investments abroad totaled $54.6 billion, or 7 percent of GNP (Wilkins 1970, 201–202). Coca Cola, Eastman Kodak, Ford, General Electric, Heinz, International Harvester, and National Cash Register (later IBM) are household names today, and all built or purchased manufacturing plants overseas between 1890 and 1913 (Wilkins 1970, table X.3, 212–213). These developments can be linked to the same transportation and communication innovations that we have been stressing throughout this book—railroad, steamship, telegraph, and cable.

Since Stephen Hymer's work in 1960, economists have come to understand that DFI represents more than simply international capital seeking out the highest returns.[10] This simple view cannot explain the cross-hauling of DFI, with U.S. firms investing in Europe and European firms investing in the United States. Rather, a firm goes multinational when it wishes to locate activities in more than one country and when it makes sense to conduct these activities within the firm rather than through the market place, such as by licensing technologies or brand names to foreign companies. There are substantial set-up costs in producing abroad for the first time, and organizations go multinational when the costs of transacting through the marketplace are even higher. When firms rely heavily on intangible assets, such as goodwill, reputation, and know-how, then it may be impossible for them to subcontract local firms to produce for them, and full-fledged MNCs emerge as a result.[11]

This microeconomic approach to the multinational enterprise predicts that companies should expand overseas cautiously and incrementally, since overseas production involves substantial start-up costs, and that DFI should be most heavily concentrated in sectors where intangible assets are important. The historical record bears out these predictions well. In the American case, the origins of direct overseas investment can be traced back to the integration of the national market, which was largely due to the railroad. Internal market integration meant that American firms could sell into a far larger market, enabling them to introduce new technologies whose fixed costs were so large that they required a national market to make them viable. Alfred Chandler's *The Visible Hand* is still the classic account of the growth of the modern U.S. corporation in this period. It stresses mass production, mass distribution, the role of the telegraph in enabling firms to coordinate activities across a wider geographical area, and the many changes in management structure that evolved to accommodate these events.

A typical firm becoming multinational would first expand within its own national market, until further expansion was impossible. It would then seek out foreign markets. Its first overseas investment was typically in distribution, replacing foreign commercial agents with its own sales staff (Wilkins 1970, 45–46). Overseas production followed only later, sometimes due to a desire to avoid tariff barriers. The most important destinations for American DFI were initially the United States' immediate neighbors, Mexico and Canada. The United Kingdom, which was culturally if not geographically close to the United States, was a popular destination (although continental tariffs often induced firms to locate there). European companies were also investing in America, particularly in the chemical industries, although such familiar names as Michelin, Fiat, and Bausch & Lomb were also involved. Indeed, the only two-digit industry in which Mira Wilkins (1986) could not locate any evidence of pre-1914 European direct investment in the United States was furniture, an industry that in the late nineteenth century possessed few intangible assets.

Then as now, MNCs helped spread new technologies internationally, especially those embodied in capital goods. The Singer sewing machine and the McCormick reaper were prominently involved in the early wave of American DFI in Europe. MNCs helped transfer silk-processing and sugar-refining technology as far afield as China, although such ventures were not always profitable (Brown 1979).

Direct foreign investment was thus another dimension of globalization that contributed to international convergence. However, we do not think that it had a very significant impact on late-nineteenth-century convergence. It is likely to be playing a much bigger role today.

Explaining Capital Market Integration

What explains the high and rising levels of international capital market integration experienced in the late nineteenth century, and what explains its disintegration in the interwar period? The answers lie with technology, institutions, and politics.

Technology

The transportation and communication revolution had a powerful impact on international capital markets, just as it did on labor and commodity markets. Lawrence Officer (1985) has shown how declining specie freight and insurance rates, as well as speedier and more reliable transatlantic transportation, played the crucial role in increasing the integration of the Anglo-American foreign exchange market. The telegraph had a direct impact on capital market integration by speeding up the transfer of information between financial centers. The quality of telegraph communication improved dramatically in the middle of the century. The first submarine cable was laid between Dover and Calais in 1851; New York and San Francisco were linked by 1864; the International Telegraph Union was established in 1865; and a permanent transatlantic cable was laid in 1866. It was not long before Europe was linked with the Far East and Australia (Mokyr 1990, 123–124; Foreman-Peck 1995, 67–68).

For arbitrage to integrate geographically distant markets, traders need price information: price differentials trigger trade or capital flows, and the flows bring prices closer together. Kenneth Garbade and William Silber (1978) describe conditions prior to the introduction of the transatlantic cable:

Participants in one market location received price information from the other center with a time delay equal to the duration of an ocean crossing, or about three weeks. . . . Investors, therefore, had to estimate the price in the foreign market which would prevail three weeks hence based on information which was already three weeks old. Since the precision of this estimate was necessarily low, it took a relatively large differential between the current price in the home market and the last available price in the foreign market to induce an investor to enter an order in the foreign market. After the opening of the trans-Atlantic cable, investors could learn of prices in the foreign market within a day, and could enter orders for execution in that market with a one day delay. . . . Differentials between the current price in the home market and the last available price in the foreign market which might have been ignored before the cable, now presented attractive arbitrage or investment opportunities. (Garbade and Silber 1978, 820)

Officer (1996, 166) shows that in fact it took only about ten days to travel between New York and Britain in 1866, but ten days was still a long time. Garbade and Silber collected London and New York prices for U.S. Treasury bonds immediately before and after the introduction of the transatlantic cable on July 27 of that year. The mean absolute price differential fell by an enormous 69 percent between April and July 1866 and between August and November 1866 (Garbade and Silber 1978, table 1, 825). There was no further decline in the differential between 1866 and 1871. The impact of the cable on market integration emerged immediately and it was enormous.

The telegraph also played a role in integrating domestic U.S. capital markets. In 1844 a line between Washington and Baltimore was established, and a line between New York and Philadephia followed in 1846, which was immediately used for speculation in stocks (Garbade and Silber 1978, 823). It had taken only a day to get information between these two cities prior to the telegraph, so its impact on price differentials was smaller than for London and New York. Nonetheless, its introduction reduced mean absolute price differences between the cities by between 24 percent and 30 percent. New York and New Orleans were farther apart, and when the telegraph linked the two cities in July 1848, mean absolute price differences fell by 40 percent.

Financial Institutions

Thirty years ago, Lance Davis (1965) argued that financial innovations were largely responsible for the increase in domestic capital market integration he documented for the United States. Specifically, Davis attributed the decline in interregional short-term interest rate differentials to the development of a national market for commercial paper, and the decline in long-term interest rate differentials to developments in the life insurance, mortgage, and national securities markets.

Most accounts of late-nineteenth-century international capital market integration stress another financial institution, the gold standard.[12] Under the system, individual countries agreed to exchange their currencies for gold at a fixed rate. The fact that gold was freely traded between these countries meant that it cost the same everywhere (give or take transport costs). The result was that countries' bilateral exchange rates were fixed by their relative gold prices. Except for wartime interruptions, Britain had been on the gold standard since the eighteenth century, Portugal adopted it in 1854, the new German Reich did the same in 1871, a host of European countries followed Germany in the 1870s, and the United States joined the major Atlantic economy players when it restored convertibility in 1879.

Many argue that the gold standard promoted international capital mobility by eliminating exchange risk. An alternative view argues that adherence to the gold standard provided a guarantee to investors that the country concerned would pursue conservative fiscal and monetary policies (Bordo and Kydland 1995; Bordo and Rockoff 1996), policies that would make potential investors more willing to risk their capital overseas (see chapter 12). The fact that capital was more mobile under the classical gold standard than subsequently has often been taken as evidence confirming these hypotheses. However, since countries were also on the gold standard for much of the interwar period, it might be argued that the gold standard by itself cannot provide an explanation for the contrast between the pre-1914 and post-1918 experiences (Eichengreen 1990). Maybe so, but the interwar gold standard was at its zenith in the late 1920s, and several pieces of evidence suggest that international capital markets were in fact much better integrated then compared with the early 1920s or the decade of the 1930s. Both the real and nominal interest rate data given in Obstfeld and Taylor (1998) and presented above document a narrowing of international interest rate differentials in the late 1920s. Based on tests specifically designed for an era in which gold had an important monetary function, Jones and Obstfeld (1997) reach the same conclusion: international capital markets were better integrated in the late 1920s than in the early 1920s.[13]

Politics

The gold standard was clearly an important part of the story, but politics also played a big role in facilitating international capital flows. First, the late nineteenth century was a remarkably peaceful and stable era, a fact that not only directly promoted international lending, but also facilitated the central bank cooperation that was important for the smooth functioning of the gold standard (Eichengreen 1992). Second, and perhaps more important, the gold standard itself was a political as well as an economic institution, something that Karl Polanyi (1944) emphasized many years ago. This political dimension largely arose from what Obstfeld and Taylor (1998) call the policy trilemma identified by the Mundell-Fleming model and summarized pithily by Polanyi as follows: "In its simplest form the problem was this: commodity money was vital to the existence of foreign trade; token money, to the existence of domestic trade. How far did they agree with each other?" (Polanyi ([1944] 1957, 193). In more modern language, the policy trilemma arises from the fact that small countries lose control over their domestic interest rates if they adopt a fixed exchange rate policy under conditions of international capital mobility. If policymakers wish to pursue an independent monetary policy, they have no choice but to impose capital controls or abandon fixed exchange rates, or do both. The gold standard was a fixed exchange rate system and further enhanced capital mobility in an already liberal age: adhering to it therefore exposed countries to the risk of industrial crisis and depression.

Barry Eichengreen (1992) has argued that the classical gold standard relied on a number of political, economic, and intellectual factors that were not present in the interwar period. Sticking to gold meant subordinating monetary policy to the goal of maintaining gold reserves and the gold parity, regardless of the domestic employment consequences. Those employment consequences may not have been too costly in the extremely flexible environment of the late nineteenth century, but that would change as the rise of trade unionism and the political left gradually increased nominal wage rigidity. Moreover, before 1914 there was a virtually unanimous consensus in favor of the gold standard, but this would also change, as macroeconomic understanding increased and the working-class vote grew more powerful. In the interwar period, it would become increasingly difficult politically to maintain the gold standard at the cost of increasing unemployment. Policymakers now had to confront the policy trilemma head-on, and they ended up abandoning international commitments in order to fulfill their domestic commitments. Capital controls (which directly impeded capital mobility) and the abandonment of the gold standard (which indirectly did the same) became the dominant policy choices during the interwar period. Eichengreen's conclusion is that the interwar breakdown of international capital markets was thus at least in part due to the spread of democracy. Polanyi (1944) went one step further and argued that the spread of democracy and the rise of the left were themselves largely a reaction to the national and international market system, yet another way in which late-nineteenth-century globalization undermined itself.

Once again in this book, we see that distribution matters for the maintenance of international economic systems.

12   International Capital Flows: Causes and Consequences

International capital markets were extremely well integrated in the late nineteenth century. Capital was highly mobile, responding flexibly to rate-of-return differentials between the capital-exporting and capital-importing nations. This chapter explains the huge size of the capital transfers and the large fluctuations in foreign investment documented in figure 11.1 and table 11.1. Were they driven by investment demand booms at the overseas periphery and slumps at the European core? Was it shifting savings supplies at the core or periphery that mattered? Or was it both? As it happens, economic historians have spent far more time explaining the cycles than they have explaining the trends (Edelstein 1982, 164). In addition, the chapter tries to explain the direction of the international capital flows. In 1990 Robert Lucas published an article with the eye-catching title, "Why Doesn't Capital Flow from Rich to Poor Countries?" in which he argued that capital flows to poor countries like India should be enormous if low capital-labor ratios really implied capital scarcity and a high marginal productivity of capital. Had Lucas looked at late-nineteenth-century experience, he would not have been surprised by the modern Indian example. After all, the vast majority of European capital export was to the labor-scarce and resource-abundant New World, not to labor-abundant Asia or even to the poorest parts of Europe.

Finally, this chapter assesses the impact of international capital flows on income distribution, peripheral growth, and international convergence. To what extent did capital mobility help poor countries catch up with rich countries, and to what extent did the interwar breakdown of international capital markets contribute to the cessation of convergence?

These, then, are the issues addressed. Although we can provide only a brief introduction to this enormous topic, we go beyond historical

description to provide an analytical assessment of the causes and consequences of late-nineteenth-century capital flows.

Explaining Late-Nineteenth-Century Capital Flows: Long-Run Determinants

Given how well integrated world capital markets were in the late nineteenth century, it is ironic that one of the most influential theories trying to explain the huge international capital flows of that time appeals
to capital market segmentation and domestic British capital market failure. The argument, put forward by the 1931 Macmillan Report, has
dominated the British literature to a large extent. The claim is that the
City of London systematically discriminated against domestic borrow-
ers, preferring instead to channel funds into overseas ventures. The
result was that domestic British industry, starved of capital, grew more
slowly than it would otherwise have done. An obvious implication of
the hypothesis is that domestic (British) rates of return must have exceeded those available on foreign investments. According to this thesis, market failure at home accounts for the huge capital export from
Britain.

The most rigorous test of the thesis has been carried out by Michael
Edelstein (1976, 1981, 1982), who tabulated capital gains and losses,
dividends, and interest payments for a sample of 566 British home and
overseas securities. His data in table 12.1 show that domestic returns
did exceed overseas returns in some periods, but that these periods
alternated with others in which overseas returns were far higher. There
is some weak evidence that these gaps rose with each subsequent boom
and slump. For example, the spread between foreign and home rates
of return on total assets rose from 2.69 percent to 3.85 percent between
the two booms of 1877–1886 and 1897–1909, and it rose from −1.02 to
−1.19 between the two slumps of 1870–1876 and 1887–1896. This evidence is consistent with the historical literature on debt and default at
the periphery: the defaults during each global slump generated rising
premiums on loans during the next boom (Lindert and Morton 1989;
Eichengreen and Lindert 1991). Note also that the interest rate gap (table 12.1) is well correlated with the long swing in capital exports from
Britain (figure 11.1) and with New World capital imports (see below).
When capital flows boomed, the gap was large and positive, the latter
presumably inducing the former. When capital flows shrank, the gap
disappeared or became negative.

Table 12.1
Realized Rates of Return, Aggregate Indexes, Selected Subperiods 1870–1913, Geometric Means (%)

	1870–1913	1870–1876	1877–1886	1887–1896	1897–1909	1910–1913
Domestic						
Equity	6.37	11.94	7.19	8.93	0.92	6.64
Preference	4.84	9.08	5.70	6.10	1.85	3.25
Debentures	3.21	4.36	4.12	4.92	1.40	1.84
Total	4.60	7.62	5.37	6.42	1.35	3.60
Nondomestic						
Equity	8.28	7.34	13.27	5.34	9.54	1.37
Debentures	4.92	6.29	6.40	5.16	3.82	1.90
Total	5.72	6.60	8.06	5.23	5.20	1.79
Nondomestic minus domestic						
Equity	1.91	−4.60	6.08	−3.59	8.62	−5.27
Debentures	1.71	1.93	2.28	0.24	2.42	0.06
Total	1.12	−1.02	2.69	−1.19	3.85	−1.81

Source: Edelstein (1981, table 4.3, 79).

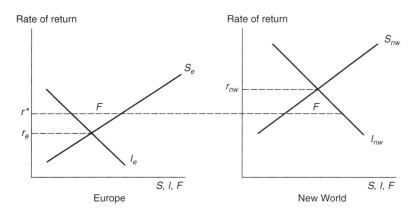

Figure 12.1
Late nineteenth century international capital market.

More important for the argument that British capital exports were due to investor (or institutional) myopia or conservatism, the *average* gap between foreign and domestic returns, over the period 1870 to 1913 as a whole, was not negative but rather was positive (1.12). This conclusion holds even when Edelstein adjusts the returns for risk. If anything, it appears that British investors were underinvesting overseas, not overinvesting as the domestic-market-failure thesis would suggest.

If domestic market failure cannot provide an explanation for British capital exports, maybe an appeal to supply and demand can. Figure 12.1 offers a stylized representation of late-nineteenth-century global capital markets. The world is divided into two: capital exporters in the European core (*e*), and capital importers at the European and New World periphery (*nw*). In each region, savings vary positively and investment negatively with interest rates. If international capital markets were completely disintegrated, the European rate of return (r_e) would be lower than the New World rate of return (r_{nw}), reflecting higher savings rates, lower investment rates, or a combination of the two. If they were completely integrated, rates of return would everywhere equal r^*, and the European core would export capital equivalent to F. The increasing levels of capital market integration documented in the previous chapter would have led to growing capital exports, but ultimately the explanation for those exports must lie in low (and declining) levels of European investment demand or New World savings supply, or high (and increasing) levels of European savings supply, or New World investment demand.

Table 12.2
Distribution of European Foreign Investment, 1913–1914

Destination	Britain	France	Germany
Russia	2.9	25.1	7.7
Turkey	0.6	7.3	7.7
Other Eastern Europe (including Austria-Hungary)	0.7	10.4	20.0
Western European periphery	1.3	11.6	7.2
Western European core	0.4	3.3	5.5
Europe (not specified)	0.5	3.3	5.1
Total Europe, including Asian Russia and Turkey	6.4	61.1	53.2
Asia and Africa, excluding Asian Russia and Turkey	25.9	21.1	12.8
Latin America	20.1	13.3	16.2
North America and Australasia	44.8	4.4	15.7
Other (not specified)	2.8	0.0	2.1
Total	100	100	100

Source: Feis (1930, 23, 51, 74).
Note: Columns may not sum to 100 due to rounding.

The most obvious explanation for the size of European capital exports is that New World investment demand was high due to labor and capital requirements associated with frontier expansion. If New World land was to produce food for European consumers and raw materials for factories, railways had to make it accessible, land had to be improved, and housing had to be provided for the new frontier communities. Since the bulk of UK overseas investment went to land-abundant and resource-abundant locations like the New World, this explanation has considerable appeal. The Americas, Australasia, and Russia took almost 68 percent of British foreign investment (table 12.2). These regions also took almost 40 percent of German foreign investment and almost 43 percent of French foreign investment (table 12.2). The amounts going to Britain's African or Asian colonies, such as West Africa, or the Straits and Malay states, were minimal in comparison. In December 1913, British capital in West Africa amounted to £37.3 million, that in the Straits settlements amounted to £27.3 million, that in British North Borneo amounted to £5.8 million, and that in Hong Kong to just £3.1 million, out of a grand total of £3,763.3 million (Feis 1930, 23). British capital typically financed railroads and other infrastructural projects, rather than activities traditionally associated with the colonies; in December 1913, only £41 million was invested in the rubber industry, and only £22.4 million was invested in the tea and coffee industries (Feis 1930, 27). The frontier was obviously an important force accounting for the enormous size of the capital flows.

Were there other forces at work as well? Contemporaries certainly thought so. In his theory of imperialism, J. A. Hobson (1902) pointed to excess British savings as being the root cause of capital exports. Hobson also thought that excess British saving (i.e., a consumption shortfall) was due to unequal income distribution. High profit shares meant high savings rates since capitalists saved a greater proportion of their income than did workers. Hobson also thought that these huge capital exports explained British imperialism; the proof of this proposition was to be found in the fact that "during the period in which British possessions had increased by 4,754 m. square miles and by a population of 88 millions, British overseas investments had also increased enormously" (Fieldhouse 1961, 190). Hobson's theory could explain growing levels of foreign investment if British inequality was on the rise, leading to rightward shifts in S_e. Unfortunately for Hobson's theory, British inequality was falling, not rising at this time (Williamson 1985, chapters 3, 4; Lindert and Williamson 1985; chapter 9 above). Furthermore, inequality was rising in the New World, which should have diminished the need for capital inflows there, at least according to Hobson's thinking (Williamson 1979, 1997a; Lindert and Williamson 1980; chapter 9 above).

Lenin (1915) agreed with Hobson that imperialism was driven by capital exports but argued that those capital exports were due to a systemic capitalist crisis that drove down domestic investment returns and ultimately would lead to the system's downfall. If by this Lenin was simply appealing to diminishing returns, there might be something to it. After all, table 12.1 does show a clear decline in domestic rates of return in Britain between 1870/76 and 1910/13, a period of industrial leadership loss and, finally, Edwardian economic failure.[1]

The frontier thesis appeals to booming overseas investment demand, Hobson appeals to excessive domestic saving, and the Marxists propose a lack of domestic investment opportunities as causing the huge capital exports documented in the previous chapter. A fourth hypothesis appeals to a lack of New World savings, relying on demography to help account for the huge capital flows (Taylor and Williamson 1994). Labor scarcity in the New World generated a labor supply response, documented in figure 12.2. The rate of growth in the economically active population (the total population minus the dependent

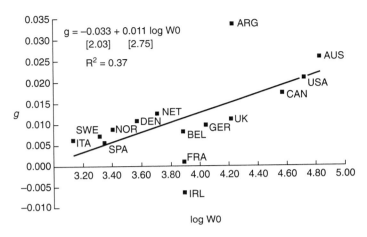

Figure 12.2
Real wages and population growth, 1870–1913. Source: Taylor and Williamson (1994), figure 1, p. 351. The growth rate of the population is g; and W0 is the real wage in 1870.

youths and elderly) grew faster in the labor-scarce New World than in the labor-abundant European periphery, with the European industrial core lying in the middle. This long-run labor supply response took two forms. First, there was the domestic response. Couples married early, had more children, and the children had higher survival rates. This would have produced enormous youth dependency burdens in the New World were it not for the second response. Mass migration partially offset these domestic dependency rate effects since it self-selected young adults. Figure 12.3 shows that it only partially offset the dependency burden, since the gap in dependency rates between the New World and the UK was very large—larger than it is today between the Third World and the OECD. Some time ago, Ansley Coale and Edgar Hoover (1958) offered a model that can be used to help explain capital flows in the pre-1914 period. This model suggests that these dependency burdens (and their absence in demographically mature Europe) should have choked off domestic savings in the New World (and augmented it in Europe), thus pushing foreign capital out of Europe and pulling it in to the New World. Taylor and Williamson (1994) show that this was indeed the case and, furthermore, that perhaps as much as two-thirds of British net foreign investment abroad might be explained by these demographic forces. It appears that capital flows during the age of high imperialism can be viewed, at least partially, as an intergenerational transfer.

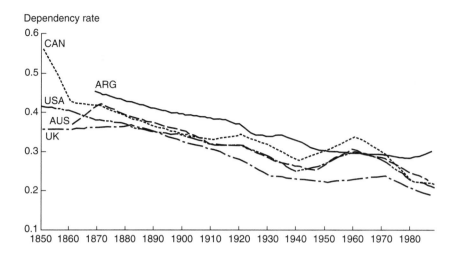

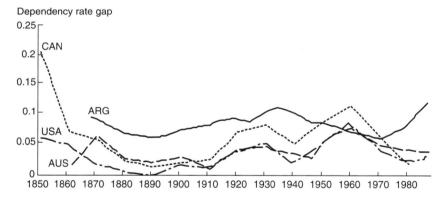

Figure 12.3
Dependency rates, 1850–1988. Source: Taylor and Williamson (1994), figure 2. The dependency rate is the share of the population aged 0–15 years. The dependency rate gap is the difference between each country's dependency rate and that of Britain.

Explaining Long Swings in International Lending

It appears that a frontier overseas, demographic forces, and a growth slowdown in Britain provide the best explanations for the huge capital flows that took place in the late nineteenth century. Furthermore, the disappearance of any one or more of these three forces would have implied a secular decline in foreign investment flows in the absence of the Great War. But what explains the large fluctuations in international

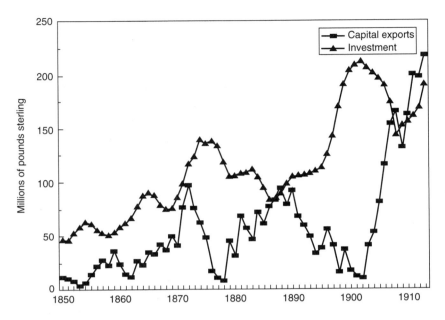

Figure 12.4
British capital exports and domestic investment, 1850–1913 (millions of pounds sterling).
Source: Jones and Obstfeld (1997). Note: Gold-adjusted current account data only avail-
able from 1869 onward.

lending (figure 12.4)? British capital exports were nearly £100 million
at their peak in 1872, before declining to a trough of only £8 million
in 1878. They rose to another peak of £95 million in 1888, fell to another
trough of only £11 million in 1902, before rising again to an astonishing
£218 million peak in 1913. New World investment demand, New
World savings supply, and disappearing investment opportunities in
the Old World associated with a growth slowdown may have determined long-run trends, but the cycle must have been driven by shorter-
run fluctuations in either supply or demand, and in either Britain or
the New World. Which of these forces was likely to have accounted
for most of the instability, or for what used to be called long swings
and Kuznets cycles (Abramovitz 1961)?

Figure 12.4 seems to rule out at least one hypothesis, since shifts in
British savings supply could not possibly have been responsible for
the long swings in British capital exports. If this were the case, then
both domestic investment and capital exports should have increased
during booms, as extra savings were made available for all investment

purposes (S_e shifts to the right in figure 12.1), and interest rates everywhere fell. There may be some evidence of this from 1909 onward, but figure 12.4 clearly shows that British domestic investment and capital exports varied inversely over the cycle, something that has long been appreciated by economic historians (Cairncross 1953, Thomas 1954, Williamson 1964, Abramowitz 1968, Easterlin 1968, Edelstein 1982). Although the British savings rate was not fixed over time,[2] cycles in overseas investment must have been driven more by shifts in home and/or overseas investment demand than by shifts in domestic (or foreign) savings.

Some have argued that British investment demand was the key exogenous factor, in which case interest rates should have declined as capital was pushed overseas by inadequate domestic investment opportunities (I_e shifts to the left in figure 12.1). Others have argued that New World investment demand was the driving force, in which case interest rates should have risen as capital was pulled into the booming New World (I_{nw} shifts to the right in figure 12.1). Table 12.1 suggests that both forces may have been at work: UK returns were lower during 1877–1886 (a capital export boom) than during 1870–1876 (a bust), while overseas returns were higher during 1877–1886 than during 1870–1876. UK returns rose again during the bust of 1887–1896, while overseas returns fell; and UK returns fell sharply during the boom of 1897–1909, while overseas returns remained steady. The evidence suggests simultaneous inward shifts in UK investment demand and outward shifts in overseas investment demand during booms, and many have argued that migration provided the link between the two. Housing demand was an important component of overall investment, and several authors, most notably Richard Easterlin (1968), have linked the long swings in capital exports to long swings in migration: when migration boomed, capital was exported from Europe, where housing demand was declining, to the New World, where housing demand was increasing. Still others have focused on railway construction. Implicit in Knick Harley's (1980) work is a view that the wheat trade may have played an important role in the cycle by stimulating railway construction on the frontier. If this is true, then it implies that prices in world commodity markets were the driving force, having quite different effects on the primary-product-producing frontier and the industrial core. We will have a lot more to say about these trade connections in chapter 13.

The Impact of Global Capital Mobility on Country Accumulation Performance

If we had good capital stock data for the whole Atlantic economy starting with 1860, we could say something quite explicit about the contribution of international capital flows to accumulation experience country by country. Unfortunately, the data are missing for most countries; Edward Wolff (1991, 571) was able to collect data for only three members of the Atlantic economy in 1870 (Germany, the United Kingdom, and the United States) and for only four members by 1913 (Italy added). Nevertheless, we can construct some rough estimates by making reasonable assumptions. The critical question is whether late-nineteenth-century capital mobility served to augment significantly the rate of accumulation in capital-scarce economies and whether accumulation in such countries was significantly reduced after World War I. Pre-1914 Scandinavia is used to illustrate the former point and post-1914 Argentina to illustrate the latter. We also explore the extent to which pre-1914 Scandinavian experience can be generalized to other members of the European periphery.

Foreign Capital Presence and Scandinavian Catch-Up Prior to 1914

Although British investors were more interested in overseas investment, there were substantial capital flows within Europe prior to 1914. France and Germany took the lead in lending to the European periphery: 61 percent of French foreign investments were in Europe at the end of 1913, and the figure for Germany was 53 percent (table 12.2). Did these capital flows help account for the catch-up by the European periphery, documented in chapter 2?

Since resource-rich Sweden absorbed exceptionally heavy doses of foreign capital, we begin there. Foreign capital was directed into social overhead construction for Swedish cities and the railroads between them, expenditures that were financed by government bond issues. French investors were the main foreign holders of the Swedish bonds. Previously we estimated the importance of British capital exports, United States capital imports, and Swedish capital imports, relative to their respective capital stocks (O'Rourke and Williamson 1995a). Capital imports over the four decades following 1870 served to make the 1910 Swedish capital stock 50 percent bigger than it would have been in their absence. Capital exports served to make the 1910 British capital stock 20 percent smaller than it would have been in their absence. The United States was a much more modest capital importer than was Sweden (capital inflows over the four decades only augmented its 1910 capital stock by a tiny 0.3 percent), so global capital markets should have contributed to Swedish catch-up on both the United States and Britain.

Using CGE models, we estimated international capital flows as having increased Swedish real wages by more than 25 percent and lowered British real wages by more than 7 percent (table 12.3, column 2). Capital flows thus accounted for 43 percent of the decline in the Anglo-Swedish wage gap and 34 percent of the decline in the U.S.-Swedish wage gap (table 12.3, columns 3 and 4). The results appear to support Eli Heckscher's contention that the capital imports between 1860 and 1910 were "a vital prerequisite for the country's rapid economic upswing" (Heckscher 1954, 210).

What about the rest of Scandinavia? The contribution of foreign capital imports to Danish convergence was likely to have been considerably smaller since foreign investment financed a smaller share of domestic accumulation there. Foreign capital imports were estimated to have made the 1910 Danish capital stock 16 percent bigger than it would have been in their absence (O'Rourke and Williamson 1995c). Norwegian capital imports were also smaller than were Sweden's (Riis and Thonstad 1989). Although Norwegian capital imports were even larger than were Sweden's after 1890, Norway was actually a net capital exporter between 1870 and 1890, so the net impact of foreign capital on the 1910 Norwegian capital stock was to raise it by "only" 17 percent, very similar to the Danish figure. The contribution of capital imports to Norwegian wage convergence on Britain and America was big—about 35 and 20 percent, respectively—but it was smaller than their contribution to Swedish wage convergence—about 43 and 34 percent, respectively. Danish experience was similar to that of Norway: capital imports accounted for about 30 and 16 percent, respectively, of Danish convergence on Britain and America.[3]

Capital inflows made a substantial contribution to Scandinavian catch-up on the leaders prior to 1914. The catch-up would have been considerably less impressive without that foreign capital. These conclusions cannot, however, be easily generalized to the rest of the European periphery.

Table 12.3
Impact of International Capital Flows on Convergence Around the Periphery, 1870–1910

Country	Cumulative impact on capital stock (1)	Impact of capital flows, 1870–1910, on real wages in 1910 (2)
Poor European Periphery		
Denmark	+16.3%	+8.2%
Norway	+17.4	+8.8
Sweden	+50.1	+25.2
Italy	Small negative?	Small negative?
Portugal	Small positive	Small positive
Spain	Small positive	Small positive
Ireland	Negative	Negative
Rich Old and New World		
Great Britain	−20.4%	−7.3%
United States	+0.3	+0.1

	Share of wage convergence, 1870–1910, on Britain explained (3)	Share of wage convergence, 1870–1910, on United States explained (4)
Denmark	30.0%	16.3%
Norway	35.1	20.0
Sweden	43.0	34.0
Italy	Positive	None?
Portugal	(None)	(None?)
Spain	(None)	(None?)
Ireland	Small positive	None

Source: O'Rourke and Williamson (1997, table 7).
Note: Three of the Italian entries and two of the Iberian entries have question marks, indicating substantial uncertainty even as to the sign of the effect. Capital flows explain none of the Iberian fallback behind the United States if capital inflows raised Iberian capital stocks by more than 0.3 percent. Although the evidence for Ireland is also weak, it is strong enough, we feel, to make unambiguous statements. Parentheses around the Iberian entries in columns 3 and 4 indicate that it is Iberian *divergence* that is being explained. Note that the results here are based on unrounded wage rates, whereas the levels in table 2.1 have been rounded.

Did Capital Flow to the Remainder of the European Periphery?

The Scandinavian experience conforms well with the predictions of simple trade theory. As a poor, capital-scarce region, Scandinavia should have exported labor and imported capital. Both forces should have increased Scandinavian capital-labor ratios and helped Scandinavia converge on richer countries such as Britain and the United States. Emigration was lower from Sweden, which imported a lot of capital, than from Norway, which imported less capital, suggesting that labor outflows and capital inflows were substitutes, which simple theory predicts.

Simple theory would also predict that capital should have flowed to other low-wage economies around the European periphery. Is this prediction born out by the evidence? Did international capital flows make a powerful contribution to living standard improvement in these countries too? These questions are difficult to answer since good (or even adequate) balance-of-payments data are rarely available for the rest of the periphery. However, what data we do have tell a surprising story.

Economic historians do not know whether Ireland exported or imported capital during the late nineteenth century since trade statistics were not collected after the customs union with Britain in the mid–1820s. The indications, however, are that postfamine Ireland ran trade surpluses and thus may have exported capital. Indeed, in his evidence to an 1895 royal commission, Robert Giffen estimated that Ireland ran a trade surplus of £5.5 million in 1893,[4] and it seems likely that Ireland was running trade surpluses for most of the nineteenth century. One cannot conclude from this fact alone that Ireland was running current account surpluses, and thus exporting capital, since the trade surpluses must have been at least partially offset by the remittance of rents to absentee landlords and by net taxes paid to the British Exchequer.[5] However, Giffen concluded that Ireland was probably a net capital exporter, and modern Irish historians have speculated that after 1860 "Ireland's position on capital account . . . moved from net debtor to net creditor status" (Kennedy 1995, 108).

In short, Ireland probably experienced net capital outflows during the late nineteenth century. Since the United States was a net capital importer, capital flows were clearly a force for Irish-American divergence rather than convergence. Since one can only assume that Britain exported even more capital than Ireland, capital flows must have been a (small) force for Anglo-Irish convergence. Capital flows may have implied both Irish catch-up and fallback, depending on which leader is being considered (table 12.3). In any case, there is no evidence suggesting anything like the Scandinavian experience here. Capital inflows cannot have made a significant contribution to Irish growth.

A similar picture emerges from official Italian statistics. True, the merchandise trade account was substantially negative throughout the period, but invisible earnings (tourism and shipping) were a partial offset—in some years enough to lead to a balance of trade surplus. Net factor income from abroad was negative prior to 1900 but positive afterward, as rising emigrant remittances came to offset income earned on foreign capital in Italy (Zamagni 1993, 126–127). Official balance of payments statistics reveal substantial capital imports in the 1860s and late 1880s, but substantial capital exports from 1894 to 1907.[6] Over the entire period between 1870 and 1913, the official statistics suggest that there were net capital exports from Italy, a force for divergence rather than convergence.

The Italian official balance of payments statistics have been questioned by Giovanni Federico and others.[7] Certainly the qualitative literature emphasizes capital imports, especially in the 1880s (when state bonds were sold) and at the turn of the century (when direct investments became more important). Nonetheless, specialists are uncertain about the evidence, and these uncertainties are reflected in table 12.3.

The conventional wisdom for Spain has been that the country ran large deficits on current account, and Broder's (1976) estimates indicate capital inflows throughout the period. However, Leandro Prados (1988, 188–197) has challenged this view. His estimates suggest almost continuous merchandise trade surpluses from 1875 to 1912.[8] Prados surmises that the current account balance was in deficit between 1850 and 1890; remittances and the merchandise trade surplus were smaller then than they were to become after 1900, and payments to foreign capital were larger. The picture that emerges from more recent work is one of deficits between 1870 and 1890, surpluses after the depreciation and tariffs of 1891, deficits around the turn of the century, and surpluses in the decade before World War I.[9] Net capital inflows must have been small (table 12.3); even Broder's figures suggest that they accounted for only around 7 percent of gross domestic fixed capital formation between 1890 and 1913. As was true for Italy, international capital flows could not have contributed much, if anything, to Spanish growth.

Current account data are also lacking for Portugal. Pedro Lains (1992) has revised the official trade statistics, making the balance of trade deficits much smaller. Appropriate accounting for emigrant remittances would also diminish Portuguese current account deficits and net capital imports. Jaime Reis's (1991) figures suggest capital inflows between 1865 and 1890. On the other hand, Salazar (1916) claimed that capital fled Portugal after the 1891 financial crisis, that it returned after the 1902 agreement with foreign creditors, but that it fled again in 1907 in response to the dictatorial government of General João. Franco.[10] The safest assessment would seem to be that capital imports can have made only a relatively small contribution to Portuguese accumulation in the late nineteenth century (table 12.3).[11]

There are three main conclusions to be drawn from this brief tour around the European periphery. First, we urgently need balance of payments data for the Celtic and Mediterranean fringes, as well as for Russia and the rest of eastern and central Europe. Second, capital flows probably did not contribute very much to the reduction of wage gaps between the United States and the European periphery, except in the case of Scandinavia; but large British capital outflows meant that international capital markets were reducing wage gaps between Britain and the entire periphery. Third, the development of global capital markets was not enough by itself to guarantee that capital would chase cheap labor. Capital inflows may have made an important contribution to Scandinavian development, but they made no contribution at all to Irish growth, probably none to Italian growth, and only a tiny contribution to Iberian growth.

Why Didn't Capital Always Flow to Poor Countries?

Why didn't Ireland, Iberia, and Italy attract large-scale capital inflows the same way that Scandinavia did? Granted, Sweden resembled New World economies in offering abundant resources (iron ore and timber), as did Norway (timber), but standard theory suggests that cheap labor is also a valuable resource. Both Portugal and Italy had lower wage rates in 1870 than did Sweden, and Spanish wages were lower than Norwegian or Danish wages (table 2.1). If lower wages meant lower capital-labor ratios, and if lower capital-labor ratios meant higher returns, then why weren't there big capital flows toward Iberia and Italy?[12]

This is precisely the point that Robert Lucas made in his famous 1990 article. He argued that if production functions were the same everywhere and if capital and labor were the only inputs into production, then rates of return to capital would be vastly greater in poor countries than in rich ones. The fact that productivity levels are fifteen times higher in the United States than in India would imply that the rate of return to capital was fifty-eight times higher in India than in the United States (Lucas 1990, 93).[13] How could international capital markets allow such huge gaps to persist?

Matthew Higgins (1993) has shown that this conundrum can in large part be resolved by allowing for different technologies across countries and correcting for differences in the price of investment goods.[14] We will see in the next section that the second correction becomes increasingly important across the twentieth century, especially for countries such as Argentina that pursued inward-looking development policies. In the late-nineteenth-century context, the first correction has considerable appeal. It is not hard to imagine that the same amount of labor and capital produced less output in Ireland than in Britain. If so, then lower Irish labor productivity would reflect lower capital-labor ratios *and* less efficient technology. While lower capital-labor ratios may suggest that Irish wages were low and Irish rates of return were high, an inefficient technology would suggest that *both* were low.

These arguments sit well with a lot of historical work showing large and unexplained productivity differentials between countries in the late nineteenth century, implying that poorly paid labor was not necessarily cheap labor. The economic historian Gregory Clark (1987) addressed the same issue as did the economist Lucas, and at about the same time. Clark presented data collected by the U.S. government just before World War I on production costs facing cotton textile mills in America, Europe, and Asia (Clark 1987, table 1, 146). The data showed huge variations in labor costs, consistent with the evidence of chapter 2. For example, weekly wage rates were $5.00 in England, but $2.70 in Spain, $0.78 in India, and $0.54 in China. Coal was cheaper in England than in the latter three countries, but this on its own could not have compensated for higher British labor costs. Assuming that cotton mills in all countries used inputs in the same proportion as did those in Britain, the profit rate should have been 8 percent in Britain, but 10.5 percent in Spain, 19 percent in India, and 22 percent in China. American mills should have recorded losses because their labor costs were even higher than in Britain. Adjusting for differential rates of capacity utilization suggests that Spanish profit rates could have been as high as 14 percent, with Indian and Chinese profit rates at 23 percent and 33 percent, respectively (Clark 1987, table 2, 148). And yet Indian and Chinese mills did not grow at anything like the rate suggested by these figures, while Mediterranean textile factories typically relied on protection to remain competitive.

Clark's explanation for this puzzle was that workers at the periphery were less productive than their counterparts in the core. Although all countries had access to the same machinery, peripheral workers operated fewer looms and spindles. For example, New England workers operated 6.5 times as much machinery as did their Greek counterparts (Clark 1987, 149–150). Peripheral workers were as efficient as American workers when they migrated to the United States, but they worked less efficiently when at home.[15] Clark hypothesized that local environmental or cultural forces were at work, reducing worker productivity in poor countries.[16]

There is also an extensive literature suggesting that factors such as these may have been responsible for Ireland's failure to attract British capital in the nineteenth century. An 1825 observer predicted that "Lancashire and Louth will form as it were one factory. . . . Whatever operations can be procured best by the human hand, I think, will be performed in Ireland, for the hand which is satisfied with the cheaper subsistence will necessarily undersell the hand not so circumstanced" (cited in Mokyr 1985, 259). This vision was never fulfilled, and Irish observers have wondered why ever since. The argument that a lack of natural resources was to blame was disposed of by Robert Kane in 1845, a conclusion backed by Joel Mokyr (1985). Nor does the argument that investors were reluctant to invest in Ireland due to the insecurity of property find support in the data. Cormac Ó Gráda (1994b, 333–334) could find no evidence that insurance premiums were higher in Ireland than in the rest of the United Kingdom. Furthermore, Ó Gráda (1994b, table 13.5, 339) has provided Irish evidence similar to that of Clark. Wage surveys for the *Gardeners' Chronicle* suggest that weekly wages for agricultural laborers in 1860 were 6.49 shillings in Ireland, 10.83 shillings in England, and 12.40 shillings in Scotland, confirming the data presented in chapter 2. However, piece rates were as high in Ireland as in Britain, if not higher. For example, the labor cost of mowing an acre of hay was 3.08 shillings in Scotland, 3.58 shillings in England, and 3.60 shillings in Ireland. The clear inference is that Irish labor, while poor, was not cheap, a claim made by contemporary observers such as Arthur Young, and low labor productivity offers an obvious explanation for this fact. Why the low labor productivity? Poor nutrition cannot provide an explanation for the period before 1845, since the prefamine Irish were better fed than the British. Mokyr (1991) suggested not only that Irish workers may have been inherently less efficient than their British counterparts, but that emigration could have systematically deprived the country of its "best" workers, a possibility we encountered in chapter 8.[17]

An alternative line of explanation blames the Mediterranean periphery's failure to attract capital on unorthodox macroeconomic policies, in particular the failure to adhere to the gold standard, which was typically due to excessive government borrowing. In Italy, the lira was inconvertible between 1866 and 1884, and again from 1894 to 1913, although Vera Zamagni (1993, 180) comments that the Italian system remained de facto tied to the gold standard during the latter period.[18] Spain suspended the convertibility of the peseta into gold in 1883, and the value of the peseta fluctuated against other currencies for the rest of the pre-1914 period. Portugal suspended convertibility in 1891. Chapter 11 argued that the gold standard facilitated international capital mobility; in its absence, exchange risk or country default risk associated with excessive government deficits might have made it difficult for Iberia and Italy to raise finance abroad.

The argument has been stated most forcefully for Spain. Pablo Martín-Aceña (1994) argued that exchange rate instability was largely to blame for Spain's failure to attract foreign capital and its consequent poor growth performance. More recently, Michael Bordo and Hugh Rockoff (1996) have explored the determinants of interest rates in a sample of capital-importing countries. Their conclusion is that "the benefits of committing to gold were significant. . . . Where commitment was high, rates were low; where commitment was low, rates were high" (Bordo and Rockoff 1996, 414). Thus, Spain and Portugal paid interest rates two or three percentage points above the British (risk-free) rate, and Italy paid one percentage point more, reflecting its policy of "shadowing the gold standard." Macroeconomic risk might well have played an important role in reducing the Mediterranean periphery's ability to attract foreign capital.

Yet exchange risk cannot be the whole story, as two examples will confirm. Ireland was on the gold standard and also was a constituent part of the United Kingdom, but these facts did not suffice to attract foreign capital. Commitment to the gold standard alone did not guarantee capital inflows. On the other hand, Argentina's adherence to the gold standard was shaky, with convertibility suspensions between 1876 and 1883 and again between 1885 and 1899 (Bordo and Rockoff 1996, 399). Argentine interest rates were over three percentage points higher than British rates as a result, but this did not prevent enormous foreign investment flows into Argentina. Exchange rate and associated risks might deter capital flows, but they did not overcome (or even dim) the considerable lure of the Argentine pampas.

Foreign Capital Absence and Argentina's Slowdown After 1914

Capital inflows into Argentina were so large prior to 1913 that foreigners owned about 48 percent of the capital stock in that year (Taylor 1992a, table 2, 913). Chapter 2 reported that Argentine wages grew rapidly during the period, so much so that they exceeded British wages in several years from 1888 onward. The Scandinavian experience, as well as standard economics, suggests that rapid Argentine wage growth must have been in large part due to those capital imports. What happened, then, when abundant world capital supplies dried up during and after the Great War?

Alan Taylor has demonstrated that Argentina's fall from First World to Third World status in the decades after the Great War can be explained largely by its failure to maintain pre-1914 levels of capital accumulation. The demographic forces mentioned earlier were particularly strong in Argentina: dependency rates were extremely high, and savings rates were consequently very low—5 percent or less between 1900 and 1929 (Taylor 1992a, table 4, 922). In the prewar period, the savings shortfall was made up by substantial capital imports, and the Argentine capital stock steadily increased. After the Great War, capital imports declined, and accumulation rates dropped off. The per annum capital stock growth rate was 4.8 percent between 1890 and 1913, 2.2 percent between 1913 and 1929, and just 1.1 percent between 1929 and 1939.[19] The result was that while Argentine capital-labor ratios rose significantly before 1913, enabling rapid increases in living standards, they actually fell between 1913 and 1939.

Taylor (1994b, 1994c, 1997) has identified two distinct phases in post-1918 Argentine economic history. In the interwar period, Argentine accumulation was constrained by its low savings rates and an inability to attract foreign capital.[20] This was initially due to the war-induced breakdown of international capital markets. Argentina's main supplier,

Britain, had incurred heavy war debts and had cashed in foreign assets. The poor state of the postwar British economy made new capital exports to Argentina unlikely. New York was the alternative source of capital, but raising money there proved difficult and expensive. New capital disappeared from Argentina, and some old capital actually pulled out. The foreign share of Argentina's capital stock fell from 48 percent in 1913 to 32 percent in 1929. Subsequently, the Great Depression intervened, inducing a shift toward protectionism and capital controls. A wave of Latin American debt defaults further reduced lending to the region.[21]

From the late 1930s onward, protectionism further slowed Argentina's accumulation rates by sharply increasing the relative price of investment goods. Taylor (1994b, 1994c, 1998) has provided abundant econometric evidence suggesting that investment is indeed inversely related to the relative price of capital goods and that most of Argentina's poor investment performance between 1960 and 1985 can be explained by the high relative price of capital goods there. And the low investment can account for as much as half of Argentina's slow growth relative to the OECD over the period (Taylor 1994c, 13–14).

Conclusion

Late-nineteenth-century world capital flows were a force for divergence, not convergence, since much capital moved to some of the richest countries in the world. European capital tended to chase after European labor as both migrated to the land-abundant and labor-scarce New World. In a few cases, capital did flow from rich to poor countries seeking out cheap labor. When this happened, the effects could be dramatic, as Scandinavian history shows. Why it did not happen more often remains one of the enduring puzzles of this period, and of the twentieth century as well.

Trade and Factor Flows: Substitutes or Complements?

Robert Mundell's seminal article, "International Trade and Factor Mobility," was published over forty years ago, and its conclusion threw down a challenge: Can history tell us whether (and when) trade and factor mobility are substitutes?[1] The challenge has assumed greater policy relevance as governments in North America and Western Europe today struggle with increasing levels of immigration from the east and the south. Americans wonder whether the North American Free Trade Agreement (NAFTA) will restrain immigration from Mexico; European Union (EU) officials hope that Europe Agreements with former communist countries and Mediterranean trade agreements with North Africa will lower immigration rates from those sending areas; and politicians in Tokyo pray that the collapse of the export-based boom in Southeast Asia will not raise Southeast Asian demands for entrance into Japan's labor markets.

In the forty years since Mundell wrote, trade theorists have come to understand that theory is ambiguous on this issue. Whether trade and factor mobility are complements or substitutes depends on the assumptions made. If ever there was an open invitation for historical research, this surely is it. Yet few efforts have been made to identify empirically the complementarity or substitutability between factor flows and trade (Wong 1988). Perhaps Atlantic economy history may prove to be a valuable guide to choosing among these assumptions. But if theory is ambiguous, history may be too: the appropriate model for one historical period may not be the appropriate model for another. After all, there may have been regime switches in history corresponding to alternative assumptions that trade theorists invoke to yield complementarity or substitutability. Nonetheless, even if history cannot identify the "right" model for thinking about international trade and factor mobility in the

1990s, it certainly can provide valuable insights into the nature of the connection.

The first section of this chapter discusses the theoretical ambiguity concerning trade and factor mobility within relatively simple models; we need to cover this ground so as to motivate the economic history. The remainder of the chapter uses that theory to explore the experience of three New World countries and seven Old World countries between 1870 and 1940.[2] We approach the data from three angles. First, we focus briefly on the Kuznets cycle in the United Kingdom and United States—those long swings in foreign lending discussed in chapter 12. Were trade and factor flows substitutes or complements over these long cycles, and is there any evidence of a regime switch around 1890 (when the U.S. frontier was officially declared closed) or after World War I when the world lapsed into autarky? Second, we use more formal econometric techniques to investigate the relationship between trade and factor flows over shorter-run business cycles, using annual data for all ten countries. Did the resource-abundant New World and resource-scarce Old World obey the same laws of complementarity or substitutability, and was there a regime switch around World War I? Third, we investigate the trade versus factor flow relationship using decade-averaged panel data, thus shifting the focus from shorter-run relationships generated by macroinstability in the time series to longer-run relationships manifested over decades and across trading partners of widely differing endowments. Finally, the chapter returns to the issues discussed in chapter 10 and asks: Did New World policymakers act as if they viewed migration and trade as substitutes?

Theory

When countries move from autarky to free trade, does the incentive for factors to migrate increase or diminish? When countries move from factor immobility to active participation in global factor markets, does the volume of trade increase or diminish? This book has documented important globalization forces after 1850: a dramatic fall in transport costs inducing a trade boom, a switch in international migration from trickle to mass, and a rise in foreign capital flows unmatched even in the 1990s. After World War I, an even more dramatic deglobalization took place. It seems to us that these historic events were big enough to justify the thought experiments posed above; theoretical questions about movements between free trade and autarky, or the reverse, are not just classroom games since they have very real historical counterparts.

Only constant returns to scale models are considered, so that trade is due solely to endowment or technology differences between countries. As we mentioned in chapter 4, this is likely to have been true of the late nineteenth century at least, given that Antoni Estevadeordal (1997) has shown that endowments do a very good job of explaining the patterns of international trade on the eve of World War I.

2 × 2 Models

The relationship between trade and factor mobility in the standard 2 × 2 model is well known. Let Britain and Ireland produce machines and textiles, using labor and capital. Textile production is relatively labor intensive, and Ireland is relatively labor abundant. Wages are initially low in Ireland and high in Britain, while profits are higher in Ireland. When trade opens up, Ireland exports textiles and imports machines. Wages rise in Ireland and fall in Britain, while profits fall in Ireland and rise in Britain, implying that trade induces factor price convergence (Ohlin 1924 reprinted in Flam and Flanders 1991). Under restrictive circumstances, there will be complete factor price equalization (Heckscher 1919; Lerner 1952; Samuelson 1949). Trade reduces or completely eliminates the incentive for labor to move to Britain and for capital to flow to Ireland, and therefore trade and factor mobility are substitutes.

Alternatively, factor mobility should tend to equalize relative factor endowments across countries, raising Irish capital-labor ratios and lowering British capital-labor ratios. Factor mobility thus erodes the basis for trade (Mundell 1957). Once again, the conclusion is that trade and factor mobility are substitutes.

As James Markusen (1983) has shown, these classic results are derived from the assumption that factor endowments alone are the basis for trade; countries are assumed to be otherwise identical. If the basis for trade is some other difference between countries, trade and factor flows can be complements, even in the context of 2 × 2 models. Markusen's most intuitive demonstration of this principle concerns differences in technology between countries. Now let Ireland and Britain have identical factor endowments, but also let technology in the British machine industry be (Hicks neutral) superior to that in the Irish machine industry; that is, Britain has discovered some new technology that gives it productivity leadership in machines, and it will have a comparative advantage in machine production. When trade opens up, Britain will export machines. An increase in capital-intensive machine production will increase the demand for capital in Britain, hence raising British profits and lowering British wages. When Ireland specializes in textiles, Irish wages rise and Irish profits fall. In equilibrium, wages are higher in Ireland, while profits are higher in Britain. Now allow factors to flow in response to factor price differentials. Capital will flow from Ireland to Britain, and labor from Britain to Ireland. In line with the Rybczynski (1955) theorem, machine production in Britain will expand still further, and British textile production will contract still further, while the opposite production responses will occur in Ireland. This will further increase British exports of machines and imports of textiles. Factor mobility has increased trade. Thus, trade and factor mobility are complements.

The Specific Factors and 3 × 2 Models

Eli Heckscher and Bertil Ohlin were motivated by the intercontinental exchange of primary products for manufactures that characterized the late nineteenth century. Land-scarce and labor-abundant Europe exported manufactured goods to the resource-abundant, labor-scarce New World, in exchange for grain, wool, raw cotton, and other agricultural products. It is difficult to rationalize such trade in the context of simple 2 × 2 models since land, labor, and capital were all relevant factors of production underlying trade in the Atlantic economy a century ago. In 1966, Peter Temin wrote a paper on the antebellum American economy in which he assumed that manufactured goods were produced with labor and capital, while food was produced with labor and land. This 3 × 2 model was fully developed shortly thereafter by Ronald Jones (1971), and dubbed the *specific-factors model of trade*. We draw attention to the cliometric antecedents of this famous model, not just out of team spirit but in order to highlight a theme of this chapter: the "correct" trade model may vary with the period being studied.

The relationship between trade and factor mobility in the specific-factors model is ambiguous. Imagine two economies, Europe and America, and to keep matters simple, assume that they differ only in their land endowments: America has more land. What does this imply for American autarkic factor prices, relative to European autarkic factor prices?[3]

One way to answer this question is to distinguish between factor mobility responses and price effects due to differences in land availability (following Corden and Neary 1982).[4] With more land, the marginal product of labor in agriculture increases and rents fall. Wages increase in both sectors, since labor moves into agriculture, where labor demand is booming, and profits fall in manufacturing, as the emigrating labor drives up capital-labor ratios and drives down capital's marginal productivity. But more land also increases the supply of food relative to the supply of manufactured goods. This will lower the relative price of food, tending to lower rents still further, but tending also to *increase* profits—perhaps enough to offset the initial fall, perhaps not. American rents will definitely be lower than European rents, but American profits may be higher or lower than European profits.

Profits in the United States will be higher if the manufacturing sector's labor force and output are larger than in Europe.[5] More land and higher per capita incomes imply a greater demand for manufactures, while a lower relative price of food implies the opposite. The net impact of an increased land endowment on profits thus depends on the relative size of these income and substitution effects.

Thus, there are two possibilities, even in this highly artificial example in which the two economies differ only in their land endowments. Either land *and* capital are cheaper in the United States than in Europe (while labor is more expensive); or U.S. land is cheaper, while U.S. capital and labor are more expensive (dual scarcity). In the first case, U.S. capital should flow to Europe, while European labor should migrate to the United States; in the second (dual scarcity) case, there is an incentive for both labor and capital to flow from Europe to America.

What does a move from autarky to free trade imply for these migration incentives? The United States exports food, and its relative price of food increases. This raises U.S. rents and lowers U.S. profits. Meanwhile, trade increases European profits but lowers European rents. In the first case (land and capital cheaper in the United States), the incentive for U.S. capital to emigrate has increased. Thus, trade and factor mobility are complements. In the second case (land cheaper but capital more expensive in the United States), the incentive for European capital to emigrate has declined. In effect, trade and factor mobility are substitutes. As for labor, the impact of relative price changes on real wages is ambiguous (recall from chapter 5 the tension between changes in nominal wages and changes in food prices): trade could be a substitute for or a complement to migration.

The same ambiguity emerges where the impact of factor flows on trade is the issue. Labor migration's impact on trade is ambiguous because it depends on migration's impact on relative outputs in Europe and the United States. Similarly, if capital is cheaper in the United States than in Europe, then capital flows from America to Europe will increase trade (increasing relative supplies of manufactured goods in Europe, and lowering them in the United States). In the dual scarcity case, capital flows to the United States will increase manufacturing and diminish agriculture there, thus lowering the volume of trade. This ambiguity has been rigorously demonstrated recently by Peter Neary (1995).

Clearly the relationship between trade and factor mobility is ambiguous in the specific-factors model. Indeed, it is clear from the discussion that trade could be a complement with migration, but a substitute for capital flows, or vice versa. To take just one example from a range of possibilities, capital flows and trade are substitutes in the dual scarcity case. This does not preclude the possibility that emigration would increase the supply of manufactures relative to food in Europe and that immigration would increase the supply of food relative to manufactures in the United States, in which case migration and trade are complements. Going from the specific factors model to a more general 3×2 model (in which land and capital, as well as labor, are mobile between sectors) only increases the range of uncertainty.[6]

Frontier Arguments

The existence of a third factor like land and other natural resources is not enough per se to generate a strong presumption of complementarity between trade and factor mobility. Such a presumption can emerge from models where the effective supply of the third factor is endogenous—a natural assumption in the context of late-nineteenth-century New World frontier economies or even of resource-rich Southeast Asian colonies. In particular, as food prices rise due to trade, there is an incentive to extend the frontier and increase the effective supply of land. However, extending the frontier requires heavy inputs of capital (to construct railroads to the interior) and labor (to build new towns in the interior). When the United States opens to trade and the relative price of food increases, the specific-factors model may conclude that profits fall. In the dual scarcity case, this lessens the incentive for capital to flow from Europe. However, if the increase in the demand for capital associated with an endogenous frontier extension is not completely off-set by the decline in manufacturing's demand, then the return to capital in the United States, and even the U.S.-European profit differential, might increase. In this case, the incentive for capital to flow to the United States would also increase. Similarly, if extending the frontier sufficiently increased the U.S. demand for labor, this might create the presumption that U.S.-European wage gaps would also increase. The existence of an endogenous frontier seems to increase the likelihood that trade and factor mobility will be complements rather than substitutes. However, the elegant models with an endogenous New World frontier that Ronald Findlay (1995) has constructed show that even in this case, trade and factor mobility can be substitutes.

Very stylized models of North-South trade can produce unambiguous complementarity. If the North exports manufactures and imports natural resources, and if northern investment in the South is required for the exploitation of the South's resources, then complementarity is assured.[7] One study argued strongly for complementarity by appealing to the fact that foreign capital is required to develop the exports of extractive industries in less developed countries (Schmitz and Helmberger 1970). John Williams (1929) also argued that foreign capital and trade were complements rather than substitutes, relying heavily on his knowledge of Argentina. Both papers argue that there are surplus resources at the frontier that require foreign investment before they can be vented onto world markets.

This frontier argument can be extended to the contemporary Third World. City building is very capital intensive, and to the extent that globalization generates an export boom of labor-intensive manufactures in the Third World, it also induces city growth (Kelley and Williamson 1984; IBRD 1995). This in turn generates heavy social overhead demand, high returns to capital, and foreign investments (Lewis 1978). Thus, trade and capital flows are complements, not substitutes.

Of course, this argument has its reverse. With the disappearance of nineteenth-century frontiers, town building slowed and railroad and other population-sensitive investment dropped off, and this, in turn, may have caused international factor mobility to subside, complementarity to vanish, and substitutability to emerge. Similarly, with the completion of twentieth-century urban social overhead in the Third World, factor mobility may subside, complementarity may vanish, and substitutability may emerge. The recent financial crisis in East and Southeast Asia may also eventually provoke such a regime switch.

Three morals emerge from this survey of what standard theory has to say about the substitutability versus complementarity question. First, theory is ambiguous. The ambiguity can be resolved only with evidence, and history is a good place to look for that evidence. Second, endogenous frontier models seem to offer a clear and historically relevant case where trade and factor mobility are more likely to be complements than substitutes. To the extent that frontier settlement is a transition process, we should look to disequilibrium transitions for evidence of complementarity. A transition has ended when a frontier has disappeared or an economy is fully urbanized. Third, the "correct" model will vary with the period being studied. Regime switches are likely to be common, especially at the beginning and the end of a transition.

With this brief survey of theory to guide us, we are ready to look at pre–World War II history in the Atlantic economy. We start with the long swing.

Time-Series Evidence: The Long Swing and Macroinstability, 1870–1940

In 1968, Moses Abramovitz gave a university lecture at the London School of Economics on "The Passing of the Kuznets Cycle," that special form of macroinstability that characterized so much of the Atlantic economy prior to 1914. Abramovitz preferred to call these events Kuznets cycles, after their discoverer (Kuznets 1930, 1958). But these fifteen to twenty-year growth surges and slowdowns were also called "long swings," and, unless interrupted by war, they typically ended in severe depressions like the mid–1870s, the mid–1890s, and the 1930s. Abramovitz and other scholars (Lewis and O'Leary 1955; Abramovitz 1961; Williamson 1964; Easterlin 1966, 1968) documented long swings in the rate of frontier settlement, capital accumulation, labor force growth, productivity advance, city building, internal and external migration, and other underlying fundamentals associated with long-run growth. Richard Easterlin (1968) went so far as to offer an explanation for the U.S. long swings based on an explicit interaction between what was then called population-sensitive investment (like housing) and labor-supply responses, the latter driven largely by endogenous mass migration. Abramovitz viewed this explanation with favor in his 1968 lecture.

These booms and busts were global in scope. Given that primary product markets always exhibit greater instability during global booms and busts, it is not surprising that the long swings were most dramatic in the resource-abundant New World. Nonetheless, they were also apparent in much of Europe, where they generated waves of urbanization and industrial growth, typically producing Old World long swings in domestic accumulation rates, which, as we saw in the previous chapter, moved inversely with those in the New World (figure 12.4). Capital flowed from Germany, France, and especially Britain during booms, and it flowed back home during busts (Cairncross 1953; Williamson 1964). The pattern appeared in the rhythm of the mass migrations, which recorded spectacular flows from Europe to the New World during booms, and net return migration during busts (D. Thomas 1941; B. Thomas 1954; Easterlin 1961; Wilkinson 1967; Williamson 1974b; Hatton and Williamson 1998). It also appeared in relative prices (Abramovitz 1961; Williamson 1964; Rostow 1978). As we have seen in chapter 3, transport costs fell globally, so every trading partner could have enjoyed steadily improving terms of trade prior to World War I; but around that trend, the New World terms of trade improved during New World booms while it slumped in Europe.

Were trade and factor mobility substitutes or complements over the long swing? Did they both rise during booms and fall during slumps? It is difficult to test this rigorously, since there are not enough long swings to justify formal statistical procedures (Harley 1980, 237); more informal techniques are required. We thus present graphical evidence for the two most important countries in the Atlantic economy community: the United Kingdom and the United States.

Railway construction on the U.S. frontier surged during booms, and Knick Harley (1980) has shown that peaks in wheat prices preceded peaks in railroad construction. This led Harley to argue that rising wheat prices were the signal for further railroad construction, which was inevitably associated with U.S. imports of labor and capital. Although the question motivating this chapter was not Harley's chief concern, the implication is that trade in wheat and factor flows were complements over the Kuznets cycle: the desire to export wheat was a key motivating factor in railroad construction, which was a key factor in stimulating capital and labor flows. In figure 13.1 we plot the long swings in U.S. immigration, U.S. capital imports, and U.S. wheat exports, between 1850 and 1913. The periods before and after 1890 are

(a)

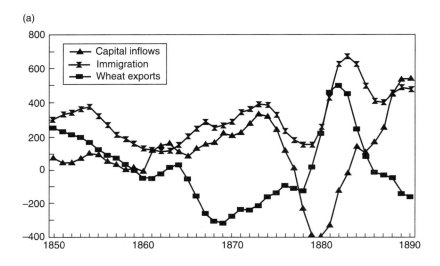

(b)

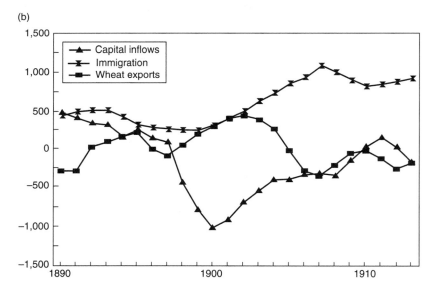

Figure 13.1
Factor flows and wheat exports, United States, (a) 1850–1890 and (b) 1890–1913. Source:
Mitchell (1995); U.S. Department of Commerce (1975); Romer (1989). Note: Capital
inflows are negative of current account, indexed to 1850 = 25, deflated by GDP deflator
(linked to wholesale price index at 1869); immigration: gross inflows, indexed to 1850 =
300; wheat exports: by weight; deviations from quadratic trend, indexed to 1850 = 250.

plotted separately, because 1890 was the year in which the U.S. Census Commissioner officially declared the U.S. frontier closed.[8]

Capital inflows and immigration were clearly complements over the long swing, as the many authors previously cited recognized. How did exports of wheat, the key frontier staple, fit into the Kuznets cycle? Such correlations are largely in the eye of the beholder but focus on the link between wheat exports and immigration in the years before 1890. The two series move in opposite directions in the late 1860s, when wheat exports slumped and immigration increased. But otherwise the two series usually move in the same direction: both fell in the late 1850s, rose in the early 1860s, and rose in the early 1870s and early 1880s, before falling sharply again. No such correlation is apparent after 1890; if anything, an inverse relationship seems more typical.

Figure 13.1 does seem roughly consistent with our earlier theoretical speculations about the role of the frontier, with a complementary relationship between trade and factor mobility appearing more clearly when the frontier was still expanding than afterward. But the evidence is rather elusive, and, in any case, we believe that aggregate trade flows matter more to the Mundell thesis than does trade in a particular export staple.

Figures 13.2 and 13.3 deal with the second objection, since they plot movements in aggregate trade flows. They illustrate the long swings for the United States and the United Kingdom, where the epochs are broken up into the prewar globalization phase and the postwar de-globalization phase. These figures clearly show the enormous instability in the time series. Migration and capital flows are highly correlated, with capital apparently chasing after labor. But these figures also offer a surprise: aggregate trade levels are *not* well correlated over the long swing with mass migration or international capital flows, and this is true whether trade is plotted as deviations from trend or not. The figures do not suggest much optimism for the complementarity hypothesis embedded in the long swing literature. Our frontier hypotheses may have held for goods produced on the frontier, but aggregate trade flows incorporated many other goods as well.

Perhaps a more elaborate empirical approach is needed to tease out such relationships as may exist in the data; if so, we need to turn our attention toward higher-frequency (e.g., annual) movements in the data. With the help of William Collins, we recently pursued two methods of measuring the association of trade volumes with factor flows in each of our ten countries' annual time series (Collins, O'Rourke, and

(a)

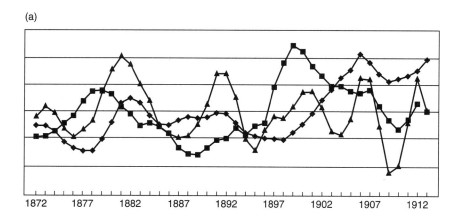

(b)

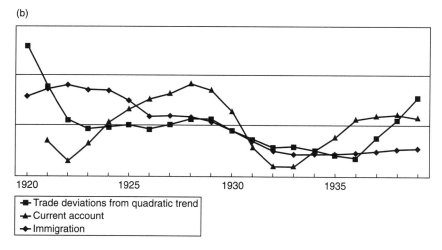

Figure 13.2
Long swings in trade and factor flows, United States, (*a*) 1872–1913 and (*b*) 1920–1939.
Note: All series are three-year moving averages and rescaled for presentataion.

Williamson 1997). First, we simply asked whether relatively large (small) factor flows are associated with relatively small (large) trade flows ceteris paribus, regardless of the direction of the factor flows. This first approach focused on magnitudes alone, and the absolute values of factor flows were entered in the regressions. But with a given endowment, should a factor inflow and a factor outflow of the same magnitude be expected to have the same impact on trade volumes? It could be argued that if trade and factor flows are substitutes, then

(a)

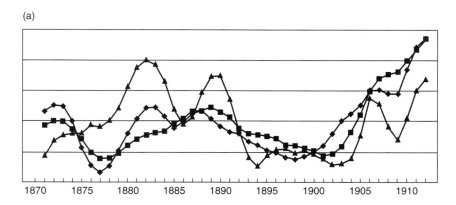

(b)

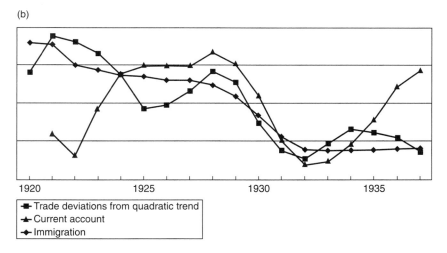

- ■ Trade deviations from quadratic trend
- ▲ Current account
- ◆ Immigration

Figure 13.3
Long swings in trade and factor flows, United Kingdom, (a) 1870–1913 and (b) 1920–1937. Note: All series are three-year moving averages and rescaled for presentation.

emigration (or capital exports) is expected to lessen trade only if labor (or capital) is leaving a relatively labor- (or capital-) abundant country. Thus, our second approach asked whether factor flows in the "right" direction (into a factor-scarce country or out of a factor-abundant country) were associated with more or less trade. The determination of factor abundance or scarcity was based on the country's share in the sample's total endowment of a given factor, relative to the country's share in the sample's total GDP. Since it turned out that these two approaches yielded much the same result, we discuss only the first.

Regressions were estimated taking the real value of trade as the dependent variable and controlling for time and time squared, which enabled us to isolate macroeconomic instability from long-run trends in the country time series. Only the key findings are discussed here since the details can be found elsewhere (Collins, O'Rourke, and Williamson 1997, tables 1a–1c). Tariff rates were introduced to reflect the fact that many of these countries retreated from globalization in the late nineteenth century and that all of these countries participated in the race toward deglobalization after World War I. We expected negative coefficients here, and our expectations were confirmed (with the odd exception of Canada). We also introduced a measure for transport costs (Isserlis 1938).[9] It almost always had the wrong sign in these regressions, presumably because transport costs were endogenous over the cycle, rising during booms as space in tramp bottoms got scarce and falling during slumps as space in tramp bottoms got abundant. We expect different signs on transport costs when these cycles and swings are removed from the data, and thus where exogenous supply-side forces are more likely to dominate.

The impact of the frontier or policy change (or both) was explored by estimating relationships for the prewar and interwar years separately. Our expectation was that complementarity would appear more frequently in the prewar decades than afterward, reflecting the disappearance of frontiers, especially for the resource-abundant New World.

Most important for the central question of this chapter are the factor flow variables. Migration is measured as gross intercontinental emigration from the European countries and gross immigration to the New World countries (except for Australia, which reports net in-migration). The current account variable is the overall current balance, divided by a GDP deflator for the sake of intertemporal comparability. So what are the coefficients on the factor mobility variables?

Tables 13.1 through 13.3 summarize the results in terms of the hypothesis being tested: Were trade and factor flows substitutes? Deriving any of these three tables from the relevant regression results (Collins, O'Rourke, and Williamson 1997, tables 1a–1c) is straightforward: a positive and significant coefficient is interpreted as complementarity, a negative and significant coefficient is interpreted as substitutability, and any coefficient not statistically different from zero is deemed neutral.[10] The regressions are performed three different ways. Table 13.1 is derived from regressions where trade levels are

Table 13.1
Complements or Substitutes over the Long Swing, 1870–1940?

	1870–1913		1919–1936	
	Trade vs. migration	Trade vs. capital flows	Trade vs. migration	Trade vs. capital flows
Australia	C	S	C	S
Canada	N	N	N	N
Denmark	N	N	N	C
France	—	N	—	N
Germany	N	N	C	C
Italy	C	S	C	C
Norway	N	N	N	S
Sweden	N	N	C	C
United Kingdom	C	N	C	N
United States	C	N	N	C

Sources: From Collins, O'Rourke, and Williamson (1997, table 1a).
Note: A positive and significant (at the 10 percent level) coefficient relating trade to factor flows in the underlying regression is designated complementary (C). A negative and significant (at the 10 percent level) coefficient on the factor flow variable is designated substitutable (S). Insignificant coefficients are designated neutral (N).

Table 13.2
Complements or Substitutes over the Long Swing, 1870–1940? (Underlying regression uses changes in trade and changes in factor flows)

	1870–1913		1919–1936	
	Trade vs. migration	Trade vs. capital flows	Trade vs. migration	Trade vs. capital flows
Australia	N	N	N	N
Canada	N	N	N	N
Denmark	N	N	N	C
France	—	N	—	N
Germany	N	N	—	—
Italy	N	N	C	C
Norway	N	N	N	N
Sweden	N	N	N	C
United Kingdom	C	N	C	N
United States	C	N	N	C

Source: From Collins, O'Rourke, and Williamson (1997, table 1b).
Note: See notes to table 13.1.

Table 13.3
Complements or Substitutes over the Long Swing, 1870–1940? (Underlying regression uses changes in trade and factor flow levels)

	1870–1913		1919–1936	
	Trade vs. migration	Trade vs. capital flows	Trade vs. migration	Trade vs. capital flows
Australia	N	N	N	S
Canada	N	C	N	N
Denmark	N	N	N	N
France	—	N	—	N
Germany	N	N	C	N
Italy	N	N	C	N
Norway	N	S	C	S
Sweden	N	N	C	N
United Kingdom	C	S	N	N
United States	N	N	S	N

Source: From Collins, O'Rourke, and Williamson (1997, table 1c).
Note: See notes to table 13.1.

regressed on factor flow levels plus the additional variables; table 13.2 is derived from regressions where changes in trade are regressed on changes in factor flows; and table 13.3 is derived from regressions where changes in trade are regressed on factor flow levels.

Neutral entries dominate all three tables (53, 78, and 71 percent in tables 13.1, 13.2, and 13.3, respectively, or 67 percent overall), suggesting that the theoretical ambiguities highlighted in the previous section find their match in empirical ambiguities. Nevertheless, complementarity is far more common than substitutability, and it accounts for 25 percent of the entries in all three tables combined. In addition, complementarity is associated twice as often with migration (34 percent) as with capital flows (17 percent). Substitutability appears in only 8 percent of the cases, and all but one of those cases involve capital flows, not migration. This distinction between capital flows and migration suggests that some factor flows are more closely related to trade than others.

So far, history soundly rejects substitutability. However, there are two unpleasant surprises that also appear in these tables. First, and contrary to prediction, complementarity was not more pervasive in the resource-abundant New World (19 percent in all three tables combined) than in the resource-scarce Old World (28 percent in all three tables combined). Second, and again contrary to prediction, complementarity was three times more common in the "postfrontier" period: complementarity occurred 36 percent of the time during the interwar years but only 14 percent of the time prior to World War I.

Our priors strongly suggested complementarity, and regime switch away from complementarity toward substitutability. The evidence rejects those priors in the sense that it supports a regime switch toward complementarity, when the disappearing frontier thesis predicted a regime switch from complementarity. To repeat, aggregate trade flows involved a lot more than just the frontier staple goods. However, perhaps the complementarity found in the interwar data is actually driven by policy, the simultaneous breakdown of international commodity and factor markets. And although there is some evidence to support prewar complementarity, we expected stronger and more comprehensive confirmation given the plausible inferences emerging from endogenous frontier arguments and the older long-swing literature. Another blow to any endogenous frontier model favoring complementarity is the finding that the New World with the frontier offers no evidence of stronger complementarity than the Old World without the frontier. In any case, the long-swing evidence certainly rejects substitutability.

Panel Data from History: The Atlantic Community, 1870–1940

This section takes another step toward filling the empirical void in the debate by exploring long-run relationships in panel data for our ten Atlantic economies between 1870 and 1940. The dependent variable in the regressions, trade volume, is now measured as the sum of imports and exports relative to GDP (as opposed to the previous section, which measured "real" trade levels for each country). One important advantage of this new trade volume measure is that it provides a simple metric for comparison across countries that does not require the difficult translation of each country's trade into a common (real) currency by exchange rates and import and export price indexes. One potential disadvantage of the new measure, however, is that it departs from Heckscher-Ohlin-Vanek theory, which relates the volume of a country's trade, *unscaled* by GDP, to the gap between its factor endowment and its factor consumption.[11]

The panel data regressions are reported in detail elsewhere (Collins, O'Rourke, and Williamson 1997, table 3), so we focus here on the central findings. Tariffs were included in the panel regression just as they were in the long-swing analysis. To reflect the substantial decline in transport costs over this period, the Isserlis index was again included in the regressions. However, since the index is identical for each country, it can be useful, potentially at least, only in explaining variation in trade and GDP shares over time. The explanatory variables of greatest interest to us were average annual net migration rates and the current account relative to GDP for each decade between 1870 and 1940.

The regressions pursued a simple question: Ceteris paribus, were larger flows of people and capital associated with higher or lower volumes of trade? Like the long-swing analysis in the previous section, the panel data provide virtually no support for the substitutability hypothesis. They do provide some limited support (once country dummies are included) for complementarity between capital flows and trade. Even when significant, however, the size of all the estimated coefficients indicates a weak economic link between factor and trade flows.[12]

Political Economy Connections: Tariffs and Immigration Restrictions

We turn now to another piece of evidence: Did New World immigration policy behave in a fashion suggesting that the decision makers of that time viewed trade and factor flows as substitutes?[13]

The Stylized Policy Facts

Chapter 10 argued that there was a gradual closing of New World doors to immigrants after the 1880s. Australia, Argentina, Brazil, Canada, and the United States all began to restrict immigration in the decades before the Great War. What was true of immigration policy was also true of trade policy. Chapter 6 identified a globalization backlash in which tariffs started to rise on the European Continent as well as in the New World. The interwar period saw a further tightening of controls on both trade and factor flows, a tightening that was to be gradually eased after 1945 by Bretton Woods, GATT, guest worker arrangements in Europe, the 1965 repeal of national origins quotas in the United States, foreign capital market deregulation, and other policy events consistent with globalization, especially after the early 1970s.

What, if any, is the relationship between trade and immigration restrictions? We saw in chapter 10 that concerns over inequality were crucial in increasing the barriers to free migration. But did New World nations pursue legislation then that suggested that politicians and voters believed that trade and immigration were substitutes? If they thought so, then they would have believed that it was no use restricting just one when workers' living standards were under threat, but rather that they had to restrict both. Alternatively, if trade and factor flows were complements, then restricting either trade or immigration would have done the trick.

Exploring the Links Between Trade and Migration Policy

Unskilled labor at the bottom of the distribution is scarce and expensive in rich countries, and that fact by itself helped make income distributions more egalitarian than in poor countries (chapter 9). Immigration from poor countries should erode unskilled labor scarcity in rich countries and raise inequality. Labor-intensive commodity imports should do the same. How should policy respond? If, driven by the presence of a frontier, trade and immigration were complements in the pre–World War I rich New World, then protection and immigration restriction need not have gone hand in hand. Such a correlation might have emerged as the frontier disappeared.

The United States was indeed protectionist, especially after the Civil War when landed and slave interests in the South had been defeated. And as we pointed out in chapter 6, other labor-scarce and resource-abundant New World countries began to protect, favoring manufacturing in particular. Canada was protectionist, especially after 1878; the state of Victoria (in Australia) was by 1866, and a federal Australia followed Victoria's lead in 1906; Argentina went that route in the 1870s, and so did Brazil. The fact that these labor-scarce frontier countries moved only gradually to restrict immigration, while they moved very quickly to protect industry, is consistent with our earlier suggestion that as the frontier closed, trade and factor flows began to switch from being complements to being substitutes. At first, protection was sufficient, but later, immigration restrictions also became necessary. However, the closing of the frontier might have mattered more directly for the immigration debate.

Americans thought the western frontier had disappeared in the 1890s, Argentineans thought the pampas had filled up shortly thereafter, Brazilians in São Paulo must have thought the same as coffee prices collapsed in the 1920s, and Canadians must have shared this view when declining grain prices brought an end to their prairie boom. Simple theory would predict that the closing of the frontier had an impact on attitudes toward immigration: the wage impact of immigration should have been lower when elastic supplies of land were available, since they could absorb new workers. The timing of New World immigration restrictions seems at least roughly consistent with this view since the really big change in attitudes toward immigration policy did not emerge until the 1890s.

Is the timing of immigration restriction adequately explained by the less elastic New World demand for labor implied by closing frontiers? Or did a changing relationship between trade and factor flows—first complements, then substitutes—also play a role? Were immigration restrictions positively associated with tariffs, as would be true if trade and factor flows were substitutes, and did the association between tariffs and migration policy change over time?

Table 10.1 reported the results of a regression, taken from Timmer and Williamson (1996), seeking to explain the determinants of immigration policy in five countries—Argentina, Australia, Brazil, Canada, and the United States—between about 1860 and 1930. It showed that immigration policy was significantly affected by the lagged dependent variable, the lagged relative position of the unskilled at the bottom of the income distribution, the lagged rise in an immigrant threat to unskilled workers' wages, and the quality of immigrants relative to natives (and previous immigrants). The remaining right-hand-side variables were insignificant, so we will not discuss them here, except for the one that is relevant to this chapter: the ratio of trade to GDP. That variable was not significantly related to immigration policy, suggesting that openness and proimmigration policies were not complements, as would be true if trade and migration were substitutes.

However, we know that the ratio of trade to GDP is a crude (and possibly misleading) index of trade policy. What happens if trade shares are replaced in the regression by average tariffs? In this case, even stronger evidence emerges to suggest that policymakers viewed trade and factor flows as complements.[14] The coefficient on average tariffs was 3.91, suggesting that a 10 percentage point increase in the average tariff was associated with an increase in the immigration policy index of 0.4; and the coefficient was statistically significant at the 12.5 percent level. Higher protectionism was associated with more liberal migration policies, not less liberal policies, during this period. Between

1860 and 1930, policy did not behave as if New World politicians and voters thought that trade and immigration were substitutes.

Was there a difference between the pre-1914 and post-1914 periods? Since we are using five-year averages, there are only fifteen observations for the latter period, and five of these overlap with the Great War. Those caveats aside, the evidence accords with our earlier suggestions that the closing of the frontier could have coincided with the emergence of a positive correlation between trade and immigration restrictions. For the pre-1914 period, the coefficient on average tariffs was positive (but insignificant); for the post-1914 period, the coefficient was large, negative, and highly significant.[15] After 1914, countries insulating themselves from trade also attempted to insulate themselves from migration flows, whereas the same had not been true before that date. In contrast with the direct evidence on trade and factor flows, the indirect evidence on policy is consistent with a regime switch, in which trade and migration changed from being complements to substitutes.

History's Lessons

The elegant model associated with Eli Heckscher and Bertil Ohlin makes the unambiguous statement that trade and factor mobility are substitutes.[16] In the absence of factor mobility, trade can serve to equalize factor prices internationally. In the presence of factor mobility, trade may disappear altogether. The issue is important for the policy implications it generates. If immigration threatens egalitarian distributions by creating labor abundance at the bottom of the distribution, immigration quotas will simply provoke more trade and a flood of "unfair competition" from unskilled workers, making labor-intensive goods in distant lands of labor surplus from which they can no longer emigrate. If rich countries retreat behind tariff walls, there will be far more immigrants hammering at their gates since opportunities for making labor-intensive export goods at home will have dried up. The economics is so plausible that it survived with little challenge over the four decades from the early post–World War I years, when Heckscher and Ohlin were writing, to 1957, when Robert Mundell published his seminal piece. In the four decades since, the challenges to that conventional wisdom have been so many that nothing but theoretical ambiguity remains.

This chapter attacks the ambiguity by exploring the experience of the Atlantic economy between 1870 and 1940. That history suggests the following lessons. When we look at annual variations in the time-series data, we find that trade and capital flows were rarely substitutes and often complements. The same was true for trade and migration. When we look at longer-run relationships in the panel data, we find once again that trade and capital flows were rarely substitutes and often complements. Trade and migration were never substitutes. When we look at immigration policy in the New World, it appears that policymakers never acted as if they viewed trade and migration as substitutes during the late nineteenth century. However, there is some evidence of a regime switch coinciding with the closing of the frontier and the interwar descent into autarky: policymakers acted more as though they viewed trade and migration as substitutes after the Great War.

Overall, the history of the Atlantic economy between 1870 and 1940 rejects the thesis that trade and factor mobility were substitutes. It is a little more comfortable with the thesis that they were complements. Whether these lessons will survive the scrutiny of better data, more data, and new econometric techniques remains to be seen, but if this chapter serves to provoke economists to look more carefully at the post–World War II experience, we shall be content.

This book began by documenting the powerful real wage convergence that characterized the years between the Great Irish Famine and the Great War. Living standards in the Old World were catching up with those in the New, while Scandinavian, Irish, and Italian living standards were catching up with those in Britain and the rest of the European industrial core. We showed how and why factor prices (and workers' living standards) converged faster than GDP per capita and average labor productivity. We then went on to assert that this convergence was intimately linked to the evolution of the Atlantic economy. We claimed that the positive correlation between globalization and convergence that emerged following the middle of the nineteenth century is not spurious but causal, at least up to World War I.

Does the evidence presented in this book justify that claim? This chapter pulls together the various threads of the argument and makes the case in one final summation. It then shows which lessons from history are relevant to current debates about globalization and which are not.

A Word About Evidence: Factor Prices Versus Output Aggregates

Macroeconomists look only at aggregate measures like GDP per capita or GDP per worker-hour when assessing the growth of nations. This book relies more heavily on factor prices, and real wage rates in particular. Chapter 2 offered four reasons for doing this, and three of them deserve repeating for the economists reading this book.

First, individuals earn wages, skill premiums, profits, and rents, not GDP per capita. Real unskilled wages are a better measure of ordinary workers' living standards than traditional macroeconomic aggregates. Second, chapters 4 through 11 offered plenty of evidence that income

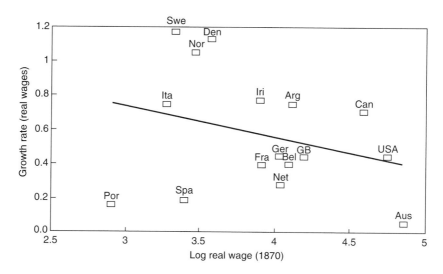

Figure 14.1
"Unconditional" real wage convergence, 1870–1913. Source: O'Rourke and Williamson
(1997, figure 1).

distribution matters for the evolution of policy. Changes that increase
average incomes may hit some groups hard, and if those losers are
sufficiently powerful, they can often successfully resist those changes.
Third, the sources of convergence can be better understood by focusing
on factor prices. Trade, migration, and capital flows all influence factor
prices directly, and thus only indirectly influence GDP per capita;
moreover, open economy forces may have a very different impact on
factor prices than alternative sources of convergence, such as technological catch-up. Factor price data therefore help us to discriminate
among alternative explanations for growth and convergence.

Atlantic Economy Convergence

Let us focus on those countries chiefly involved in the late-nineteenth-
century catch-up on the leaders, the poor economies on the western
European periphery.[1] Table 2.2 documented the great variety in country experience around the periphery. Some, like Ireland, converged on
the economic leaders at about the expected rate; some, like the Scandinavian trio, converged at a ferocious rate; some, like Italy, converged
at a much more sedate pace, a convergence that was delayed, coming
mainly at the end of the epoch; and some, like the Iberian pair, failed
to converge at all. Figure 14.1 puts this performance into perspective

by comparing each country with the predictions of the simplest unconditional convergence model (indicated by the regression line). The figure confirms that relative to the regression line, the Scandinavians
(Swe, Den, Nor) were overachievers, the Irish (Irl) caught up at about
the rate predicted by their initial income, and the Italians (Ita) caught
up a little more slowly. Support for the unconditional convergence hypothesis would have been much stronger in this Atlantic economy sample had the Iberians been excluded, since they failed. With the Iberians
gone (Por and Spa), the slope of the regression line would have been
far steeper. It also would have been much steeper if the United States
and Canada (Can) were excluded, since they bucked the convergence
tide, and they would have been even farther above a regression line
that excluded the Iberian pair. Australia (Aus) did badly, even relative
to the unconditional convergence line. There was very little variance
among the European leaders (Fra, Bel, Ger, Net, GB), and in spite of
the volumes that have been written about British failure, its growth
performance is almost exactly on the unconditional convergence line.

To what extent can this variance in catching up around the periphery
be explained by the open economy forces emphasized in this book?
The discussion is made more concrete in this chapter by exploring the
determinants of individual country catch-up or fallback relative to the
economic giants of the day, Great Britain and the United States. To
what extent did Scandinavian participation in the growing world economy explain its success? To what extent did Iberian efforts to insulate
themselves from these forces explain its failure? And what about Ireland and Italy, lying in the middle of the range? How much of the
catch-up and fallback around the periphery can be explained simply
by each country's ability and willingness to emigrate?

The Role of Education

One way to assess the importance of open economy forces is to ask
how well they do compared with other potential sources of growth.
One popular candidate, emphasized by economic historians and new-
growth theorists alike, is education. In his 1981 presidential address to
the Economic History Association, Richard Easterlin thought that lack
of education was the central reason that the whole world was not developed. Moses Abramovitz (1986), Robert Barro (1991), and others
have found that education has been an important determinant of
late-twentieth-century growth, and that convergence is apparent only

after controlling for initial educational levels and other conditioning factors. Anticipating this recent empirical growth literature on the late-twentieth-century experience, Lars Sandberg (1979) argued that Sweden's success a century ago was due to its status as an "impoverished sophisticate": a poor but highly educated country, it was poised and ready to converge on the industrial core. Similarly, Carlo Cipolla documented relatively high literacy levels in Scandinavia and concluded that "more literate countries were the first to import the Industrial Revolution" (Cipolla 1969, 87). More recently, Gabriel Tortella (1994) has blamed poor education for the dismal economic performance of the Mediterranean basin.

We recently tried to evaluate these claims for the nineteenth century by estimating convergence equations, conditional on schooling (O'Rourke and Williamson 1997). Part A of table 14.1 confirms that education was positively associated with growth and that convergence conditional on initial education is stronger than unconditional convergence.

What really interests us, however, is the contribution of education to convergence.[2] How much of Scandinavian catch-up and Iberian fallback was due to their initial human capital endowment? The answer takes the education coefficients in part A of table 14.1 and applies these coefficients to educational levels around the European periphery, in Britain and in the United States.[3] This makes it possible to calculate the growth differential between core and periphery countries that is due to *differences* in human capital endowment. This due-to-schooling differential is then expressed as a percentage of the total growth differential observed between 1870 and 1913 (part B of table 14.1).

Let us start with the Scandinavians, where the schooling thesis has had the greatest following. A moment's reflection should make it clear that education cannot explain much of Scandinavia's catch-up on Britain or the United States, since the latter two also benefited from high levels of education. Thus, schooling accounted for only about 8 percent of Danish catch-up on Britain, 6 percent of Norwegian catch-up, and 5 percent of Swedish catch-up (according to the enrollment data, and even less if the literacy data are used). Education accounted for none of the Scandinavian catch-up on the United States, according to the enrollment data.

Since Ireland and Italy were less well educated than Britain and the United States, none of the Irish and Italian catch-up can be explained by good education, but the absence of faster catch-up there might be explained by poor education. Very poor Iberian education *can* account for a significant proportion of the peninsula's fallback relative to Britain and the United States. Relative to Britain, the figures are 10 percent for Spain and 58 percent for Portugal. On average, 34 percent of Iberian fallback relative to Britain can be explained by poor enrollment rates. Over 70 percent of Iberian fallback relative to the United States can be attributed to the same cause.

Good and bad schooling help explain convergence and divergence around the European periphery a century ago, but they help explain these patterns only in Scandinavia and Iberia, and in only one case, Iberia, do they explain very much. Globalization forces mattered far more.

The Role of Migration

Recall how we have assessed the impact of globalization throughout this book. Rather than relying solely on correlations apparent in the data, we also measured the size of the shocks associated with late-nineteenth-century globalization, and then derived the impact of those shocks by imposing them on well-specified models of these Atlantic economies. This second method was used to assess the impact of mass migration in chapter 8. The impact on the labor force was measured for both sending and receiving countries, and then the impact of these labor force shocks on real wages and GDP per capita was calculated using both computable general equilibrium models and econometric methods. The analysis suggested that emigration in postfamine Ireland accounted for as much as half of observed real wage growth and over one-quarter of observed income per capita growth after 1851. Emigration increased real wages in Sweden by 8 to 12 percent between 1870 and 1910. U.S. immigration lowered real wages by between 8 and 15 percent. Mass migration accounted for all of Irish real wage convergence on the United States and for between 25 and 40 percent of Swedish convergence. Using the econometric estimates, it looks like mass migration prior to the Great War probably accounted for about 70 percent of the overall real wage convergence observed in the Atlantic economy as a whole.

Another way to use this evidence is to ask how well it explains individual country performance around the poor European periphery. Table 14.2 summarizes the relevant information for those economies, as well as for Britain and the United States. The first column reports the

Table 14.1
Conditional Convergence for the Late Nineteenth Century

	Coefficients on:			
	---	---	---	---
Sample	Log 1870 value	Log schooling variable	R^2	N
A. Convergence regressions				
A.1 Unconditional convergence equations				
1870–1913, real wage Figure 1	−0.177 (1.101)		0.08	16	0.005
1870–1913, GDP per worker-hour	−0.025 (0.255)		0.01	14	0.001
A.2 Using enrollment rate estimates				
1870–1913, real wage	−0.258 (1.352)	0.192 (0.813)	0.12	16	0.007
1870–1913, GDP per worker	−0.277** (3.361)	0.446* (4.537)	0.65	14	0.008
A.3 Using literacy rate estimates				
1870–1913, real wage	−0.350** (2.076)	0.534** (2.026)	0.30	16	0.010
1870–1913, GDP per worker	−0.167 (1.479)	0.292** (2.016)	0.27	14	0.004

average net migration rates, the second reports the cumulative impact of migration on the 1910 domestic labor force, and the third reports its impact on real wages in 1910.[4] The columns show that emigration had a huge effect on Italian and Irish real wages, very large effects on Scandinavian, and especially Norwegian, real wages, and only small effects on British and Iberian real wages. Columns 4 and 5 report our bottom line: the share of the observed real wage convergence on Britain and the United States accounted for by mass migration.

The figures for Ireland and Italy are enormous: mass migration accounted for *all* of the convergence on the United States for those two countries and for 65 to 87 percent of their convergence on Britain. The amazing characteristic of these two countries is that they seem to have relied exclusively on emigration to achieve some catch-up on the leaders. Portugal and Spain, on the other hand, were unable or unwilling to exploit these emigration possibilities. A significant share of their divergence from Britain is explained by "underemigration" (up to 3.5 percent for Spain and about 17 to 30 percent for Portugal). The "none" in parentheses under column 5 means that although mass migration

Table 14.1   (continued)

| Country | Real wage growth using: | |
	Enrollment	Literacy
B. Convergence impact		
B.1 Share of growth gap, periphery versus Britain, explained by schooling		
Denmark	8	5
Norway	6	5
Sweden	5	4
Italy	None	None
Portugal	(58)	(All)
Spain	(10)	(All)
Ireland	None	None
B.2 Share of growth gap, periphery versus United States, explained by schooling		
Denmark	None	9
Norway	None	9
Sweden	None	8
Italy	None	None
Portugal	(94)	(All)
Spain	(51)	(All)
Ireland	None	5

Source: O'Rourke and Williamson (1997, tables 3, 5).
Note: The results in part B are calculated by dividing the growth gap in question into the coefficient on the schooling variable times the difference in the log of education in the two countries being compared. Parentheses around the Iberian entries in part B indicate that it is Iberian *divergence,* not convergence, that is being explained. Note that the results here are based on unrounded wage rates, whereas the levels in table 2.1 have been rounded.
t = statistics in parentheses.
* Significant at 1 percent.
** Significant at 5 percent.
*** Significant at 10 percent.

should have helped produce Iberian convergence on the United States, divergence factors overwhelmed these forces. That is, mass migration cannot explain any of the Iberian fallback on the United States. Scandinavia lies between these extremes: on average, 8 percent of the Scandinavian convergence on Britain, and a little more than two-fifths of the convergence on the United States, was due to mass migration. The contribution of emigration to convergence was biggest for the poorest Scandinavian country, Norway, just as one might have predicted.

Table 14.2
Impact of Mass Migration on Convergence Around the Periphery, 1870–1910

Country	Net labor migration rate, 1870–1910 (per 000 per annum) (1)	Cumulative impact on labor force, 1910 (2a)	(2b)	Impact of migration, 1870–1910, on real wages (3a)	(3b)
Poor European Periphery					
Denmark	3.67	14%		+7.6%	+9.6%
Norway	6.93	24		+9.7	+16.4
Sweden	5.55	20	18%	+7.5	+12.3
Italy	12.21	39		+28.2	
Portugal	1.40	5		+4.3	
Spain	−1.53	6		+5.9	
Ireland	14.84	45		+31.9	
Rich Old and New Worlds					
Great Britain	2.97	11	10	+5.6	+6.6
United States	+5.31	+24	+21	8.1	15.1

Country	Share of wage convergence, 1870–1910, on Britain explained (4a)	(4b)	Share of wage convergence, 1870–1910, on United States explained (5a)	(5b)
Denmark	3.9%	5.7%	31.9%	49.2%
Norway	8.9	20.0	40.6	67.7
Sweden	2.9	8.4	24.6	41.4
Italy	67.8	64.8	All	All
Portugal	(16.7)	(29.6)	(None)	(None)
Spain	(None)	(3.5)	(None)	(None)
Ireland	86.9	83.6	All	All

Note and sources: Columns 1, 2a, and 3a are from table 8.1. Columns 2b and 3b are from O'Rourke and Williamson (1995a; 1995d, appendix 6), and the assumption that the Swedish labor force wage elasticity applied in Denmark and Norway. Columns 4 and 5 are derived from column 3 and the wage data underlying O'Rourke and Williamson (1997). Parentheses around the Iberian entries in columns 4a–5b indicate that it is Iberian *divergence* that is being explained. Note that the results here are based on unrounded wage rates, whereas the levels in table 2.1 have been rounded.

Mass migration explains a very large share of the catch-up and its absence around the European periphery. Why did emigration rates vary so much? Why did Iberia fail to exploit this powerful source of catch-up? Chapter 7 showed that a culture-specific "Latin" explanation is not needed to explain those low rates in Iberia, but rather that it can be explained by weak demographic pressure; lack of industrialization; low emigration in the 1870s and earlier, cutting off remittances that would have been an important source of finance for young Iberians pondering emigration in the 1880s or 1890s; and an exchange rate policy that served to make migration more expensive. Thus, it was the Irish and the Scandinavians who were best able to exploit emigration as a convergence force, not the Iberians, who had the most to gain from mass migration.

The Role of International Capital Flows

Chapter 12 argued that international capital flows were on balance a force for divergence in the late nineteenth century, flowing from the low-wage Old World to the high-wage but resource-rich New World. They thus contributed to the North American surge in relative living standards, bucking the convergence trend. True, the low-wage Scandinavian economies also managed to attract capital inflows, but note that this was especially true of resource-rich (iron and timber) Sweden. Recall the message of table 12.3, which showed the contribution of international capital flows to convergence and divergence around the western European periphery. Capital inflows boosted Scandinavian capital stocks significantly, especially in Sweden; Ireland (and possibly Italy) may actually have *exported* capital; and capital inflows had only a small impact on Iberian capital stocks. The net result was that while capital flows can explain between 30 and 43 percent of Scandinavian convergence on Britain and between 16 and 34 percent of Scandinavian convergence on the United States, they made no contribution to Irish (and possibly Italian) living standards, and boosted Iberian real wages only marginally. This failure of international capital flows to act as a systematic force for convergence is not unique to this period and remains a subject of debate and controversy. But surely one explanation is that nineteenth-century financial capital was used primarily to construct social overhead: railroads, harbors, municipal improvements, and so on. Thus, those countries catching up that were also experiencing really big emigrations did not undergo the kind of social overhead investment booms that required financial capital from London, Paris, and Amsterdam to make up big domestic savings shortfalls.

The Role of Trade

Chapter 6 noted the tremendous diversity in trade policies around the late-nineteenth-century European periphery. As part of the United Kingdom, Ireland remained a free trader throughout; Denmark also pursued relatively liberal policies, while Sweden and Norway adopted moderate protection; Italy was more protectionist; and Iberia was extremely protectionist. Can the contrast between Scandinavian catch-up and Iberian fallback be explained by trade policy?

Recall the strategy adopted to answer questions such as these: calculate the price shocks associated with declining transport costs and changing tariff levels, and then impose those price shocks on computable general equilibrium models of individual economies. Table 14.3 summarizes our earlier results on the impact of commodity market integration on real wages and living standards around the European periphery, and in Britain and the United States. The decline in transatlantic transport costs boosted British wages by some 20 percent but left U.S. wages relatively unchanged: commodity market integration was a powerful force for Anglo-American real wage convergence. On the other hand, integration with global commodity markets had a smaller effect on Swedish real wages. Anglo-Swedish price convergence boosted Swedish real wages by a mere 1.9 percent, accounting for only about 3 percent of the decline in the Anglo-Swedish wage gap. Transatlantic price convergence increased Swedish real wages by a bigger but still modest 6.2 percent, accounting for a little less than one-tenth of the Swedish catch-up on the United States. From what we know about the trade policies of the three Scandinavian countries, Heckscher-Ohlin effects were probably larger in Norway than in Sweden, and a lot larger in Denmark. This is reflected by the entries in table 14.3.[5]

What about the rest of the European periphery? The computable general equilibrium model used in chapter 8 to assess the impact of emigration on Irish living standards can also be used to calculate the impact of declining transatlantic price gaps. What would Irish real wages have been in 1908 if transatlantic price gaps had remained constant in the four decades after 1870, rather than declining as they actually did? When these counterfactual price shocks are imposed on the

Table 14.3
Impact of Commodity Market Integration on Convergence Around the Periphery, 1870–1910

Country	Impact of commodity market integration, intra-European, 1870–1910, on real wages (1)	Impact of commodity market integration, transatlantic, 1870–1910, on real wages (2)
Denmark	>1.9%	>6.2%
Norway	>1.9	>6.2
Sweden	1.9	6.2
Italy	Positive?	Negative?
Portugal	Positive?	Negative?
Spain	Positive?	Negative?
Ireland	Negative?	−8.8
	Share of wage convergence, 1870–1910, on Britain explained (3)	Share of wage convergence, 1870–1910, on United States explained (4)
Denmark	>3.9%	>12.1%
Norway	>4.4	>13.9
Sweden	3.1	9.4
Italy	Positive?	None?
Portugal	(None?)	(Positive?)
Spain	(None?)	(Positive?)
Ireland	None?	None

Note and sources: O'Rourke and Williamson (1997, table 9). Parentheses around the Iberian entries in columns 3 and 4 indicate that it is Iberian *divergence* that is being explained. Note that the results here are based on unrounded wage rates, whereas the levels in table 2.1 have been rounded.

Irish model, real Irish wages increase by 9.6 percent, implying that declining transatlantic price gaps *lowered* Irish real wages by 8.8 percent.[6] In agricultural Ireland, the negative impact of cheap food on labor demand dominated the positive impact of a lower cost of living. Table 14.3 thus indicates that Heckscher-Ohlin forces actually increased the Irish-American wage gap; they did not contribute to Irish-American convergence at all.

We have not estimated the evolution of Anglo-Irish commodity price gaps but suspect that commodity market integration across the Irish Sea led mostly to an increase in Irish animal product prices, as rail and steamships helped Irish farmers meet the growing British urban demand for breakfast foods. This may have reduced the demand for Irish labor still further if Irish animal husbandry was land intensive. To evaluate the hypothesis more carefully, we would need an Irish model that distinguished between tillage and pasture (the current version has only one agricultural sector), and we would need price information that is currently unavailable. Table 14.3 reflects our uncertainty.

The Mediterranean countries present even more uncertainty. As before, we would like to distinguish between transatlantic and intra-European commodity market integration. If the Irish experience is any guide, then the transatlantic effect, by lowering grain prices, may have been to lower Mediterranean wages; after all, chapter 6 was able to report how cheap grain served to lower French real wages. Intra-European integration may have had the opposite effect by increasing the output of labor-intensive Mediterranean products (such as olives and wine) and labor-intensive industrial and mining activities in Italy and Spain. Table 14.3 thus suggests that while transatlantic integration may have contributed to the Iberian divergence observed, intra-European integration probably contributed nothing to the observed divergence since it should have led to convergence. We admit that this is purely speculative.[7]

Measuring commodity market integration at various points around the European periphery and calculating its impact on individual countries should get major research priority. But what we know so far suggests that these forces did not play a consistent role in contributing to catch-up and falling behind around the periphery. Indeed, cheap grain on its own probably contributed to intra-European divergence, increasing real wages in urban Britain but lowering them in more agricultural economies. While trade made a significant contribution to Scandinavian real wage catch-up, elsewhere in continental Europe the contribution was far more modest, and sometimes negative.

Globalization and Convergence: A Summary

Table 14.4 offers a final assessment of the sources of catch-up and fallback around the European periphery. The table confirms that open economy forces were crucial in explaining patterns of relative growth during the late nineteenth century. Mass migration and international

Table 14.4
Sources of Catch-Up and Fall Back Around the European Periphery, 1870–1910 (in percent)

	Schooling	Mass migration	Capital flows	Trade	Residual
How much of real wage convergence (or divergence) on Britain explained?					
Denmark	5–8	3.9–5.7	30.0	>3.9	<52.4–57.2
Norway	5–6	8.9–20.0	35.1	>4.4	<34.5–46.6
Sweden	4–5	2.9–8.4	43.0	3.1	40.5–47.0
Italy	0	64.8–67.8	Positive	Positive?	<32.2–35.2
Portugal	(58–all)	(16.7–29.6)	(0)	(0?)	(0–25.3)
Spain	(10–all)	(0–3.5)	(0)	(0?)	(0–90.0)
Ireland	0	83.6–86.9	Small positive	0?	<13.1–16.4
How much of real wage convergence (or divergence) on America explained?					
Denmark	0–9	31.9–49.2	16.3	>12.1	<13.4–39.7
Norway	0–9	40.6–67.7	20.0	>13.9	<0–25.5
Sweden	0–8	24.6–41.4	34.0	9.4	7.2–32.0
Italy	0	All	0?	0?	0
Portugal	(94–all)	(0)	(0?)	(Positive?)	(0–6)
Spain	(51–all)	(0)	(0?)	(Positive?)	(0–49)
Ireland	0–5	All	0	0	0

Note and sources: From tables 4.1 (parts B.1 and B.2), table 14.2 (columns 4a–5b), table 12.3 (columns 3 and 4), and table 14.3 (columns 3 and 4). Parentheses around the Iberian entries indicate that it is Iberian *divergence* that is being explained. Note that the results here are based on unrounded wage rates, whereas the levels in table 2.1 have been rounded.

capital flows served to explain between a third and a half of the Scandinavian catch-up on Britain; they explained between 48 and 88 percent of the Scandinavian catch-up on the United States; they explained over two-thirds of the Irish and Italian catch-up on Britain; and they explained all of the Irish and Italian catch-up on the United States. A failure to send out enough emigrants, and to import enough capital, explained an important part of Iberian failure. Iberian isolation did contribute to its failure during this period, but it was factor market isolation that mattered most. Oddly enough, debates about comparative performance around the periphery have said little about factor market integration. Our results suggest that the ability to exploit international factor markets was *the* crucial variable determining relative performance.

The libraries are full of debates over nineteenth-century tariff policies and their impact on performance. Given that fact, we were surprised to find that the contribution of trade to convergence was uniformly so small. But that is the tentative answer emerging from table 14.4. It was small even under free trade regimes, as in Ireland and Denmark. Declining transport costs are unlikely to have explained much more than 5 percent of Scandinavia's catch-up on Britain, or 15 percent of Scandinavia's catch-up on the United States. Heckscher and Ohlin predicted that trade should have led to rapid European real wage convergence on the New World. They were right for Britain, since the impact was big. They were wrong everywhere else, since the impact was small.

The last column of table 14.4 reports the residual after the first four columns are added up. The entries for Scandinavia seem plausible: about half of the catch-up on Britain can be explained by globalization and schooling combined; superior total factor productivity growth must explain the other half, and it was most important for Denmark. Reasonably enough, the residual—and thus, presumably, superior total factor productivity growth—accounts for a much smaller share of Scandinavian catch-up on the dynamic U.S. economy. The table suggests that none of the Irish or Italian catch-up on the United States was due to superior rates of Irish or Italian total factor productivity growth, which again seems plausible. The range for Spain is much too big to conclude anything, but it looks as if only a small proportion of the Portuguese fallback can be attributed to *slower* rates of Portuguese total factor productivity growth.

What Are the Lessons from History?

This book demonstrates the causal link between globalization and convergence in the late-nineteenth-century Atlantic economy. It remains to be seen whether the interwar disintegration of the world economy was responsible for the breakdown of convergence and whether open economy forces have been mainly responsible for the renewed convergence observed since 1950. Our priors are that open economy forces are still important. We hope that this book has supplied some methodological hardware that should be useful in nailing down the thesis for the more data-abundant decades since 1950.

Despite these caveats, there are several lessons that can be drawn from the late-nineteenth-century Atlantic economy, and they are directly relevant to current debates over convergence and the distributional consequences of globalization.

The Convergence Debate

While economic historians have examined the long-run convergence record for some time, *convergence* recently became a buzzword among economists as a result of contributions to what is now called endogenous growth theory. It is well known that the simple Solow growth model predicts long-run convergence, at least for countries with similar savings rates, population growth rates, and other fundamentals. It is equally well known that the data in the Penn World Tables show no unconditional convergence for the world as a whole. There are three ways to deal with these facts. One is to argue that the Solow model is inadequate and that endogenous growth models should replace it. A second is to argue that the Solow model, in which labor and capital are the only factors of production, is unnecessarily limited. Additional factors of production, like human capital, are necessary to make the model really effective. Furthermore, different countries have different investment, education, and population growth rates, and thus are converging to different steady states. This "augmented Solow model" approach has spawned a vast literature on conditional convergence. The issue is not whether countries converge but whether they converge conditional on attitudes toward thrift, commitments to education, quality of institutions, geographic location, and demographic preferences.

The third possible response to the absence of convergence at the global level is to argue that open economy forces have a lot more to do with convergence than growth theory admits. Indeed, the conditional convergence literature is usually discussed in the context of the closed economy. While trade policy variables have certainly entered the analysis, the dominant metaphor is still that of different economies growing in isolation from each other. We believe that the catching up of poor countries with rich may have as much to do with open economy linkages as with any other force identified by growth theory. Jeffrey Sachs and Andrew Warner (1995a) argue this case for the late twentieth century: there *is* convergence among those economies that have adopted open trading policies, but not among countries that have remained protectionist. The lack of unconditional convergence poses a problem for the simple Solow model. The lack of conditional convergence poses a problem for the augmented Solow model. Neither eventuality poses a problem for the open economy perspective: where there has been openness, there has been convergence; where there has been autarky, there has been either divergence or cessation of convergence.

Wicksell, Heckscher, Ohlin, and other Scandinavian economists argued that open economy forces had a lot to do with Scandinavian convergence on rich countries like Britain and America. In constructing their argument, they developed the essential insights of neoclassical trade theory. Their theory is static, but it is not incompatible with dynamic theories of growth, as Gene Grossman and Elhanan Helpman (1991) or Ronald Findlay (1995) have shown. Our aim has been to illustrate how these simple Scandinavian insights can explain a large share of the growth variance around the late-nineteenth-century Atlantic economy. Yet it was globalization in factor markets that mattered most prior to World War I, especially globalization of labor markets. Thus, one must be cautious in applying lessons of history to the present, where mass migrations are so much more modest.

We also had a methodological goal in mind when writing this book. The conditional convergence literature rarely goes beyond cross-country correlations and standard hypothesis testing. It looks for conditional convergence in the sample as a whole. When it explores open economy forces, it simply correlates growth with summary measures of openness. We believe that it is essential to go beyond these correlations, since they rarely distinguish between the impact of open commodity markets and open factor markets, and since they often conceal as much as they reveal. Here are two illustrations of the latter point.

First, explanations for the diversity of growth rates are as interesting as whether the conditional convergence line slopes up or down. The fact that late-nineteenth-century convergence depends largely on Scandinavian success is not a problem for us. It is the difference in performance of *all* members of the Atlantic economy that matters to us, and globalization forces can explain a lot of these differences.

Second, it is not enough to show that openness is correlated with growth. Economists and historians both need to examine whether the mechanisms that theory says should have linked the two were actually in operation during a given era, and if so, they need to quantify the impact of these mechanisms on convergence. How much migration was there in the late nineteenth century? Was it big enough to have had a large impact on wage and labor productivity gaps? What about the impact of capital flows? What about the impact of declining transport costs? We have tried to quantify these linkages for the Atlantic economy, and in so doing concluded that they were central to late-nineteenth-century experience. Moreover, our results understate the contribution of globalization to convergence since we have not quantified the impact of international technology transfers.

The Trade and Inequality Debate

This book has devoted a lot of space to the distributional consequences of late-nineteenth-century globalization. There are three lessons of history relevant to late-twentieth-century debates about the impact of what contemporary economists call North-South[8] trade and migration on inequality.

First, trade *can* have dramatic effects on income distribution, and this is possible even when it is a small share of GDP. Trade accounted for a smaller share of GDP everywhere in the Atlantic economy in 1913 than in 1987 (table 3.1). Yet late-nineteenth-century trade led to a 50 percent fall in British rents and a 20 percent rise in British real wages. Cheap grain would have led to a fall in Swedish and German land rents of around 15 percent had not protection muted that globalization impact. Low trade shares do not constitute proof that trade does not matter for income distribution. *If* trade has increased inequality in the present-day OECD—and we stress the word *if*—it has done so by changing commodity prices, a point well understood by international economists active in that debate.

Second, the impact of trade on income distribution can vary enormously depending on the structure of the economy in question, as well as on the size of the shock. The late-nineteenth-century distinction between the land-abundant New World and the land-scarce Old World is as stark as the distinction between the skill-abundant North and the skill-deprived South today. But trade did not have the same impact on factor prices everywhere a century ago, even within the Old World. Britain, France, Ireland, and Sweden were all land-scarce, labor-abundant economies when viewed in a global context, but there were many more differences among them that mattered. Those differences meant that declining transatlantic transport costs increased British real wages a lot, increased Swedish wages a little, and reduced Irish and French wages. It would be surprising if trade had the same distributional impact today on economies as diverse as the United States, Japan, the European core, and the European periphery, even though all these countries are rich compared with the Third World.

Third, although globalization did contribute to increased inequality in labor-scarce New World countries a century ago, it was migration that was doing the bulk of the work, not trade. That fact may offer some solace to those worried about trade and inequality in the North today, although what is true for one era is not necessarily true for another.

Globalization Backlash: A Cautionary Tale

A third focus of this book has been the political implications of globalization, and the lessons are sobering. Politicians, journalists, and market analysts have a tendency to extrapolate the immediate past into the indefinite future, and such thinking suggests that the world is irreversibly headed toward ever greater levels of economic integration. The historical record suggests the contrary.

The interwar decades saw a return to autarkic trade policies, the breakdown of international capital markets, and an end to mass migration. Global capital markets have only recently regained the ground they lost during that era, and migration is unlikely *ever* to regain the levels achieved prior to World War I. It would be comforting to think that interwar deglobalization was an exogenous shock, brought about by the onset of the Great War, events that had nothing at all to do with the globalization forces that had been at work previously. Were this true, we could reason that interwar autarkic reactions could be avoided today, so long as the international community keeps the peace. The evidence presented in this book suggests that this view of interwar deglobalization is both incorrect and misleading. The correct view is that a political backlash developed in response to the actual or perceived distributional effects of globalization. The backlash led to the reimposition of tariffs and the adoption of immigration restrictions, even before the Great War. Far from being destroyed by unforeseen and exogenous political events, globalization, at least in part, destroyed itself.

European tariffs on agricultural imports were adopted in direct response to the fall in land rents associated with globalization, while New World immigration controls were erected to combat the increased inequality to which the mass migrations gave rise, or were thought to have given rise. The record suggests that unless politicians worry about who gains and who loses, they may be forced by the electorate to stop efforts to strengthen global economy links, and perhaps even to dismantle them.

A Final Word

The globalization experience of the Atlantic economy prior to the Great War speaks directly and eloquently to globalization debates today. Economists who base their views of globalization, convergence, inequality, and policy solely on the years since 1970 are making a great mistake. We hope that this book will help them to avoid that mistake—or remedy it.

Appendix	Trade Theory and Computable General Equilibrium Models

This appendix provides a brief introduction to the computable general equilibrium (CGE) models used in the book. It indicates how they are related to the simple trade models taught to undergraduate students. The appendix does not attempt to provide a self-contained exposition of trade theory, because these are already available elsewhere. Rather, it indicates how the two most important textbook models treat the relationship between globalization and income distribution, the major theme of this book. Our account is restricted to constant returns to scale models, since comparative advantage provides a good explanation for late-nineteenth-century trade patterns.[1]

The Heckscher-Ohlin-Samuelson (2 × 2) Model

Heckscher and Ohlin had a general trade model in mind when deriving their theories, but the Heckscher-Ohlin-Samuelson (HOS) model used in the classroom is a very special one, and in certain respects the two Swedes would have had difficulty recognizing it.

The model assumes that there are two countries, two commodities, and two factors of production. As in chapter 13, call the countries Britain and Ireland, the commodities textiles and machines, and the factors of production labor and capital. Assume that machine production is relatively capital intensive and that Ireland is relatively labor abundant. Also assume that labor and capital are perfectly mobile within each country, so that wages and profits are the same in each sector.

All constant returns to scale general equilibrium models can be characterized by the following sets of equations: (1) for every sector, price equals average cost so that there are no supernormal profits; (2) for every commodity or factor of production, demand equals supply; (3) for every consumer, income equals expenditure. These three sets of equations are typically solved simultaneously, but in the case of the 2×2 HOS model, they can be solved recursively as follows.

First, the price-equal-cost equations can be used to solve for domestic factor prices, assuming that both commodities are produced. Under the assumption of constant returns to scale, average cost depends on factor prices alone; thus, average cost in each sector is a function of wages and profits only. The price of textiles in each country equals the average cost of producing textiles, which is a function of wages and profits, and the same is true in the machinery sector. We have

$$p_T = c_T(w, r), \tag{1}$$

$$p_M = c_M(w, r), \tag{2}$$

where p_T and p_M are the prices of textiles and machines, w and r are wages and profits, and c_T and c_M are the average cost functions in the two sectors.

Commodity prices in both sectors are given by world market conditions: they are exogenous in a small, open economy. Thus, if both commodities are produced and both equations 1 and 2 hold, then we have enough information to solve for wages and profits (since there are two equations with which to solve for two unknowns).

Factor prices determine factor proportions in both sectors. Given factor proportions in both sectors and total factor endowments, the full employment conditions for labor and capital can be used to solve for output levels. Finally, factor prices and endowments determine income; income, commodity prices, and preferences determine the consumption of each commodity; and trade in each commodity is equal to the difference between output and consumption.

It is equations 1 and 2 that are crucial here. As long as both commodities are produced, factor prices are completely determined by commodity prices (assuming that cost functions remain unchanged). This implies four important theorems.

First, trade affects income distribution by changing commodity prices. As globalization proceeds, import prices fall and export prices rise, and from equations 1 and 2, wages and profits will change. Even in more general trade models, this theorem continues to hold: for traded goods sectors, prices are given by world market conditions, and thus average costs in those sectors are exogenously determined. Factor prices do not depend on import volumes, or export volumes, or total trade volumes, or import penetration rates; they depend on commodity prices.

Second, factor supplies do not affect income distribution in the HOS model, as long as both commodities are produced. As Edward Leamer (1995) puts it, the derived demand for factors of production will be infinite under these conditions. An increase in a country's labor supply will lead to an expansion of labor-intensive textile production, which will absorb the extra labor without any need for a fall in wages. Clearly, as long as this is true, neither international migration nor international capital flows will have any impact on income distribution. Since the econometric evidence cited in chapter 8 suggests that labor demand elasticities were less than infinite, the CGE models we use will have to avoid this second implication of the HOS model.

Incorporating nontraded goods into the model does not change the second theorem. Equations 1 and 2 continue to determine wages and profits, and these then determine nontraded goods prices through the cost-equals-price equations for nontraded sectors. The theorem also continues to hold in models where n factors of production produce n traded goods, where n is any number greater than 2.

Third, if both countries produce both goods and use the same technology, they will share the same cost functions, and if there are no trade costs, so that commodity prices are identical in the two countries, then both countries face identical equations 1 and 2. In that case, factor prices are clearly also equal across countries. This is the famous factor price equalization (FPE) theorem, although as Leamer (1995) points out, the word *equalization* seems to refer to a process, whereas the FPE theorem refers to only equilibrium outcomes.

This book is concerned with the process of factor price convergence, induced by (among other things) commodity price convergence. The FPE theorem is thus not particularly relevant to the book. Of greater interest is the fourth theorem that emerges from the HOS model, the Stolper-Samuelson theorem, mentioned in chapter 4 and used elsewhere in the book. If the relative price of textiles falls, then resources shift out of labor-intensive textiles into capital-intensive machinery production, the demand for labor falls and that for capital rises, and wages fall and profits rise. Similarly, if the relative price of textiles rises, then wages will rise and profits will fall. The implication of the theorem is that commodity price convergence can induce factor price convergence. If the barriers to trade between Ireland and Britain decline, then relative textile prices will fall in Britain and rise in Ireland. Initially high Irish profits and British wages will fall, while initially low Irish wages and British profits will rise. Factor prices will converge internationally.

The Sector-Specific Factors (2 × 3) Model

The sector-specific factors (SSF) model has already been described in chapters 5 and 13. There are two sectors—call them agriculture and industry—producing food and manufactures. Labor is again mobile between sectors, but land can be used only in agriculture, and capital can be used only in industry. There are three factors of production, each earning its own rate of return, but only two price-equals-cost equations. We need another equation to determine factor prices. In short, factor prices must also be determined by the full employment conditions, and thus factor supplies influence factor prices and income distribution. Of course, commodity prices (and thus trade) still affect distribution, as we have seen in chapter 5. For example, a decline in food prices will lead to a decline in nominal wages, a decline in real rents, and an increase in real profits, with the effect on real wages being ambiguous (chapters 5 and 6).

The SSF model is thus flexible enough to allow both trade and factor endowments (and thus global factor mobility) to influence income distribution. However, its structure is still very simple, a virtue that enables trade theorists to derive clear predictions from it. Robert Fogel pointed out several of these simplifications in a famous article published more than thirty years ago (Fogel 1967): in the real world, capital is used in agriculture as well as in industry, land is used in industry as well as in agriculture, and food is processed by manufacturing; none of these realities is allowed in the simple SSF model. The important point is that expanding the model in these directions could overturn several of its predictions. For example, imagine that capital is an input into both industry and agriculture. A decline in food prices leads to a decline in agricultural output and an increase in manufacturing output. The latter effect will tend to increase the return to capital, as in the SSF model, but the former effect will tend to lower it. Which effect dominates is purely an empirical matter.

Computable General Equilibrium Models

Our response to Fogel's important contribution is to specify our empirical trade models in a sufficiently general manner that, insofar as is possible, the qualitative impact of trade and factor mobility on income distribution is not determined by model structure alone, but by the model's theoretical structure and the data used to calibrate it. A variety of CGE models are used in this book, individually tailored to deal with different questions, but most of them share several key features. Essentially they are augmented versions of the SSF model. They are illustrated here by the British model used to derive the impact of commodity price convergence in chapter 4.

The model incorporates two traded sectors, agriculture (A) and manufacturing (M), and one nontraded sector, services (S). There are three factors of production: labor, land, and capital. As in the SSF model, land is used only in agriculture, but capital is perfectly mobile among all three sectors. Moreover, labor is only imperfectly mobile between agriculture and the rest of the economy, reflecting the reality of large urban-rural wage gaps during this period.[2] Agricultural and nonagricultural wages are thus free to differ in this specification. An imported intermediate input (reflecting inputs of goods such as raw cotton) is also used in manufacturing, while manufactured goods are used as inputs into the nontraded sector.

We thus have the following three price-equals-cost equations:

$$p_A = c_A(w_A, r, d), \tag{3}$$

$$p_M = c_M(w_{NA}, r, p_I), \tag{4}$$

$$p_S = c_S(w_{NA}, r, p_M), \tag{5}$$

where p_A, p_M, and p_S are the prices of the three domestically produced goods; c_A, c_M, and c_S are the average cost functions in the three sectors; w_A and w_{NA} are agricultural and nonagricultural wages; r and d are profits and rents; and p_I is the price of imported intermediates.

Britain is assumed to be small in world commodity markets, so traded agricultural and manufactured goods prices are exogenous. Nontraded goods prices are, however, determined by domestic supply and demand. Equations 3 and 4 are not sufficient to determine the four factor prices in the model (r, d, w_A, and w_{NA}). The specification thus allows for factor mobility, as well as trade, to have an impact on factor prices and income distribution.

This model was the first one we constructed in the course of the research for this book, and subsequent models have elaborated on its basic structure (for a recent example, see O'Rourke 1997, which discusses the French, British, and Swedish models, whose results are reported in chapter 6). Nevertheless, several key features of the model have carried over to CGE models constructed for other countries or time periods. First, all the models distinguish between agricultural and nonagricultural labor, although labor is partially mobile between town and countryside. Second, capital is assumed to be mobile throughout the economy. Third, land is used only in agriculture. Fourth, we incorporate as many intermediate inputs as the data allow. Fifth, factor prices are never assumed to be independent of factor supplies. This is avoided by having more factors than traded goods, as above; or by assuming that domestic, imported and exported goods are imperfect substitutes for each other; or by assuming some combination of the two. The latter "Armington" assumption implies that the commodity prices facing domestic producers are not exogenous, even in traded goods sectors.

More detailed descriptions of the CGE models used in the book can be found in the journal articles cited in the text, and in the working papers cited therein.

Notes

Chapter 2

1. These are wage rates, usually weekly, rather than annual earnings. As such, they do not reflect changes in unemployment generated by industrial crisis or changes in seasonal labor utilization rates. They are therefore most effective in speaking to long-run changes in the cost of labor and living standards.

2. Purchasing power parity, or PPP, calculations are difficult but essential to be sure that the same yardstick is being used to compare the purchasing power of the wage received in one country with that in the next. The idea is to construct some average market basket and then to cost out that basket by applying prices for the same commodites country by country. See Williamson (1995).

3. Of course, such a statement involves a value judgment, but so does the decision to focus on average incomes alone.

4. The statistic C is defined as the variance of real wage rates across countries, divided by the square of their mean, equivalent to the coefficient of variation, but easier to decompose.

5. Per capita incomes were still quite a bit higher in England, but real wages were quite a different matter.

6. For example, Robert Margo (1992) has nothing to say about the impressive antebellum U.S. real wage growth performance compared to Britain and the rest of Europe.

7. And thus Maddison (1982, 92) calls it the "liberal" phase.

8. The time series in figure 2.2 labeled I-13 and N-15 will be discussed below.

9. Abramovitz (1986, 398), O'Rourke (1989, 1995a), and Boyer, Hatton, and O'Rourke (1994) all make the same point.

10. For the classic paper, see Watkins (1963).

11. Abramovitz (1986, table 1, 391) found the same.

12. See also Abramovitz (1986, 395) and Wolff (1991, 569).

Chapter 3

1. As late as 1874, steamships carried 90 percent of the ginger, 90 percent of the pop-pyseed, 90 percent of the tea, and 99 percent of the cowhides from Calcutta to Britain, but only 40 percent of the jute cuttings and one-third of the rice (Fletcher 1958, 561).

2. Gilpin (1975), Kindleberger (1973), and Krasner (1976) are just three of a vast number of references on the topic.

3. These figures imply that transport costs from Chicago to Liverpool were about 19 percent of the New York wheat price in 1868.

4. Harley's (1980) data tell a similar story.

5. This section draws heavily on O'Rourke and Williamson (1994).

6. Harley (1992c) also finds transatlantic price convergence for meat.

7. Sugar was the only exception to the price convergence rule. It should also be noted, however, that the decline in raw cotton price differentials was very modest.

8. Surprisingly, there is no evidence of price convergence for Swedish export-oriented industries such as iron and lumber. We have no explanation for this anomaly, although Marvin McInnis (1993) has warned about the problems of comparability surrounding lumber prices in world markets at this time.

9. The appearance of the Suez Canal and cost-reducing innovations on seagoing transport prior to 1914 did not completely free Asia from the tyranny of distance. Radelet, Sachs, and Lee (1997) have shown that growth performance even in the late twentieth century is still influenced by whether a country is landlocked, by the length of its coastline, and by its distance from Tokyo, New York, and Europe.

Chapter 4

1. The factor price equalization (FPE) theorem states that in equilibrium, given a variety of restrictive assumptions, factor prices will be equal across countries. Clearly such equilibriums are not observed in practice. In this chapter we do not test the FPE theorem (which relates to equilibrium outcomes) but the looser intuition that commodity price convergence induces factor price convergence (which relates to a process), put forward by Heckscher and Ohlin. See Leamer (1995) on the process-outcome distinction and the appendix to this book.

2. Sweden switched to protection relatively late, which is why it is included, somewhat arbitrarily, in the "free trade" group. See chapter 6.

3. Based on O'Rourke, Taylor, and Williamson (1996, table 2, 505), which reports predicted values from regressions run on time and time squared, of the time series underlying the figures. Spanish figure updated, reflecting the revisions to Williamson's (1995) wage database underlying O'Rourke and Williamson (1997).

4. Lawrence and Slaughter (1993) and Leamer (1994, 1995) are among the economists who have made this point most forcefully.

5. There are various surveys available in the literature. Dervis, DeMelo, and Robinson (1982) offer one for development. Shoven and Whalley (1984) offer another for trade and

public finance, as well as a more recent overview (1992). James (1984), Thomas (1987), and O'Rourke (1995b) offer others for economic history.

6. On the other hand, Davis (1995) shows that intraindustry trade can also be accounted for by more traditional models in which trade is driven by technological differences as well as factor endowments.

7. Indeed, recent papers by Davis, Weinstein, Bradford, and Shimpo (1997) and Harrigan (1997) also find strong empirical support for the Heckscher-Ohlin view of trade, based on late-twentieth-century data.

8. Estevadeordal (1997) considers endowments of capital, land, minerals, and skilled and unskilled labor.

9. This section draws on O'Rourke and Williamson (1994, 1995b).

10. Such a formulation is entirely consistent with the worldview of Heckscher and Ohlin, who were concerned with the intercontinental exchange of agricultural for manufacturing goods. It is not consistent with the "Heckscher-Ohlin-Samuelson" model of international trade, which assumes only two goods and two factors of production. In our British model, for example, there are two traded goods (agriculture and manufacturing), one nontraded good, and three factors of production (land, labor, and capital), while in the U.S. model there is a second agricultural sector (industrial crops). The British model is thus closer in spirit to the sector-specific factors model described in the econometric section below; but unlike that model, it allows for capital to be used in agriculture as well as industry and incorporates intermediate inputs. The CGE models differ from simple textbook trade theory in other ways. See the appendix, which gives a simple account of the "Heckscher-Ohlin-Samuelson" and sector-specific factors models, as well as the British and U.S. models used in this chapter.

11. O'Rourke and Williamson (1995b, 921). These estimates are derived from simple partial equilibrium models of the world markets for food and manufactured goods: world supply for each of these commodities must equal world demand, where the world is divided into the Old and New Worlds. Supply and demand in each region depend on local prices: Old World food prices equal New World prices plus transport costs, while New World manufactured goods prices equal Old World prices plus transport costs. See O'Rourke and Williamson (1994, 1995b). The method requires information about the share of various commodities in agricultural and manufacturing output in the two countries, as well as information about the production and consumption of manufactures and food in the Old and New Worlds, and estimates of supply and demand elasticities for the two commodities. It would, of course, be more intellectually satisfying to model the impact of technological change in the transportation sector directly, in the context of a CGE model of the global economy, but the data needed for such an exercise are not available.

12. O'Rourke and Williamson (1995b, revised table 3, 922).

13. O'Rourke and Williamson (1995a, table 2.4, 203).

14. The section draws heavily on joint work with Alan Taylor (O'Rourke, Taylor, and Williamson 1996).

15. More generally, the three-factor two-good model could be used to motivate the equation we estimate, although in this case the sign of the effect of prices on the wage-rental ratio is indeterminate (Thompson 1985, 1986). See O'Rourke, Taylor, and Williamson (1996).

16. The textbook specific factors model assumes a particularly simple production structure so that analytical results can be easily derived. Recall that the CGE model was able to incorporate several real-world additions to the model: intermediate inputs, capital inputs into agriculture, and imperfectly mobile labor. It makes sense to rely on simpler general equilibrium models when deriving equations to be estimated econometrically.

17. Note that this specification treats the economy-wide Solow residual as exogenous, rather than incorporating a model of biased technological change, as is implicit in the work of Habakkuk (1962).

18. The arithmetic is trivial. Let national income (Y) equal the sum of wages (wL, the wage per worker times the total labor force) and land rents (rD, rent per hectare times total hectares), ignoring skills, capital and all else: $Y = wL + rD$. Then per worker income growth is (where an asterisk refers to the percentage growth over the full fifteen years):

$$Y^* - L^* = w^*\theta_L + L^*(\theta_L - 1) + r^*\theta_D.$$

We assume that labor (θ_L) and land's share (θ_D) exhausted national income and that labor got 60 percent. We also assume that land hectarage was fixed and that labor force growth (assumed equal to population growth) was 7.6 percent between 1850 and 1870 (Maddison 1995, 106).

Chapter 5

1. The first argument can be traced back to Porter (1851, 139, 141–142) and McCulloch (1837, 1:551). The second is discussed below.

2. Animal products had a tariff of only 5.3 percent, and effective protection on manufacturing was probably negative (Williamson 1990b, 128–129). Solar and van Zanden (1996) estimate a higher rate of protection on animal products, but grain tariffs are of chief concern in this chapter.

3. Assuming that Britain was a sufficiently important player in global raw materials markets.

4. The foreign elasticity of demand for British exports is taken to be 1.1, as estimated by Irwin (1988); the foreign elasticity of raw materials supply is taken to be 0.5 (similar to estimates of U.S. cotton supply elasticities). World prices of grains and nongrains are still taken to be exogenous.

5. Feinstein (1972, table 118) cited in Ó Gráda (1994a, table 6.1).

6. O'Rourke (1997b) presents some preliminary findings on the connection between tariffs and growth in the late nineteenth century.

7. O'Rourke (1989, appendix 3.1 and 1991, table 4, 412); Ó Gráda (1993, table 29, 154). See Turner (1996) for an extensive discussion of postfamine trends in Irish agriculture.

8. The Rybczynski theorem states, roughly, that those sectors that use a given factor of production relatively intensively will benefit most by an economy-wide increase in the endowment of that factor. Thus, an increase in land-labor ratios would have favored Irish land-intensive pastoral activities, while a decline in the land-labor ratio would have favored Irish labor-intensive tillage activities.

9. The average Anglo-American real wage gap in the 1830s was 52.8 percent. It was to get bigger in the 1840s and 1850s, before the convergence up to the mid-1890s.

Chapter 6

1. Several sections of this chapter rely heavily on O'Rourke (1997a).

2. Imperial China forgot the art of building large ships between 1430 and 1553, having previously reached the east coast of Africa, but this politically induced move toward isolation remains the exception rather than the rule (Jones 1981, 204–205).

3. Bairoch (1989) provides an excellent introduction, and we draw largely on his work in this account. Tracy (1989) is another good source.

4. Cotton, wool, and flax were among the agricultural raw materials that escaped heavy tariffs, ensuring high effective rates of protection for the import-competing textile industries.

5. It did, however, impose tariffs on various manufactured goods: manufactured textiles faced duties of between 20 and 25 percent (Bairoch 1989, 81).

6. Denmark protected its manufacturing sector more than is commonly recognized, and Norwegian protection was quite high on the eve of World War I.

7. Late-nineteenth-century tariffs were specific. They are converted to their ad valorem equivalents by dividing the specific tariff by a notional world price, set equal to the domestic price minus the specific tariff.

8. Note the even higher protection for German oats.

9. Note that the wheat price data cited here are not quite the same as those used earlier by O'Rourke and Williamson (1994). This fact accounts for the modest differences between the wheat price gaps reported here and those reported in chapter 3 (which relied on the alternative data).

10. European prices are market averages, while U.S. prices are for particular grades of grain. U.S. wheat prices were adjusted in an attempt to correct for this discrepancy. Trends in transatlantic price gaps will be reliable unless the mix of European wheat grades was changing significantly and systematically over time.

11. As we saw in chapter 5, these conclusions assume that world prices were exogenous and that the country concerned was "small" in world commodity markets. Continental European economies were indeed "small" in this sense, and so was Britain by the 1870s.

12. This was not universally the case; for example, the picture in France was mixed. The discussion that follows in the text is based on Bairoch (1989).

13. The econometric estimates range between 0.46 and 0.52, and control for the capital-labor ratio, the land-labor ratio, the economy-wide Solow residual, and meat and manufactured goods prices.

14. CGE estimates suggest a similar impact on Swedish rents but a much smaller impact on French rents (4 percent).

15. Note that a relatively large proportion of Sweden's agricultural labor force worked in the forestry sector, which helps explain why Swedish real wages would have been largely unaffected by this price shock, rather than lowered, as in France.

16. For surveys of the U.S. debate, see Taussig (1888) or Ashley (1905), on which the following section largely draws.

17. The western states were rewarded by internal improvements financed by the tariff revenues.

18. The objection might have been made (as it was during the Gore-Perot debate on NAFTA) that low-wage labor is not necessarily cheap: competitiveness depends not just on wages but on labor productivity, and this is typically higher in high-wage economies. Indeed, in a well-known article, Gregory Clark (1987) provided evidence that cotton mill workers were a lot more productive in high-wage than in low-wage economies in 1910, and that this productivity advantage could not be explained by superior technology or higher capital-labor ratios. We return to this argument in chapter 12.

19. This situation would change drastically later, as Egypt and India became important suppliers. Note the similarity with the British case, discussed in chapter 5. Both countries enjoyed an initial period of market power, which eventually disappeared in the face of foreign competition.

20. Leonard Tilley, the new finance minister, speaking in 1879 (cited in McDiarmid 1946, 161).

21. Oddly enough, modern analysis suggests that the Victorian tariffs would have reduced employment since Victorian export industries were actually more labor intensive than Victorian import industries (Siriwardana 1991).

Chapter 7

1. This chapter draws heavily on a collaboration between Timothy Hatton and one of us (Hatton and Williamson 1998, chapters 2, 3).

2. Australia and Brazil offer good counterexamples. Both went through periods when generous subsidies were used to encourage immigration. To a lesser but still significant extent, the same was true of Argentina and Canada. Chapter 10 will have far more to say about these issues.

3. Note that table 7.2, row B, reports Swedish figures of 36.7 and 59.9, respectively, for the 1870s and 1900–1913, a bit different from the figures of 33 and 56 reported in the text. The explanation is that not all Swedes went to the United States, which is the comparison reported in the text. To repeat, table 7.2, row B, reports the country wage relative to a weighted average of all destination regions for that country.

4. Taylor (1994a) offers detailed evidence of this segmentation, and its impact on real wage convergence and divergence in the Atlantic economy was profound. Although migration from Europe to the New World certainly closed the gap between the two, it also served to widen the gap between Latin America and North America.

5. Guinnane (1997) offers further evidence that late-nineteenth-century Irish demographic trends were not, as often supposed, deviant but consistent with rational economic behavior.

6. Chapter 13 will see whether this proposition can be generalized to the Atlantic economy as a whole or whether the complementarity is a Spanish eccentricity.

Chapter 8

1. This chapter relies heavily on a collaboration between Timothy Hatton and one of us (Hatton and Williamson 1998, chapters 8–10).

2. Mokyr and Ó Gráda (1982) provide a survey of the literature.

3. The model also assumes increasing returns to scale, an assumption still unsupported by the nineteenth-century evidence.

4. The evidence on the latter point is mixed (Mokyr and Ó Gráda 1982).

5. The following section draws heavily on a collaboration between George Boyer, Timothy Hatton, and one of us (Boyer, Hatton, and O'Rourke 1994).

6. By the 1950s at least, the assumption of capital mobility would evidently have been preferred by the Irish Commission on Population, which observed, "Irish capital formed part of the world market and Irish industrial projects had to compete for capital with the opportunities for investment, not only in Great Britain but throughout the world" (1954, 26).

7. Even perfect capital mobility is only a partial offset. After all, more capital and labor in the no-emigration world would have to work with the same amount of land. This would be especially important in agrarian economies like Ireland, Sweden, and other emigrating countries, where (fixed) land endowments were such important inputs to economy-wide output performance.

8. Using the average 21 percent figure for emigration-induced Irish wage increases.

9. These wage comparisons are based on three-year averages centered around 1870 and 1910. Swedish real wages in 1870 (as shown in table 2.1) were unusually low.

10. Again, based on three-year averages centered on 1870 and 1910.

11. The United States absorbed 90 percent of the Danish emigrants and 97 percent of the Norwegian emigrants.

12. The term comes from Sidney Pollard (1978), who characterized the Irish in early industrializing Britain in the same way. Williamson (1986) disagreed. The exchange between Pollard and Williamson over the impact of the Irish immigrants on British workers from the 1820s to the 1850s exactly parallels this later debate in America.

13. The smaller labor market effects cited elsewhere in this chapter for the United States (immigration raised the labor force by 24 percent in 1910, table 8.1) exclude the children of the foreign-born, while they are included here.

14. This result was also confirmed using a CGE model for the 1890–1913 period (Williamson and Lindert 1980).

15. And thus immigration lowered real wages by 8 percent. Note again that this labor force estimate counted the children of immigrants.

16. This section draws heavily on Taylor and Williamson (1997).

17. Note the similarity between the econometric estimates in table 8.1 and the CGE estimates for Ireland, Sweden, and the United States reported earlier.

18. Readers who suspect that these large impacts are driven by unusually small labor demand elasticities estimated on late-nineteenth-century evidence should be reassured

by a reading of Taylor and Williamson (1997), from whence these results are taken: the elasticities estimated on late-nineteenth-century evidence fall right in the middle of those estimated for the post–World War II period (Hammermesh 1993).

19. Barriers to exit did exist in countries outside our Atlantic economy sample; for example, most emigration from Russia was illegal. On this, and for a more detailed discussion of migration policy, see Foreman-Peck (1992) and chapter 10.

Chapter 9

1. This chapter draws heavily on Williamson (1997a).

2. The impact on overall southern inequality is ambiguous, since in some cases basic skilled wages may rise relative to unskilled wages, while in other cases they may fall.

3. The academic literature on the topic has exploded, and the 1995 *World Development Report* was primarily devoted to the issue.

4. Some evidence on late-nineteenth-century inequality trends has been collected by economic historians since Simon Kuznets published his presidential address to the American Economic Association in 1955. For surveys, see Brenner, Kaelble, and Thomas (1990), Williamson (1991, chapter 1), and Lindert (1997). They seem to offer some support for the view that inequality was on the rise in the United States before World War I while it had been falling in Britain since the 1860s. But the Atlantic economy coverage is not sufficiently comprehensive to be used in the pre-1914 discussion that follows. The documentation does improve in coverage and quality for the interwar period.

5. Recent studies of the Third World globalization-inequality connection also tend to focus on wage inequality, and sometimes even on only urban wage inequality. This is a big mistake for countries where rural wage employment is significant and landed interests are powerful. Surely the economic position of landlords and rural labor matters in economies where agriculture is one-fifth, one-quarter, or even one-third of the economy.

6. We invoke poetic license here. Recall that the "wage-rental ratio" is being approximated by the ratio of wage rates to farm land values. Farm rents are documented only for Britain in our eleven-country Atlantic economy sample, while farm land values are documented for all of them (O'Rourke, Taylor, and Williamson 1996).

7. This was certainly true of Europe, Argentina, and the American South, but less true for the American Midwest and Canada, where the family farm dominated.

8. The Kuznets curve is to be distinguished from the Kuznets cycle, which we will meet in chapters 12 and 13.

9. Chapter 6 offered one possible explanation for this finding. Free trade in grain raised real wages in highly industrial Britain, thus lowering inequality, but it lowered real wages in more heavily agricultural France, thus raising inequality.

Chapter 10

1. This chapter draws heavily on two collaborations involving Ashley Timmer and one of us (Timmer and Williamson 1996, 1998).

2. And they had been very high in the United States since the Civil War (chapter 6).

3. After World War II, a focus on human rights developed; most Western countries changed their immigration policies to provide for special consideration of political refugees. Prior to the 1930s, such classifications did not exist.

4. This, it turns out, is a reasonable assumption by the 1890s, at least for U.S. manufacturing (Hanes 1993, 1996).

5. In 1890, 54 percent of the U.S. labor force was in agriculture. The share was also 54 percent in Canada in 1891, but a bit lower in the rest of the immigrating overseas regions like Argentina (21 percent in 1895), Australia (38 percent in 1901), and New Zealand (40 percent in 1896). See Mitchell (1983, 150–159).

6. WTOY is plotted by the dotted line in each graph. Note also that the Australia (AUW-TOY2) index is lagged two years, while the Canadian (CAWTOY4) and United States (USWTOY4) indexes are both lagged four years. These offered the best fits in the regression analysis.

7. About 60 percent of the total emigration out of Europe was to the United States (Hatton and Williamson 1998, chapter 2), and about 70 percent of the total emigration to our five-country New World sample was to the United States.

8. Furthermore, the econometric estimates of this effect are likely to be biased downward since open immigration policy implies more immigrants and lower WTOY, as we have seen in chapter 9.

9. These results emerged in the individual countries' time series. The panel data regression reported in table 10.1 uses two immigrant quality variables: IMWAGE is the wage in the country of origin, and THREAT uses information on both quality and quantity. IMWAGE has the wrong sign in the panel data regressions, and THREAT has the right sign.

Chapter 11

1. Based on data given in Jones and Obstfeld (1997).

2. For example, Japanese and German current account surpluses in the mid- and late 1980s peaked at around 4 or 5 percent of GDP (IMF 1997, 165).

3. For the years 1885–1910; based on data kindly supplied by Alan Taylor.

4. In addition to this Anglo-American evidence, Craig and Fisher (1997, 208–219) show that both real and nominal interest rates were "generally pretty strongly correlated" (p. 220) across European countries between 1870 and 1913.

5. Australia, Belgium, Canada, France, Germany, Italy, the Netherlands, Sweden, the United Kingdom, and the United States. The estimates that follow in the text are taken from Obstfeld and Taylor (1998, table 11.3, 366).

6. Lothian (1995) presents similar evidence on real interest rates, but finds no great change in the dispersion of nominal interest rates from 1880 onward.

7. In addition, Jones and Obstfeld (1997) provide improved current account data and improved versions of the Feldstein and Horioka test for the pre-1945 period, both designed to take proper account of the role of gold flows in an era when gold was a significant reserve asset.

8. Taken from the *Economist* (November 22, 1997).

9. Published in English as Servan-Schreiber (1968).

10. Hymer's dissertation was published later (Hymer 1976). What has become a vast literature on the subject is ably surveyed in Caves (1996).

11. Vertically integrated MNCs arise for different reasons, of the type identified by Oliver Williamson (1971).

12. Eichengreen (1996) provides a highly readable introduction to the subject.

13. The issue is not quite settled, however, given that Taylor's (1996a) evidence reproduced in figure 11.3 suggests the opposite (based, however, on a different sample of countries).

Chapter 12

1. However, the Hobson-Lenin explanation for imperialism is at odds with the evidence that British capital went to the frontier rather than to Britain's African or Asian colonies (Fieldhouse 1961, 199).

2. For example, savings amounted to around 9 percent of GDP in the early 1850s, but around 15 percent of GDP in the early 1870s (figure 11.1; Edelstein 1982).

3. The Danish and Norwegian figures were derived on the assumption that capital stock-wage elasticities were the same throughout Scandinavia.

4. BPP (1896, 174, supplement to table 3). When official Irish trade statistics began to be compiled in 1904, they showed a mixed pattern but with deficits more common up to 1913.

5. See, for example, the discussion in the 1895 Royal Commission's minutes of evidence (BPP 1896, 3–4) or Solar (1979, 24).

6. The Italian capital import figures are given in Fenoaltea (1988, table 4, 620–621).

7. In personal communications.

8. The exceptions being 1876 and 1883 (Prados 1988, 252–254).

9. Based on unpublished estimates by Prados.

10. Cited in Lains (1992, 215–216).

11. Mata (1995) suggests that capital inflows can have had only a small aggregate impact on the Portuguese economy, but that they were important in particular sectors. His estimates suggest that foreign capital accounted for 12 percent of net investment between 1851 and 1890 and 42 percent of net investment between 1891 and 1913. However, he uses official trade statistics. Lains's revisions would imply much smaller percentages.

12. The same question may apply to Russia and the rest of eastern and central Europe.

13. This assumes a common Cobb-Douglas technology and a capital share of 0.4.

14. Higgins's work has since been updated by Taylor (1996b).

15. Of course, it may be that the best and the brightest workers emigrated, an untestable but commonly asserted hypothesis.

16. Higgins's suggestion is that total factor productivity is lower in some countries than in others, while Clark is concerned with the efficiency of labor; still, the two arguments are clearly similar.

17. The latter suggestion is pursued theoretically in O'Rourke (1992).

18. Bordo and Rockoff (1996, 398) argue that this was more true after 1903.

19. Taylor (1992a, table 3, 919).

20. A further factor inhibiting Argentine accumulation in the interwar period was the collapse of primary product prices after their wartime peak, lowering investment demand.

21. Argentina was the only major Latin American debtor not to default, but the benefits it gained by playing by the rules were slender (Jorgensen and Sachs 1989).

Chapter 13

1. This chapter is a revision and abridgment of a collaboration involving William Collins (Collins, O'Rourke, and Williamson 1997).

2. The sample includes Australia, Canada, Denmark, France, Germany, Italy, Norway, Sweden, the United Kingdom, and the United States.

3. The treatment here follows Findlay (1995, chapter 1).

4. Corden and Neary (1982) consider the impact of a Hicks-neutral technological improvement in one sector and distinguish between the resource movement and spending effects of the associated boom.

5. With a fixed capital stock, output can increase only if the labor force increases and, consequently, capital-labor ratios fall.

6. Thompson (1985, 1986), for example, has shown that price movements can have paradoxical effects on rents and profits.

7. Such a model was outlined some time ago by Kemp and Ohyama (1978), even though they were interested in a different set of issues.

8. Immigration figures are gross; capital inflows are simply the negative of the current account, deflated by the GNP price deflator (spliced onto the wholesale price index which is used for years prior to 1869). Wheat exports are measured as deviations from a quadratic trend. All three series are rescaled for presentational purposes, and three-year moving averages are used in order to smooth out the series somewhat.

9. It is, appropriately, a deflated freight rate index, but it is a generic worldwide index rather than a country-specific index.

10. Tables 13.1 through 13.3 use a 10 percent level in the hypothesis testing, but the same qualitative results emerge when a 5 percent level is used. The only difference is that in the latter case, some complementarity results fall into the neutral category. In short, the substitutability hypothesis is still defeated. Those readers who have been paying attention to Deirdre McCloskey (1998) and Edward Leamer (1998b) lately should take note here. The complementarity result would hold more strongly if we ignored t-statistics altogether. For the prewar period, twenty-four of the twenty-seven migration coefficients

are positive, while fourteen of the thirty capital flow coefficients are positive. For the interwar period, twenty-two of the twenty-six migration coefficients are positive, while nineteen of the twenty-nine capital flow coefficients are positive.

11. Nevertheless, an effort was made to develop a measure of the distance between endowment and factor consumption points that includes the necessary scaling; see Collins, O'Rourke, and Williamson (1997, 15–16).

12. This finding is echoed in the empirical literature on trade, foreign domestic investment, and multinational corporations (Grubert and Mutti 1991).

13. This section draws heavily on Timmer and Williamson (1996).

14. The tariff data for Australia, Canada, and the United States were taken from Collins, O'Rourke, and Williamson (1997). The Brazilian tariff data were available only from 1900 on and were derived from Mitchell (1983). Argentine tariffs were available only from 1895 and were derived from customs duty data in Mitchell (1983) and trade data in Taylor (1997). Details of the regressions cited in this section are available on request.

15. The coefficient suggested that a 10 percentage point increase in average tariffs was associated with an enormous 6.8 point decline in the migration policy index.

16. At least, the 2×2 version of Heckscher-Ohlin theory makes such a statement.

Chapter 14

1. This section draws heavily on O'Rourke and Williamson (1997).

2. This appears to place us in the Leamer (1998) and McCloskey (1998) camp: our ultimate interest is in the economic impact of the factors alleged to cause growth, not simply the statistical significance of the beta coefficient in some conditional convergence equation.

3. In the discussion, we emphasize results based on enrollment rates, since these are probably superior to our literacy rate estimates; see O'Rourke and Williamson (1997).

4. Columns headed "a" in table 14.2 report the labor force shocks given in Taylor and Williamson (1997) and that paper's econometric estimates of the real wage impact (as reported in table 8.1). Columns headed "b" report the independent labor force and CGE impact estimates in O'Rourke and Williamson (1997, table 6).

5. The Danish and Norwegian numbers are not always identical to the Swedish numbers, since the same increase in the domestic wage will imply different percentage changes in wage gaps for different countries.

6. This counterfactual implies that Irish agricultural prices would have been 21.4 percent higher than they actually were in 1908, while imported manufactured goods would have been 9.8 percent cheaper than they actually were.

7. When future research makes this assessment for Iberia properly, it will need to sort out the independent influence of tariffs and an undervalued domestic currency.

8. The North-South rhetoric refers to labor-scarce, rich, industrial economies versus labor-abundant, poor, agricultural economies. North always overlaps with temperate, and South almost always overlaps with tropical.

Appendix

1. We also assume away such complications as factor intensity reversals, since our purpose is to provide intuition rather than rigorous proof.

2. This is done by endowing the representative consumer with "raw" labor, which is transformed into agricultural and nonagricultural labor by an artifical sector characterized by a constant elasticity of transformation production function. The allocation of labor between sectors is thus responsive to wage gaps, but not perfectly so (i.e., the elasticity of transformation is finite, rather than infinite).

References

Abramovitz, M. (1961). ''The Nature and Significance of Kuznets Cycles.'' *Economic Development and Cultural Change* 9, 3:225–248.

Abramovitz, M. (1968). ''The Passing of the Kuznets Cycle.'' *Economica* 35:349–367.

Abramovitz, M. (1986). ''Catching Up, Forging Ahead, and Falling Behind.'' *Journal of Economic History* 46 (June):385–406.

ADB (Asian Development Bank). (1997). *Emerging Asia*. Manila: Asian Development Bank.

Aghion, P. (1998). ''Inequality and Economic Growth.'' In P. Aghion and J. G. Williamson, *Growth, Inequality and Globalization: Theory, History and Policy: The Mattioli Lectures.* Cambridge: Cambridge University Press.

A'Hearn, B. (1996). ''Institutions, Externalities, and Economic Development: Cotton Textiles and Regional Disparities in 19th Century Italy.'' Paper presented to the II Congress of the European Association of Historical Economics, Ca' Foscari University of Venice, January 19–20.

Ahluwalia, M. (1976). ''Inequality, Poverty and Development.'' *Journal of Development Economics* 3(4):307–342.

Akerman, S. (1976). ''Theories of Migration Research.'' In H. Rundblom and H. Norman (eds.), *From Sweden to America: A History of the Migration*. Minneapolis: University of Minnesota Press.

Alesina, A., and R. Perotti. (1994). ''The Political Economy of Growth: A Critical Survey of the Recent Literature.'' *World Bank Economic Review* 8, no. 3:351–371.

Allen, R. C. (1979). ''International Competition in Iron and Steel, 1850–1913.'' *Journal of Economic History* 49:911–937.

Anderson, J. E. (1995). ''Tariff Index Theory.'' *Review of International Economics* 3, no. 2: 156–173.

Anderson, J. E., and J. P. Neary. (1994). ''Measuring the Restrictiveness of Trade Policy.'' *World Bank Economic Review* 8 (May):151–169.

Arrow, K. J. (1962). ''The Economic Implications of Learning by Doing.'' *Review of Economic Studies* 29 (June):155–173.

Ashley, P. (1905). *Modern Tariff History: Germany–United States–France*. New York: E. P. Dutton.

Baer, W. (1964). "Regional Inequality and Economic Growth in Brazil." *Economic Development and Cultural Change* 12(April):268–285.

Bailey, W. B. (1912). "The Birds of Passage." *American Journal of Sociology* 18:391–397.

Baines, D. E. (1985). *Migration in a Mature Economy*. Cambridge: Cambridge University Press.

Baines, D. E. (1991). *Emigration from Europe, 1815–1930*. London: Macmillan.

Bairoch, P. (1972). "Free Trade and European Economic Development in the Nineteenth Century." *European Economic Review* 3:211–245.

Bairoch, P. (1976). "Europe's Gross National Product: 1800–1975." *Journal of European Economic History* 5 (May–August):273–340.

Bairoch, P. (1989). "European Trade Policy, 1815–1914." In P. Mathias and S. Pollard (eds.), *The Cambridge Economic History of Europe*, vol. 8. Cambridge: Cambridge University Press.

Bairoch, P. (1993). *Economics and World History: Myths and Paradoxes*. Chicago: University of Chicago Press.

Baldwin, R. E. (1969). "The Case Against Infant Industry Protection." *Journal of Political Economy* 77 (May–June):295–305.

Bardini, C., A. Carreras, and P. Lains. (1995). "The National Accounts for Italy, Spain and Portugal." *Scandinavian Economic History Review* 43, no. 1:115–146.

Barkin, K. D. (1970). *The Controversy over German Industrialization, 1890–1902*. Chicago: University of Chicago Press.

Barro, R. J. (1991). "Economic Growth in a Cross Section of Countries." *Journal of Political Economy* 106 (May):407–443.

Barro, R. J. (1996). "The Determinants of Economic Growth." *Lionel Robbins Lecture*, London School of Economics (February 20–22).

Barro, R. J., and X. Sala-i-Martin. (1991). "Convergence Across States and Regions." *Brookings Papers on Economic Activity* 1:107–182.

Barro, R. J., and X. Sala-i-Martin. (1992). "Convergence." *Journal of Political Economy* 100 (April):223–252.

Barro, R. J., and X. Sala-i-Martin. (1995). *Economic Growth*. New York: McGraw-Hill.

Bateman, F., and T. Weiss. (1976). "Manufacturing in the Antebellum South." *Research in Economic History* 1:1–44.

Bateman, F., and T. Weiss. (1981). *A Deplorable Scarcity*. Chapel Hill, N.C.: University of North Carolina Press.

Baumol, W. (1986). "Productivity Growth, Convergence and Welfare: What the Long-Run Data Show." *American Economic Review* 76 (December):1072–1085.

Baumol, W. J., S. A. B. Blackman, and E. N. Wolff. (1989). *Productivity and American Leadership: The Long View*. Cambridge, Mass.: MIT Press.

Bayoumi, T. (1989). "Saving-Investment Correlations: Immobile Capital, Government Policy or Endogenous Behavior?" *International Monetary Fund Staff Working Paper WP/ 89/66*, Washington, D.C. (August).

Bhagwati, J. N., and D. A. Irwin. (1987). "The Return of the Reciprocitarians: U.S. Trade Policy Today." *World Economy* 10:109–130.

Bils, M. (1984). "Tariff Protection and Production in the Early U.S. Cotton Textile Industry." *Journal of Economic History* 44, no. 4:1033–1045.

Blainey, G. (1966). *The Tyranny of Distance: How Distance Shaped Australia's History*. Rev. ed. Melbourne: Macmillan.

Bloom, D. E., and J. G. Williamson. (1997). "Demographic Transitions and Economic Miracles in Emerging Asia." NBER Working Paper No. 6268, National Bureau of Economic Research, Cambridge, Mass., November.

Board of Trade. (1903). "Memoranda, Statistical Tables and Charts Prepared in the Board of Trade . . . Foreign Trade and Industrial Conditions." *Parliamentary Papers* 67, Cd. 1761.

Bordo, M. D., and F. E. Kydland. (1995). "The Gold Standard as a Rule: An Essay in Exploration." *Explorations in Economic History* 32 (October):423–464.

Bordo, M. D., and H. Rockoff. (1996). "The Gold Standard as a 'Good Housekeeping Seal of Approval.'" *Journal of Economic History* 56, no. 2:389–428.

Borjas, G. (1994). "The Economics of Immigration." *Journal of Economic Literature* 32 (December):1667–1717.

Borjas, G., R. B. Freeman, and L. F. Katz. (1992). "On the Labor Market Impacts of Immigration and Trade." In G. Borjas and R. B. Freeman (eds.), *Immigration and the Work Force: Economic Consequences for the United States and Source Areas*. Chicago: University of Chicago Press.

Bourguignon, F., and C. Morrisson. (1991). *External Trade and Income Distribution*. Paris: OECD.

Boyer, G. R., T. J. Hatton, and K. H. O'Rourke. (1994). "Emigration and Economic Growth in Ireland, 1850–1914." In T. J. Hatton and J. G. Williamson (eds.), *Migration and the International Labor Market, 1850–1939*. London: Routledge.

Brandt, L. (1985). "Chinese Agriculture and the International Economy, 1870–1913: A Reassessment." *Explorations in Economic History* 22:168–180.

Brandt, L. (1993). "Interwar Japanese Agriculture: Revisionist Views on the Impact of the Colonial Rice Policy and Labor-Surplus Hypothesis." *Explorations in Economic History* 30:259–293.

Brenner, Y. S., H. Kaelble, and M. Thomas. (1990). *Income Distribution in Historical Perspective*. Cambridge: Cambridge University Press.

BPP. (1893–1894). *Royal Commission on Labour: The Agricultural Labourer, Assistant Commissioners' Reports on the Agricultural Labourer*. Vol. 4, *Ireland*. London: HMSO (C. 6894).

BPP. (1896). *Royal Commission on the "Financial Relations Between Great Britain and Ireland." Second Volume of Minutes of Evidence*. London: HMSO (C. 8008).

Broder, A. (1976). "Les Investissements Etrangers en Espagne au XIXe Siècle: Méthodologie et Quantification." *Revue d'Histoire Economique et Sociale* 54, no. 1:29–63.

Brown, S. R. (1979). "The Transfer of Technology to China in the Nineteenth Century: The Role of Direct Foreign Investment." *Journal of Economic History* 39 (March):181–197.

Buchinsky, M., and B. Polak. (1993). "The Emergence of a National Capital Market in England, 1710–1880." *Journal of Economic History* 53 (March):1–24.

Bulmer-Thomas, V. (1994). *The Economic History of Latin America Since Independence*. Cambridge: Cambridge University Press.

Burns, A. (1954). *The Frontiers of Economic Knowledge*. Princeton, N.J.: Princeton University Press.

Cairncross, A. (1953). *Home and Foreign Investment*. Cambridge: Cambridge University Press.

Cairnes, J. E. (1873). *Political Essays*. London: Macmillan.

Cameron, R. (1989). *A Concise Economic History of the World from Paleolithic Times to the Present*. New York: Oxford University Press.

Capie, F. (1983). "Tariff Protection and Economic Performance in the Nineteenth Century." In J. Black and L. A. Winters (eds.), *Policy and Performance in International Trade*. London: Macmillan.

Capie, F. (1994). *Tariffs and Growth: Some Insights from the World Economy, 1850–1940*. Manchester: Manchester University Press.

Caron, F. (1979). *An Economic History of Modern France*. London: Methuen.

Carlsson, S. (1976). "Chronology and Composition of Swedish Emigration to America." In H. Rundblom and H. Norman (eds.), *From Sweden to America; A History of the Migration*. Minneapolis: University of Minnesota Press.

Cassing, J., T. J. McKeown, and J. Ochs. (1986). "The Political Economy of the Tariff Cycle." *American Political Science Review* 80, no. 3 (September):843–862.

Caves, R. E. (1971). "International Corporations: The Industrial Economics of Foreign Investment." *Economica* 38 (February):1–27.

Caves, R. E. (1996). *Multinational Enterprise and Economic Analysis*. 2d ed. Cambridge: Cambridge University Press.

Chambers, E. J., and D. F. Gordon. (1966). "Primary Products and Economic Growth: An Empirical Measurement." *Journal of Political Economy* 74:315–322.

Chandler, A. D. (1977). *The Visible Hand: The Managerial Revolution in American Business*. Cambridge, Mass.: Belknap Press.

Cipolla, C. M. (1969). *Literacy and Development in the West*. London: Penguin.

Clark, G. (1987). "Why Isn't the Whole World Developed? Lessons from the Cotton Mills." *Journal of Economic History* 47, no. 1:141–173.

Coale, A. J., and E. Hoover. (1958). *Population Growth and Economic Development in Low-Income Countries*. Princeton, N.J.: Princeton University Press.

Coale, A. J., and S. C. Watkins. (eds.). (1986). *The Decline of Fertility in Europe*. Princeton, N.J.: Princeton University Press.

Collins, W. J. (1996). "Regional Labor Markets in British India." Mimeo. Cambridge, Mass.: Department of Economics, Harvard University.

Collins, W. J. (1997). "When the Tide Turned: Immigration and the Delay of the Great Migration." *Journal of Economic History* 57 (September):607–632.

Collins, W. J., K. H. O'Rourke, and J. G. Williamson. (1997). "Were Trade and Factor Mobility Substitutes in History?" NBER Working Paper No. 6059, National Bureau of Economic Research, Cambridge, Mass., June.

Collins, W. J., and J. G. Williamson (1999). "Capital Goods Prices, Global Capital Markets and Growth." Presented to the ASSA meetings, New York, January 3–5.

Coppa, F. J. (1970). "The Italian Tariff and the Conflict Between Agriculture and Industry: The Commercial Policy of Liberal Italy, 1860–1922." *Journal of Economic History* 30, no. 4:742–769.

Corden, W. M., and J. P. Neary. (1982). "Booming Sector and De-Industrialization in a Small Open Economy." *Economic Journal* 92:825–848.

Cortes-Conde, R. (1979). *El Progreso Argentino, 1880–1914*. Buenos Aires: Editorial Sudamericana.

Crafts, N. F. R., and T. C. Mills. (1994). "Trends in Real Wages in Britain, 1750–1913." *Explorations in Economic History* 31 (April):176–194.

Crafts, N. F. R., and M. Thomas. (1986). "Comparative Advantage in U.K. Manufacturing Trade 1910–1935." *Economic Journal* 96 (September):629–645.

Crafts, N. F. R., and G. Toniolo. (1996). *Economic Growth in Europe Since 1945*. Cambridge: Cambridge University Press.

Craig, L. A., and D. Fisher. (1997). *The Integration of the European Economy, 1850–1913*. New York: St. Martin's Press.

Crouzet, F. (1964). "Wars, Blockade, and Economic Change in Europe, 1792–1815." *Journal of Economic History* 24:567–588.

David, P. A. (1970). "Learning by Doing and Tariff Protection: A Reconsideration of the Case of the Ante-bellum United States Cotton Textile Industry." *Journal of Economic History* 30, no. 3:521–601.

David, P. A. (1975). *Technical Choice, Innovation and Economic Growth*. Cambridge: Cambridge University Press.

Davis, D. R. (1992). "Essays in the Theory of International Trade and Economic Growth." Ph.D. dissertation, Columbia University.

Davis, D. R. (1995). "Intra-Industry Trade: A Heckscher-Ohlin-Ricardo Approach." *Journal of International Economics* 34 (November):201–226.

Davis, D. R. (1996). "Trade Liberalization and Income Distribution." Mimeo. Cambridge, Mass.: Harvard University (June).

Davis, D. R., D. E. Weinstein, S. C. Bradford, and K. Shimpo. (1997). "Using International and Japanese Regional Data to Determine When the Factor Abundance Theory of Trade Works." *American Economic Review* 87 (June):421–446.

Davis, L. E. (1965). "The Investment Market, 1870–1914: The Evolution of a National Market." *Journal of Economic History* 25 (September):355–399.

DeCanio, S. J., and J. Mokyr. (1977). "Inflation and Wage Lag During the American Civil War." *Explorations in Economic History* 14 (October):311–336.

Deininger, K., and L. Squire. (1996). "A New Data Set Measuring Income Inequality." *World Bank Economic Review* 10:565–591.

DeLong, J. B. (1988). "Productivity Growth, Convergence and Welfare: Comment." *American Economic Review* 78 (December):1138–1154.

DeLong, J. B. (1992). "Productivity Growth and Machinery Investment: A Long-Run Look 1870–1980." *Journal of Economic History* 52, no. 2:307–324.

DeLong, J. B., and L. Summers. (1991). "Equipment Investment and Economic Growth." *Quarterly Journal of Economics* 106:445–502.

Dervis, K., J. DeMelo, and S. Robinson. (1982). *General Equilibrium Models for Development Policy*. Cambridge: Cambridge University Press.

Diaz-Alejandro, C. F. (1970). *Essays on the Economic History of the Argentine Republic*. New Haven, Conn.: Yale University Press.

Dowrick, S., and D.-T. Nguyen. (1989). "OECD Comparative Economic Growth 1950–85: Catch-Up and Convergence." *American Economic Review* 79 (December):1010–1030.

Dunlevy, J. A., and H. A. Gemery. (1977). "The Role of Migrant Stock and Lagged Migration in the Settlement Patterns of Nineteenth Century Immigrants." *Review of Economics and Statistics* 59:137–144.

Dunlevy, J. A., and H. A. Gemery. (1978). "Economic Opportunity and the Responses of Old and New Immigrants in the United States." *Journal of Economic History* 38:901–917.

Durlauf, S. N., and P. Johnson. (1992). "Local versus Global Convergence Across National Economies." Paper presented to the Conference on Economic Fluctuations, National Bureau of Economic Research, Cambridge, Mass., July.

Easterlin, R. A. (1960). "Interregional Differences in Per Capita Income, Population, and Total Income, 1840–1950." In *Trends in the American Economy in the Nineteenth Century*. Princeton, N.J.: Princeton University Press.

Easterlin, R. A. (1961). "Influence on European Overseas Emigration Before World War I." *Economic Development and Cultural Change* 9:33–51.

Easterlin, R. A. (1966). "Economic-Demographic Interactions and Long Swings in Economic Growth."*American Economic Review* 56:1063–1104.

Easterlin, R. A. (1968). *Population, Labor Force and Long Swings in Economic Growth*. New York: National Bureau of Economic Research.

Easterlin, R. A. (1971). "Regional Income Trends 1840–1950." In R. W. Fogel and S. L. Engerman (eds.), *The Reinterpretation of American Economic History*. New York: Harper and Row.

Easterlin, R. A. (1981). "Why Isn't the Whole World Developed?" *Journal of Economic History* 41:1–19.

Eckaus, R. (1961). "The North-South Differential in Italian Economic Development." *Journal of Economic History* 20:285–317.

Edelstein, M. (1976). "Realized Rates of Return on U.K. Home and Overseas Portfolio Investment in the Age of High Imperialism." *Explorations in Economic History* 13:283–329.

Edelstein, M. (1981). "Foreign Investment and Empire 1860–1914." In R. Floud and D. N. McCloskey (eds.), *The Economic History of Britain Since 1700*, vol. 2. Cambridge: Cambridge University Press.

Edelstein, M. (1982). *Overseas Investment in the Age of High Imperialism*. New York: Columbia University Press.

Edelstein, M. (1994). "Foreign Investment and Accumulation, 1860–1914." In R. C. Floud and D. N. McCloskey (eds.), *The Economic History of Britain Since 1700*, vol. 2. Cambridge: Cambridge University Press.

Eichengreen, B. (1990). "Trends and Cycles in Foreign Lending." In H. Siebert (ed.), *Capital Flows in the World Economy*. Tubingen: Mohr.

Eichengreen, B. (1992). *Golden Fetters: The Gold Standard and the Great Depression, 1919–1939*. Oxford: Oxford University Press.

Eichengreen, B. (1996). *Globalizing Capital: A History of the International Monetary System*. Princeton, N.J.: Princeton University Press.

Eichengreen, B., and P. H. Lindert. (1991). *The International Debt Crisis in Historical Perspective*. Cambridge, Mass.: MIT Press.

Eichengreen, B., and R. Portes. (1986). "Debt and Default in the 1930s." *European Economic Review* (June):599–640.

Eltis, D. (1983). "Free and Coerced Transatlantic Migrations: Some Comparisons." *American Historical Review* 88:251–280.

Erickson, C. (1990). "Emigration from the British Isles to the U.S.A. in 1841: Part 2. Who Were the English Emigrants?" *Population Studies* 44:21–40.

Estevadeordal, A. (1997). "Measuring Protection in the Early Twentieth Century." *European Review of Economic History* 1:89–125.

Ethier, W. (1982). "Decreasing Costs in International Trade and Frank Graham's Argument for Protection." *Econometrica* 50:1243–1268.

Eversley, Lord. (1907). "The Decline in the Number of Agricultural Labourers in Great Britain." *Journal of the Royal Statistical Society* 70:267–306.

Faini, R. (1991). "Regional Development and Economic Integration." In J. da Silva Lopes and L. Beleza (eds.), *Portugal and the Internal Market of the EEC*. Lisbon: Banco de Portugal.

Faini, R., and A. Venturini. (1994a). "Italian Migrations: The Pre-War Period." In T. J. Hatton and J. G. Williamson (eds.), *Migration and the International Labor Market, 1850–1939*. London: Routledge.

Faini, R., and A. Venturini. (1994b). "Migration and Growth: The Experience of Southern Europe." Centre for Economic Policy Research Discussion Paper 964, CEPR, London.

Fairlie, S. (1965). "The Nineteenth Century Corn Law Reconsidered." *Economic History Review* 18:562–575.

Fairlie, S. (1969). "The Corn Laws and British Wheat Production, 1829–76." *Economic History Review* 22:88–116.

Federico, G. (1988). "Commercio Estero e 'Periferie': Il Caso dei Paesi Mediterranei." *Meridiana* 4:163–196.

Federico, G. (1992). "El Comercio Exterior de los Paises Mediterraneos en el Siglo XIX." In L. Prados de la Escosura and V. Zamagni (eds.), *El Desarrollo Económico en la Europa del Sur: España e Italia en Perspectiva Histórica*. Madrid: Alianza.

Federico, G., and G. Toniolo. (1991). "Italy." In R. Sylla and G. Toniolo (eds.), *Patterns of European Industrialization*. London: Routledge.

Feenstra, R., and G. Hanson. (1995). "Foreign Investment, Outsourcing and Relative Wages." In R. C. Feenstra, G. M. Grossman, and D. A. Irwin (eds.), *Political Economy of Trade Policy: Essays in Honor of Jagdish Bhagwati*. Cambridge, Mass.: MIT Press.

Feinstein, C. H. (1972). *National Income, Expenditure and Output of the United Kingdom*. Cambridge: Cambridge University Press.

Feis, H. (1930). *Europe, the World's Banker 1870–1914*. New Haven, Conn.: Yale University Press.

Feldstein, M., and C. Horioka. (1980). "Domestic Saving and International Capital Flows." *Economic Journal* 90 (June):314–329.

Feliciano, Z. (1995). "Workers and Trade Liberalization: The Impact of Trade Reforms in Mexico on Wages and Employment." Mimeo. Department of Economics, Queens College of CUNY, Flushing, New York.

Fenoaltea, S. (1988). "International Resource Flows and Construction Movements in the Atlantic Economy: The Kuznets Cycle in Italy, 1861–1913." *Journal of Economic History* 48, no. 3:605–637.

Ferenczi, I., and W. F. Willcox. (1929). *International Migrations*, vol. 1. New York: National Bureau of Economics Research.

Fieldhouse, D. K. (1961). " 'Imperialism': An Historiographical Revision." *Economic History Review* 2d ser.,14, no. 2:187–209.

Findlay, R. F. (1995). *Factor Proportions, Trade, and Growth*. Cambridge, Mass.: MIT Press.

Fishlow, A. (1989). "Conditionality and Willingness to Pay: Some Parallels from the 1890s." In B. Eichengreen and P. H. Lindert (eds.), *The International Debt Crisis in Historical Perspective*. Cambridge, Mass.: MIT Press.

Fitzpatrick, D. (1983). "Irish Farming Families Before the First World War." *Comparative Studies in Society and History* 25:339–374.

Flam, H., and M. J. Flanders. (1991). *Heckscher-Ohlin Trade Theory*. Cambridge, Mass.: MIT Press.

Fletcher, M. E. (1958). "The Suez Canal and World Shipping, 1869–1914." *Journal of Economic History* 18:556–573.

Floud, R. C. (1994). "Britain, 1860–1914: A Survey." In R. C. Floud and D. N. McCloskey (eds.), *The Economic History of Britain Since 1700*, vol. 2. Cambridge: Cambridge University Press.

Fogel, R. W. (1967). "The Specification Problem in Economic History." *Journal of Economic History* 27 (September):283–308.

Foreman-Peck, J. S. (1992). "A Political Economy of International Migration, 1815–1914." *Manchester School* 60:359–376.

Foreman-Peck, J. (1995). *A History of the World Economy*. Harvester Wheatsheaf: Hempstead, England.

Frankel, J. A. (1982). "The 1807–1809 Embargo Against Great Britain." *Journal of Economic History* 52, no. 2:291–308.

Freeman, R. (1995). "Are Your Wages Set in Beijing?" *Journal of Economic Perspectives* 9 (Summer):15–32.

Friedman, M. (1992). "Do Old Fallacies Never Die?" *Journal of Economic Literature* 76 (December):2129–2132.

Galenson, D. (1984). "The Rise and Fall of Indentured Servitude in the Americas: An Economic Analysis." *Journal of Economic History* 44:1–26.

Garbade, K. D., and W. L. Silber. (1978). "Technology, Communication and the Performance of Financial Markets: 1840–1975." *Journal of Finance* 33 (June):819–832.

Geary, R. C. (1935–36). "The Future Population of Saorstát Eireann and Some Observations on Population Statistics." *Journal of the Statistical and Social Inquiry Society of Ireland* 15:15–32.

Gerschenkron, A. (1943). *Bread and Democracy in Germany*. Berkeley: University of California Press.

Gerschenkron, A. (1962). *Economic Backwardness in Historical Perspective*. Cambridge, Mass.: Harvard University Press.

Gibbon, P., and C. Curtain. (1978). "The Stem Family in Ireland." *Comparative Studies in Society and History* 20:429–453.

Gilpin, R. (1975). *U.S. Power and the Multinational Corporation: The Political Economy of Foreign Direct Investment*. New York: Basic Books.

Girard, L. (1966). "Transport." In H. J. Habbakuk and M. M. Postan (eds.), *The Cambridge Economic History of Europe*, vol. 6: *The Industrial Revolution and After: Incomes, Population and Technological Change*. Cambridge: Cambridge University Press.

Goldin, C. (1994). "The Political Economy of Immigration Restriction in the United States, 1890 to 1921." In C. Goldin and G. D. Libecap (eds.), *The Regulated Economy: A Historical Approach to Political Economy*. Chicago: University of Chicago Press.

Goldin, C., and F. D. Lewis. (1975). "The Economic Costs of the American Civil War: Estimates and Implications." *Journal of Economic History* 35:299–326.

Goldin, C., and R. A. Margo. (1992). "The Great Compression: The Wage Structure in the United States at Mid-Century." *Quarterly Journal of Economics* 107:1–34.

Good, D. F. (1984). *The Economic Rise of the Habsburg Empire, 1750–1914*. Berkeley: University of California Press.

Goodwin, B. K., and T. J. Grennes. (1998). "Tsarist Russia and the World Wheat Market." *Explorations in Economic History* 35:405–430.

Goreux, L. M. (1956). "Les Migrations Agricoles in France Depuis un Siècle et leur Relation avec Certains Facteurs Economiques." *Etudes et Conjuncture* 11 (April):327–376.

Gould, J. D. (1979). "European Inter-continental Emigration, 1815–1914: Patterns and Causes." *Journal of European Economic History* 8:593–679.

Gould, J. D. (1980a). "European Inter-continental Emigration. The Road Home: Return Migration from the U.S.A." *Journal of European Economic History* 9:41–112.

Gould, J. D. (1980b). "European Inter-continental Emigration: The Role of 'Diffusion' and 'Feedback.' " *Journal of European Economic History* 9:267–315.

Gourevitch, P. (1986). *Politics in Hard Times: Comparative Responses to International Economic Crises*. Ithaca, N.Y.: Cornell University Press.

Green, A. G. (1995). "A Comparison of Canadian and U.S. Immigration Policy in the Twentieth Century." In Don J. DeVoretz (ed.), *Diminishing Returns: The Economics of Canada's Recent Immigration Policy*. Toronto: Laurier Press.

Grossman, G., and E. Helpman. (1991). *Innovation and Growth in the Global Economy*. Cambridge, Mass.: MIT Press.

Grubb, F. (1994). "The End of European Servitude in the United States: An Economic Analysis of Market Collapse, 1772–1835." *Journal of Economic History* 54:794–824.

Grubert, H., and J. Mutti. (1991). "Taxes, Tariffs and Transfer Pricing in Multinational Corporate Decision Making." *Review of Economics and Statistics* 73:285–293.

Guinnane, T. W. (1992). "Intergenerational Transfers, Emigration, and the Rural Irish Household System." *Explorations in Economic History* 29:457–476.

Guinnane, T. W. (1997). *The Vanishing Irish: Households, Migration, and the Rural Economy in Ireland, 1850–1914*. Princeton, N.J.: Princeton University Press.

Guinnane, T. W., and R. I. Miller. (1996). "Bonds Without Bondsmen: Tenant-Right in Nineteenth-Century Ireland." *Journal of Economic History* 56, no. 1:113–142.

Habakkuk, H. J. (1962). *American and British Technology in the Nineteenth Century*. Cambridge: Cambridge University Press.

Hamilton, A. (1791). *Report on Manufactures*. In S. McKee Jr. (ed.) (1934), *Papers on Public Credit, Commerce and Finance by Alexander Hamilton*. New York: Columbia University Press.

Hammermesh, D. (1993). *Labor Demand*. Princeton, N.J.: Princeton University Press.

Hanes, C. (1993). "The Development of Nominal Wage Rigidity in the Late Nineteenth Century." *American Economic Review* 83:732–756.

Hanes, C. (1996). "Immigrants' Relative Rate of Wage Growth in the Late Nineteenth Century." *Explorations in Economic History* 33:35–64.

Hanley, S. B., and K. Yamamura. (1977). *Economic and Demographic Change in Preindustrial Japan, 1600–1868*. Princeton, N.J.: Princeton University Press.

Hardach, K. W. (1967). *Die Bedeutung wirtschaftlicher Factoren bei die Wiedereinfürung der Eisen- und Getreidezölle on Deutschland 1879*. Berlin.

Harley, C. K. (1980). "Transportation, the World Wheat Trade, and the Kuznets Cycle, 1850–1913." *Explorations in Economic History* 17 (July):218–250.

Harley, C. K. (1988). "Ocean Freight Rates and Productivity, 1740–1913: The Primacy of Mechanical Invention Reaffirmed." *Journal of Economic History* 48:851–876.

Harley, C. K. (1992a). "The Antebellum American Tariff: Food Exports and Manufacturing." *Explorations in Economic History* 29, no. 4:375–400.

Harley, C. K. (1992b). "International Competitiveness of the Antebellum American Cotton Textile Industry." *Journal of Economic History* 52, no. 3:559–584.

Harley, C. K. (1992c). "The World Food Economy and Pre–World War I Argentina." In S. N. Broadberry and N. F. R. Crafts (eds.), *Britain in the International Economy, 1870–1939*. Cambridge: Cambridge University Press.

Harrigan, J. (1997). "Technology, Factor Supplies, and International Specialization: Estimating the Neoclassical Model." *American Economic Review* 87 (September):475–494.

Harrison, A. (1996). "Openness and Growth: A Time Series, Cross-Country Analysis for Developing Countries." *Journal of Development Economics* 48:419–447.

Hatton, T. J. (1995). "A Model of UK Emigration." *Review of Economics and Statistics* 77: 407–415.

Hatton, T. J., and J. G. Williamson. (1993). "After the Famine: Emigration from Ireland 1850–1913." *Journal of Economic History* 53:575–600.

Hatton, T. J., and J. G. Williamson. (1994a). "Late-Comers to Mass Emigration: The Latin Experience." In T. J. Hatton and J. G. Williamson (eds.), *Migration and the International Labor Market, 1850–1939*. London: Routledge.

Hatton, T. J., and J. G. Williamson. (1994b). "What Drove the Mass Migrations from Europe in the Late Nineteenth Century?" *Population and Development Review* 20:1–27.

Hatton, T. J., and J. G. Williamson. (1995). "The Impact of Immigration on American Labor Markets Prior to the Quotas." NBER Working Paper No. 5185, National Bureau of Economic Research, Cambridge, Mass., July.

Hatton, T. J., and J. G. Williamson. (1997). "Italian Emigration in a Globally Integrating Atlantic Economy." Unpublished manuscript. Harvard University.

Hatton, T. J., and J. G. Williamson. (1998). *The Age of Mass Migration: An Economic Analysis*. New York: Oxford University Press.

Hayami, Y., and V. W. Ruttan. (1971). *Agricultural Development*. Baltimore: Johns Hopkins University Press.

Head, K. (1994). "Infant Industry Protection in the Steel Rail Industry." *Journal of International Economics* 37:141–165.

Heckscher, E. F. (1919). "The Effect of Foreign Trade on the Distribution of Income." *Ekonomisk Tidskrift*, 497–512.

Heckscher, E. F. (1954). *An Economic History of Sweden*. Cambridge, Mass.: Harvard University Press.

Helleiner, E. (1994a). "From Bretton Woods to Global Finance: A World Turned Upside Down." In R. Stubbs and G. Underhill (eds.), *Political Economy and the Changing Global Order*. Toronto: McClelland and Steuert.

Helleiner, E. (1994b). *States and the Reemergence of Global Finance: From Bretton Woods to the 1990s*. Ithaca, N.Y.: Cornell University Press.

Helpman, E., and P. R. Krugman. (1985). *Market Structure and Foreign Trade*. Cambridge, Mass.: MIT Press.

Higgins, M. D. (1993). "Why Capital Doesn't Flow from Rich to Poor Countries." Mimeo. Cambridge, Mass.: Harvard University.

Higgins, M., and J. G. Williamson. (1997). "Age Structure Dynamics in Asia and Dependence on Foreign Capital." *Population and Development Review* 23, no. 2:261–293.

Higgins, M., and J. G. Williamson. (1999). "Inequality the World Around: Cohort Supply, Kuznets Curves, Globalization and Other Forces." (forthcoming).

Hirschman, A. O. (1958). *The Strategy of Economic Development.* New Haven, Conn.: Yale University Press.

Hirschman, A. O. (1970). *Exit, Voice, and Loyalty: Responses to Decline in Firms, Organizations, and States.* Cambridge, Mass.: Harvard University Press.

Hobson, J. A. (1902). *Imperialism: A Study.* London: Nisbet.

Huber, J. R. (1971). "Effect on Prices of Japan's Entry into World Commerce After 1858." *Journal of Political Economy* 79:614–628.

Hurd, J. (1975). "Railways and the Expansion of Markets in India, 1861–1921." *Explorations in Economic History* 12:263–288.

Hussain, A., and K. Tribe (1981). *Marxism and the Agrarian Question,* vol. 1: German Social Democracy and the Peasantry, 1890–1907. Atlantic Highlands, N.J.: Humanities Press.

Hvidt, K. (1975). *Flight to America.* New York: Academic Press.

Hymer, S. H. (1976). *The International Operations of National Firms: A Study of Direct Foreign Investment.* Cambridge, Mass.: MIT Press.

IBRD. (1983). *The World Development Report 1983.* Washington, D.C.: World Bank.

IBRD. (1995). *The World Development Report 1995.* Washington, D.C.: World Bank.

IMF. (1997). *World Economic Outlook.* Washington, D.C.: International Monetary Fund.

Imlah, J. A. H. (1958). *Economic Elements in the Pax Britannica: Studies in British Foreign Trade in the Nineteenth Century.* Cambridge, Mass.: Harvard University Press.

Ireland. Commission on Emigration and other Population Problems. (1954). *Reports.* Dublin: Stationery Office.

Irwin, D. A. (1988). "Welfare Effects of British Free Trade: Debate and Evidence from the 1840s." *Journal of Political Economy* 96 (December):1142–1164.

Irwin, D. A. (1989). "Political Economy and Peels's Repeal of the Corn Laws." *Economics and Politics* 1 (Spring):41–59.

Irwin, D. A. (1993). "Free Trade and Protection in Nineteenth-Century Britain and France Revisited: A Comment on Nye." *Journal of Economic History* 53 (March):146–152.

Irwin, D. A. (1994). "The Political Economy of Free Trade: Voting in the British General Election of 1906." *Journal of Law and Economics* 36:75–108.

Irwin, D. A. (1996a). *Against the Tide: An Intellectual History of Free Trade.* Princeton, N.J.: Princeton University Press.

Irwin, D. A. (1996b). "Changes in U.S. Tariffs: Prices or Policies?" NBER Working Paper No. 5665, National Bureau of Economic Research, Cambridge, Mass., July.

Isserlis, L. (1938). "Tramp Shipping Cargoes and Freights." *Journal of the Royal Statistical Society* 101, pt. 1:304–417.

James, J. A. (1978). "The Welfare Effects of the Antebellum Tariff: A General Equilibrium Analysis." *Explorations in Economic History* 15:231–256.

James, J. A. (1981). "The Optimal Tariff in the Antebellum United States." *American Economic Review* 71, no. 4:726–734.

James, J. A. (1984). "The Use of General Equilibrium Analysis in Economic History." *Explorations in Economic History* 21:231–253.

Jones, C. I. (1994). "Economic Growth and the Relative Price of Capital." *Journal of Monetary Economics* 34:359–382.

Jones, E. L. (1981). *The European Miracle: Environment, Economies and Geopolitics in the History of Europe and Asia.* Cambridge: Cambridge University Press.

Jones, M. T., and M. Obstfeld. (1997). "Saving, Investment, and Gold: A Reassessment of Historical Current Account Data." NBER Working Paper No. 6103, National Bureau of Economic Research, Cambridge, Mass., July.

Jones, R. W. (1971). "A Three-Factor Model in Theory, Trade, and History." In J. N. Bhagwati et al. (eds), *Trade, Balance of Payments, and Growth.* Amsterdam: North-Holland.

Jorgensen, E., and J. Sachs. (1989). "Default and Renegotiation of Latin American Foreign Bonds in the Interwar Period." In B. Eichengreen and P. H. Lindert (eds.), *The International Debt Crisis in Historical Perspective.* Cambridge, Mass.: MIT Press.

Kamphoefner, W. D. (1976). "At the Crossroads of Economic Development: Background Factors Affecting Emigration from Nineteenth Century Germany." In I. A. Glazier and L. de Rosa (eds.), *Migration Across Time and Distance.* New York: Holmes and Meier.

Kang, K. H., and M. S. Cha. (1996). "Imperial Policy or World Price Shocks? Explaining Interwar Korean Living Standards." Paper presented to the Conference on East and Southeast Asian Economic Change in the Long Run, Honolulu, April 11.

Karlstrom, U. (1985). *Economic Growth and Migration During the Industrialization of Sweden: A General Equilibrium Approach.* Stockholm: Stockholm School of Economics.

Kelley, A. C., and J. G. Williamson. (1984). *What Drives Third World City Growth?* Princeton, N.J.: Princeton University Press.

Kemp, M. C., and M. Ohyama. (1978). "On the Sharing of Trade Gains by Resource-Poor and Resource-Rich Countries." *Journal of International Economics* 8:93–115.

Kennedy, K. A. (1995). "The National Accounts for Ireland in the Nineteenth and Twentieth Centuries." *Scandinavian Economic History Review* 43, no. 1:101–114.

Kero, R. (1991). "Migration Traditions from Finland to North America." In R. J. Vecoli and S. M. Sinke (eds.), *A Century of European Migrations, 1830–1930.* Urbana: University of Illinois Press.

Keynes, J. M. (1936). *The General Theory of Employment, Interest and Money.* London: Macmillan.

Kindleberger, C. P. (1951). "Group Behavior and International Trade." *Journal of Political Economy* 59:30–46.

Kindleberger, C. P. (1973). *The World in Depression*. Boston: Little, Brown.

Kindleberger, C. P. (1975). "The Rise of Free Trade in Western Europe, 1820–1875." *Journal of Economic History* 35:20–55.

Kindleberger, C. P. (1978). *Economic Response: Comparative Studies in Trade, Finance and Growth*. Cambridge, Mass.: Harvard University Press.

Kitchen, M. (1978). *The Political Economy of Germany, 1815–1914*. London: Croom Helm.

Kosters, M. H. (1994). "An Overview of Changing Wage Patterns in the Labor Market." In J. Bhagwati and M. H. Kosters (eds.), *Trade and Wages: Leveling Wages Down?* Washington, D.C.: AEI Press.

Krasner, S. D. (1976). "State Power and the Structure of International Trade." *World Politics* 28:317–347.

Krueger, A. (1978). *Liberalization Attempts and Consequences*. Cambridge, Mass.: Ballinger.

Krugman, P. (1991a). *Geography and Trade*. Cambridge, Mass.: MIT Press.

Krugman, P. (1991b). "Increasing Returns and Economic Geography." *Journal of Political Economy* 99, no. 3:483–499.

Krugman, P., and R. Lawrence. (1994). "Trade, Jobs and Wages." *Scientific American* (April):22–27.

Krugman, P. R., and A. Venables. (1990). "Integration and the Competitiveness of Peripheral Industry." In C. Bliss and J. Braga de Macedo (eds.), *Unity with Diversity in the European Community*, Cambridge: Cambridge University Press.

Krugman, P. R., and A. Venables. (1995). "Globalization and the Inequality of Nations." NBER Working Paper No. 5098, National Bureau of Economic Research, Cambridge, Mass., April.

Kuuse, J. (1971). "Mechanization, Commercialization and the Protectionist Movement in Swedish Agriculture, 1860–1910." *Scandinavian Economic History Review* 19, no. 1:23–44.

Kuznets, S. (1930). *Secular Movements in Production and Prices*. New York: National Bureau of Economic Research.

Kuznets, S. (1955). "Economic Growth and Income Inequality." *American Economic Review* 45:1–28.

Kuznets, S. (1958). "Long Swings in the Growth of Population and in Related Economic Variables." *Proceedings of the American Philosophical Society* 102, no. 1:25–52.

Lains, P. (1992). "Foreign Trade and Economic Growth in the European Periphery: Portugal, 1851–1913." Ph.D. dissertation, European University Institute.

Landes, D. (1969). *The Unbound Prometheus: Technological Change and Industrial Development in Western Europe from 1750 to the Present*. Cambridge: Cambridge University Press.

Latham, A. J. H., and L. Neal. (1983). "The International Market in Rice and Wheat, 1868–1914." *Economic History Review* 36:260–275.

Lawrence, L., and M. Slaughter. (1993). "International Trade and American Wages in the 1980s: Giant Sucking Sound or Small Hiccup?" *Brookings Papers on Economic Activity, Microeconomics* 2:161–226.

Leamer, E. E. (1994). "Trade, Wages and Revolving Door Ideas." NBER Working Paper No. 4716, National Bureau of Economic Research, Cambridge, Mass., April.

Leamer, E. E. (1995). "The Heckscher-Ohlin Model in Theory and Practice." *Princeton Studies in International Finance* 77 (February).

Leamer, E. E. (1998a). "Measures of Openness." In R. E. Baldwin (ed.), *Trade Policy Issues and Empirical Analysis*. Chicago: University of Chicago Press.

Leamer, E. E. (1998b). "The State of Play: What's Significant?" Paper delivered at the annual meetings of the American Economic Association, Chicago, January 3–5.

Lee, J.-W. (1993). "International Trade, Distortions, and Long-Run Economic Growth." *IMF Staff Papers* 40:299–328.

Lee, J.-W. (1995). "Capital Goods Imports and Long-Run Growth." *Journal of Development Economics* 48:91–110.

Leff, N. H. (1972). "Economic Development and Regional Inequality: Origins of the Brazilian Case." *Quarterly Journal of Economics* 86, no. 2 (May):243–262.

Leff, N. H. (1992). "Economic Development in Brazil, 1822–1913." First Boston Working Paper FB-92-02, Columbia University, New York.

Lenin, V. I. (1915). *Imperialism, the Highest State of Capitalism*. Moscow: Foreign Languages Publishing House.

Leontief, W. W. (1953). "Domestic Production and Foreign Trade: The American Capital Position Re-Examined." *Proceedings of the American Philosophical Society* 97 (September): 332–349.

Lerner, A. P. (1952). "Factor Prices and International Trade." *Economica* 19, no. 73:1–15.

Lévy-Leboyer, M., and F. Bourguignon. (1990). *The French Economy in the Nineteenth Century*. Cambridge: Cambridge University Press.

Lewis, W. A. (1949). *Economic Survey, 1919–1939*. London: George Allen and Unwin.

Lewis, W. A. (1954). "Economic Development with Unlimited Supplies of Labour." *Manchester School of Economic and Social Studies* 22:139–191.

Lewis, W. A. (1978). *The Evolution of the International Economic Order*. Princeton, N.J.: Princeton University Press.

Lewis, W. A., and P. J. O'Leary. (1955). "Secular Swings in Production and Trade, 1870–1913." *Manchester School of Economic and Social Studies* 13, no. 2:113–152.

Liepmann, H. (1938). *Tariff Levels and the Economic Unity of Europe*. London: Allen and Unwin.

Lindert, P. H. (1978). *Fertility and Scarcity in America*. Princeton, N.J.: Princeton University Press.

Lindert, P. H. (1994). "Unequal Living Standards." In R. C. Floud and D. N. McCloskey (eds.), *The Economic History of Britain Since 1700*, vol. 1. Cambridge: Cambridge University Press.

Lindert, P. H. (1997). "Three Centuries of Inequality in Britain and America." In A. B. Atkinson and F. Bourguignon (eds.), *Handbook of Income Distribution*. Amsterdam: North-Holland.

Lindert, P. H., and P. J. Morton. (1989). "How Sovereign Debt Has Worked." In J. D. Sachs (ed.), *Developing Country Debt and the World Economy*. Chicago: University of Chicago Press.

Lindert, P. H., and J. G. Williamson. (1983). "English Workers' Living Standards During the Industrial Revolution: A New Look." *Economic History Review*, 2d ser., 36 (February): 1–25.

Lindert, P. H., and J. G. Williamson. (1985). "English Workers' Living Standards: A Reply to Crafts." *Journal of Economic History* 45 (March):145–153.

List, F. (1841). *The National System of Political Economy*. Translated by S. S. Lloyd 1991. Original ed., London: Longman's, Green; reprinted Fairfield, N.J.: Augustus M. Kelley.

Lothian, J. R. (1995). "Capital Market Integration and Exchange-Rate Regimes in Historical Perspective." Mimeo. Fordham University.

Lucas, R. E. (1988). "On the Mechanics of Economic Development." *Journal of Monetary Economics* 22 (July):3–42.

Lucas, R. E. (1990). "Why Doesn't Capital Flow from Rich to Poor Countries?" *American Economic Review* 80 (May):92–96.

Maddison, A. (1982). *Phases of Capitalist Development*. Oxford: Oxford University Press.

Maddison, A. (1989). *The World Economy in the 20th Century*. Paris: OECD.

Maddison, A. (1991). *Dynamic Forces in Capitalist Development: A Long-Run Comparative View*. Oxford: Oxford University Press.

Maddison, A. (1994). "Explaining the Economic Performance of Nations." In W. Baumol, R. Nelson, and E. Wolff (eds.), *Convergence of Productivity: Cross-National Studies and Historical Evidence*. New York: Oxford University Press.

Maddison, A. (1995). *Monitoring the World Economy, 1820–1992*. Paris: OECD Development Centre Studies.

Magee, S. P., W. A. Brock, and L. Young. (1989). *Black Hole Tariffs and Endogenous Policy Theory*. New York: Cambridge University Press.

Mankiw, N. G., D. Romer, and D. N. Weil. (1992). "A Contribution to the Empirics of Economic Growth." *Quarterly Journal of Economics* 107 (May):407–437.

Margo, R. (1992). "Wages and Prices During the Ante Bellum Period: A Survey and New Evidence." In R. E. Gallman and J. Wallis (eds.), *American Economic Growth and Living Standards Before the Civil War*. Chicago: University of Chicago Press.

Markusen, J. R. (1983). "Factor Movements and Commodity Trade as Complements." *Journal of International Economics* 13:341–356.

Marshall, A. (1920). *Principles of Economics*. 8th ed. London: Macmillan.

Martín-Aceña, P. (1994). "Spain During the Classical Gold Standard Years, 1880–1914." In M. D. Bordo and F. Capie (eds.), *Monetary Regimes in Transition*. Cambridge: Cambridge University Press.

Marvel, H. P., and E. J. Ray. (1983). "The Kennedy Round: Evidence on the Regulation of International Trade in the United States." *American Economic Review* 73, no. 1:190–197.

Marx, K. (1977). *Capital*, vol. 1. New York: Vintage Books.

Massey, D. S. (1988). "Economic Development and International Migration in Comparative Perspective." *Population and Development Review* 14:383–413.

Mata, E. (1995). "Foreign Investments in the Portuguese Economy from the Middle Nineteenth Century Till the First World War." Paper presented to XV Encontro da Associação Portuguesa de História Económica e Social, Evora.

Mayhew, A. (1972). "A Reappraisal of the Causes of Farm Protest in the United States, 1870–1900." *Journal of Economic History* 32:464–476.

McCloskey, D. N. (1970). "Did Victorian Britain Fail?" *Economic History Review*, 2d ser., 23 (December):446–459.

McCloskey, D. N. (1973). *Economic Maturity and Entrepreneurial Decline*. Cambridge, Mass.: Harvard University Press.

McCloskey, D. N. (1980). "Magnanimous Albion: Free Trade and British National Income, 1841–1881." *Explorations in Economic History* 17 (July):303–320.

McCloskey, D. N. (1998). "The State of Play: Statistical Significance, Blackboard Theory, and the Stagnation of Modern Economics." Paper delivered at the annual meetings of the American Economic Association, Chicago, January 3–5.

McCraw, T. K. (1984). *Prophets of Regulation*. Cambridge, Mass.: Belknap Press.

McCulloch, J. R. (1837). *A Statistical Account of the British Empire*. London: C. Knight and Co.

McDiarmid, O. J. (1946). *Commercial Policy in the Canadian Economy*. Cambridge, Mass.: Harvard University Press.

McGouldrick, P., and M. Tannen. (1977). "Did American Manufacturers Discriminate Against Immigrants Before 1914?" *Journal of Economic History* 37:723–746.

McInnis, M. (1993). "Britain in the World Market for Timber." Paper presented at the EHE Conference on Market Integration, Lerici, Italy, April 1–4.

McInnis, M. (1994). "Immigration and Emigration: Canada in the Late Nineteenth Century." In T. J. Hatton and J. G. Williamson (eds.), *Migration and the International Labor Market, 1850–1939*. London: Routledge.

McKeown, T. J. (1983). "Hegemonic Stability Theory and 19th Century Tariff Levels in Europe." *International Organization* 37:73–91.

McLean, I. W., and J. J. Pincus. (1983). "Did Australian Living Standards Stagnate Between 1890 and 1940?" *Journal of Economic History* 43 (March):193–202.

Meade, J. (1955). *Trade and Welfare*. London: Oxford University Press.

Metzer, J. (1974). "Railroad Development and Market Integration: The Case of Tsarist Russia." *Journal of Economic History* 34:529–550.

Metzler, L. A. (1949). "Tariffs, the Terms of Trade, and the Distribution of National Income." *Journal of Political Economy* 57 (February):1–29.

Mitchell, B. R. (1983). *International Historical Statistics: The Americas and Australasia*. Detroit, Mich.: Gale Research Company.

Mokyr, J. (1985). *Why Ireland Starved: A Quantitative and Analytical History of the Irish Economy, 1800–1850.* London: George Allen & Unwin.

Mokyr, J. (1990). *The Lever of Riches: Technological Creativity and Economic Progress.* New York: Oxford University Press.

Mokyr, J. (1991). "Dear Labor, Cheap Labor, and the Industrial Revolution." In P. Higonnet, D. S. Landes, and H. Rosovsky (eds.), *Favorites of Fortune: Technology, Growth, and Economic Development Since the Industrial Revolution.* Cambridge, Mass.: Harvard University Press.

Mokyr, J., and C. Ó Gráda. (1982). "Emigration and Poverty in Prefamine Ireland." *Explorations in Economic History* 19, no. 4:360–384.

Molinas, C., and L. Prados. (1989). "Was Spain Different? Spanish Historical Backwardness Revisited." *Explorations in Economic History* 26:385–402.

Moreda, V. P. (1987). "Spain's Demographic Modernization, 1800–1930." In N. Sanchez-Albornoz (ed.), *The Economic Modernization of Spain, 1830–1930.* New York: New York University Press.

Mukerji, K. (1969). "Land Prices in Punjab." In K. K. Chaudhuri (ed.), *Trends of Socio-Economic Change in India, 1871–1961.* Simla: Indian Institute of Advanced Study.

Mundell, R. A. (1957). "International Trade and Factor Mobility." *American Economic Review* 47, no. 3:321–335.

Murray, A. E. (1970). *A History of the Commercial and Financial Relations Between England and Ireland from the Period of the Restoration.* Rev. of 1903 ed. New York: Burt Franklin.

Myrdal, G. (1957). *Economic Theory and Underdeveloped Regions.* London: Duckworth.

Neal, L. (1985). "Integration of International Capital Markets: Quantitative Evidence from the Eighteenth to Twentieth Centuries." *Journal of Economic History* 45 (June):219–226.

Neal, L. (1990). *The Rise of Financial Capitalism: International Capital Markets in the Age of Reason.* Cambridge: Cambridge University Press.

Neal, L., and P. Uselding. (1972). "Immigration: A Neglected Source of American Economic Growth: 1790–1912." *Oxford Economic Papers* 24:68–88.

Neary, J. P (1995). "Factor Mobility and International Trade." *Canadian Journal of Economics* 28 (special issue):S4–S23.

Nelson, R. R., and G. Wright. (1992). "The Rise and Fall of American Technological Leadership." *Journal of Economic Literature* 30 (December):1931–1964.

Nicholas, S., and P. R. Shergold. (1987). "Human Capital and the Pre-Famine Irish Emigration to England." *Explorations in Economic History* 24, no. 2:158–177.

North, D. C. (1958). "Ocean Freight Rates and Economic Development, 1750–1913." *Journal of Economic History* 18:538–555.

Nye, J. V. (1991). "The Myth of Free-Trade Britain and Fortress France." *Journal of Economic History* 51 (March):23–46.

O'Brien, G. (1921). *The Economic History of Ireland from the Union to the Famine.* London: Longmans, Green.

Obstfeld, M. (1995). "International Capital Mobility in the 1990s." In P. B. Kenen (ed.), *Understanding Interdependence: The Macroeconomics of the Open Economy*. Princeton, N.J.: Princeton University Press.

Obstfeld, M. (1997). "The Great Depression as a Watershed: International Capital Mobility over the Long Run." NBER Working Paper No. 5960, National Bureau of Economic Research, Cambridge, Mass., March.

Obstfeld, M., and A. M. Taylor. (1998). "The Great Depression as a Watershed: International Capital Mobility in the Long Run." In M. D. Bordo, C. D. Goldin, and E. N. White (eds.), *The Defining Moment: The Great Depression and the American Economy in the Twentieth Century*. Chicago: University of Chicago Press.

Officer, L. H. (1985). "Integration in the American Foreign-Exchange Market, 1791–1900." *Journal of Economic History* 45 (September):557–585.

Officer, L. H. (1996). *Between the Dollar-Sterling Gold Points: Exchange Rates, Parity and Market Behavior*. Cambridge: Cambridge University Press.

Ó Gráda, C. (1993). *Ireland Before and After the Famine: Explorations in Economic History*. Manchester: Manchester University Press.

Ó Gráda, C. (1994a). "British Agriculture, 1860–1914." In R. C. Floud and D. N. McCloskey (eds.), *The Economic History of Britain Since 1700*, vol. 2. Cambridge: Cambridge University Press.

Ó Gráda, C. (1994b). *Ireland, 1780–1939: A New Economic History*. Oxford: Oxford University Press.

Ó Gráda, C., and K. H. O'Rourke. (1996). "Irish Economic Growth, 1945–1988." In N. F. R. Crafts and G. Toniolo (eds.), *Economic Growth in Europe Since 1945*. Cambridge: Cambridge University Press.

Ó Gráda, C., and K. H. O'Rourke. (1997). "Migration as Disaster Relief: Lessons from the Great Irish Famine." *European Review of Economic History* 1, no. 1:3–25.

Ohlin, B. (1933). *Interregional and International Trade*. Cambridge, Mass.: Harvard University Press.

O'Rourke, K. (1989). "Agricultural Change and Rural Depopulation: Ireland, 1845–1876." Ph.D. dissertation, Harvard University.

O'Rourke, K. (1991). "Rural Depopulation in a Small Open Economy: Ireland 1856–1876." *Explorations in Economic History* 28 (October):409–432.

O'Rourke, K. (1992). "Why Ireland Emigrated: A Positive Theory of Factor Flows." *Oxford Economic Papers* 44:322–340.

O'Rourke, K. (1994a). "Did Labor Flow Uphill? International Migration and Wage Rates in 20th Century Ireland." In G. Grantham and M. MacKinnon (eds.), *Labor Market Evolution: The Economic History of Market Integration, Wage Flexibility and the Employment Relation*. New York: Routledge.

O'Rourke, K. (1994b). "The Repeal of the Corn Laws and Irish Emigration." *Explorations in Economic History* 31 (January):120–138.

O'Rourke, K. (1994c). "The Economic Impact of the Famine in the Short and Long Run." *American Economic Review (Papers and Proceedings)* 84 (May):309–313.

O'Rourke, K. (1995a). "Emigration and Living Standards in Ireland Since the Famine." *Journal of Population Economics* 8:407–421.

O'Rourke, K. (1995b). "Computable General Equilibrium Models and Economic History." Paper delivered to the New Directions in History Roundtable, 20th annual meeting, SSHA, Chicago, November 16–19.

O'Rourke, K. (1997a). "The European Grain Invasion, 1870–1913." *Journal of Economic History* 57 (December):775–801.

O'Rourke, K. (1997b). "Tariffs and Growth in the Late 19th Century." CER Working Paper WP97/18, Department of Economics, University College Dublin, July.

O'Rourke, K. H., A. M. Taylor, and J. G. Williamson. (1996). "Factor Price Convergence in the Late Nineteenth Century." *International Economic Review* 37 (August):499–530.

O'Rourke, K. H., and J. G. Williamson. (1994). "Late 19th Century Anglo-American Factor Price Convergence: Were Heckscher and Ohlin Right?" *Journal of Economic History* 54 (December):892–916.

O'Rourke, K. H., and J. G. Williamson. (1995a). "Open Economy Forces and Late 19th Century Swedish Catch-Up: A Quantitative Accounting." *Scandinavian Economic History Review* 43, no. 2:171–203.

O'Rourke, K. H., and J. G. Williamson. (1995b). "Erratum." *Journal of Economic History* 55, no. 4:921–922.

O'Rourke, K. H., and J. G. Williamson. (1995c). "Education, Globalization, and Catch-Up: Scandinavia in the Swedish Mirror." *Scandinavian Economic History Review* 43, no. 3:287–309.

O'Rourke, K. H., and J. G. Williamson. (1995d). Open Economy Forces and Late 19th Century Scandinavian Catch-up. *HIER Discussion Paper 1709*, Harvard University, Cambridge, MA.

O'Rourke, K. H., and J. G. Williamson. (1997). "Around the European Periphery 1870–1913: Globalization, Schooling and Growth." *European Review of Economic History* 1 (August):153–191.

O'Rourke, K. H., J. G. Williamson, and T. J. Hatton. (1994). "Mass Migration, Commodity Market Integration and Real Wage Convergence." In T. J. Hatton and J. G. Williamson (eds.), *Migration and the International Labor Market, 1850–1939*. London: Routledge.

Perotti, R. (1996). "Growth, Income Distribution and Democracy." *Journal of Economic Growth* 1 (June):149–187.

Polanyi, K. (1944). *The Great Transformation: The Political and Economic Origins of Our Time*. New York: Rinehart.

Pollard, S. (1978). "Labour in Great Britain." In P. Mathias and M. M. Postan (eds.), *The Cambridge Economic History of Europe*, vol. 7: The Industrial Economies: Capital, Labour, and Enterprise, pt 1. Cambridge: Cambridge University Press.

Pope, C. (1972). "The Impact of the Ante Bellum Tariff on Income Distribution." *Explorations in Economic History* 9:375–421.

Pope, D., and G. Withers. (1994). "Wage Effects of Immigration in Late-Nineteenth-Century Australia." In Timothy J. Hatton and Jeffrey G. Williamson, (eds.), *Migration and the International Labor Market, 1850–1939*. London: Routledge.

Porter, G. R. (1851). *The Progress of the Nation*. London: C. Knight and Co.

Prados de la Escosura, L. (1982). *Comercio Exterior y Crecimiento Economico en Espana 1826–1913*. Madrid: Banco de Espana.

Prados de la Escosura, L. (1988). *De imperio a nacion: Crecimiento y atraso economico en Espana 1780–1930*. Madrid: Alianza.

Prados de la Escosura, L., T. Sanchez, and J. Oliva. (1993). "De Te Fabula Narratur? Growth, Structural Change and Convergence in Europe, 19th and 20th Centuries." Working Paper No. D–93009, Ministerio de Economia y Hacienda, Madrid, December.

Putnam, R. D. (1993). *Making Democracy Work: Civic Traditions in Modern Italy*. Princeton, N.J.: Princeton University Press.

Quah, D. (1993). "Galton's Fallacy and Tests of the Convergence Hypothesis." *Scandinavian Journal of Economics* 95, no. 4:427–443.

Radelet, S., J. Sachs, and J.-W. Lee. (1997). "Economic Growth in Asia." In Asian Development Bank (ed.), *Emerging Asia*. Manila: Asian Development Bank.

Rae, J. (1834). *Statement of Some New Principles of Political Economy*. Boston: Hilliard, Gray.

Redford, A. (1926). *Labour Migration in England, 1800–1850*. Manchester: Manchester University Press.

Reis, J. (1991). "The Gold Standard in Portugal, 1854–1891." Paper presented to the Conference on the Gold Standard in the Periphery, 1854–1939. Lisbon, Universidade Nova de Lisboa.

Revenga, A. (1992). "Exporting Jobs: The Impact of Import Competition on Employment and Wages in U.S. Manufacturing." *Quarterly Journal of Economics* 107:255–284.

Reynolds, L. (1985). *Economic Growth in the Third World, 1850–1980*. New Haven, Conn.: Yale University Press.

Richardson, J. D. (1995). "Income Inequality and Trade: How to Think, What to Conclude." *Journal of Economic Perspectives* 9 (Summer):33–55.

Riis, C., and T. Thonstad. (1989). "A Counterfactual Study of Economic Impacts of Norwegian Emigration and Capital Imports." In I. Gordon and A. P. Thirlwall (eds.), *European Factor Mobility: Trends and Consequences*. London: Macmillan.

Rivera-Batiz, L. A., and P. M. Romer. (1991). "Economic Integration and Endogenous Growth." *Quarterly Journal of Economics* 106:531–555.

Robbins, D. (1996). "Trade, Trade Liberalization and Inequality in Latin America and East Asia—Synthesis of Seven Countries." Mimeo. Cambridge, Mass.: Harvard Institute for International Development.

Roehner, B. M. (1994). "Les Mecanismes d'interdependance spatiale entre marches du blé au XIXe siècle." *Histoire, Economie et Société* 2:343–394.

Rogowski, R. (1989). *Commerce and Coalitions: How Trade Effects Domestic Political Arrangements*. Princeton, N.J.: Princeton University Press.

Romer, P. (1986). "Increasing Returns and Long-Run Growth." *Journal of Political Economy* 94 (October):1002–1037.

Romer, P. (1989). "Capital Accumulation in the Theory of Long-Run Growth." In R. J. Barro (ed.), *Modern Business Cycle Theory*. Cambridge, Mass.: Harvard University Press.

Rostow, W. W. (1978). *World Economy: History and Prospect*. Austin: University of Texas Press.

Rostow, W. W. (1990). *Theorists of Economic Growth from David Hume to the Present*. Oxford: Oxford University Press.

Rybczynski, T. M. (1955). "Factor Endowments and Relative Commodity Prices." *Economica* 22, no. 88:336–341.

Sachs, J. D., and A. Warner. (1995a). "Economic Reform and the Process of Global Integration." *Brookings Papers on Economic Activity, I*, Brookings Institution, Washington, D.C.

Sachs, J. D., and A. Warner. (1995b). "Natural Resource Abundance and Economic Growth." NBER Working Paper No. 5398, National Bureau of Economic Research, Cambridge, Mass., December.

Salazar, A. de O. (1916). *O Ágio do Ouro: Sua Natureza e Suas causas, 1891–1915*. Coimbra: Imprensa da Universidade.

Samuelson, P. A. (1949). "International Factor-Price Equalization Once Again." *Economic Journal* 59 (234):181–197.

Sanchez-Alonso, B. (1995). *Las Causas de la Emigracion Española, 1880–1930*. Madrid: Alianza Editorial.

Sanchez-Alonso, B. (1998). "What Slowed Down the Mass Migration from Spain in the Late Nineteenth Century?" Paper presented to the Conference on Long Run Economic Change in the Mediterranean Basin, Istanbul, Turkey, June 4–7.

Sandberg, L. G. (1979). "The Case of the Impoverished Sophisticate: Human Capital and Swedish Economic Growth Before World War I." *Journal of Economic History* 39:225–241.

Schmitz, A. P., and P. Helmberger. (1970). "Factor Mobility and International Trade: The Case of Complementarity." *American Economic Review* 60, no. 4:761–767.

Semmingsen, I. (1960). "Norwegian Emigration in the Nineteenth Century." *Scandinavian Economic History Review* 8:150–160.

Semmingsen, I. (1972). "Emigration from Scandinavia." *Scandinavia Economic History Review* 20:45–60.

Servan-Schreiber, J. J. (1968). *The American Challenge*. New York: Atheneum.

Shergold, P. R. (1982). *Working-Class Life: The "American Standard" in Comparative Perspective, 1899–1913*. Pittsburgh: University of Pittsburgh Press.

Shoven, J. B., and J. Whalley. (1984). "Applied General Equilibrium Models of Taxation and International Trade: An Introduction and Survey." *Journal of Economic Literature* 22:1007–1051.

Shoven, J. B., and J. Whalley. (1992). *Applying General Equilibrium*. Cambridge: Cambridge University Press.

Shughart, W., R. Tollison, and M. Kimenyi. (1986). "The Political Economy of Immigration Restrictions." *Yale Journal on Regulation*, 51, no. 4.

Siriwardana, A. M. (1991). "The Impact of Tariff Protection in the Colony of Victoria in the Late Nineteenth Century: A General Equilibrium Analysis." *Australian Economic History Review* 31, no. 2:45–65.

Slaughter, M. J. (1995). "The Antebellum Transportation Revolution and Factor-Price Convergence." NBER Working Paper No. 5303, National Bureau of Economic Research, Cambridge, Mass., October.

Smeeding, T. M., and J. Coder. (1995). "Income Inequality in Rich Countries During the 1980s." *Journal of Income Distribution* 5:13–29.

Smith, M. S. (1980). *Tariff Reform in France, 1860–1900.* Ithaca, N.Y.: Cornell University Press.

Smith, T. C. (1973). "Pre-Modern Economic Growth: Japan and the West." *Past and Present* 60 (August):127–160.

Solar, P. M. (1979). "The Agricultural Trade Statistics in the Irish Railway Commissioners' Report." *Irish Economic and Social History* 6:24–40.

Solar, P. M. (1987). "Growth and Distribution in Irish Agriculture Before the Famine." Ph.D, dissertation, Stanford University.

Solar, P., and J. Van Zanden. (1996). "With and Without the Corn Laws: Ireland, Holland and Agricultural Protection in the Mid-Nineteenth Century." Paper presented to the II Congress of the EAHE, Venice, January 19–20.

Solow, B. L. (1971). *The Land Question and the Irish Economy, 1870–1903.* Cambridge, Mass.: Harvard University Press.

Solow, R. M. (1956). "A Contribution to the Theory of Economic Growth." *Quarterly Journal of Economics* 70 (February):65–94.

Stigler, G. J. (1982). *The Economist as Preacher and Other Essays.* Chicago: University of Chicago Press.

Stokey, N. L. (1991). "Human Capital, Product Quality, and Growth." *Quarterly Journal of Economics* 106:587–616.

Summers, R., and A. Heston. (1991). "The Penn World Table (Mark 5): An Expanded Set of International Comparisons, 1950–1988." *Quarterly Journal of Economics* 106 (May): 327–368.

Taussig, F. W. (1888). *The Tariff History of the United States: A Series of Essays.* New York: Putnam's.

Taylor, A. M. (1992a). "External Dependence, Demographic Burdens, and Argentine Economic Decline After the Belle Epoque." *Journal of Economic History* 52 (December):907–936.

Taylor, A. M. (1992b). "Argentine Economic Growth in Comparative Perspective." Ph.D. dissertation, Harvard University.

Taylor, A. M. (1994a). "Mass Migration to Distant Southern Shores." In T. J. Hatton and J. G. Williamson (eds.), *Migration and the International Labor Market, 1850–1939.* London: Routledge.

Taylor, A. M. (1994b). "Tres Fases del Crecimiento Económico Argentino." *Revista de Historia Económica* 12, no. 3:649–683.

Taylor, A. M. (1994c). "Three Phases of Argentine Economic Growth." NBER Historical Paper No. 60, National Bureau of Economic Research, Cambridge, Mass., October.

Taylor, A. M. (1995). "Debt, Dependence and the Demographic Transition: Latin America in to the Next Century." *World Development* 23, no. 5:869–879.

Taylor, A. M. (1996a). "International Capital Mobility in History: The Saving-Investment Relationship." NBER Working Paper No. 5743, National Bureau of Economic Research, Cambridge, Mass., September.

Taylor, A. M. (1996b). "Sources of Convergence in the Late Nineteenth Century." NBER Working Paper No. 5806, National Bureau of Economic Research, Cambridge, Mass., October.

Taylor, A. M. (1997a). "Argentina and the World Capital Market: Saving, Investment, and International Capital Mobility in the Twentieth Century." NBER Working Paper No. 6302, National Bureau of Economic Research, Cambridge, Mass., December.

Taylor, A. M. (1998). "On the Costs of Inward-Looking Development: Historical Perspectives on Price Distortions, Growth, and Divergence in Latin America from the 1930s to the 1980s." *Journal of Economic History* 58, no. 1:1–28.

Taylor, A. M., and J. G. Williamson. (1994). "Capital Flows to the New World as an Intergenerational Transfer." *Journal of Political Economy* 102 (April):348–371.

Taylor, A. M., and J. G. Williamson. (1997). "Convergence in the Age of Mass Migration." *European Review of Economic History* 1:27–63.

Temin, P. (1966). "Labor Scarcity and the Problem of American Industrial Efficiency in the 1850s." *Journal of Economic History* 26 (September):277–298.

Thistlethwaite, F. (1960). "Migration from Europe Overseas in the Nineteenth and Twentieth Centuries." Paper presented to the 11th Congress International des Sciences Historiques, Rapports, Upsalla.

Thomas, B. (1954). *Migration and Economic Growth*. Cambridge: Cambridge University Press.

Thomas, B. (1972). *Migration and Urban Development*. London: Methuen.

Thomas, D. S. (1941). *Social and Economic Aspects of Swedish Population Movements*. New York: Macmillan.

Thomas, M. (1987). "General Equilibrium Models and Research in Economic History." In A. Field (ed.), *The Future of Economic History*. Boston: Kluwer-Nijhoff.

Thompson, H. (1985). "Complementarity in a Simple General Equilibrium Production Model." *Canadian Journal of Economics* 18, no. 3:616–621.

Thompson, H. (1986). "Free Trade and Factor-Price Polarization." *European Economic Review* 30:419–425.

Timmer, A., and J. G. Williamson. (1996). "Racism, Xenophobia or Markets? The Political Economy of Immigration Policy Prior to the Thirties." NBER Working Paper No. 5867, National Bureau of Economic Research, Cambridge, Mass., December.

Timmer, A., and J. G. Williamson. (1998). "Immigration Policy Prior to the Thirties: Labor Markets, Policy Interactions and Globalization Backlash." *Population and Development Review* 24 (December):739–771.

Tipton, F. B. (1976). *Regional Variations in the Economic Development of Germany During the Nineteenth Century*. Middletown, Conn.: Wesleyan University Press.

Toniolo, G. (1977). "Effective Protection and Industrial Growth: The Case of Italian Engineering 1896–1913." *Journal of European Economic History* 5:659–673.

Torrens, R. (1844). *The Budget: On Commercial and Colonial Policy*. London: Smith, Elder.

Tortella, G. (1994). "Patterns of Economic Retardation and Recovery in South-Western Europe in the Nineteenth and Twentieth Centuries." *Economic History Review* 47, no. 1: 1–21.

Tracy, M. (1989). *Government and Agriculture in Western Europe 1880–1988*. 3rd ed. New York: Harvester Wheatsheaf.

Turner, M. (1996). *After the Famine: Irish Agriculture, 1850–1914*. Cambridge: Cambridge University Press.

Ufford, E. M. (1984). "Patterns of Transition in U.S. Net Foreign Investment 1869–1913." Senior honors thesis, Harvard University.

Uselding, P. (1971). "Conjectural Estimates of Gross Human Capital Inflow to the American Economy." *Explorations in Economic History* 9:49–61.

Vamvakidis, A. (1997). "How Robust Is the Growth-Openness Connection? Historical Evidence." Mimeo. Cambridge, Mass.: Harvard University.

Vaughan, W. E. (1984). *Landlords and Tenants in Ireland, 1848–1904*. Dundalk: Dundalgan Press.

Vedovato, C. (1990). "Economic Stagnation and Easy 'Exit': The Italian South from Unification to the 1950s." *Scandinavian Economic History Review* 38, no. 1:74–94.

Verdier, T. (1994). "Models of Political Economy of Growth: A Short Survey." *European Economic Review* 38 (April):757–763.

Viner, J. (1950). *The Customs Unions Issue*. New York: Carnegie Endowment for International Peace.

Walker, M. (1964). *Germany and the Emigration, 1816–1885*. Cambridge, Mass.: Harvard University Press.

Watkins, M. H. (1963). "A Staple Theory of Economic Growth." *Canadian Journal of Economics and Political Science* 29 (May):141–158.

Webb, S. B. (1977). "Tariff Protection for the Iron Industry, Cotton Textiles and Agriculture in Germany, 1879–1914." *Jahrbücher für Nationalökonomie und Statistik* 192, no. 3–4: 336–357.

Webb, S. B. (1980). "Tariffs, Cartels, Technology, and Growth in the German Steel Industry, 1879 to 1914." *Journal of Economic History* 40, no. 2:309–329.

Webb, S. B. (1982). "Agricultural Protection in Wilhelminian Germany: Forging an Empire with Pork and Rye." *Journal of Economic History* 42, no. 2:309–326.

Whelan, K. (1995). "Krugman's Economic Geography and the Long-Run Effects of the Great Irish Famine." Mimeo. Cambridge, Mass.: Massachusetts Institute of Technology.

Whitney, W. G. (1968). "The Structure of the American Economy in the Late Nineteenth Century." Ph.D. dissertation, Harvard University.

Wicksell, K. (1882). *Om utvandringen: Dess betydelse och orsaker*. Stockholm: Albert Bonniers Forlag.

Wilkins, M. (1970). *The Emergence of Multinational Enterprise: American Business Abroad from the Colonial Era to 1914*. Cambridge, Mass.: Harvard University Press.

Wilkins, M. (1986). "European Multinationals in the United States: 1875–1914." In A. Teichova, M. Lévy-Leboyer, and H. Nussbaum (eds.), *Multinational Enterprise in Historical Perspective*. Cambridge: Cambridge University Press.

Wilkinson, M. (1967). "Evidences of Long Swings in the Growth of Swedish Population and Related Economic Variables, 1860–1965." *Journal of Economic History* 27, no. 1:17–38.

Wilkinson, M. (1970). "European Migration to the United States: An Econometric Analysis of Aggregate Labor Supply and Demand." *Review of Economics and Statistics* 52:272–279.

Williams, J. H. (1929). "The Theory of International Trade Reconsidered." *Economic Journal* 39 (154):195–209.

Williamson, J. G. (1964). *American Growth and the Balance of Payments, 1820–1913*. Chapel Hill: University of North Carolina Press.

Williamson, J. G. (1965). "Regional Inequality and the Process of National Development." *Economic Development and Cultural Change* 13, 4, pt. 2 (July), Supplement.

Williamson, J. G. (1974a). "Watersheds and Turning Points: Conjectures on the Long Term Impact of Civil War Financing." *Journal of Economic History* 34 (September):636–661.

Williamson, J. G. (1974b). "Migration to the New World: Long Term Influences and Impact." *Explorations in Economic History* 11:357–390.

Williamson, J. G. (1974c). *Late Nineteenth Century American Development: A General Equilibrium History*. Cambridge: Cambridge University Press.

Williamson, J. G. (1979). "Inequality, Accumulation and Technological Imbalance: A Growth-Equity Conflict in American History?" *Economic Development and Cultural Change* 27 (January):231–253.

Williamson, J. G. (1980a). "Unbalanced Growth, Inequality and Regional Development: Some Lessons from American History." In V. Arnold (ed.), *Alternatives to Confrontation: A National Policy Towards Regional Change*. Lexington, Mass.: Heath.

Williamson, J. G. (1980b). "Greasing the Wheels of Sputtering Export Engines: Midwestern Grains and American Growth." *Explorations in Economic History* 17 (July):189–217.

Williamson, J. G. (1982). "Immigrant-Inequality Trade Offs in the Promised Land: Income Distribution and Absorptive Capacity Prior to the Quotas." In B. Chiswick (ed.), *The Gateway: U.S. Immigration Issues and Policies*. Washington, D.C.: American Enterprise Institute.

Williamson, J. G. (1985). *Did British Capitalism Breed Inequality?* London: Allen and Unwin.

Williamson, J. G. (1986). "The Impact of the Irish on British Labor Markets During the Industrial Revolution." *Journal of Economic History* 46:693–720.

Williamson, J. G. (1988). "Migrant Selectivity, Urbanization, and Industrial Revolutions." *Population and Development Review* 14:287–314.

Williamson, J. G. (1990a). *Coping with City Growth During the British Industrial Revolution*. Cambridge: Cambridge University Press.

Williamson, J. G. (1990b). "The Impact of the Corn Laws Just Prior to Repeal." *Explorations in Economic History* 27 (April):123–156.

Williamson, J. G. (1991). *Inequality, Poverty, and History: The Kuznets Memorial Lectures*. Oxford: Basil Blackwell.

Williamson, J. G. (1995). "The Evolution of Global Labor Markets Since 1830: Background Evidence and Hypotheses." *Explorations in Economic History* 32:141–196.

Williamson, J. G. (1996). "Globalization, Convergence and History." *Journal of Economic History* 56 (June):1–30.

Williamson, J. G. (1997a). "Globalization and Inequality, Past and Present." *World Bank Research Observer* 12 (August):117–135.

Williamson, J. G. (1997b). "Growth, Distribution and Demography: Some Lessons from History." NBER Working Paper No. 6244, National Bureau of Economic Research, Cambridge, Mass., October.

Williamson, J. G. (1998a). "Real Wages and Relative Factor Prices Around the Mediterranean Basin, 1500–1940." Paper presented at the Conference on Long Run Economic Change in the Mediterranean Basin, Istanbul, Turkey, June 4–6.

Williamson, J. G. (1998b). "Real Wages and Relative Factor Prices in the Third World 1820–1940: Asia." HIER Discussion Paper No. 1844, Department of Economics. Harvard University, Cambridge, Mass. (August).

Williamson, J. G., and P. H. Lindert. (1980). *American Inequality: A Macroeconomic History*. New York: Academic Press.

Williamson, O. E. (1971). "The Vertical Integration of Production: Market Failure Considerations." *American Economic Review* 61 (May):316–325.

Wolff, E. N. (1991). "Capital Formation and Productivity Convergence over the Long Term." *American Economic Review* 81 (June):565–579.

Wong, K.-Y. (1983). "On Choosing Among Trade in Goods and International Capital and Labor Mobility: A Theoretical Analysis." *Journal of International Economics* 14:223–250.

Wong, K.-Y. (1988). "International Factor Mobility and the Volume of Trade: An Empirical Study." In R. Feenstra (ed.), *Empirical Methods for International Trade*. Cambridge, Mass.: MIT Press.

Wood, A. (1994). *North-South Trade, Employment and Inequality: Changing Fortunes in a Skill-Driven World*. Oxford: Clarendon Press.

Wood, A. (1995). "How Trade Hurt Unskilled Workers." *Journal of Economic Perspectives* 9 (Summer):57–80.

Wood, A. (1997). "Openness and Wage Inequality in Developing Countries: The Latin American Challenge to East Asian Conventional Wisdom." *World Bank Economic Review* 11, no. 1:33–57.

Wright, G. (1986). *Old South, New South: Revolutions in the Southern Economy Since the Civil War*. New York: Oxford University Press.

Wright, G. (1990). "The Origins of American Industrial Success, 1879–1940." *American Economic Review* 80 (September):651–668.

Yasuba, Y. (1978). "Freight Rates and Productivity in Ocean Transportation for Japan, 1875–1943." *Explorations in Economic History* 15:11–39.

Yasuba, Y. (1996). "Did Japan Ever Suffer from a Shortage of Natural Resources Before World War II?" *Journal of Economic History* 56:543–560.

Young, A. (1991). "Learning by Doing and the Dynamic Effects of International Trade." *Quarterly Journal of Economics* 106:369–405.

Zamagni, V. (1993). *The Economic History of Italy, 1860–1990*. Oxford: Clarendon Press.

Zevin, R. B. (1992). "Are World Financial Markets More Open? If So, Why and With What Effects?" In T. Banuri and J. B. Schor (eds.), *Financial Openness and National Autonomy: Opportunities and Constraints*. Oxford: Clarendon Press.

Index